Disaster Policy and Emergency Management in Russia

Disaster Policy and Emergency Management in Russia

Boris Porfiriev

Nova Science Publishers, Inc.
Commack New York

Editorial Production: Susan Boriotti
Assistant Vice President/Art Director: Maria Ester Hawrys
Office Manager: Annette Hellinger
Graphics: Frank Grucci and John T'Lustachowski
Information Editor: Tatiana Shohov
Book Production: Ludmila Kwartiroff, Christine Mathosian and Tammy Sauter
Circulation: Maryanne Schmidt
Marketing/Sales: Cathy DeGregory

Library of Congress Cataloging-in-Publication Data available upon request

ISBN 1-56072-421-8

Copyright © 1998 by Nova Science Publishers, Inc.
6080 Jericho Turnpike, Suite 207
Commack, New York 11725
Tele. 516-499-3103   Fax 516-499-3146
E-Mail: Novascience@earthlink.net
Web Site: http://www.nexusworld.com/nova

All rights reserved. No part of this book may be reproduced, stored in a retrieval system or transmitted in any form or by any means: electronic, electrostatic, magnetic, tape, mechanical photocopying, recording or otherwise without permission from the publishers.

The authors and publisher haven taken care in preparation of this book, but make no expressed or implied warranty of any kind and assume no responsibility for any errors or omissions. No liability is assumed for incidental or consequential damages in connection with or arising out of information contained in this book.

This publication is designed to provide accurate and authoritative information with regard to the subject matter covered herein. It is sold with the clear understanding that the publisher is not engaged in rendering legal or any other professional services. If legal or any other expert assistance is required, the services of a competent person should be sought. FROM A DECLARATION OF PARTICIPANTS JOINTLY ADOPTED BY A COMMITTEE OF THE AMERICAN BAR ASSOCIATION AND A COMMITTEE OF PUBLISHERS.

Printed in the United States of America

CONTENTS

List of Tables vii
List of Figures ix
Foreword, Enrico L. Quarantelli xi
Preface xiii
About the Author xvii

Chapter 1. Emergencies, Disasters and Catastrophes: Development Trends and Conceptualization 1

Armed Conflicts, Major Natural Hazards and Technological Accidents in the World and Russia: Increasing Threat to Security and Safety of Communities and Societies 2
Emergencies and Disasters as Research and Management Categories 28
Pre-conditions and Underlying Causes of Emergencies, Disasters and Catastrophes. Developmental Phases of An Emergency 36
Classification of Emergencies 47

Chapter 2. The Concept of the Emergency Management Cycle 63

Emergency Management Strategies: Goals. Types and Priorities 63
Emergency Management Mechanism: Stages, Functions and Agents 78

Chapter 3. State Emergency Management Policy in Russia: Legal Basis and Organizational Issues 97

The Legal Basis of Emergency and Disaster Policy: Trends in the World and Russia 97
The State Emergency and Disaster Policy and Organization of Emergency Management in Russia 112

**Chapter 4. Emergency Management in Russia in Practice:
Case Studies of the 1990s** **131**

Aftermath and Response to the Radiation Accident at the Siberian Chemical
    Complex: Reminiscent of Chernobyl? 131
Preparedness, Response to and Recovery from a Major Fire at the
    Kamski Car Plant 153
Preparedness and Organizational Response of Communities and Authorities
    to the Neftegorsk Earthquake Disaster 170

Afterword 191

Annex 1 195

Annex 2 197

Annex 3 199

References 201

Index 223

LIST OF TABLES

Table 1	Vulnerability of the Russian Cities to the Most Dangerous Geophysical Hazards	12
Table 2	The Number of Emergencies in Russia, 1990-1996	20
Table 3	The Number of Killed in Emergencies in Russia, 1990-1996	22
Table 4	The Rates of Growth of the Number of Emergencies in Russia	24
Table 5	Percentage of Emergencies in Russia by The Type of Hazard	24
Table 6	Percentage of Technological Accidents in Russia by Domain of Hazard	25
Table 7	Percentage of Killed in Technological Accidents in Russia by Source of Death	25
Table 8	Emergency Criteria	31
Table 9	Typology of Hazards (Threats) to the Security (Safety) of a Social System	50
Table 10	Typology of Social Systems Vulnerability	55
Table 11	Typology of Emergencies	56
Table 12	Typology of Emergencies by Scale of Effect in the Russian Federation	60
Table 13	Types of Emergency Management Goals by Objective of Protection	66
Table 14	Types of Emergency Management Goals By a Source of Hazard	67
Table 15	Management Policies Typology	68
Table 16	Typology of Emergency Management Strategies	70
Table 17	Efficiency of Management Strategies by Type of Emergencies	75
Table 18	Stages, Phases and Functions of Emergency Management Strategies	77
Table 19	Fields of Responsibility of the Main Emergency Management Agents	90
Table 20	Radiation Dosage and Area Contaminated by the SCC Accident	141
Table 21	Radiation Dose and Number of Persons Irradiated While the SCC Accident	145
Table 22	The Neftegorsk Earthquake Disaster Effect	176
Table 23	Professionals Involved in Response to the Earthquake Disasters in Kobe and Neftegorsk	182

LIST OF FIGURES

Figure 1	The Number of Natural Disasters Which Involved Substantial Economic in 1963 – 1992	4
Figure 2	Percentage of Economic Losses in 1965 – 1992	5
Figure 3	Economic Losses / Insured Losses Incurred by Substantial Natural Hazards Worldwide in 1960 - 1993	6
Figure 4	Economic Losses Incurred by Substantial Natural Hazards Worldwide in 1965 – 1992	6
Figure 5	The Number of Killed in Substantial Natural Disasters Worldwide in 1965 – 1992	8
Figure 6	The Number of Affected in Substantial Natural Disasters Worldwide in 1965 – 1992	8
Figure 7	The World Regional Structure of Economic Losses in 1965 – 1992	9
Figure 8	The Frequency of the World Major Technological Accidents (50 or More Killed in Each)	13
Figure 9	The Number of Killed in the Major Technological Accidents Worldwide in 1900 - 1990	16
Figure 10	The Number of Evacuated During the Major Technological Accidents in 1969 – 1987	16
Figure 11	The Case-Load of Diphtheria in the Former Soviet Union and the CIS	26
Figure 12	The Causal Chain of the Origin and Development of an Emergency	38
Figure 13	Integral Classification of Emergencies	49
Figure 14	Organizational Structure of the RUSPRE	116
Figure 15a	The Structure of Functions Carried Out by the Federal Government Bodies Within the RUSPRE	118
Figure 15b	The Structure of Functions Carried Out by the Key Subsystems of the RUSPRE	118
Figure 16	The MES Regions and Case Studies Localization	122
Figure 17	Organizational Structure of the MES	124

Figure 18	The Total Number of Lines in the Stories on KamAZ Big Fire Published in the Russian Most Circulated Newspapers From 15 April to 5 October, 1993	**168**
Figure 19	The Number of Stories on KamAZ Big Fire Published in the Russian Most Circulated Newspapers From 15 April to 5 October, 1993	**169**
Figure 20	The Number of Lines in the Stories on KamAZ Big Fire Published in the Russian Most Circulated Newspapers From 15 April to 5 October, 1993	**171**
Figure 21	The Structure of the Search and Rescue Personnel Involved in Response to the Neftegorsk Earthquake	**180**
Figure 22	The Efficiency of Search and Rescue Operations During the Neftegorsk Earthquake Disaster	**184**

FOREWORD

This is an interesting and worthwhile monograph for several reasons. For one, it is written by someone from a society somewhat different than is typical of almost all who have previously published on the more theoretical and general aspects of disasters and emergency management. The great majority of such writers have been from West European or North American societies with relatively stable social systems, long established democratic types of government, and with very strong private sectors. Dr. Porfiriev of course is from Russia, the major component of the former Soviet Union, and as such is living in a very turbulent social setting which and has been undergoing the transition from an authoritarian regimen to a democracy, and from primarily a state run economic system to a more mixed type. The importance here is not so much the personal history of the author of the volume under discussion but that he is analyzing emergencies and disasters, the emergency planning and management issues from the rather different background and experience of the Soviet Union and its transformation to Russia. As such, Dr. Porfiriev necessarily reflects a perspective on the aforementioned issues that is simply personally if not professionally unfamiliar to almost all previous writers on the topics he discusses, and therefore an experiential perspective presented by him is relatively different from that of most scholars.

Second, this volume is a useful contribution because of the wealth of information it provides historically on disasters and emergency management in the former Soviet Union and into the present time Russia. As the author himself points out, much of what he writes about was mostly unknown even to Soviet citizens for decades. Thus, it is noted, and I think almost publicly for the first time, that there had been major disasters unknown to anyone except in very limited official circles and the impacted populations themselves. For example, mentioned are the earthquake in 1948 which may have resulted in 110,000 fatalities, as well as a tsunami in 1952 which may have killed 10,000 persons, and a radiation accident in 1957 that affected at least 250,000 people. In addition, in the last chapter of this book, Dr. Porfiriev presents us three very detailed case studies which illustrate the range of emergencies and crises the contemporary Russia has more recently undergone. For anyone interested in comparative descriptions and analyses of disasters and emergency policy and management, this can not be but a very welcomed addition to the research literature.

Third, and related to the second reason, this monograph is of interest because of what its author reports on the historical and legal development of the emergency management system in the former Soviet Union and current Russia. Included is an extensive exposition of the regulatory and legal aspects of the system, a topic which has been little addressed in the Western literature on the subject involved. The data and its comprehensive analysis are not only of value for comparative research studies, but also because they contribute to the surfacing of important questions about the universality of disaster related phenomena. Along some lines, what Porfiriev notes is quite similar to what many Western observers have said about their own national emergency management systems. On the other hand, there are issues discussed by the author which are less obvious or even nonexistent in more Western type societies. It is unclear, and it is not a matter which Dr. Porfiriev could have addressed, whether these differences stem from the traumatic social transition in a Soviet Union reducing to a Russia, or whether they are specifically associated in some way with Russian values and norms (or maybe even historical experiences), or whether they result from the different kinds of social systems involved (for example, Russia is not as industrialized / urbanized as most Western type countries). These and similar kinds of questions are suggested by some of the content of this book. What behaviors are universal, what are social system type specific, and what are country particular? Disaster researchers have not done well in answering such questions, but this volume reinforces the idea that they should be asked and answered.

The disaster field is fortunate that Dr. Porfiriev has brought to bear in this monograph his sophisticated treatment, his extensive knowledge of the literature (in both Russian as well as other sources), and his willingness to range widely in covering different topics. Disaster researchers ought to be able to do better studies because of the contributions of this book. Along some lines, it is what some of us in the area started to think about at the height of the Cold War in the 1960s and 1970s when we wondered if there were counterpart colleagues in the Soviet Union. However, intensive efforts by Swedish, German and American scholars to make direct contact were total failures. Only in the very late 1980s were initial contacts made between social science disaster researchers, among the very first being between ourselves and the author of this monograph. These initial contacts have started to bear fruit, in particular in terms of joint editing the volumes on social science research of emergencies and disasters in the former Soviet Union and contemporary Russia. One of these entitled *Social Science Research on Mitigation of and Recovery from Disasters and Large Scale Hazards in Russia* has been just edited by Dr. Porfiriev and ourselves while another volume entitled *An Annotated Inventory of the Social Science Research Literature in the Former Soviet Union and Contemporary Russia* was put together by slightly earlier by Alla Mozgovaya and ourselves. However, this monograph by Dr. Porfiriev is a final demonstration that the intellectual isolation and separation generated by the Cold War is completely over, and we in the West are now getting exposure to what is being produced in the emergency and disaster area in Russia. We are especially fortunate in that this book by Dr. Porfiriev is not only quantitatively extensive but even more important that it is of such high quality.

E. L. Quarantelli
Research Professor
Disaster Research Center,
University of Delaware.
Newark, Delaware 19716 USA
23 August 1997

PREFACE

For many decades federal emergency and disaster policy and management has been an important but one of the least publicized and studied aspect of the national policy in the former Soviet Union. Being considered by the top state officials from the narrow viewpoint of state security and civil defense until the late 1980s, emergencies and disasters which occurred in the country until that time were kept secret even from the Russian citizens let alone the rest of the world. The official media reported them only in case of the major disasters but always specified that there were no fatalities nor serious destruction.

Another important characteristic of federal policy in this area was its fragmentation with particular ministries responsible for their own set of functions primarily associated with social order, fire safety and state security. The mitigation and preparedness were carried out within the command-and-control administration model by the respective bodies to prevent and cope with possible mass disturbances, riots and enemy attack with using mass destruction weapons while the rescue of lives and property in the event of natural and technological emergencies and disasters were the prerogative of the emergency services (fire, police, medical care and so forth) within the local authorities and the army.

The historical confluence of the crucial political changes in the former Soviet Union in the mid 1980s (known everywhere as *perestroika*) and the worlds worst radiation disaster in Chernobyl, transpired to become the turning point in the aforementioned governmental policy and public perception of safety and security issues. The major earthquake disaster in Armenia in December 1988 necessitated reconsideration of the previous inefficient policy in the field of public protection and institutionalization of emergency management activities both in peace time and war time as an independent, although organic area within the national security policy framework.

This was followed by tremendous work on the development and enforcement of new laws and regulations, restructuring and establishing new organizational units with the emergency management state committees succeeded by the special respective ministry being the most important innovation. The dissolution of the Soviet Union in 1991 followed by a deep and lasting economic crisis in Russia and the other CIS countries considerably impeded and restrained the progress of the new policy. In Russia during the 1990s, the development and building of the Unified State System for Emergencies Prevention and Response (RUSPRE) has already proved its efficiency both nationally and internationally although much more needs to be done to make it really comprehensive and effective.

These drastic changes in the policy of the former Soviet Union and contemporary Russia and the emergence of the emergency and disaster research as a new important area of both academic and practical social studies are closely and intrinsically associated. Until *perestroika* and Chernobyl, these studies, especially sociological, psychological and economic disaster research literature, were confined to rare manuals and popular articles on civil defense while the natural science and technical monographs were plentiful. The first Russian monograph on organizational and economic issues of emergency management in the Soviet Union was published as recently as 1991 (Porfiriev, 1991a).

Although in the recent years the number of publications on this subject has substantially increased, research monographs which might combine the analysis of commonalties and peculiarities of emergencies origin and development with that of the legal, organizational and economic issues of emergency policy and management in Russia, in particular in the light of the global context of these problems, are still lacking. In this book I hope to compensate this lacuna as far as possible, at least for a Western reader who knows even less about both the research and its results and practical policy in the field under discussion, in particular due to the so-called language barrier.

With this in mind, I have chosen a systems approach as the basic methodological tool of this study which puts the particular analysis of disasters and emergency management into a more general analytical framework of development policy and decision making within a certain type of a social system. Therefore the study follows a deductive logic which implies reasoning from the general to the specific.

It starts with a general analysis of the relationship between emergencies and/or disasters and development both in the world and Russia. This especially reveals the past, recent and expected trends in qualitative and quantitative changes in the pattern of threats to the integral security of a social system and its vulnerability to hazardous impacts and goes to the conceptualization and typology of emergencies (Chapter 1). At this point it is worth special noting that in this book the concept of emergency differs from its everyday usage as a synonym of accident and is close to what has been called a disaster in the US sociological literature although they are not identical. The categories of disaster and catastrophe which imply a qualitatively more severe degree of gravity of an event or occasion's effect for a given social system are also extensively used throughout this study.

The latter is continued by the analysis of the emergency management concept which involves a systemic set of prevention, mitigation and alleviation strategies which should be developed and later on implemented via a cycle of certain stages and measures including prevention and mitigation, preparedness, response and recovery. Russia is used in this case as the main illustration of the key principles and points of this concept (Chapter 2).

This is followed by a substantive analysis of emergency and disaster policy and management in contemporary Russia. First, the legal basis of the aforementioned RUSPRE system which has been being built there since 1992 is scrutinized within the framework of the main approaches applied to the world practice in the legal regulation of emergency management. This is followed by the detailed discussion of the organizational structure and key functions of the RUSPRE (Chapter 3).

Finally Chapter 4 involves three cases of major radiation, fire and earthquake emergencies and disasters which occurred in the first half of the 1990s in Russia and a comprehensive analysis of preparedness, response to and recovery from these provided by the local, regional and federal authorities and the RUSPRE.

This work could not have been done without the helpful and generous assistance of a number of individuals and organizations. My greatest appreciation must go first to Professor Anatoly Mikeev from the Academy of Management of the Ministry of Internal Affairs of the Russian Federation and the Chief of the Fire Service of the former Soviet Union. He was not only been a close collaborator while writing the section on the big fire at the KamAZ truck assembly plant and but also a friend throughout the whole writing of this book and our joint teaching in the aforementioned academy many times providing me with his huge practical experience and friendly assistance at different times during the course of the study.

Professor Enrico Quarantelli from Disaster Research Center (DRC) of the University of Delaware (USA) deserves my special sincere thanks for his continuous valuable and kind multiyear cooperation and indispensable support of my emergency and disaster research efforts, and this book for which he has written the foreword in particular. I have benefited much from both the classic works on the sociology of disaster and fruitful discussions of disaster theory and practice with him and his outstanding colleagues from the DRC during my visits to the United States. I owe my special gratitude to Professors Joanne Nigg and Kathleen Tierney, co-directors of the DRC, Research Professor Russell Dynes and Diane Murray, the DRC Secretary, both for their hospitality and research support.

I also thank geographers, Professor Sergey Miagkov, from the Moscow State University, my *alma mater*, and Professor David Alexander from Amherst University in Massachusetts, the USA, as well as Professor, Dr. Uriel Rosenthal, Professor of Government from the University of Leiden the Netherlands, for their helpful comments on certain draft sections of the study, and Dr. Alexey Voskressenskiy, from the Institute for Far Eastern Studies of the Russian Academy of Sciences for moral and organizational support.

And last, but not the least, I owe a special debt to my family, especially to my wife and daughter, for their patience and encouragement that made this book possible. To my deepest regret my father, who was an exacting but always a gentle first reader of my papers and who provided indispensable moral support for my research studies including this monograph died just as I completed the book. I commemorate this book to this wonderful man and his enormous influence on my life.

Special credit goes to several institutions which provided organizational support for this study. First, is the Institute for Systems Analysis of the Russian Academy of Sciences, especially its Department of Organizational Management Systems headed by Professor Vladimir Leksin, which supported my efforts throughout the five years of the study. The Netherlands Institute for Advanced Studies (NIAS) of the Royal Dutch Academy of Sciences and Arts (KNAW) deserves special appreciation for providing me the unique opportunity to work there on this book in Spring 1996 as a TRIS Fellow. Computer and logistics support came from my colleagues and friends in two Russian research and engineering companies, namely PRIN and ESPAR-Analyst Ltd.

Grateful acknowledgment is made for permission to quote extensively from my case study papers on major radiation accident in 1993 (1996c) (copyright © 1996 by Springer-Verlag New York Inc.) and earthquake disaster at the in 1995 in Russia (1996b) (copyright © 1996 by Blackwell Publishers Ltd.). Both papers have been updated and in addition the first one substantially revised. I have also cited briefly with respective permission from my theoretical papers on the national security concept (1992a) (copyright © 1992 by Springer-Verlag New York Inc.) and disaster and disaster areas (1995) (copyright © 1995 Research Committee on Disasters, International Sociological Association).

I owe my special gratitude to the editors and publisher of this book for their patience and indispensable efforts to make its initial English version readable to the Western audience. To the extent that this monograph has merit, considerable credit must be given to them and the other individuals and organizations mentioned above. Flaws, errors and other imperfections which remain should be considered as my personal responsibility. To all who assisted this endeavor, I hope that the result does credit to our efforts.

Boris N. Porfiriev

ABOUT THE AUTHOR

Boris Porfiriev has been involved in emergency and disaster research since 1977 when he got his bachelor's degree in economic geography from the Moscow State University and started his studies on the topic of environmental disasters and crisis at the Russian Academy of Sciences. Since 1985 he has been working there as a Leading Researcher at the Institute for Systems Analysis where from he received his doctor's degree in economy and public administration in 1990. In addition, in 1994 he became a Professor at the Academy of Management of the Ministry of Internal Affairs of the Russian Federation. His experience includes emergency and environmental research with over 150 research articles on these topics, as well as teaching and consulting on emergency and crisis management issues. He has also been serving as an expert on these topics for several governmental and parliamentary committees including the widely acclaimed Investigatory Commission on Chernobyl.

CHAPTER 1

EMERGENCIES, DISASTERS AND CATASTROPHES: DEVELOPMENT TRENDS AND CONCEPTUALIZATION

The history of mankind gives evidence that the development of human civilization has never been smooth and non-contradictory. While progress has been going on and contributing to a solution of a certain set of crucial problems, the latter have been overplayed by other issues no less important and urgent. These fluctuations in the developmental process necessitated for, and have been escorted by, conspicuous changes in societies' management strategies including revision of existing priorities and models of political, social and economic as well as scientific and technological development, innovations in planning and public administration instruments, disappearance of some functions and organizations and emergence of the other.

In certain moments of this process, the existing contradictions between nature and human society and within society itself, cumulate and sharpen. This considerably augments the burden load impact on, and aggravates the risk to the sustainability of the social systems. This includes increasing the frequency and scale of adverse effects of the military and acute social conflicts, industrial accidents and environmental contamination, natural hazards and their combined impact on societies and communities. This means that with numerous risks to social and economic stability, the development of the role of situations which sever the collective routines of thousands of people and change them into emergencies and disasters and therefore require urgent responses, conspicuously increases both in quantitative and qualitative terms.

This chapter starts with an overview of development trends of the main threats to social and political security: wars and armed conflicts as most dangerous and devastating conflict-type hazards, and major natural hazardous occasions and technological accidents as the most debilitating non-conflict crisis events, and analysis of their impact on social systems both globally and in the former Soviet Union and contemporary Russia. Then the destructive effects of the impact is scrutinized in terms of the social system vulnerability in order to develop the conceptualization and typology of emergency, disaster and catastrophes as research and management categories and study the prerequisites for, mechanism and phases of emergency development.

ARMED CONFLICTS, MAJOR NATURAL HAZARDS AND TECHNOLOGICAL ACCIDENTS IN THE WORLD AND RUSSIA: INCREASING THREAT TO SECURITY AND SAFETY OF COMMUNITIES AND SOCIETIES

From a historical perspective, natural hazards and wars have been the most long term and disastrous threats to the very existence of humankind. Since the first communities appeared on the Earth they have been increasingly confronted and impacted by multifaceted hazardous natural agents that considerably changed and/or destroyed whole civilizations which had been loosely protected at that time. The situation was substantially aggravated by more and more conflict behavior of the people struggling for new living space and resources and killing each other, primarily civilian populations, and thus augmenting vulnerability of the social systems (societies and communities). Given that only the entire history of human civilization has seen only rare periods of peace, it is no wonder that the cumulative disastrous effect of wars and armed conflicts on security and safety of social systems has surpassed that of natural hazards.

Regional and world wars have produced the greatest human and material losses. Tentative and incomplete estimates show that more than 600 wars and armed conflicts, each leading to at least more than 1,000 killed, have occurred within the last 500 years while the total number of their victims has exceeded 160 million. These include 10 million killed in World War I, which also inflicted 30 billion US$ of direct economic damages. World War II resulted in 55 million killed and 315 billion US$ of direct economic losses, respectively (1945 prices). After this war, regional wars and armed conflicts have taken the lives of more than 25 million people while tens of millions became refugees. In the mid 1980s, there were about 13 million refugees in the world as a result of religious, national and other conflicts primarily in developing countries (Sivard, 1991: 22-25; Smirnov, 1988: 12-13).

Despite initial enthusiasm at the end of the "Cold War" in the late 1980s, the number of regional crises in the 1990s have not been reduced noticeably. Their total number has remained in the range of 40 to 50 per year with the conflicts each involving more than 1,000 killed, mainly in developing countries. This has been dominating the world scene. It is important, however, that while the total number of these conflicts in the late 1980s - 1990s has not substantially changed, on the contrary in Europe, primarily in former Yugoslavia and the Soviet Union, the latter have increased from two in 1990 to eight in 1993 and 1994 (*World Disasters Report* 1995: 107-110).

The former Soviet Union and Russia have been especially suffering from wars and armed conflicts. From the total number killed in these events in the world during the last 500 years, Russia and the former USSR account for more than 35 million or nearly 22%, including six million or 60% of all killed in World War I and more than 27 million or nearly a half of the total fatalities in World War II.

The latter turned out to be a real national disaster and for the bulk of the regions in the European part of the Soviet Union it was a catastrophe. This war killed about 14% of the country's population and destroyed more than one third of the national wealth. The USSR's direct economic damages skyrocketed to 679 billion rubles while Russia lost 255 billion. These figures do not include nearly 2,000 billion rubles of economic costs, which involve military expenditures and income losses by the national economy as a result of the war (1941 prices). Totally or partly were destroyed were 1,710 cities and towns, more than 70,000 villages and hamlets and 6 million buildings that made about 25 million people homeless or 13% of the national population (*Narodnoie Khoziaistvo* SSSR, 1987: 45-46). While it took from 10 to 12 years to reconstruct and completely recover the economic power of the Soviet Union, many demographic, social and psychological consequences of World War II have not yet been overcome.

Although the human and material losses incurred by the post war armed conflicts in the former Soviet Union have been incomparably inferior in absolute terms than those in World War

II, the gravity of their effects on the social systems in affected regions in relative terms is quite comparable. According to some estimates, armed conflicts which have occurred at the territory of the former Soviet Union and contemporary Russia in 1986-1997 inflicted direct economic damages accounting for at least 20 billion to 30 billion US$, resulting in nearly one million refugees and more than 100,000 killed, mainly in the North Caucasus, in the Chechen Republic. Thus the latter has lost about 10% of its population and 12% has become refugees (many of them Russians).

Considering the overall social and economic crisis in Russia in the 1990s, it would hardly be a mistake to suppose that the economic rehabilitation of the affected region to the pre-conflict level would take no less time than the recovery of the former Soviet Union after World War II. The political, social and psychological aftermath of the conflicts will be felt both by affected people and the Russian population as a whole much longer.

Even those relatively short periods when human society was living peacefully can hardly be seen through rose-colored glasses. Natural hazards, epidemics (although of different diseases) and in recent decades more and more destructive technological accidents as well as their combined impact on humans and their environment have been increasingly jeopardizing social systems security and safety. The scale and gravity of human and economic losses incurred by these dangerous occasions are comparable with the figures, which refer to wars and armed conflicts.

In 1965-1995, major natural hazards, technological accidents and compound hazardous occasions of mixed origin sources affected more than three billion people worldwide including six million killed and inflicted total economic direct damages of 1,300 to 1,500 billion US$. Within the same period, millions of people were forced to leave their native places as a result of the continuing destruction of natural resources and degradation of environmental quality. They have become a new class of 'environmental refugees' which nowadays accounts for more than 10 million. Given this and considering that conflict-type events have been especially and profoundly studied by scholars of international and national (Russian) security, it seems reasonable to pay much more attention to the non-conflict emergencies.

A NEW VERSION OF AN OLD DANGER: INCREASING VULNERABILITY TO MAJOR NATURAL HAZARDS

Contrary to the wide-spread opinion of technocrats and technological optimists in the 1970s that modern civilization diminished the risk of hazardous natural phenomena, existing and accumulating empirical knowledge shows evidence that the contemporary world has become more vulnerable to this kind of impact, primarily to that one which gives birth to major or substantial disasters. According to the UN statistical criteria, the latter involved either direct economic losses exceeding 1% of the yearly gross national product or GNP (A); or the number of affected (casualties) surpassing 1% of the country's population (B) or the number of killed over 100 (C) (see: Disasters Around the World, 1994).

As Fig. 1 shows, between 1965 and 1992 the number of substantial natural disasters grew unevenly but more or less steadily and more than quadrupled in terms of degree of economic damage (criterion A) and increased 3.5-fold and more than doubled in terms of the proportion of the population affected and number of killed (criteria B and C, respectively).

Given this fact and considering the major disasters which occurred later on, in particular earthquakes in the USA (Northridge) in 1994, Japan (Kobe) and Russia (Neftegorsk, Sakhalin Island) in 1995, in Iran (Meshed) in 1997 as well as floods in the USA in 1993, in Europe and Russia in 1995 and 1996, in China in 1997 and so forth, I believe that the existing trend will last at least to the end of the 20th century.

The trend also manifests accelerated rates of growth of the number of substantial natural hazards, primarily floods, windstorms, droughts and earthquakes which have caused considerable economic damage (see Fig. 2).

This acceleration has been especially pronounced since the late 1980s when between 1987 and 1996, 15 disasters with a cost of insured losses each exceeding 1 billion US$ occurred, mostly in industrialized countries, while before 1987 there was only one such an event (Domeisen, 1995).

This naturally results in a substantial increase in the volume of economic damages worldwide. The latter jumped from 40 billion US$ in 1960s to 70 billion US$ in 1970s and 120 US$ in the 1980s thus tripled within 30 years. If inflation is discounted, this increase would be more spectacular and reach 5-fold for total economic losses and soar to 12-fold for insured losses. Thus the rates of economic damages inflicted by substantial natural hazards in the last 30 years surpassed those of the number of such hazards by 20% at least that reveals a growing vulnerability of the world community to natural disasters. Totally within 1965 and 1992 the latter, mainly windstorms, earthquakes and floods, incurred economic damage of 340 billion US$ (Berz, 1993; *Disasters Around the World*, 1994; Pisano, 1995) (see Fig. 2, 3 and 4).

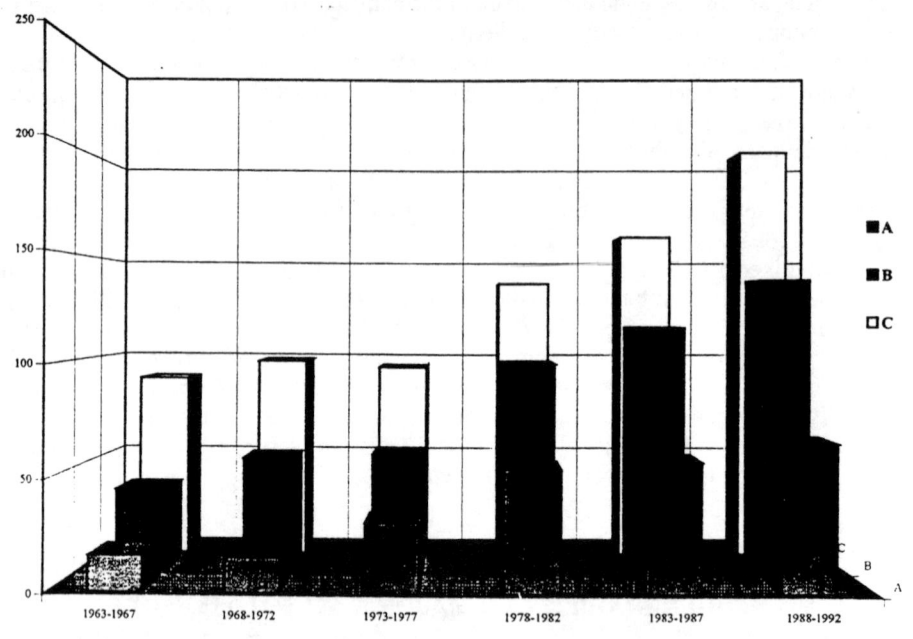

For explanations of A, B and C criteria see the text.

Fig. 1 The Number of Natural Disasters Which Involved Substantial Economic Losses (A), the Number Killed (B) and Affected Population (C) Worldwide in 1963-1992

Source (Disasters 1994)

Considering the major disasters occurred from 1993 to 1997 and that average annual insured loss incurred by them between 1990 and 1994 only amounted to 10 billion US$, I believe that estimated economic damages in the 1990s would skyrocket to 300-350 billion US$.

However important the pace and absolute figures of economic losses are, the social impact of the major natural hazards should be considered as really paramount. As Fig. 5 shows, the absolute number and the rates of increase of those affected and killed in these disasters have been no less spectacular than those for economic damages.

The number killed fluctuated between 1965 and 1992 reaching a maximum in 1970-1972 when the drought in the Sahel region in Africa led to more than 1.2 million deaths. In general in the last 30 years this natural hazard was responsible for more than a half of the total number of killed in substantial natural disasters worldwide, while most of the rest have been caused by windstorms and earthquakes (see Fig. 4).

A

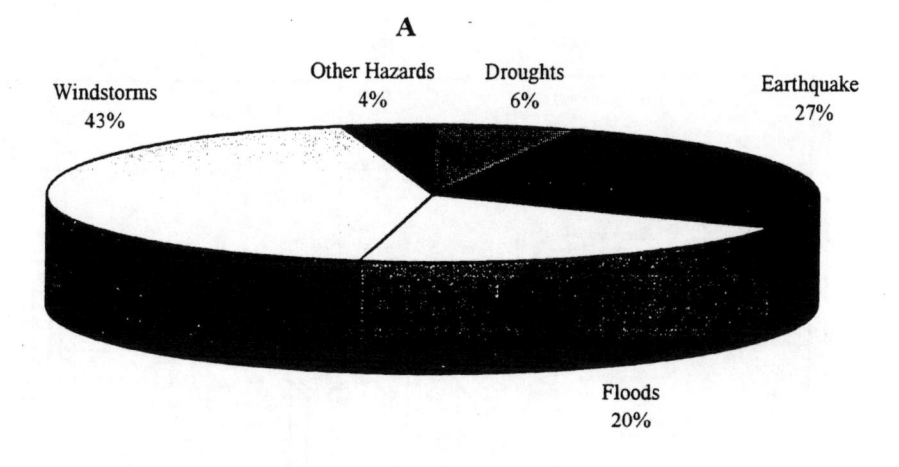

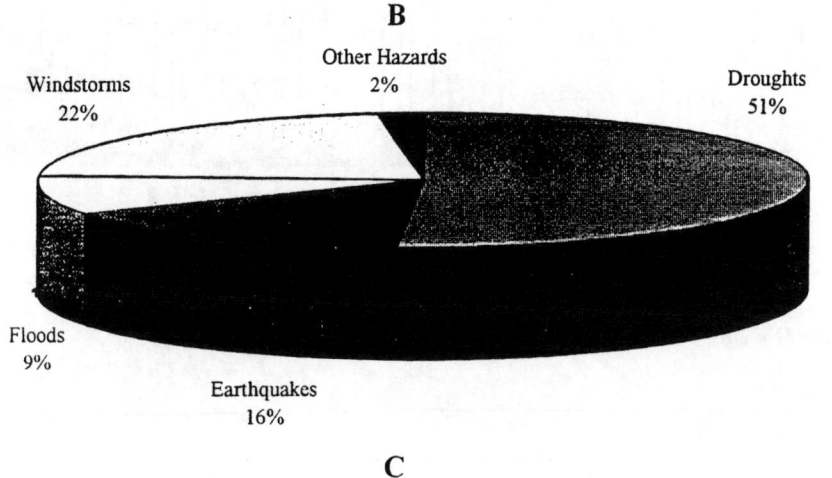

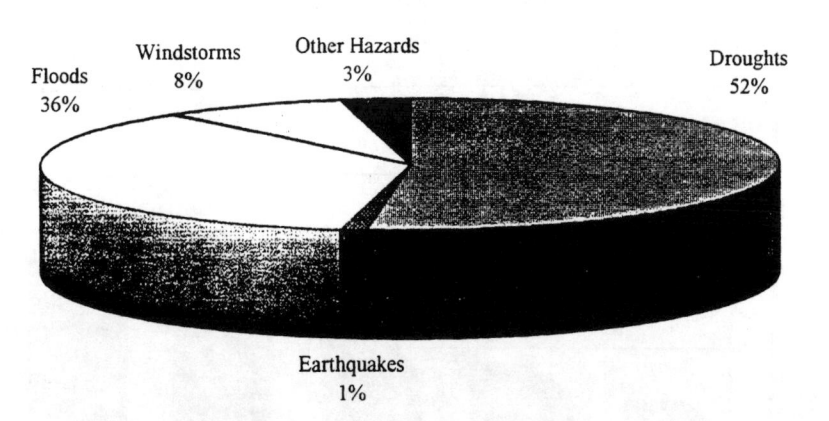

- Windstorms 43%
- Other Hazards 4%
- Droughts 6%
- Earthquake 27%
- Floods 20%

B

- Windstorms 22%
- Other Hazards 2%
- Droughts 51%
- Floods 9%
- Earthquakes 16%

C

- Floods 36%
- Windstorms 8%
- Other Hazards 3%
- Droughts 52%
- Earthquakes 1%

Fig. 2. Percentage of Economic Losses (A), Killed (B), and Affected (C) by Substantial Natural Hazards Worldwide by Hazard Agent in 1965-1992

Source (Disasters 1994)

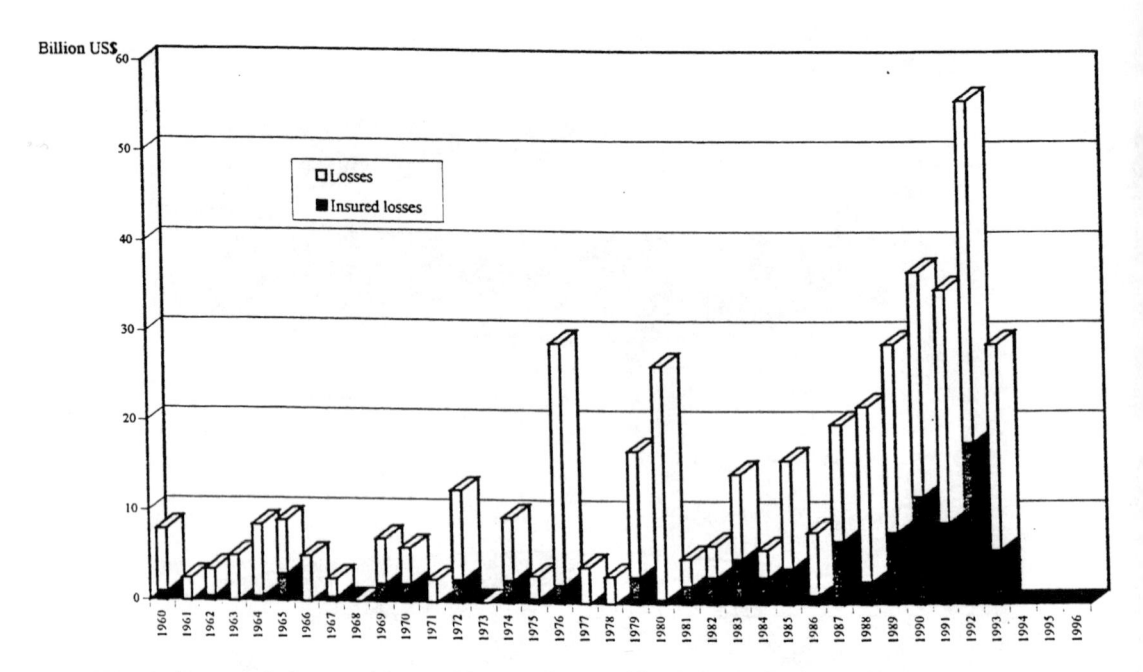

Fig. 3. Economic Losses / Insured Losses Incurred by Substantial Natural Hazards Worldwide in 1960-1993

Source (Pisano, 1995)

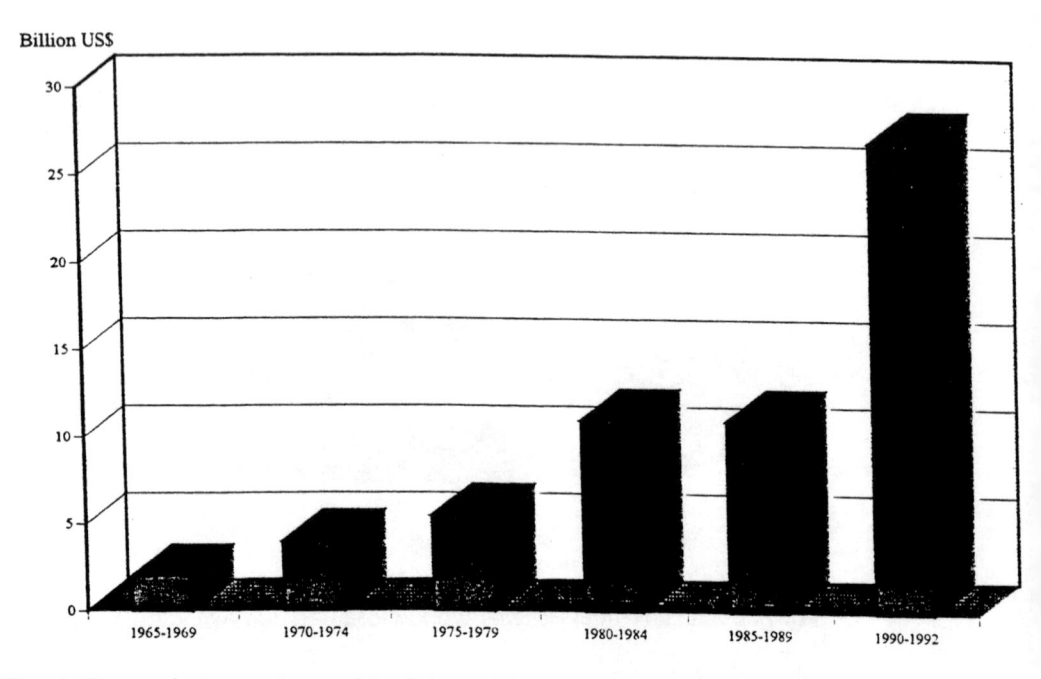

Fig. 4. Economic Losses Incurred by Substantial Natural Hazards Worldwide in 1965-1992

Source (Disasters, 1994)

The number of affected has been steadily increasing from estimated 40 million annually in the 1960s to 100 million in the 1970s and to more than 160 million in the 1980s and thus more than quadrupled within the same period. The total number of affected, primarily by droughts and floods, exceeded that of those killed, by a factor of almost 1,000. For most of these people, survival after a disaster occurs is becoming more and more difficult leaving them even less protected against future shocks. Considering that in the last 30 years the rate of growth of the number of those affected has exceeded by 10% that of the number those of category B natural disasters, the gradually increasing degree of both populations' involvement and vulnerability of the social systems worldwide is absolutely apparent.

Although the trend, which manifests itself in terms of economic and social effects of the major natural disasters, is really a global one, it masks the great discrepancies in the degree of vulnerability existing between various geographical regions and countries with different levels of economic development. The available data shows that the developing countries of Africa and Asia are the most socially vulnerable while more industrialized countries and economic leaders from America, Asia and Europe are the most economically vulnerable to the major natural hazards with Asia continuing to be the most disaster prone region in the world (see Fig. 6).

The structure of casualties and economic losses incurred by substantial natural disasters are evidence about the close correlation between the social and economic vulnerability, and demographic factors and economic development level. Countries with large populations suffer more disaster casualties and economic damages in absolute terms. For example, Bangladesh, China and India have the greatest records of those killed and affected in Asia in the last 30 years while Brazil, Peru and Argentina in America and the former Soviet Union in Europe have been at the top of respective disasters "black lists" (*World Disasters Report* 1995: 104).

However, much more important is the fact that the economic power of these and some other mostly impacted countries considerably yields to that of the world leaders and therefore the former can not afford an effective protection system against major natural hazards for their peoples. Consequently, the developing countries where two thirds of the world's population lives suffers the most debilitating effects of the hazards concentrating 95% of the total disaster related victims (both killed and affected) and nearly 40% of the economic losses worldwide (Clarke and Munasinghe, 1995) (see Fig. 7)

In these countries substantial natural disasters account for an estimated 1% of the total human mortality while direct economic damages inflicted by geophysical extreme events only account for between 2% and 3% of their total GNP. The same losses related to GNP in per capita terms are 20 times greater than in industrialized countries while the proportion of aggregate economic costs (losses and expenditures on civil protection) to GNP reaches as high as from 15% to 20% Clarke and Munasinghe, 1995; Harris, Hohenemser and Kates, 1985).

Contrary to that, the developed countries show a much lower degree of vulnerability to substantial natural hazards especially in terms of casualties while the situation looks much more serious in terms of economic damages (see Fig. 7). As the US data shows, in the early 1990s the number of natural disaster casualties accounted for between 0.05% and 0.1% of the total human mortality and direct and indirect economic losses associated with these disasters were in the order of 1% of the GNP. However, what is really remarkable is the conspicuous increase of the degree of vulnerability in the last three decades, especially in economic terms. The average annual number of deaths in substantial natural disasters in the USA between 1965 and 1985 tripled while insurance payouts in 1990-1994 more than quadrupled those accumulated in the 1980s which themselves were quadruple those of the 1970s. According to some estimates, by the year 2000 annual direct economic losses will skyrocket to average nearly 40 billion US$ (Clarke and Munasinghe, 1995; Harris, Hohenemser and Kates, 1985; Petak, 1985).

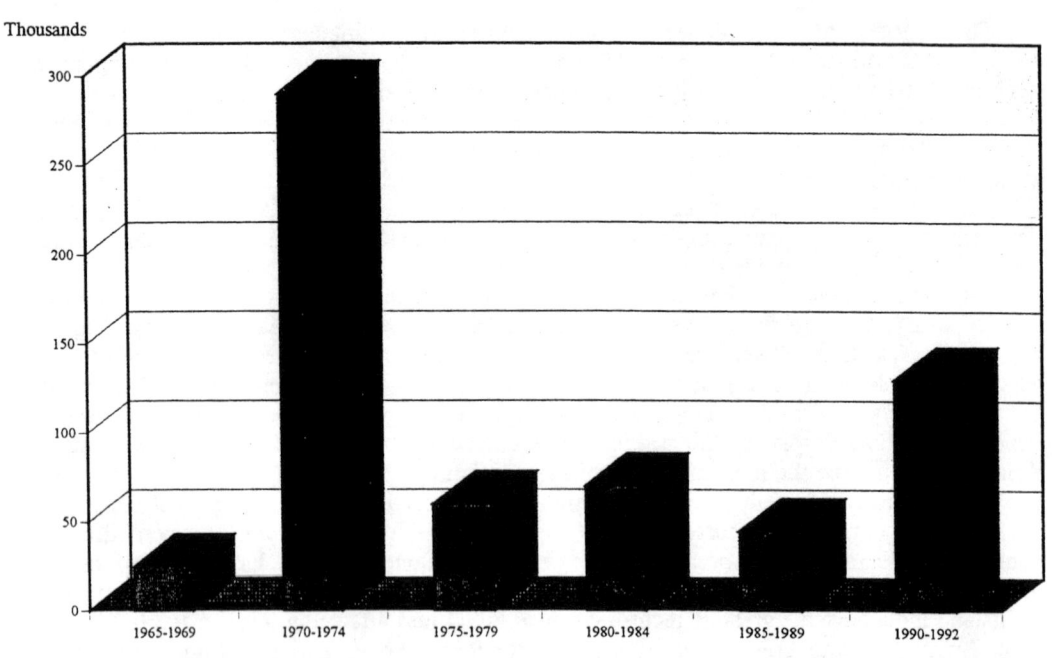

Fig. 5. The Number of Killed in Substantial Natural Disasters Worldwide in 1965-1992

Source (Disasters 1994)

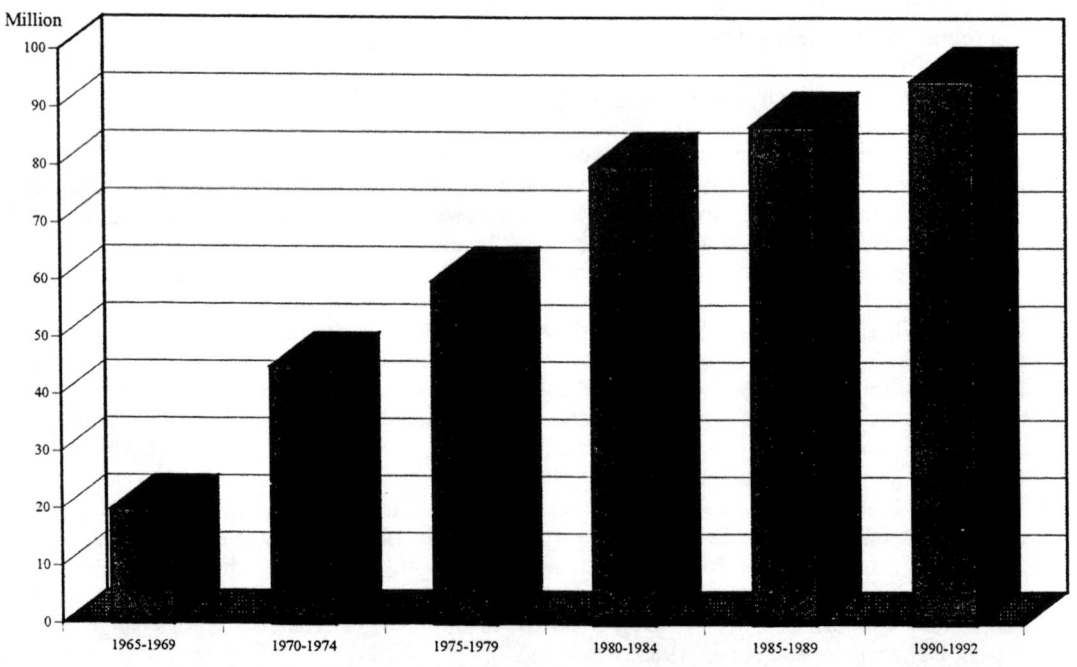

Fig. 6. Number of Affected in Substantial Natural Disasters Worldwide in 1965-1992

Source (Disasters)

A

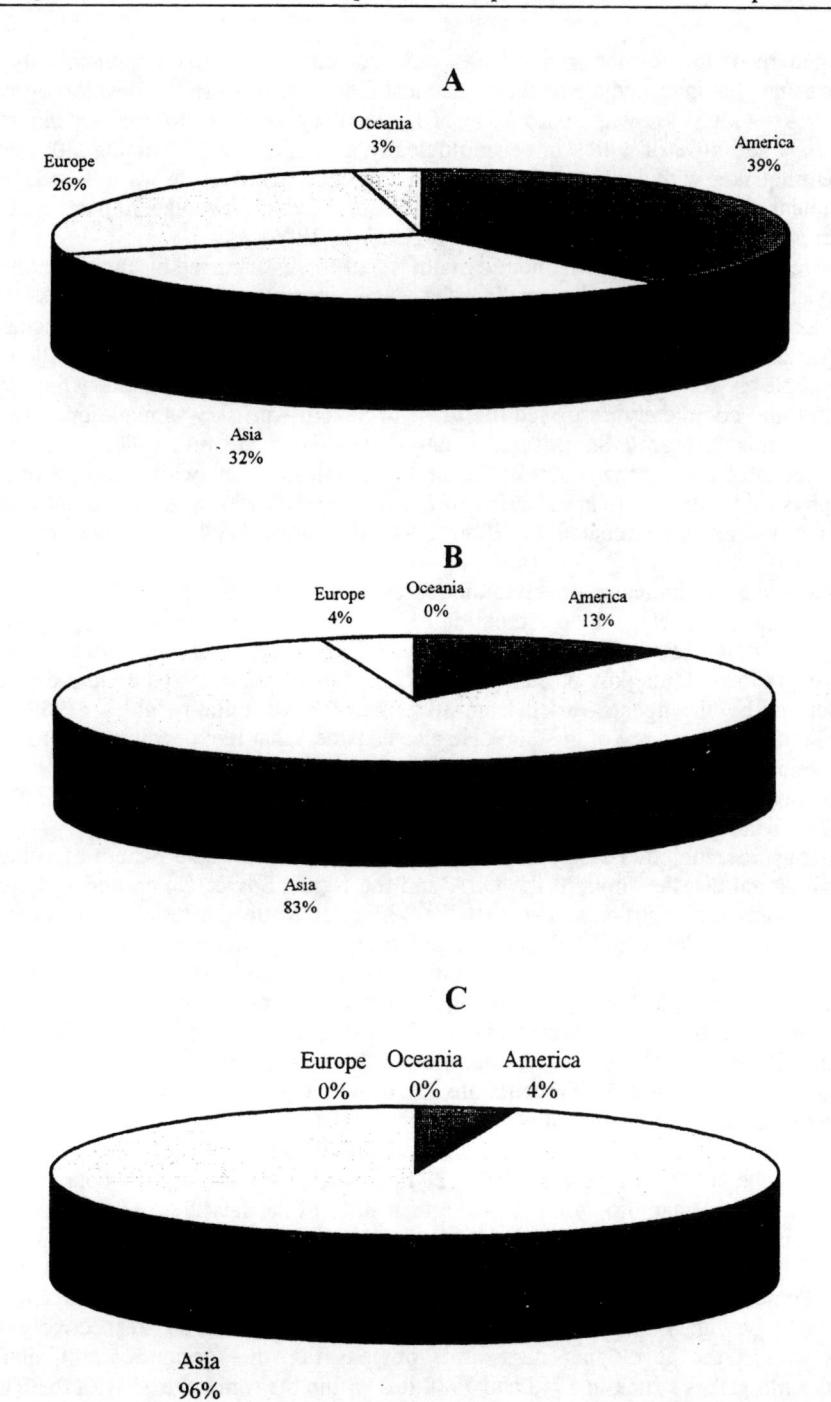

- Oceania 3%
- America 39%
- Europe 26%
- Asia 32%

B

- Europe 4%
- Oceania 0%
- America 13%
- Asia 83%

C

- Europe 0%
- Oceania 0%
- America 4%
- Asia 96%

Fig. 7. The World Regional Structure of Economic Losses (A), the Number Killed (B) and Affected (C) in substantial Natural Disasters in 1965-1992.

Source (Disasters, 1994)

The pattern of the former Soviet Union and contemporary Russia vulnerability to natural hazards is somewhat intermediate between the most industrialized and the developing countries of the world. As widely known, about 70% of its territory is prone to various natural hazards. Between 30% and 40% of it lies in seismologically unstable zones including 20% of the areas prone to earthquakes with a magnitude exceeding 7 on the Richter scale while floods provoke the most frequent and economically devastating disasters which average impact 50,000 square kilometers per year (*Gosudarstvennii Doklad o Zaschite*, 1996).

However, much less is known about casualties and losses incurred by major natural disasters before the late 1980s given that the very fact that such calamities and their damages ever occurred was kept secret for many decades. For example, the truth about the major earthquake disaster in 1948 in Ashkhabad (Turkmen Republic within the former Soviet Union) which killed more than 110,000 people as well as tsunami disaster in 1952 in the Far East of Russia which killed more than 10,000 and completely destroyed the town of Severo-Kurilsk was made open to the public only after glasnost appeared. Some assessments show that in the mid-1980s substantial natural disasters accounted for less than 0.1% of the total national mortality while direct economic losses from geophysical hazards were in the order of 2% of the GNP with average annual damages from floods alone reaching an estimated 1 billion US$ (Babourin, 1990; *Gosudarstvennii Doklad o Zaschite*, 1996).

I believe that the indicator of economic losses as a proportion to the GNP should be even greater considering monetary underestimation of state and especially non-state property damages from major natural hazards, in particular by the official sources in the former Soviet Union. Russian geographer S. Miagkov presumes that in late 1980s - early 1990s annual direct economic losses incurred by the agents varied from 30 billion to 50 billion rubles (1989 prices) and accounted for from 3% to 5% of the GNP. He also considers that if expenditures on mitigation and civil protection are involved, the total economic costs associated with natural disasters would soar to an estimated 75-100 billion rubles per year in average or from 7% to 9% of the GNP (Miagkov, 1995: 183). I believe the latter indicator to be on the order of 5% of the GNP.

At first glance, the cited assessments provide grounds to treat the pattern of vulnerability to substantial natural disasters both in the USA and the former Soviet Union and nowadays Russia as rather economically destructive than socially 'killing'. While the ratio between the percentage of economic losses related to GNP and the percentage of the number of killed by geophysical agents in the total mortality vary from 10:1 to 20:1 in the USA and from 30:1 to 50:1 in the former Soviet Union and Russia, the analogous indicator in developing countries is less by an order of magnitude and fluctuates around 2:1. However, such a conclusion for the former Soviet Union and Russia would be somewhat hasty. In certain important respects, its type of vulnerability to natural hazards is much more like developing countries, especially considering the proximity of respective indicators of economic losses related to GNP.

The historical data on major earthquake hazard vulnerability may corroborate this point even better. During the 20th century more than 1,120 fatal earthquakes affected 70 countries and caused a loss of life of more than 1,5 million. More than 80% of the fatalities occurred in six countries both in the first and second halves of the century. Those were China, Japan, Iran, Italy, USSR and Turkey in 1900-1949 and China, Guatemala, Iran, Peru, Turkey and USSR (CIS) in 1950-1997 (Coburn, Pomonis and Spense, 1993 with author's amendments). Given that the earthquake disasters in Italy, Japan and Turkey occurred in 1908, 1923 and 1930, respectively when these countries were at the developing stage, it is obvious that the former Soviet Union the most disastrous earthquakes struck in 1948 and 1988 lies within the same cluster with the Third World countries.

In addition, if the social vulnerability is measured in comparative terms, the available data on major earthquakes of almost the same magnitude occurred in 1989 in Loma Prieta, in the United States, in Gissar valley in Tadjikistan and Spitak (in December 1988) in Armenia, both in the former Soviet Union, show that the ratio of the number of killed was 63:1,000:25,000 or roughly 1:16:397, respectively. Just to illustrate, the often cited analogous ratio between Japan and Peru is estimated 1:50.

If this indicator is transformed into another one which involves proportions of casualties in total number of affected, the difference in the degree of vulnerability would be represented more correctly but the gap would keep no less impressive. Given that California in the United States, Kobe prefecture in Japan and Sakhalin Island in the Far East of Russia are located in areas with the same range of seismicity, the earthquakes which struck with almost the same magnitude in 1994 in Northridge, and in 1995 in Kobe and Neftegorsk should be considered as a correct comparison. The ratio of fatalities in relative terms between them would reach 1:30:200. However if economic vulnerability measured as a value of direct economic losses incurred by these disasters is compared, the ratio between the cited cases would change to the opposite that is 200:33:1 (see also Chapter 4).

The peculiarities of the former Soviet Union and Russia as well as world regional differences in terms of their vulnerability to natural hazards stressed earlier are most explicit in the urban areas, in particular in the coastal zones, which concentrate the increasing percentage of both population and economic wealth. In the 1960s estimated 30% of the world population were living in cities while in 1995 this proportion reached 42% or 2.4 billion in absolute figures. Considering that at least 80% of the population growth in the 1990s has been occurring in urban zones it is no wonder that by the year 2000 half of the world citizens will be living in these zones crowded into 3% of the earth's land area (*Cities at Risk*, 1996).

Such a concentration of people has been drastically increasing the demand for land in the cities of the world. The latter in its turn has been resulting in using unsuitable terrain (floodplains, unstable slopes and grounds, etc.) prone to natural hazards, in disrupting natural drainage channels and geomorphologic stability thus augmenting the flood, inundation and landslide risk. In addition a high concentration of urban dwellers increases their exposure to extreme meteorological events like windstorms (hurricanes, tornadoes and so forth).

The situation is further aggravated by continuing rapid population growth in the cities of developing countries where 80% of the world's urban residents will live by 2005 with 85% of the number of the world largest cities also located there as early as by year 2000. This will considerably increase vulnerability of the Third World urban communities where mostly poor people with no protection against natural hazards live. When disasters strike, their living conditions tremendously worsen and become critical. Thus poverty and vulnerability to disasters reinforce each other creating something like a vicious circle hard to overcome (*Cities at Risk*, 1996; Clarke and Munasinghe, 1995).

At the same time the cities in the most developed countries which account for almost 80% of their total population (against 30% in developing countries) are also at risk of natural disasters. While the Third World urban areas accumulate the bulk of the national poverty the cities in industrialized countries concentrate material wealth including buildings and constructions which are mostly in jeopardy in case of major natural hazards impact while people are relatively more protected. If again earthquakes are used as an example, those which occurred in 1980s and 1990s in California and in 1995 in Kobe, besides direct destruction also provoked serious industrial accidents and especially fires. This caused the greatest economic damages including 30 billion US$ in case of Northridge and more than 100 billion US$ in Kobe - the costliest disaster ever - though the number of fatalities was far from hitting the historical records. The mentioned secondary effects of the major natural disasters, which besides burning of residential and industrial buildings, also involve environmental contamination not only enlarge total economic losses but hurt the recovery works making them more lasting, sometimes for many years.

In the former Soviet Union and present day Russia, cities have been accounting for 73% of the total population compared to 52% in 1960, many of them located in areas prone to substantial natural hazards (see Table 1). The pattern of the urban area vulnerability to these hazards is also somewhat intermediate between the two types discussed earlier. On the one hand, rapid urbanization has been facilitating accumulation of people with relatively modest income with little property of their own and inadequately protected against substantial natural shocks. On other hand,

Type of natural hazard	Natural hazard	Number of cities in jeorpady	Average annual economic losses (billions of rubles 1991 prices)	
			Per event	Per year
Hydrometeorological	Floods	746	1.1	2.0-2.5
	Windstorms	500	0.02	0.005
	Tsunamis	9	0.1	0.003
Geological	Landslides	725	0.02	1.5-2.0
	Earthquakes	103	20	1.0-1.5
	Avalanches	5	0.5	0.01
	Mudflows	9	0.1	0.001

Table 1. Vulnerability of Russian Cities to the Most Dangerous Geophysical Hazards

the demographic pressure is much lower and concentration of material wealth potentially subjected to natural hazards impact is comparatively greater in absolute terms than in developing countries.

Besides urbanization increasing vulnerability of the social systems worldwide stems from changing of the origin of natural hazards with less and less of them resulting from 'purely' geophysical and other natural extreme events but rather from a combination of these and non-natural (social and technological) factors. Trying to change nature and intensively develop natural resources with the knowledge of natural laws lacking or insufficient, human civilization created and has been using more and more powerful technological complexes. This creates very complicated compound systems with the laws for functioning even more unknown or poorly understood. This augments uncertainty and unpredictability of the behavior of these systems and therefore increases both technological and combined (involving natural, technological and social factors simultaneously) or compound threats to security and safety of societies and communities.

INCREASING MENACE OF DISASTERS AND CATASTROPHES TECHNOLOGICAL AND COMPOUND HAZARDS IMPACT ON VULNERABILITY OF THE SOCIAL SYSTEMS

The role of technological and then compound threats towards social system security has been conspicuously increasing in the post-war decades. Accelerated rates of industrial growth during this period have been accompanied by involvement of huge amounts of hazardous and explosive materials. As academician Valeriy Legasov, a well known Russian expert and the R&D leader on the special governmental task force responsible for emergency management organization while the Chernobyl radiation accident in the early phases of response and recovery, put it in late 1980s:

'In the world energy power industry alone, almost 10 billion tons of fuel have been extracted, stored and processed annually which means amounts of potentially flammable and explosive substances which are comparable with the destructive force of nuclear armaments accumulated during the whole history of humankind. Toxic chemicals (arsenic, phosgene, ammonia and others) have been stored, transported in volumes amounting to from hundreds of billions to thousands of billions lethal doses that exceed by one or two orders of magnitude, those of accumulated radioactive materials in comparable terms' (Legasov, 1987a).

The historical data on the major technological accidents which have occurred after the World War II, prove that when the potential hazard has been transformed into actual disasters and catastrophes the devastating effects of the latter and those of the warfare operations are really proximate. For example, using chlorine as a combat weapon by German troops during World War I, in 1915 killed and injured more than 100,000 while the major chemical accident in Bhopal (India) in 1984 lead to 220,000 casualties. The nuclear bombing in Hiroshima and Nagasaki in 1945 affected an estimated 250,000 and 140,000 people, respectively, while about 270,000 were affected during the radiation accident at the nuclear industrial complex "Maiak" in the shadow town of Cheliabinsk-65 (now Ozersk) in the Cheliabinsk region (South Urals) in 1957 and about 4 million in the former Soviet Union alone during the Chernobyl radiation disaster in 1986.

The analysis of the data on the major technological accidents which occurred in the 20th century, although sometimes incomplete and inconsistent, reveal that the frequency and impact pattern of these dangerous occasions has been much more uneven than those of the substantial natural hazards. However, in historical perspective it shows evidence of the alarming trend of conspicuous growth of their number and increasing vulnerability of the social systems worldwide towards their impact. If the criteria of 50 or more killed, or 100 or more injured or 2,000 or more evacuated, which are considered by some experts as indicators of technological disasters, are used for description of these accidents, it would transpire that estimated two thirds of those have occurred in the last 30 years with almost 40% of them took place within 1980-1997 alone. (Assessments are based on: Porfiriev, 1991a: 14-16; Portnoff, 1989; Shrivastava, 1992: 9-11 and Russian TV in 1995-1997). As Fig. 8 shows since late 1970s the frequency of the major technological accidents augmented by an order of magnitude during a decade although later on it has somewhat decreased.

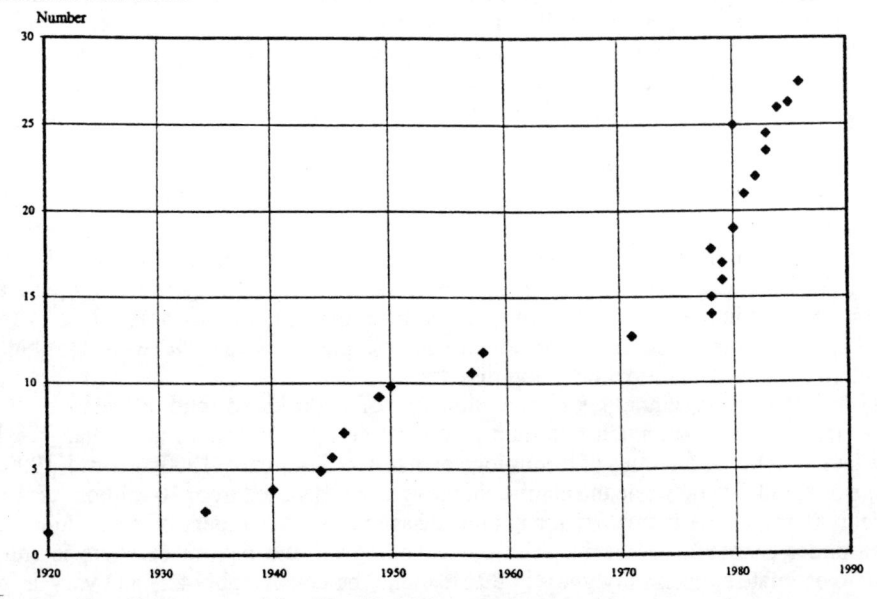

Fig. 8. The Frequency of the World Major Technological Accidents (50 or more killed in each)
Source (Portnoff, 1989 with the author's amendments.)

OECD statistics which are based on other criteria of technological disasters also corroborate the trend of increasing frequency of these dangerous occasions worldwide. The criteria consider as technological disasters the accidents in industry and transportation which lead to 100 or more killed, 400 or more injured, 35,000 or more evacuated or 70,000 or more lacking potable water sources and are close to the earlier cited criteria of natural disasters. The average annual number of these major technological accidents jumped from one between 1974 and 1978, to two within 1979, and 1983 then exceeded three from 1984 to 1988 and kept in this range within 1989 and 1995, thus having multiplied at least 3-fold in the last 20 years (Portnoff, 1989 and author's estimates).

More detailed and comprehensive historical data however illustrate the nonuniformity of the rates of growth of the number of major technological accidents occurred in 1970s and 1980s in selected world industries. In the chemical industry, the frequency of those accidents increased from an annual three to four on average between 1940 and 1970 to 15 between 1970 and 1975 and to almost 30 within 1975-1985 and then dropped, while in oil processing industry the number of major accidents which occurred between 1940-1980 augmented 7-fold in the period 1980-1990. Similarly the number of shipwrecks involving transportation of chemical and petrochemical products which involved toxic spills risks, increased by a factor of three from the mid-1970s to the mid-1980s, but have been stagnating for the last 15 years. The frequency of the major accidents which involved rupture of pipelines between 1980 and 1990 doubled those occurred from 1960 to 1980. But at the same time the number of these accidents has not substantially changed or even decreased from 1970s to 1990s in some other hazardous industries, for example during crude oil and toxic chemicals transportation by railway and trucks (Porfiriev, 1991a: 14-16, 27; Teyes, 1987; Simeons, 1985/86; Shrivastava, 1992: 10-12).

Along with the growing number and rates of major technological accidents worldwide in the last 30 years, their economic and social impact has been also augmented although more unevenly with the highest indicators in the 1980s. However the general increasing trend is apparent, thus proving the principal conclusion on growing vulnerability of modern human civilization to industrial and compound risks.

Unfortunately, accurate data which represents dynamic statistical rows of respective dangerous situations and its social and especially economic costs for the last three decades, are lacking. Moreover the available relevant data published by some UN sources and International Red Cross and Red Crescent Federation are rather scattered, too general and sometimes dubious, not saying a word about the often-missing statistics on economic damages incurred by major technological accidents. In this respect the situation looks even worse than in the case of the frequency of these accidents. However, I believe the available data albeit fragmentary, may serve as a basis for reliable assessments concerning the effects of the impact and degree of vulnerability of affected social systems.

These estimates show evidence that the number of fatalities of technological disasters which occurred between 1950 and 1997 has at least tripled those which occurred from 1990 to 1949 with half of those taking place within the period of 1980-1997 alone. The picture becomes more spectacular and comprehensive if the relevant number of injured, evacuated and affected are involved. The estimated proportion of injured and evacuated during major technological accidents in the last 25 years in the total number of those in the 20th century as a whole accounts for almost two thirds while the same indicator for affected people exceeds 90% with the bulk of the contribution from the Chernobyl radiation disaster.

Nevertheless, in absolute terms the numbers of both killed and affected in the major technological accidents, are much less than those caused by substantial natural hazards. I believe that the total number of fatalities of technological disasters from early 1960s to mid 1990s was in the range of 8,000-10,000 while the number of those affected varied from 10 million to 12 million that yield to respective indicators for natural disasters by two orders of magnitude. The gap between direct economic losses incurred by technological and natural disasters is much more difficult to estimate although my guess is that it should be considerably less and vary in the range of 1:40 and 1:50.

The situation however will change dramatically if not only the largest technological accidents are considered as disasters but all technologically based or technologically induced compound hazardous occasions including those responsible for everyday environmental contamination, are taken into account. Supposing that a modest 3% of the world's GNP is a correct assumption to assess the contribution of the hazardous events, the total direct and indirect economic losses excluding the costs associated with increased mortality and morbidity between 1963 and 1993 would skyrocket to estimated 1,200 billion US$. At the same time, the respective number of casualties would jump to approximately 20 million estimating that the modest 10% of the total mortality is caused by these events in industrialized countries and between 1% and 2% in the rest of the world. (For argumentation of these assumptions see: Harris, Hohenemser and Kates, 1985; Porfiriev, 1997).

However interesting or dubious all these speculations are, they should not obscure the three things most important from the viewpoint of the degree of impact and social system vulnerability to the major technological accidents. One of these is the long term trend of increasing social and economic impact of these highly hazardous occasions which more frequently than before makes them real disasters and catastrophes. Although not fully sufficient to illustrate the gravity of this impact, Fig. 9 and 10 show certain evidence concerning its scale and thus may serve as corroboration of the point.

No less important is that in the 20th century, the world's largest technological disasters both in social, economic and environmental terms occurred in the last 30 years. Suffice it to cite the examples of the major oil tanker shipwrecks of "Amoco Cadiz" in 1978 and "Atlantic Empress" and "Aegean Captain" collision in 1979 that lead to the spill into the seas of 223,000 and 300,000 tons of crude oil, respectively, and the greatest surface oil spill ever of 130,000 tons in 1994 in Komi Republic in Russia; the largest industrial explosions in Cubatao, Brazil and San Juan Ixuatepec, Mexico both in 1984 and near Ufa, (former Soviet Union, now Russia) in 1989 that killed more than 500 people each and so forth. The latter turned out to be the worst accident in the history of the world pipeline transportation resulting in 645 killed including 181 children and affecting nearly 2,000 people.

I believe however that the major disasters in chemical and nuclear industries which involve the most dangerous toxic and radioactive substances would be the most convincing evidence of the gravity of the trend under discussion. In this respect in the chemical industry events incidents worth remembering are the major accident in Seveso, Italy in 1976 which resulted in emission of almost 7,000 lethal doses of dioxin into the air, contamination of the area of 18 km^2 at least, evacuation of 1,000 people and affected nearly 200 more; and the earlier mentioned world worst industrial disaster in Bhopal, India in 1984 which affected more than 200,000 people including more than 6,000 killed and 20,000 injured. In addition one should also cite the largest chemical accident and fire in Europe at 'Sandoz' plant near Bazel, Switzerland in 1986 that caused the poisoning of 300 km of the Rhine river, death of water fauna and fish and disturbed the social routines of almost 20 million people as well as accidents at chemical plants in Shanghai, China; Shibenik, former Yugoslavia and Tour, France which occurred in 1987 and 1988 and lead to serious water contamination and evacuation of 30,000; 60,000 and 200,000 people, respectively (Portnoff, 1989).

In the former Soviet Union the explosion of a tank with liquid ammonia at the "Azot" fertilizer plant and the following fire at the NPK compound fertilized store house in Ionava, Lithuania in 1989 lead to a release into the air of more than 7,000 tons of this toxic substance and considerable quantities of nitrogen oxide and other hazardous materials formed in a cloud of 30 km long and more than 300 m wide which moved tens of miles over the territory of this republic. The explosion and fire alone killed seven and injured almost 50 people while several thousands more were evacuated (Kapeliushniy, 1989; Solarev, 1989; Stroganov, 1989). The consequences could have been much more serious if a different wind arose given that this disaster was the world's greatest chemical accident in terms of the volume of the deadly hazardous release: the latter exceeded by 175-fold that in Bhopal where 40 tons of methylizocyanate escaped into the atmosphere.

Within the relatively short 50-year history of the world nuclear industry, including the nuclear power industry, four major accidents with serious social (medical) and economic repercussions occurred in Great Britain (Windscale, 1957), United States (Three Mile Island, 1979) and the former Soviet Union (Cheliabinsk-65 in 1957 and Chernobyl in 1986). The two latter have been

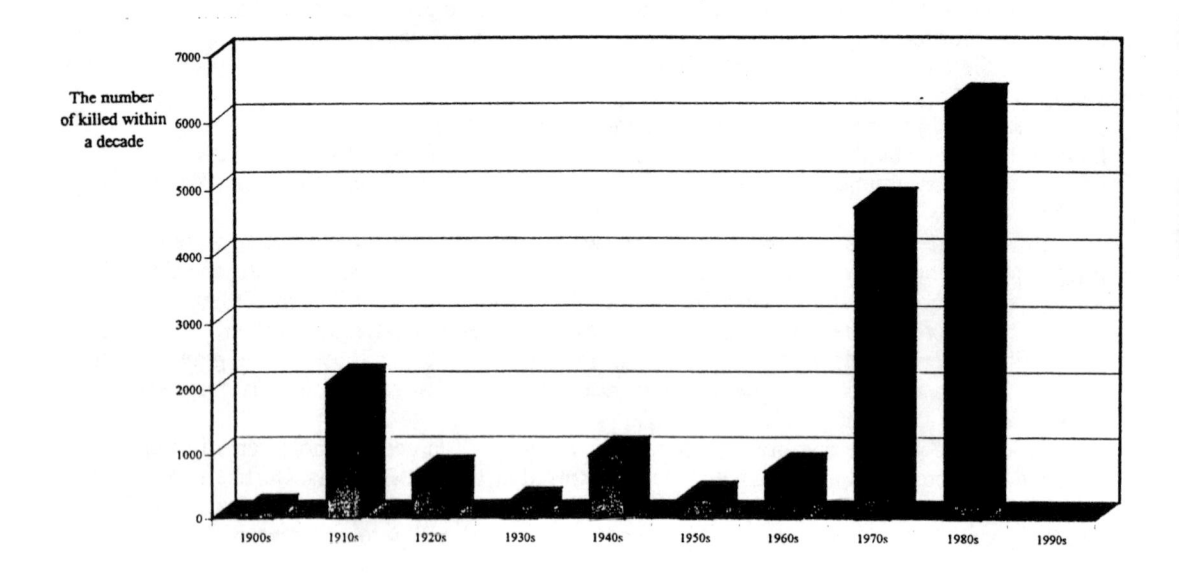

Fig. 9. The Number of Killed in the Major Technological Accidents Worldwide in 1900-1990

Source (Shrivastava, 1992)

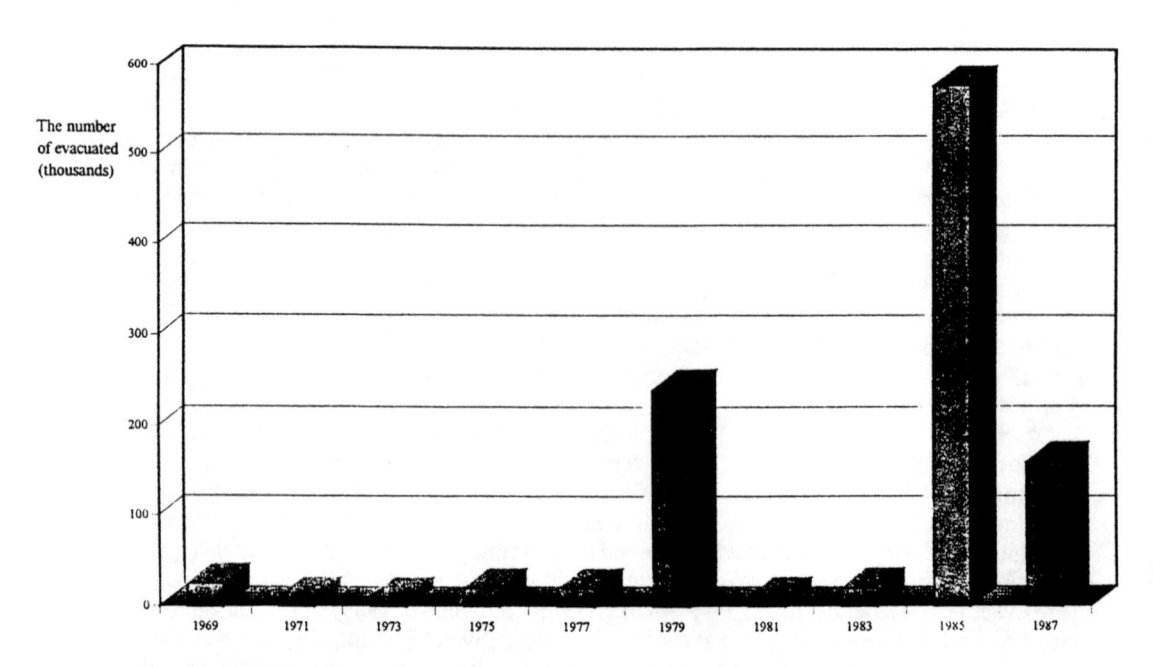

Fig. 10. The Number of Evacuated During the Major Technological Accidents in 1969-1987

Source (Shrivastava, 1992)

the worst cases ever resulting in total radioactive contamination of 22 regions or 80,000 km^2 in Russia alone which account to 0.5% of the national territory where more than 3 million people or 2% of the national population live. Given this and the fact that the affected area also amounts to an estimated 16% or 17% of such territories in the world, Russia should be considered as the most radioactive contaminated country on the Earth.

The explosion of a tank with radioactive wastes at the 'Maiak' military plant in the former secret town of Cheliabinsk-40 (now Ozersk) in the South Urals resulted in emission into the air of more than 2 million Curies (Ci) of Sr^{90} and Cs^{137} which formed a radioactive plume 105 km long and from 6 to 8 km wide. The fallout from this plume affected more than 220,000 people with 10,000 of them evacuated from 23 villages and hamlets, contaminated almost 15,000 km^2, destroyed 160 km^2 of arable lands and involved expenditures on relocation and compensations alone amounting to 200 million rubles (1989 prices) or about 70 million US$ at least (Nikipelov et al, 1989).

As noted elsewhere, the Chernobyl radiation disaster, which was initiated by an explosion at the nuclear power plant in 1986, and aggravated later due to inadequate response and recovery policy in the former Soviet Union, turned out to be the greatest technological catastrophe in the 20th century. The explosion lead to a release of more than 50 million Ci of iodine, cesium, strontium, plutonium and other radioactive materials which resulted in a global dose of about 600,000 persons Sievert (Sv) 40% of this loaded upon the former Soviet Union (currently the CIS) population. The disaster killed 31 employees and emergency workers, more than 200 were hospitalized with clinical syndromes attributable to radiation and almost 120,000 were evacuated soon after the explosion. The territory within a 2,000-km radius was subjected to radioactive fallout including areas in 20 countries and 29 regions (oblasts, krayas and republics) in the former Soviet Union alone with 19 of them in Russia, 5 in Byelorus and Ukraine each. In total an estimated 8 to 10 million people worldwide were affected including more than six million in the former Soviet Union with three million of them living in Russia (*Poiasnitelnaia Zapiska*, 1993; Sweet, 1996).

Ten years after the accident, no reliable data concerning mortality directly attributable to Chernobyl radiation disaster existed. The available assessments made between 1990 and 1996 ranged from official and absolutely untrustworthy 31 casualties to a modest 500 and soar to 30,000- the latter being proposed by Greenpeace activists and not accepted by most of the specialists. My own estimate for 1990, which was based on fragmentary statistics on mortality among the so-called liquidators (emergency workers and police officers) between 1986 and 1989 showed that the number of casualties was around 1,000 (Porfiriev, 1991b).

However, given that later on the consequences of the radiation load on human health will be aggravated and really increased, I believe that in late 1990s the number of post-impact casualties will augment from 3 to 4-fold at least and reach the figure between 3,500 and 4,000 as the most conservative guess including those died from radiation and other reasons directly tied with the disaster. By far the greatest health problem to have turned up so far, has been the hugely elevated incidence of thyroid cancer among children. The total number of cases among children under 15 in Byelorus, Ukraine and parts of Russia most contaminated (Briansk and Kaluga regions) increased from 1981-1985 to 1986-1994 by a factor of 80-100 or almost by two orders of magnitude (Sweet, 1996).

No less impressive have been economic damages incurred by the Chernobyl disaster. About 1.5 million square hectares of agricultural lands with the density of Cs^{137} exceeding 5 Ci / km^2 have been excluded from exploitation, while according to official sources direct economic losses by 1990 reached 10 billion rubles or more than 3 billion US$. Expert estimates (see, for example, Koriakin, 1990) show both direct and indirect economic costs, excluding expenditures on medical treatment and compensation to affected people, by the year 2000 will soar to 250 billion rubles or more than 80 billion US$, thus making Chernobyl one of the costliest radiation disasters ever.

As in case of natural disasters, the last but not the least important thing to stress is the intertwining and interdependence of social system vulnerability both to major technological and compound hazards, and the level of economic development of different regions and countries of the world. Accelerated industrialization along with technological progress and urbanization along with growing complexity of social systems contributed decisively to the general global trend of increasing technological and compound risks. At the same time, peculiarities in historical, cultural and political domains which have influenced considerably economic progress and level of development have predetermined substantial variations in degree and pattern of these risks and vulnerability of the social systems.

The available data show that America has been keeping its leadership, accounting for 31% of the total number of major technological accidents which involved 10 or more deaths, and/or 100 or more affected(the criteria used by the Center for Research on the Epidemiology of Disasters, CRED) and occurred in the world between 1969 and 1993 and 41% of the total economic losses incurred by these accidents from 1989 to 1993. European countries have concentrated 28% and 48% respectively while the respective proportions of Asia have been 31% and 7% the rest being spread between Africa and Oceania (*World Disaster Report 1995*: 103, 106).

The analysis of these data reveal the long term trend of a gradual decrease of the proportion of American states in the total number of technological disasters, primarily in the USA and Canada, while the proportions of European countries, in particular the former Soviet Union (currently the CIS countries), and especially Asian states have been increasing. This means that the contribution of the most developed countries to the global list of technological disasters has been diminishing while the rest of the world has been augmenting its share. The proportion of the OECD members in the total number of the largest technological accidents (in accordance with the OECD criteria cited above) dropped from an estimated 46% during 1974-1983 to 25% between 1984 and 1994 while their share in total economic damages inflicted by these accidents still exceeded a half.

Respectively the proportions of the former socialist block and developing countries in the total number of technological disasters jumped from an estimated 54% within 1974-1983 to 75% between 1984 and 1994 with about 60% of these provided by the latter. The former Soviet Union and contemporary Russia have demonstrated an accelerated increase of their input into the world inventory of technological disasters with its share reaching estimated 15-16%. At the same time the developing countries have accounted for almost 80% of the casualties of these and other non-natural disasters between 1969 and 1993. As far as the affected people are concerned, the former Soviet Union and Switzerland have provided the main contribution due to the Chernobyl radiation and the Sandoz chemical disasters. (Estimates are based on: Porfiriev, 1991a: 14-16; Portnoff, 1989; World Disasters Report 1995: 99-105).

All these show evidence that although the most industrialized countries of the world are still conspicuously jeopardized to major technological threats, particularly in economic terms, the developing countries, mainly the new industrializing states in Latin America and Asia, are especially affected by these and other hazards while the former Soviet Union and nowadays Russia has become increasingly and substantially vulnerable to the threats.

The reasons for this are multifaceted but the bulk of them are bound with the existent and even widening of educational, scientific and technological gaps between the most industrialized countries and the rest of the world. Since late 1960s these countries have been the pioneers in implementation of a new development strategy based on microelectronics, information science and technology, new materials and so on which also required and have been accompanied by new management approaches. This decisively facilitated their historical transition from industrial system which involved energy and substance transformation - the main technological risk factors - to an information and information technology intensive system.

Without going into a comprehensive analysis of this crucial transition (detailed discussion of this issue see in: Arab-Ogli, 1986; Bell, 1973; Naisbitt, 1982; Toffler, 1980) one important issue should be especially noted. Given the inverse relationship between the risk of major technological accidents and information within the society management system, these new production systems and development strategies contribute positively to the general trend of an increase in the degree of the society's protection capacity and a decrease of its vulnerability, however, being principally incapable to provide 100% technological safety and security and safety as a whole.

Contrary to that fact the rest of the world, including the former Soviet Union and contemporary Russia, have been following the outmoded development strategy which involves predominantly resource and labor intensive rather than information based production and management technologies and is resistant to other innovations and structural changes. As a result, before the vulnerability of these countries, in particular those relatively more industrialized and populous - Brazil and Mexico in America, India in Asia and the former Soviet Union in Europe, - to the major technological hazards considerably increased within 1970s and 1980s. These four countries accounted for almost 88% or seven out from the eight largest technological accidents registered from 1983 to 1996 worldwide including the earlier cited cases in Cubatao, San Juan Ixuatepec and Bhopal in 1984, Chernobyl in 1986 and Ufa in 1989 which killed more than 500 people each.

Considering the conspicuous role of the former Soviet Union in the issue under discussion in the 1980s and the drastic changes which occurred there after its dissolution in 1991, it becomes especially interesting and important to analyze and estimate the vulnerability of communities and society to the major technological and compound threats in Russia in the 1990s. The data from Russian official sources, primarily the Ministry of the Russian Federation for Civil Defense, Emergencies and Natural Disaster Response (MES) show that the impact of these agents on the social systems and their ambiance has been great. Unfortunately, the incompleteness and inconsistency of this data makes it very difficult to evaluate more or less precisely the contribution of each type of hazard into the total disaster effect on the national economy and security. It is especially hard in relation to compound hazards originating from both natural and non-natural (technological and/or social) sources. The available data provide the opportunity to delineate trustworthy only the impact of the so-called natural and social (na-soc) hazards including epidemic and epizootic. At the same time, disasters like those provoked by the major earthquakes in Spitak or Neftegorsk mentioned earlier or by large forest and peat fires have been still registered officially by the MES as 'natural emergencies' although this is either only a part of the truth as in a former case or very far from reality as in the case of forest fires: 90% of these in Russia being man-made.

In addition, the most complicated problems with official statistics in Russia in the 1990s dealt with inadequate criteria used to assess the scale and gravity of the hazards impact. For several years these criteria which involved the number of killed (two persons or more), casualties or affected (10 persons or more), value of economic damage (500,000 rubles or more, 1992 prices or approximately 20,000 US$ or more) and some other indicators (environmental, geophysical, etc.) have been used for registration of hazardous occasions as 'emergencies' as a whole without their further specification and special delineation of large scale emergencies, disasters and catastrophes which are the subject of this book. Although the situation should have turned to the better in 1996 when emergencies scale classification was approved by a special governmental order (see further on) this was not enforced till the end of 1997 and by that time nothing had changed. Therefore the following tables and graphs, which are based on official data sources and illustrate the comparative frequency and degree of impact of technological and other hazards in Russia should be treated with reservations and caution.

Given all this, it is possible nevertheless to make a general conclusion that despite a relative decrease of frequency and proportion of technological accidents and compound (na-soc) hazardous occasions in the total number of emergencies, they have been undoubtedly dominating in the 1990s (Tables 4 and 5).

Between 1992 and 1996 alone the total number of emergencies exceeded 7,000 with almost 140,000 people affected including about 12,000 of them killed. By my estimate, these basically involved local emergencies with an average number of affected of 15 persons each while the large-scale emergencies and disasters have constituted only a small percentage. Technological and compound accidents account to more than 4/5 of the total number of emergencies and 3/4 of their fatalities (Tables 2 and 3).

The most numerous have been fires and explosions at industrial and energy power plants as well as municipal facilities and residential buildings which also account for increasing proportion of all the casualties caused by technological accidents: 48% in 1996 against 20% in 1992. At the same time the latter indicator for transportation accidents (including those occurred at roads, railways, pipelines and in the air) which still dominate in terms of fatalities has been diminishing:

Table 2. The Number of Emergencies in Russia, 1990-1996

Emergencies[a]	1990	1991	1992	1993	1994	1995	1996
(1)	(2)	(3)	(4)	(5)	(6)	(7)	(8)
Railway accidents	73	80	101	91	88	52	23
Shipwrecks	113	97	3	11	22	13	23
Air crashes	18	18	20	14	15	14	18
Accidents at the main pipelines	...	114	43	32	55	48	62
Road, crossroads and bridge accidents	115	430	171	153	177	184	153
Total transportation accidents	*319*	*739*	*338*	*301*	*357*	*311*	*279*
Industrial infrastructure accidents	13	...	40	50	69	42	68
Incidents at the nuclear power plants	...	...	6	3	7	11	...
Accidents resulting in toxic and radioactive emissions	53	38	75	83	73	78	74
Fires, explosions at industrial and municipal facilities	380	397	515	446	565	583	537
Other (finding of toxic, radiation sources and ammunition)	...	...	30	13	14	46	54
Total industrial accidents	*446*	*435*	*666*	*595*	*728*	*760*	*733*
TOTAL TECHNOLOGICAL ACCIDENTS	**765**	**1174**	**1004**	**896**	**1085**	**1071**	**1012**

Table 2 (Continued)

(1)	(2)	(3)	(4)	(5)	(6)	(7)	(8)
Earthquakes, landslides	...	...	55	51	70	83	81
Windstorms (cyclones, hurricanes), avalanches, floods	...	...	64	48	108	122	129
Forest and peat fires	...	...	25	35	33	44	79
TOTAL NATURAL HAZARDS AND DISASTERS	...	...	*144*	*134*	*211*	*249*	*289*
Mass infectious diseases and poisonings	...	...	80	105	149	145	74
Epizootic	...	...	14	15	...	35	26
Other compound emergencies	...	...	31	31	32	20	22
TOTAL COMPOUND EMERGENCIES	...	...	*125*	*142*	*181*	*200*	*122*
GRAND TOTAL	...	...	*1273*	*1172*	*1477*	*1520*	*1423*

[a] The hazardous occasions involving 10 persons or more affected each (see: Pravitelstvo. Postanovleniye, 1996b).

Source: Compiled from: (Gosudarstennii Doklad, 1996a, 1996b; Chrezvichainiye Situatsii, 1994; Spravka, 1997)

Table 3. The Number Killed in Emergencies in Russia, 1990-1996

Emergencies[a]	1990	1991	1992	1993	1994	1995	1996
(1)	(2)	(3)	(4)	(5)	(6)	(7)	(8)
Railway accidents	8	20	54	32	47	24	23
Shipwrecks	...	6	2	51	...	20	47
Air crashes	155	167	287	320	270	243	282
Accidents at the main pipelines	...	...	3	1	1	2	6
Road, crossroads and bridge accidents	...	120	643	513	620	620	517
Total transportation accidents	*163*	*313*	*989*	*917*	*938*	*909*	*875*
Industrial infrastructure accidents	...	...	13	31	0	10	2
Accidents resulting in toxic and radioactive emissions	...	...	24	4	16	24	5
Fires, explosions at industrial and municipal facilities	...	...	210	320	585	717	775
Other (finding of toxic, radiation sources and ammunition)	...	...	...	...	6	8	14
Total industrial accidents	...	...	*247*	*355*	*607*	*759*	*796*
TOTAL TECHNOLOGICAL ACCIDENTS	...	...	**1236**	**1272**	**1545**	**1668**	**1671**

Table 3 (Continued)

(1)	(2)	(3)	(4)	(5)	(6)	(7)	(8)
Earthquakes, landslides	...	...	...	...	11	1999	2
Windstorms (cyclones, hurricanes), avalanches, floods	...	...	...	...	84	23	24
Forest and swamp fires	...	...	...	...	...	...	20
TOTAL NATURAL HAZARDS AND DISASTERS	...	...	...	...	*95*	*2022*	*46*
Mass infectious diseases and poisonings	...	...	89	102	767	949	361
Epizootic	...	...	...	...	...	...	...
Other compound emergencies	...	...	...	...	...	...	...
TOTAL COMPOUND EMERGENCIES	...	...	*89*	*102*	*767*	*949*	*361*
GRAND TOTAL	...	...	1325	1374	2407	4639	2078

[a] See footnote to Table 2

Emergencies [a]	1991	1992	1993	1994	1995	1996
Technological	1.00	0.86	0.76	0.92	0.91	0.86
Natural and compound	1.00	1.07	1.10	1.56	1.78	1.64

Table 4. The Rates of Growth of the Numbers of Emergencies in Russia
Source: Table 2

Emergencies	1992	1993	1994	1995	1996
Technological	78.9	76.5	73.5	70.4	71.1
Natural	11.3	11.4	14.3	16.4	20.3
Compound	9.8	12.1	12.2	13.2	8.6
TOTAL	100.0	100.0	100.0	100.0	100.0

Table 5. Percentage of Emergencies in Russia by the Type of Hazard

Source: Table 2

Accidents' Domain	1990	1991	1992	1993	1994	1995	1996
Transportation	41.7	62.9	33.7	33.6	32.9	29.0	27.6
Industrial, energy power and municipal facilities	58.3	37.1	63.4	64.3	65.9	69.7	72.4
TOTAL	100.0	100.0	100.0	100.0	100.0	100.0	100.0

Table 6. Percentage of Technological Accidents in Russia by Domain of Hazard

Source: Table 2

Source of death	1992	1993	1994	1995	1996
Transportation accidents	80.0	72.1	60.7	54.5	52.4
Accidents at the Industrial, energy power and municipal facilities	20.0	27.9	39.2	45.5	47.6
TOTAL	100.0	100.0	100.0	100.0	100.0

Table 7. Percentage of Killed in Technological Accidents in Russia by Source of Death

Source: Table 3

up to 52% from 80%, respectively with simultaneous decrease to 28% from 42% of their share in the total number of technological emergencies (see Tables 6 and 7).

As to compound emergencies, the general trend of their gradually increasing proportion both in the total number of emergencies and fatalities caused by them in Russia in the 1990s is apparent. In the mid-1990s these proportions for epidemic and epizootic (na-soc compound emergencies) alone were almost equal and vary from 10% to 11%. However, these figures are far from revealing the real role of compound hazards, which as mentioned earlier involve a much broader gamut of extreme events and occasions, as catalysts of emergencies and disasters. Given the crucial role of human activities, both as risk sources and social and environmental vulnerability factors, I believe that from as early as the 1970s compound emergencies have been the dominating type among all the emergencies, disasters and catastrophes in the former Soviet Union and contemporary Russia. In the 1990s the degree of this vulnerability has been further increasing. Suffice it to cite the available data on epidemics between 1993 and 1997 the incidence of tuberculosis in Russia augmented by almost 60% while the case-load of diphtheria in Russia and other CIS countries jumped more than five-fold from 1992 to 1994 alone (see Fig. 11).

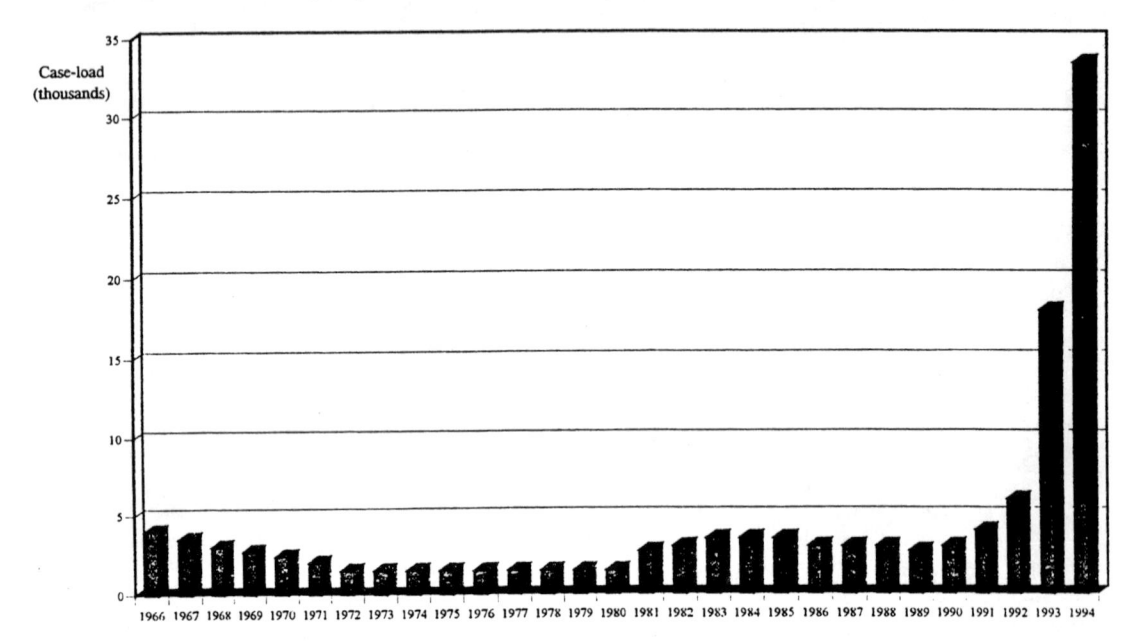

Fig. 11. The Case-Load of Diphtheria in the Former Soviet Union and the CIS

Source: (World Disaster Report, 1995)

Thus in the case of natural disasters in terms of the social system vulnerability to technological and compound threats, Russia and other countries of the former Soviet Union occupy a somewhat intermediate position between the most industrialized and the bulk of the much less developed countries of the world. On one hand this stems from continuing implementation of the previous development policy based on resource intensive and still considerable but physically and technologically obsolete production facilities.

The historical changes in the West which resulted from transfer of the bulk of industries and the whole society to R&D intensive and information technologies since late 1960s - early 1970s have only slightly touched the former Soviet Union and Russia being confined there only to the military and space sectors of economy. Most of the economy, including the key industries, remained as if it was left in the antecedent technological epoch which has been a logical consequence of preservation of the existing political system. This backwardness was especially and painfully pronounced in the industries which have been directly involved or closely associated with technological safety and security.

On the other hand, the deformations and loopholes in development policy in the former Soviet Union in the last 20 years have been further aggravated in Russia in the 1990s by the deep social and economic crisis there which has followed and accompanied the dissolution of the USSR in 1991. The crisis has lead to a sharp economic recession, shrinking of investments in technological modernization and personnel upgrading including those for strengthening of industrial safety and substantially reduced expenditures on public or social safety, in particular on mitigation of epidemic and morbidity increase through mass vaccinations and better nutrition for children.

Besides other things, the enumerated problems have meant the depreciation of the main production facilities from 70% to 90% in mid 1990s in the high risk industries, for example, in the petrochemical, fuel and energy power industries. In Russian industry as a whole, 60% of the main production facilities were depreciated by more than a half, the same indicator for another 20% of those facilities soared to 75% while the rest of 20% of them were completely or even over depreciated. The situation has been expected to worsen by the year 2000 when the number of facilities with the highest rates of depreciation will increase by 10% (Mikeev, 1996b: 15-16; Yelokhin and Chernopliokov, 1994).

This unpleasant picture is supplemented by conspicuous declining of technological and production discipline, in particular as a result of hard drinking and alcoholism. The latter alone is responsible for up to 40% of all industrial injuries which have reached dangerous levels. Nowadays the number of injured per each 1,000 workers and employees in Russia exceeds the respective index in the UK, Germany, USA and Japan by a factor of 1.5 to 8-fold. These factors substantially contribute to the gap of 3-fold to 7-fold which exists between Russia and the countries in terms of industrial personnel fatalities from technological accidents (Mikeev, 1996b: 13; V Rossii, 1996). For example, loopholes in technological and production discipline were the trigger of the 1993 radiation accident in Seversk, the most serious after Chernobyl (see Chapter 4).

At last one more specifically Russian manifestation and consequence of the deep social and economic crisis in the 1990s there is worth consideration as a factor contributing to increasing social vulnerability to technological and compound impact agents. The decline in the living standards of the majority of the Russian population along with the bankruptcy of many state enterprises, including those in high risk industries, made impossible on time payments for municipal services (electricity, heat, gas and water supplies).

The disconnection of industrial consumers from the main lifelines used by local producers as a penalty have lead to dangerous breaks at many high risk facilities including those with nuclear technologies which could lead to large emergencies and disasters. The same penalty used against residential consumers forced persons trying to restore the disconnected gas supply tubes themselves without proper safety measures. As a result in the two towns of Leningrad oblast (region): Svetogorsk and Priozersk, in 1996 alone gas explosions killed 41 persons and severely destroyed two residential buildings leaving homeless dozens of people.

The facts and figures discussed earlier show that increasing vulnerability of the social systems to the growing impact of compound hazards which involve a combination of technological and social agents sometimes mixed with natural factors is most pronounced in societies in transition to the new development strategy. These are the regions and countries with complicated political and social situations and a level of economy somewhat intermediate between the most developed and the bulk of developing countries of the world. In some respects Russia is a typical, but in much more respects, a specific case within this group. At the same time, the trend of increasing vulnerability is common for all types of modern societies including the most prosperous and results from their inadequate management capacity to cope with the pace and impact force of both old and new threats to public safety and security. Thus the problems dealing with the deep understanding of the commonalties and peculiarities of the mechanism of development of emergencies, disasters and catastrophes as well as of emergency management, are becoming more and more pressing.

EMERGENCY AND DISASTER AS RESEARCH AND MANAGEMENT CATEGORIES

The threats or real impact of the major unscheduled and extraordinary events or agents including large scale social conflicts, technological accidents, natural and compound hazards on the vulnerable elements of the social systems - that is densely populated, inadequately protected, often highly urbanized and industrialized areas - break normal social routines of communities, aggravate social, psychological and sometimes political tensions, and incur economic losses thus creating a dramatic situation full of uncertainty and complexity which requires immediate, decisive and comprehensive response actions. To describe this situation or set of occasions several terms are used in research and normative literature including: crisis, emergency, disaster and collective stress. Substantive interpretation of these terms is paramount both on methodological grounds which predetermine the conceptual system structure and from a practical perspective for giving a description of the subject area and mission of a management process.

Among the terms, crisis, emergency and disaster are most widely used in research literature in the West where the problems of social system management in unscheduled conditions have been studied as long as half a century or more. The concept of a 'crisis' which implies a serious threat to the basic structures or the fundamental values and norms of a social system which - under time pressure and highly uncertain circumstances - necessitates making critical decisions (Rosenthal, 1986; Shrivastava, 1992: 5) is used as a most general category to characterize critical situations when a direct threat to human life and health may exist but is not a compulsory requisite. The latter may be illustrated by examples of governmental, economic, personal crisis and so forth.

In other circumstances, which are at the focus of my analysis when such a direct threat, either real or perceived exists, and protection of human lives, health and material wealth is needed, the other two concepts have been used. The Western, especially US scholars: sociologists and representatives of the natural sciences (geographers, geologists, etc.) whose publications have been dominating in the field under discussion prefer the term 'disaster' while the practitioners (administrators and managers, police and fire workers an so on) also widely use the term 'emergency'. In Europe, including Russia, the latter is preferably used both by researchers and practitioners.

Given the different historical and cultural traditions, including linguistic peculiarities existing between and within countries and subjective preferences of individual researchers, it is no wonder that the universal term to describe a certain set of extraordinary occasions is lacking. However, far more important is whatever expression is used, the substantive phenomena being discussed must be the same. The analysis of conceptualizations and definitions of both 'disaster' and 'emergency' existing in different cultural domains reveals that to a considerable extent these concepts are close to each other. In the last half of a century, social scientists starting from encyclopedic and everyday usage of both words have increasingly attempted to conceptualize them as a part of situation generated by natural and man-made agents. In fact the theoretical work and empirical research on the social aspects of disasters is more or less equivalent of the social scientific analysis and applied studies of emergencies (Quarantelli, 1990: 1).

This does not mean that differences and peculiarities in interpretations of the phenomena under discussion are no longer valid. In particular, numerous variations of 'disaster' can be found elsewhere in the English research literature which has employed this category most widely. Gilbert proposes to sum up all disaster's conceptualizations within three paradigms as a: a) result of external force impact; b) result of social vulnerability; c) result of uncertainty (Gilbert, 1995). Pelanda, in turn, suggested embracing all definitions of disaster into three categories based on interpreting it as a: a) result or negative social and environmental impacts; b) state (condition) of a collective stress of a community; c) contradiction between capacity to cope with destructive agents and their negative impacts (Pelanda, 1982a).

This typology reflects three conceptual dimensions: causal, descriptive and normative, which I believe to be absolutely correct but somewhat insufficient and needing additional "axes".

Conceptualizing and defining disaster, some researchers who prefer static rather than dynamic approach consider a disaster as a discrete happening and base their definitions of this category viewing it either as an occasion (Dynes, 1988; Quarantelli, 1987a, 1987b, 1992a) or an event (Fritz, 1961; Kreps, 1989a, 1989b) or phenomenon (Horlick-Jones et al, 1991a; 1991b; 1993; Kroll-Smith and Couch, 1990). At the same time a few of them also refer to the "principle of continuity" thus involving a time scale into their concept of disaster (Quarantelli and Dynes, 1977).

Meanwhile, some scholars using the dynamic approach to disaster treat it as a category of action (Dombrowsky, 1981) while others try to combine both of the approaches within some kind of generic or ecological concept consider disaster as a certain social state/condition (crisis or vulnerability) (see Barton, 1969; Gilbert, 1991; Kroll-Smith, Couch, 1991; Lagadec, 1991; Pelanda, 1982b).

Further developing from this "nucleus" to an extensive definition of disaster and starting from earlier mentioned causal logic, some of them, primarily geographers, consider it as a reason for the following social disruptions or disorders (Alexander, 1991; Kroll-Smith, Couch, 1990; Foster, 1980). This description sets forth an exogenous or outward type concept of disaster that designates it by physical agents that usually come from nature (i.e. outside the community) and thus treating it as a natural disaster like everyday conversations.

Social scientists using the same causal logic display a wider gamut of interpretations of disaster. They consider it as a social construction, though all of them fit their view within an endogenous or inward-type concept of disaster. A few of them treat disaster as a result of social processes or social consequences that create (give birth to sources of danger or hazard) or increases the vulnerability of a social system to hazardous impacts (Pelanda, 1982; Perrow, 1984; Tierney, 1989; Quarantelli, 1987b, 1992a). This vulnerability may display itself either in the form of a collective stress situation (Barton, 1970) or a crisis within social system per se (Lagadec, 1988; Rosenthal, 1986), or inconsistency between the capacities of the latter and the demands of a disaster situation in terms of both response and recovery (Kreps, 1984; Pelanda, 1982b; Turner, 1978, 1979).

Other scholars consider disaster as a combination of reasons, whatever their origin (natural, technological, social, political) and results, both physical and social (Horlick-Jones et al, 1991a; 1991b; 1993; Kreps, 1989a, 1989b). The latter approach for a long time has been also supported by Guibert White, an outstanding American geographer. It should also be added that along with descriptive and normative interpretations of disaster embedded in Pelanda's typology, sometimes it is viewed as a statistical category. For example, UNDRO designates disaster as:

> the probability of occurrence within a specified period of time and within a given areas of potentially damaging phenomenon (UNDRO, 1982)

But Dynes, among four different meanings, stresses three as indicators either of physical or social damage or negative evaluation in general (Dynes, 1993).

Maybe somebody can view it in a different way, but I do not consider the variety of disaster conceptualizations and definitions as absolute and find them really deficient and inconsistent. Though they are really different and thus often noncomplimentary there are still substantial grounds to treat them as complanary, i.e. lying within the same categorical domain (to continue a mathematical analogy). As Quarantelli and Kreps put it, there is considerable agreement, or much more agreement than disagreement, among scholars about the essence of what a disaster is (Quarantelli, 1992a; Kreps, 1989b).

With minor exceptions I believe that all variations in explanation of disaster reflect rather the researchers' professional backgrounds, specifics tasks or goals of concrete studies, as well as indistinct terminology of individuals than discrepancy in the very meaning of disaster. Some scholars starting to answer to the question "what disaster is" further simply substitute or confuse it with other questions like "what disaster does", "how does society act under conditions of disaster", etc. that should of course be considered as relevant but still not definitely the original question (see Britton, 1987; Drabek, 1986; Fritz, 1961; Kreps, 1984; Quarantelli, 1987a, 1987b).

That is why I argue that while further discussion on conceptualization and definition of both emergency and disaster is underway, one of the most important issues to be considered is the very clear delineation of initial or starting premises, and the limitations of each study. First of all, it is crucial to distinguish its task function or, in other words, applied/pragmatic and theoretical/conceptual orientations based on ontological and epistemological grounds, respectively.

Within the latter approach, a social scientist or system analyst tries to develop a conceptually-based definition of emergency and/or disaster as such using either broad (system or interdisciplinary) or specific (disciplinary) approaches and attempts to balance cognitive, including psychological, and empirical aspects. Within the pragmatic orientation of the study, its author who is normally a decision-making analyst (supporter), engineer or natural scientist (geographer, geologist, etc.) attempts to develop a rather operational framework or/and definition of concepts necessary for elaborating laws, rules, and regulations as well as plans and measures to mitigate prepare, respond to and recover from concrete crisis.

The research methodology and methods of the two different types of studies on conceptualizing and defining emergency and/or disaster should also be expected to be quite different. The conceptual-focused ones involve generic-type complex approaches and theories (system, sociological, linguistic, information, risk, multicriterial decision-making in conditions of uncertainty, etc.) reflecting both objective and subjective (perception) aspects of crisis. At the same time, pragmatic-oriented studies apply common sense, as well as heuristic and simple logic, approaches based on a limited number of objective criteria. These are aimed at explicitly revealing those basic features and stages of life history of specific emergency and/or disaster that permit developing the normative and regulation documents.

No less different would be the form (shape) of the outcome or results of the mentioned functions or orientations of the study. In a pragmatic-type study, it may vary from a 'working' definition of the key concept simply to introduce further action program or measures proposed (see UNDRO definition of disaster above), to presenting a framework of the noted documents; from "narrow" or "subjective" version of what emergency and/or disaster is sometimes with explicit quantitative criteria (e.g. see: Clement, 1989) to recommendations for and concrete drafts of laws, rules, regulations, plans, etc.

In a conceptual-oriented study, one should obtain an extensive definition of emergency and/or disaster which distinguishes them from both routine and other crisis situation or occasions and is based on a verbal description with all or a few key qualitative (implicit) criteria mentioned above. Within this kind of a study, and remembering that in Russia both theorists and practitioners widely use the word 'emergency' to describe a situation or set of occasions of collective stress and substantial economic losses resulting from various hazardous impacts, I would try to introduce my own conceptualization of both emergency, disaster and catastrophe as social research and management categories.

To start with, it is noteworthy to mention that the ideological postulates which existed for decades in the former Soviet Union prescribed that in a socialist state no mass emergencies and disasters could occur in principle except minor accidents. Large accidents and natural calamities that happened were kept secret and forbidden to be published in mass media. When it was impossible to hide the information completely, the state-controlled newspapers, radio and TV communicated that a hazardous event, for example flood or fire, occurred with no casualties and damages. These information vacuum seriously deterred research in the field under discussion and for a long time open publications have been lacking.

That is why the term 'emergency' and its conceptualization as a social and management science category appeared in research and normative literature of the former Soviet Union only decades after the disaster conceptions discussed above were developed and published in the West, first of all in the United States. In the former Soviet Union, the concept 'emergency' as a research and management category initially was introduced by the author in his brochure (Porfiriev, 1989) and further developed in his monograph (Porfiriev, 1991). I proposed to base both emergency definition and conceptualization on seven qualitative criteria which were further characterized by 15 general descriptors (see Table 8).

Table 8. Emergency Criteria

Criteria	Description of real and/or perceived characteristics
(1)	(2)
◆ Expectability and predictability of impact	• Real or perceived unexpectedness of manifestation
◆ Social and environmental (including health) impact and effects	• Casualties, increase in communities' morbidity, epidemics • Contamination of environment, potable water and food hazardous for human health
◆ Social and psychological impact and effects	• Collective stress (fear, phobia, depression, etc.), uncertainty frustration and anxiety among affected persons and neighboring communities while culmination or emergency • Frustration and anxiety among affected persons and neighboring communities in the post-culmination or post-emergency period
◆ Social impact and effects	• Breaking of normal routines of communities including everyday water, food and other key consumer goods supplies, providing medical care, working places, decrease or temporarily suspension of economic activities • Rupturing of lifelines (water, electricity, gas supplies)

Table 8. *(Continued)*

(1)	(2)
◆ Public relations and political impact and effects	• Temporarily conspicuous increase in media coverage and public awareness • Increasing of social and political tensions and intensiveness of discussions and comments both at the national parliament and government and internationally
◆ Economic impact and effects	• Considerable economic losses in physical and/or monetary terms • Damages of engineering systems and technological complexes ("normal accidents') • Considerable damage to natural resources, agricultural lands and livestock • Considerable expenditures to be spent on recovery and compensations
◆ Organizational impact and response requirements	• Uncertainty and complexity of the occasion (happening) which predetermine: a) increasing complexity of decision making b) urgency of response (decision making) c) necessity of evacuation, search and rescue, special medical care activities

Table 8. *(Continued)*

(1)	(2)
	d) involvement of numerous and different types of organizations and personnel
	e) using of special technical devices and mechanisms for control and response
◆ Multiplicity (comprehensiveness) of effects and response	• Heterogeneity and multiplicity of chain (ripple-type) effects incurred upon various fields of activities and authority and organizational levels (e.g. substitution of building codes, land use planning schemes and operation manuals for hazardous technological facilities by more reliable and sophisticated; rejection or suspension of implementation of a large scale R&D program: nuclear, space, etc.)

Systemic integrity of these criteria should be considered as their crucial attribute: the whole set of them should be met with none of the criteria missing to treat an event or occasion as an emergency situation or simply as an emergency. In this respect special attention should be drawn to the criterion of multiplicity (comprehensiveness) of the consequences of and response to a hazardous impact. It is focused on a variety of ripple or chain effects generated by this impact in communities and societies including social, psychological, economic, environmental, political and some other as one of the main characteristics of an emergency.

For example, in the former Soviet Union, the large scale accident at the Chernobyl nuclear power plant in 1986 lead not only to the death of dozens, hospitalization of hundreds and evacuation and relocation of hundreds of thousands in the first weeks after the explosion, but to multibillion expenditures on alleviation of the aftermath and compensation to the affected people. It also resulted in suspension of both construction and starting of the exploitation of the new nuclear power units, reconsideration of respective federal training and R&D programs, in particular concerning nuclear reactor RBMK-1000 which involved considerable changes in its safety design and substantial additional expenditures on accelerated development of the new generation or reactors. All these could not but impact negatively on the economic development in the early stages of perestroika and deterred the initiation of economic reforms in the former Soviet Union in the late 1980s (Abalkin, 1988).

Similarly, already in contemporary Russia the major earthquake in Neftegorsk, Sakhalin Island in 1995 not only involved almost 2,000 fatalities, several hundred were evacuated and hospitalized, and total destruction of the town of Neftegorsk. It also forced reconsideration of the previous official seismological zoning scheme of the Far East region of Russia, starting of large scale inspection of buildings and construction in terms of their consistency to existing standards, and acceleration of the development of the Federal Seismological Monitoring and Forecasting System of the Russian Federation. An analogous ripple or chain effect of the major hazard impact was typical for the radiation accident at the Siberian chemical complex in Seversk and the large scale fire at the KamAZ truck engine plant in the middle Volga region both in 1993, which fortunately did not result in fatalities and mass evacuation although such a threat was quite real (see Chapter 4 for detailed discussion).

Contrary to the criteria of an emergency, systemic integrity is not a necessary requirement for the 15 descriptors which are used for qualitative characteristics of these criteria (see Table 8). In certain emergencies, some of the descriptors can be missing. In the examples cited above, the whole gamut of descriptors including 'the increasing of social and political tensions both nationally and internationally' are represented in the case of Chernobyl radiation disaster while in the rest of the cases, the latter descriptor along with another one, 'considerable damage to natural resources, agricultural lands and livestock', is lacking.

Using the proposed criteria as a concept basis, I defined emergency as:

> a set of occasions or situation which really is, or perceived as, unexpected, disrupting normal social activities, involving direct threats to the safety of a social system or its units and substantial economic losses, provoking uncertainty and collective stress thus necessitating an urgent response and extraordinary countermeasures (Porfiriev, 1989: 20-21).

Whatever apt or infelicitous, the proposed definition of emergency was elaborated within a conceptual-oriented approach and consequently is used in this book as an important part of the theoretical basis. From a methodological viewpoint, it is important in that it seems to allow a delineation between routine and emergency situations, on the one hand, and between emergency and other forms of crisis irrespective of their causes, on the other hand.. The emergency's main distinctive features include: (a) a breaking of the collective routines of social units (i.e., communities and societies) and their normal environment; (b) real or perceived threat to the latter urging extraordinary, often unplanned measures to cope with the situation and protect people.

The "a" descriptor distinguishes emergency from both ordinary occasions and accidents which are unforeseen happenings that often result in injuries, losses and damages. These may involve both social units (as an emergency does) or individuals (which an emergency does not). The "b" descriptor delineates an emergency among other crisis or crisis situations which do not always involve unexpectedness and direct threat to the safety and security of a social system or its units, for example in the case of a economic, governmental crisis and so on. These in turn do not require urgent and extraordinary measures to save or protect people, rather shifting the emphasis on mid-term actions to reverse the situation for the better.

The early conceptualization and definition of emergency proposed by the author later were followed by numerous interpretations by Soviet and then Russian scholars and legislators who paraphrased or emphasized certain aspects (see Broushlinskiy and Semikov, 1990; Mikeev, 1990; Mikhailov, Paschenko and Souldin, 1991; Vasilkevich, 1991). In 1990, emergency was for the first time defined prescriptively within a special regulation of the former Soviet Union government as:

> a situation at a facility or in a certain area of land or water caused by an accident, catastrophe, natural and ecological disaster, epidemic, epizootic and epiphytotic which results or may result in considerable losses, casualties and disrupting the living conditions of people (Sovet Ministrov, 1990).

A year later this was practically repeated in governmental regulation #261 of the Russian Federation and then reformulated at the highest legislative level in Russia in the 1994 Federal Act on Protection of People and Territories Against Natural and Technological Emergencies which designated the latter as:

> a situation in a certain area which results from an accident, natural hazard, catastrophe, natural or other disasters that may incur and have incurred fatalities, damages to human health or the environment, considerable material losses and have disrupted the living conditions of the people (Federalnii Zakon, 1994: para 1).

This act has also yielded definitions of the two key emergency management concepts, 'prevention' and 'liquidation', the former being formulated as:

> a set of measures taken in advance, in order to decrease to a possible maximum degree, the risk of emergency origin and to protect human health, and reduce the magnitude of environmental and material damages in case an emergency strikes,

while the latter concept was respectively designated as:

> rescue and other urgent response activities which are carried out in case of an emergency to save lives and protect human health, reduce the magnitude of environmental and material damages as well as to localize the emergency areas and stop the hazardous impact of the agents most typical for the affected areas (Federalnii Zakon, 1994: para 1).

As could be easily seen, both normative conceptualizations are somewhat confusing and narrow. The former interpretation mixes prevention and preparedness which should be separated from each other as representing qualitatively and chronologically different management phases, while the latter interpretation is restricted to response activities leaving aside recovery efforts. These important issues will be extensively discussed in Chapter 2. However, at this point it is worth noting that the following analysis involves the well-established four-unit management model including mitigation (prevention), preparedness of, response to and recovery from emergency or/and disaster.

In addition, if the author's and normative formulations of emergency cited earlier are compared with the well known conceptualizations of disaster in research literature in the West, primarily in the USA, the essential similarity between them would easily come to the light. I believe that my own interpretation of emergency is very close to the modern conceptions of disaster in terms of both of them stressing real or perceived unexpectedness, disruption of social routines and necessitating extraordinary protection and rescue measures.

However, these conceptualizations differ in that I label as an emergency all kinds of crisis occasions which directly jeopardize the safety and security of a social unit irrespective of the source of crisis and type of crisis response, while many existing disaster conceptions have distinguished the latter among other crisis situations using the criteria of its originating only from natural and technological hazards and involving only consensus or non-conflict type of response with social conflicts as a source being separated.

In this respect these disaster conceptions are concordant with emergency interpretation in para 1 of the Russian federal act cited above which treats an emergency as a result of natural and technological impact but, contrary to the former, puts the disruption of normal social activities in last place and does not mention at all the necessity of urgent response measures to be taken. Undoubtedly, the distinction between conflict and non-conflict occasions within crises is logical and substantive both from the viewpoint of consideration of the crisis origin and types of response.

Nevertheless, this leaves room for some serious methodological and practical problems which may arise in particular if a war is used as a case. In terms of response, it is surely a consensus-type event and should be considered as a national (federal) disaster. At the same time, a war is both a result and manifestation of an open armed conflict and within the theoretical and logical framework, can not be labeled as a disaster.

This means, first, that the disaster conceptualizations under discussion need further specifications which would distinguish peacetime and wartime crises. Secondly, a more clear-cut distinction between emergency and disaster conceptualizations is still an important research and practical issue for social science and management policy. Maybe some prominent disaster sociologists are right when they consider these concepts as very close or even synonymous, each of them being preferably used depending on a country or professional area peculiarities? I believe this is true while a crisis is viewed as a discrete happening within a static-type methodological approach.

However, the picture changes as soon as a dynamic-type approach is applied which treats a crisis as a developing process and presupposes a distinction between emergency and disaster as different states (both phases and gravity degrees) of a social system crisis. I reckon this type of analytical framework as more appropriate and fruitful for a comprehensive analysis of emergencies and disasters from the management or public administration perspective and therefore use it as a basis for further discussion.

PRE-CONDITIONS AND UNDERLYING CAUSES OF EMERGENCIES, DISASTERS AND CATASTROPHES. DEVELOPMENTAL PHASES OF AN EMERGENCY

From the viewpoint of emergency management, in particular, mitigation and preparedness planning, the analysis of their pre-conditions and causes is no less important than their conceptualization and definition as a social research and management objective. In general the origin of any emergency involves three necessary pre-conditions. These include, first, availability of a social unit (community or society) which serves an objective of the hazardous impact. Secondly, existence of the sources of such impact or hazards (threats) themselves which may emerge and act both within and out from a given social system. Thirdly, exposition of a given social system and its ambiance to the impact.

The enumerated pre-conditions are necessary but insufficient for the initiation of an emergency. The other two prerequisites are also needed. One of them involves the impact agents or risk factors both tangible (release of social or physical energy or hazardous and toxic substances) or intangible (information dissemination) in respective quantity (concentration) or quality (orientation) which directly threatens human lives and health and are generated by the functioning sources of a hazard.

Another prerequisite implicates inadequate protection or vulnerability of a given social system against the impact agents or risk factors. The key role of vulnerability in explaining both the origin and the essence of an emergency or a disaster has been emphasized by many respected

Western scholars cited above and I completely share this point considering it as being very important for conceptualization of these specific crisis occasions.

PRE-CONDITIONS AND CAUSES

The development of necessary and sufficient pre-conditions and their transformation into a real emergency is a causal chain process, which starts from a given social system choosing of appropriate strategies, means and methods to meet its basic needs and interests (see Fig. 12). In the most general way these include: social and political strategy or development model, organizational framework and economic instruments, technological and technical decisions. Their choice and implementation facilitate reaching the key development targets including the social system's security and safety as a common interest and goal of all its units or elements involved. At the same time, they also contribute decisively to emergence and a level of risk of the hazardous sources within the society, on one hand, and its and concrete social groups degree of vulnerability to the impact of both endogenous and exogenous threats, on other hand.

Thus, the accelerated development of the military and industrial complex in the former Soviet Union as well as in the USA, Great Britain, Germany during and especially after the World War II not only strengthened the military power of these countries but also meant the construction of more and more dangerous industrial facilities. Thus the task of creating modern and sophisticated weapons and defense systems mainly for military objectives for decades has been considerably overweighing the task of providing safety to their own industrial personnel and neighboring communities. Given this, it seems quite natural that, as mentioned earlier, some of the largest technological accidents in the 20th century have occurred at these facilities.

This example also elucidates the ambiguity or even the paradox nature of society's choosing of an appropriate mechanism to meet its basic needs and interests of certain social groups. This is manifested, first, in its role in the origin for pre-conditions of emergencies. The development and implementation of technological decisions which have been oriented on protecting people against military threats, at the same time have been transferred into a source of considerable industrial hazards fraught with future accidents and emergencies. The well-known effect of high dam construction to protect people against high water and increasing the risk of major flood disaster may also be used as another illustration of the point.

Secondly, the ambivalence and discrepancy of decision-making within a social system is manifested in its facilitating the conditions favorable to increasing the risk of hazardous agents or factors and/or exposition of the system to their impact (see Fig. 12). For example, choosing of the CFC (chlorofluorocarbons) as a coolant in refrigerators and a filler in sprays in 1960s - 1970s has lead to a substantial increase in the release of ozone depleting substances into the air thus loosening the protective capability of the 'ozone shield' and considerably augmenting exposure of communities in some regions of the world to ultraviolet irradiation. Similarly, the use of explosions for coal and oil development in seismologically unstable areas has contributed to or accelerated the release of tectonic energy forces and aggravated the debilitating effect of major earthquakes as it was in Germany in late 1970s and at Sakhalin Island in Russia in 1995.

The process of a social system (society, community) choosing of an appropriate mechanism, especially its organizational, economic and technological means and methods, to meet both its basic needs and interests of certain social groups is strongly influenced by the way of thinking and acting of the key decision makers, that is public administrators, business, political and other leaders and managers representing the interests of the politically and economically dominant social groups or units. In the former Soviet Union and in contemporary Russia, technocratic types of both thinking and acting has been prevalent among the bulk of these key decision-makers.

In a broad sense this type of thinking and acting, which has been widely spread not only among the Russian political and business establishment but in many highly developed and developing countries as well, is characterized not only by superior technology over man and human values, but of the means and methods over the goal, of tactical aims and targets over the main goal or strategic mission, of symbol over reality, as well (Zinchenko, 1989). Such categories

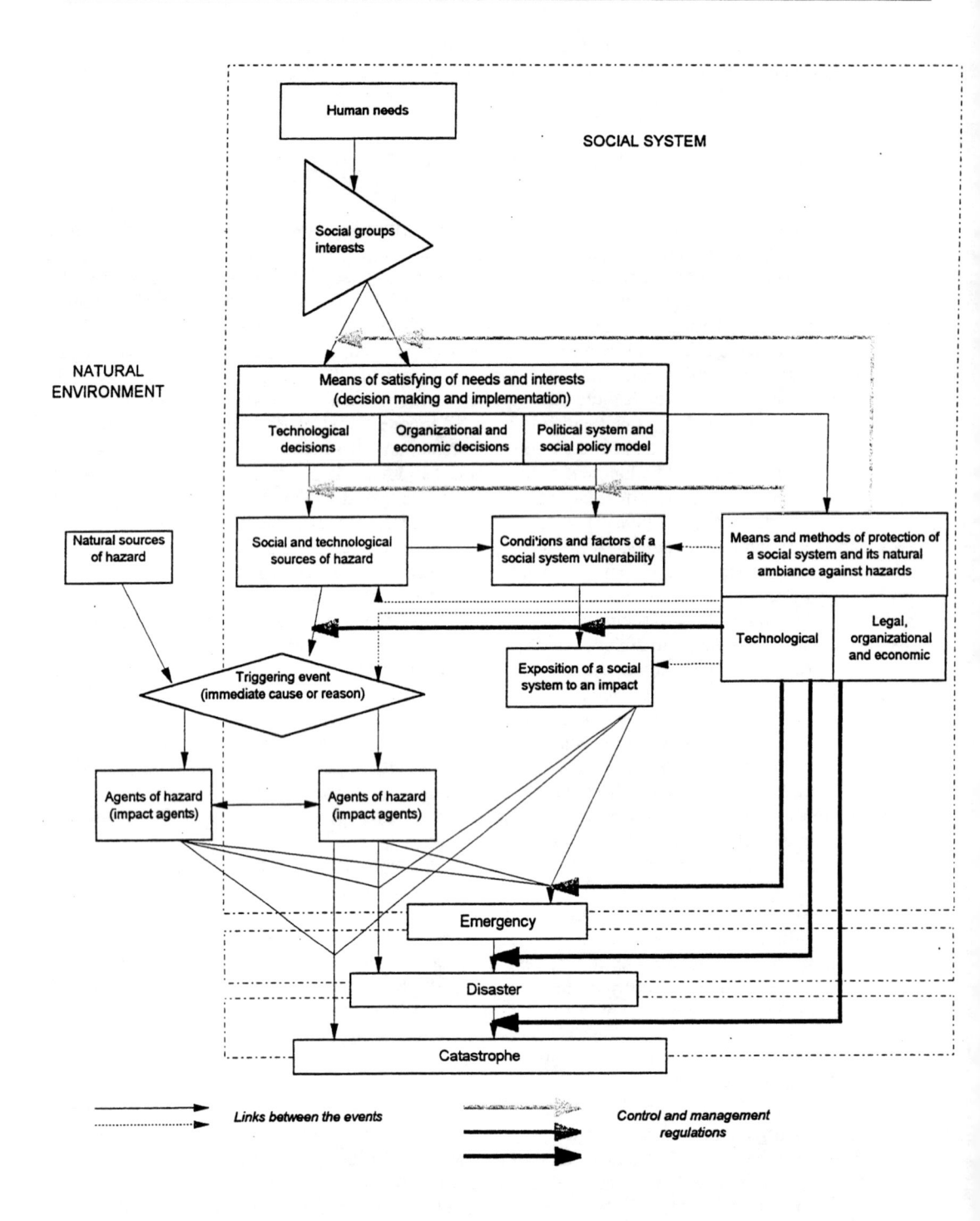

Fig 12. The Casual Chain of the Origin and Development of an Emergency.

as human conscience, morale, empathy, social responsibility and even the value of human life itself are then the least important. In the former Soviet Union and nowadays Russia this has been further aggravated by a monopoly of a certain number of industries and corruption at all levels of public administration.

All this has been leading to more or less pronounced perversion of the real needs and interests of large sections of public and Russian society as a whole, including the fundamental imperative for security and safety, in the sake of the interests of a relatively narrow group of privileged representatives of administrative and bureaucratic and industrial circles including administrators of some state and private companies while making and carrying out the decisions. This distortion takes various forms. From the perspective of systems analysis of the deep causes of and vulnerability of communities to technological emergencies and disasters in the former Soviet Union and contemporary Russia, in particular the most important of these forms include the following three.

One of them involves the construction of 'prestigious' gigantic facilities profitable to organizations, customers and contractors, but unnecessary for neighboring communities and society as a whole, including environmentally unsound and technologically unsafe entities paid for from the federal budget. These projects were represented by the erection of the Baikal paper complex, the huge dam in Kara-Bogaz-Gol Bay in the Caspian Sea, initiating of construction projects on diverting the Siberian rivers flow from the Russian North to the South, to the Middle Asia republics and so on in the former Soviet Union in the 1970s and 1980s, while in Russia in the 1990s the trans-rapid railway Moscow - St. Petersburg is especially worth noting. As Academician Boris Paton, one of the most respected authorities in engineering science and technology in the former Soviet Union, put it:

'These [facilities] are only a part of the unnecessary complexes of the public economy. They have not only been debilitating the conditions for environmental security but have also failed to perform their direct economic functions' (Paton, 1986).

Indeed, the Baikal paper complex, the ministry of the paper industry of the former Soviet Union, justified its construction and development in the 1970s using the argument that the national aviation industry supposedly needed the cellulose cord to produce aircraft wheels. However, the aircraft construction companies preferred to use metallic cord as more reliable. This made the argument invalid and the very existence of the paper complex at the bank of the world famous lake both economically not expedient and environmentally hazardous.

Similarly, currently and in the foreseeable future there is no need to construct the earlier mentioned trans-rapid railway given that the functioning railways from Moscow to St. Petersburg have been used ineffectively, in particular due to unreasonable transportation tariffs. If the new railway is built in early 2000s - while some of its parts have been really under construction in mid-1990s despite lacking necessary auditing and thanks to lobbying of this project by motivated bureaucrats in the federal government - these tariffs would undoubtedly be higher. This means that the construction of the facility would absorb hundreds of millions of US dollars from the federal budget and is initially unprofitable ignoring its technological safety and substantial environmental impact on the protected areas of Valdai valley in the European part of Russia.

Another manifestation of the distortion of interests during technocratic, bureaucratic and monopolistic making and implementing of decisions concerning risky facilities, include the construction and exploitation of entities which have been necessary for the economy of the former Soviet Union and nowadays Russia but involved obsolete construction and hazardous production technologies in order to save money on safety costs. These may be illustrated with the examples of the majority of the pipelines, the Astrakhan and Orenburg gas complexes, industrial wastewater treatment facilities and others which were built mainly in the 1960s and 1970s and are still actively used.

Until the late 1980s this practice was strongly motivated by state policy which directly prescribed increasing gross (absolute) volume of production as prestigious and financially viable. In conditions of a centralized economy and absolute state monopolistic ownership of enterprises, this policy encouraged everybody to thrive to produce more and more without considering both the quality of the final product and technological and especially environmental safety. Thus, such an impetus was typical for the enterprises of the former Soviet Union ministries of construction for oil and gas industries, energy, railways and others.

The effect of this economic policy in terms of technological and environmental safety of many hazardous facilities was felt later in the 1990s in Russia. Moreover it has been further aggravated under the pressure of the deep and lasting social and economic crisis which has involved Russia and the other CIS countries primarily as a result of the chosen means and methods of political and economic reforms. The latter have not yet provided for safety upgrading of the aging nor new industrial and transportation facilities and, the most important, for public safety considering the lessons of the largest technological emergencies and disasters in the 1980s. In addition, the crisis has diminished the resource potential needed for this task. As mentioned above, all this has resulted in accelerated depreciation of equipment including that in high-risk industries and an increasing accident rate and industrial injuries.

Last but not least, the perversion of public interest and technocratic, bureaucratic and monopolistic methods of making and implementing decisions concerns construction and exploitation of hazardous facilities which have been needed by the national economy but have been deployed in environmentally and socially vulnerable areas including neighboring areas with especially sensitive ecosystems, etc. These decisions substantially impact the safety level of industrial plants and adjacent and even more distant communities.

In the former Soviet Union and contemporary Russia, such industrial complexes have been represented by both thermal and nuclear energy power plants. Especially addressing the issue of the nuclear power plant location, Nickolai Dollezhal and Yuriy Koriakin, the authoritative Russian nuclear energy power experts, as early as in late 1970s stressed that those plants had been constructed almost exclusively in the European part of the former Soviet Union, to the West of Volga river in the densely populated and environmentally overloaded areas where 60% of the country's citizens lived. They also pointed to the existing opportunities to deploy energy power plants in areas with less population density and more favorable environmental conditions (Dollezhal and Koriakin, 1979). However, these and analogous precautions were ignored and soon the Chernobyl radiation disaster occurred. Unfortunately, this problem is still very much alive in Russian industrial policy in energy and other hazardous industries.

The discussed distortions within the decision making and implementation refer not only to the deep causes of technological accidents, but have more general connotations and are important for understanding social system vulnerability to natural and compound hazards as well. They naturally stem from the non-participative, closed-type procedure of taking decisions which directly or indirectly impact on sensitivity and protectability of a community or society against multiple threats.

It is not so crucial if this kind of decision making is generated within a party and state (as in the former Soviet Union) or administrative and bureaucratic types of a social system (as in Russia) or within large corporations (as in many transnational companies in the West). In all these cases the society as a whole loses real control over economic and technological policies which results in perversions and loopholes in decision making. When the latter involve the complex systems, either technological (high risk industries) or organizational (civil protection, social order, etc.), which are especially important or responsible for social system security and safety, this in turn conspicuously increases the risk of major accidents fraught with large scale emergencies and disasters.

This scenario is not the outcome of incompetence or ill intentions of certain decision-makers, even top managers and chief executives. The personality factor is manageable by substituting the less professional decision-maker by a more trained and reliable one. The main problem, however, is rooted in a drawback which is intrinsic for large closed-type organizational systems working for their own interest. In order to provide conditions which facilitate favorable decision taking in such a system the information is subjected to distortions.

These distortions provided by filtering and hiding the 'unpleasant' data which show the negative sides of the expected outcome and, contrary to that, stressing the positive aspects of implementing a proposed decision. The cutting off of unfavorable information is made at various levels of the organizational hierarchy, primarily by the middle and upper middle managers. They justify this behavior arguing that this unpleasant information represents only a minor fraction of the total data base, that it is impossible to take everything into account bearing in mind the limited funds, time and so on. If anybody, including mass media representatives, want to attract attention to such information they are considered as troublemakers and their opinion is attempted to be isolated. In such a situation individual honesty and competence are usually found to be insufficient to preclude making of potentially hazardous decisions (Bella, 1987). It is paramount that the characteristic is organic for such organizational system is originally predetermined by corporate or other narrow interests.

Taking and implementing decisions within closed-type large organizational systems is distinguished by one more feature which is directly associated with the development of pre-conditions and deep causes of emergencies. This includes underestimating or neglecting the role of an individual, a rank-and-file worker, engineer or manager which is reduced to a plain function of a 'screw' in a mechanism of decision implementation. In such conditions there is little if any ethical and economic motivation for creative, effective and safe work. As a result, within this type of organizational systems the working moral, business culture and competence tend towards a sharp decrease (Prigozhin, 1989: 101).

In turn this gives rise to irresponsibility and carelessness which has been one of the main causes and triggers of emergencies in the former Soviet Union and current Russia. These include the earlier cited major disasters in Chernobyl, Spitak and Nefegorsk and less devastating, but much more numerous accidents, in particular those which occurred at the chemical complex in Seversk in 1993 and at the nuclear missile cruiser 'Petr Velikiy' in 1996 when a steam explosion killed five and thermally injured more than 10 sailors (Litovkin, 1996). Although the mentioned and other emergencies are chronologically separated sometimes by decades, their causes are much alike each other.

For example, in Spitak, Leninakan (Guemri) and Neftegorsk in early 1970s, construction workers stole cement and allowed obvious defects in strengthening the walls while building residential houses which were completely destroyed by the earthquakes in 1988 and 1995, respectively. Almost 20 years after the criminally careless construction works in Armenia and Sakhalin Island, serious flaws were allowed by the Baltic shipbuilding workers in St. Petersburg in 1989 while welding the steam pipe bridging the main turbine of the cruiser 'Petr Velikiy' with its safe valve. They used improper steel parts which were half as thick as required by the standards. It is noteworthy that in these and many other similar cases, the low quality of works was ignored by superintendents and numerous examining commissions which were interested in the earliest possible completion date.

The process of making and implementing decisions which provide for meeting of society's basic needs and the specific interests of certain of its social groups consist of the development of sources of threats and vulnerability of social systems to hazardous impact, however, it creates only pre-conditions of emergencies. In order that the latter can really occur, two more things are needed.

One of them presumes that the pre-conditions should coincide in time and space with the most devastating effect of emergencies and disasters being reached while the conjunction of what sociologists call 'social time' and 'social space'. This means occasions when the least protected subsystem or unit of a given social system (community, social group, and family) are concentrated in an area most intensively or severely impacted at a certain moment in time. As an example, one may cite the urbanized areas, especially districts crowded with lower income and least protected people caught by a residential fire, industrial accident, flood or riot.

Another indispensable condition of an emergency includes a trigger or direct cause (see Fig. 12). This may arise within or out from a given social system and often, though not always, serve as a catalyst for a chain of events ending with an emergency. In recent decades there have been more cases when a hazardous occasion or event which has lead to an emergency or disaster and perceived as natural (earthquake, flood, etc.) has been triggered by economic activities. On the other side of the coin, some technological accidents both at civil and military facilities (for example, at the Chernobyl nuclear power plant or at the Shikhani plant for chemical weapon destruction) have initiated or catalyzed social tensions resulting in mass civil disturbances or other forms of social and political emergencies.

The triggers of emergencies are multiple. Among those which are concerned with technology and engineering facilities, specialists have most often cited: industrial accidents, environmental contamination, product tampering and product sabotage (Shrivastava, 1992: 6). However, from a more general perspective, the main role has been traditionally assigned to so-called human errors. These have been considered by the bulk of both statisticians and management experts as a principal direct cause of technological accidents excluding social and political conflicts.

Human errors have nearly always been implicated as erroneous actions of the personnel of complex engineering systems (see Kotik, 1987: 9-10, 14) leaving in the shade the origin of such actions. Are these generated by personnel incompetence or carelessness? In those cases the 'erroneous' actions of rank-and-file employees and minor officials should be considered as a consequence primary 'error' of superintendents and city mayors who are really responsible for that. Or do these 'errors' result from the false assessment of an extraordinary situation by operation personnel, for example by nuclear or chemical reactor operators or stem from equipment design drawbacks, in particular ergonomic loopholes? If so, such actions mean the loopholes in the cadre training and R&D policy in the respective industries where the chief executive officers and top administrators should share responsibility with the operators who have caused their own death and the death of other people. But perhaps the core of everything is rooted in a different domain? Accentuation of the word 'human error' contributes little to answering these questions.

Empirical analysis shows that the agents and factors providing for the so-called human error usually act synergistically which can be corroborated by the results of investigations of the earlier cited major radiation accidents at Chernobyl nuclear power plant, Siberian chemical complex in Seversk (for detailed discussion see: Legasov, 1988; Nesterenko, 1993 and Chapter 4 of this book) and other technological, social and compound emergencies both in Russia and abroad (see, for example, the classic work by Perrow, 1984; Rosenthal et al, 1989).

In addition, in many cases the emergency trigger has absolutely nothing to do with personnel manipulations and could even hardly be labeled as real 'error'. Suffice it to note criminal actions like terrorism which have been specially targeted on a facility demolition like bombing of the residential building in Kaspiisk in 1996, railway stations in Arzamas and Piatigorsk in 1997 in Russia or analogous well-known cases in the West.

That is why while the direct causes of emergencies are discussed it would be more correct to analyze the role of the 'human factor' or, much better, the social motivation or hidden motives of the action or actions which resulted in a tragic conclusion than to simply to point to the 'human error'. Besides, this would integrate into a single chain deep prerequisites and direct causes or triggering events which are intrinsically tied and have both lead to a tragic end.

It is especially important to note that technocratic biased decision makers in Russia, while taking measures to prevent and respond to emergencies, have been continuing to rely too much upon more and more sophisticated technologies like built-in safety equipment, 'fool-proof' systems with multiple redundancy and so forth. Undoubtedly, such a measure actually substantially reduces the possibility of a technical fault but does not guarantee against loopholes in the hazard forecasting and emergency management strategy and tactics. In addition, there are serious financial, organizational and technological constraints for boundless modernization and diffusion of the technologies.

At last, in many cases further sophistication of protection and response (warning. extinguishing, etc.) including increasing automatization would not fully exclude man from operational control thus retaining the necessary integrated safety and emergency management approach. The latter requires a comprehensive policy which balances the modern engineering and information technologies with skilled operational and strategic management including upgrading of the top public administrators and other key decision-makers.

Given this, however, the objective impossibility of complete and final solution of the 'human factor' problem while providing safety and security for a social system should be explicitly stressed. This primarily results from complexity of both a social system and its units including collective and individual behavior, natural (ecological) and engineering systems and the interaction between them which each time in a specific way recreates the emergency's pre-conditions and causes including triggering events. For this very reason 'zero risk' is principally impossible and accidents and emergencies are becoming 'normal accidents' and emergencies (see Perrow, 1984: 62-63).

The attempt to understand more deeply why the complexity has been leading to emergencies would again take us back to the mechanism of making and implementing decisions in a certain organizational and social system. This would imply detailed discussion of a more general issues of the political and social domain and development strategies of a given community or society, which form a basis for and to a substantial degree predetermine, organizational, economic and technological means and methods of taking and implementing the above- mentioned decisions.

It goes without saying that these could not be considered as unique prerequisites and factors of emergencies given the limited knowledge base existing in many fields and areas of human activities. This, in particular, diminishes both the possibility and accuracy of forecasting a great number of hazardous events and assessing their impact on human health and material values (for example, some natural phenomena or radiation low dose effect)thus decreasing the efficiency of emergency preparedness and response. In this respect only practice, and the gradual accumulation of empirical data could help to find the truth. However, it is crucial to realize that in many other cases, when the forecast and accurate risk assessment both of a hazard and decision to cope with it have been possible and even made, the prevention and preparedness activities have either failed or were not efficient enough. This means the lack of adequate feedback within the decision making system thus impeding changing the pre-conditions and causes which have facilitated the development of and contributed negatively to the prevention of and preparedness for an emergency.

PHASES OF EMERGENCY DEVELOPMENT

An analysis of the causes and course of emergency development provides for delineation of the main phases within this process. Disaster specialists have consistently made efforts to classify these stages and used as one of the prevailing ones a scheme which included: pre-disaster, warning, emergency, rehabilitation, recovery and reconstruction phases (Cuny, 1983: 40). No less consistent attempts have been made by crisis scholars and experts who have distinguished, respectively: prevention, mitigation and preparedness as pre-crisis stages, response or crisis decision making as a crisis stage and recovery as a post-crisis stage (Rosenthal et al, 1989: 14-22). However useful these classifications, they mark out the phases of the disaster or crisis management but not their emergency development stages.

Some other classifications seem to better distinguish the periodization of emergency development but also not to a full degree. For example, Legasov proposed delineating three stages within the development of a technological accident which might create an emergency or disaster situation. These include: gradual accumulation of shortcomings in the normal of an engineering system, triggering event (a brake or flaw) and the accident or emergency itself (Legasov, 1987b).

Although this classification corresponds to the causal chain of events within an emergency development, I can hardly agree with it absolutely. Given that the distinguishing of phases within any process presumes fixing certain periods or states which are clear-cut and separated chronologically, the triggering event must be treated rather as a moment than an independent stage. It may be attached either to the phase of accumulation of flaws and imperfections as their 'last drop' or to the accident itself as an initiating event. At the same time, as has been noted above, the delineation of a trigger is crucial while studying the causes of an emergency.

Similar arguments should be taken as important reservations while considering the interesting classifications proposed by Fink, Shrivastava and some other authorities in crisis management. Along with prodromal, acute crisis and chronic crisis stages which I completely agree with, they have also distinguished one more stage, crisis resolution, treating it as a final result rather than a process of crisis regulation (see Fink, 1986: 20, 25; Shrivastava, 1992: 6-7). It is also worth adding that the crisis resolution stage is a characteristic of the final goal of crisis management rather than the process of development of these occasions which should be clearly distinguished.

Given this some other scholars, in particular Rosenthal and his colleagues (see Rosenthal et al, 1989: 14-22), believe it more correct to keep only the first three stages within the proposed periodization namely: pre-crisis, trans-crisis and post-crisis stages. They label the latter in such a way considering that thanks to the response taken measures the crisis occasion should be succeeded by a qualitatively different, normal situation. However, in the case of inefficient or lacking response the trans-crisis or acute crisis stage, if the previous classification is used, would turn rather to chronic-crisis while the normal situation would be still craved for.

Given all this I believe it expedient to split the emergency development process into three stages: the origin or prodromal phase, the culmination (acute crisis or emergency per se) phase and post-culmination or the post-emergency phase.

If one comes back to the causal chain of its development, the emergency origin phase involves the availability of a set of occasions and pre-conditions which preceded and facilitated its 'birth' and include the development of the sources of hazard and factors contributing to or aggravating social system vulnerability (see Fig. 12).

This process usually takes the form of gradual accumulation of various hazardous events and occasions like flaws and minor accidents in engineering systems, seismic tension within tectonic geological systems, social and political tension and minor conflicts within social systems and so on. These step by step erode the security and safety status of a social system and its units thus creating favorable conditions for potential emergencies and disasters The increasing frequency of such events and occasions may serve as one of the warning indicators of the forthcoming major emergency and used for its forecasting.

If the origin of a technological emergency is taken as an example, in the former Soviet Union, in particular at the Astrakhan gas complex due to the poor quality of equipment and construction the main technological lines were suspended 210 times in 1987 and 163 times in 1988 while accidents occurred there forced the whole complex to be stopped 28 times and 21 times, respectively. Each of those had been escorted by a torch release of hydrogen sulfide and sulfur dioxide into the air which amounted to 1 million tons annually and surpassed the permissible levels by a dozen-fold. One of these releases killed four workers and injured many more people in the neighboring communities. In 1989, this resulted in an emergency situation when the huge 5 billion US$ industrial complex functioned only at 15% of its capacity (Gaidar and Yaroshenko, 1988; *Radi Zdoroviia*, 1989; *Experti Vozrazhaiut*, 1989).

Similarly, the defects and imperfections of the compressor equipment at another gas complex in Orenburg caused numerous torch releases of sulfur dioxide into the air in 1975-1988. Twice these lead to emergencies which involved 42 seriously injured and evacuation of all the remaining dwellers from the neighboring hamlet of Muzhichiia Pavlovka in 1987 and 10 persons injured and temporal evacuation of another 1,200 dwellers from the village of Nikolskoie in 1989 (*Vibros Gaza*, 1989; *Gazovaia Ataka*, 1989; Usoltsev and Kharitonova, 1988).

In the same year of 1989, the first cracks were detected at the oil pipeline Vozeiskoie - Yaroslavl while in 1991 these resulted in minor oil spills. Between 1991 and 1994 the frequency and volume of oil spills substantially increased which was followed by the corporation, Komineft, being sued 10 claims amounting to 40 million rubles (4 million US$). In early 1995 a major accident caused by rupture of the pipeline resulted in the spill of more than 100,000 tons of oil over a large area of Komi Republic in the North of Russia and considerable contamination of the Kolva and Usa rivers (Isk, 1995).

The practical identification and chronological delineation of the origin stage of emergency development is not an easy task. Some experts admit that in the case of technological accidents it may last for minutes or days (Legasov, 1987b). However, the empirical data shows evidence that the ripening of pre-conditions and accumulation of flaws and imperfections have usually taken much more time: from a few years, as was the case at the radiation accident at Chernobyl nuclear power plant, spills from the oil pipeline in Komi Republic and the big fire at the KamAZ truck plant, to a few decades as occurred in the cases of the compound disaster in the Aral Sea region and radiation accident at the Seversk chemical complex (see Azimov, 1986 and Chapter 4).

Given this, it is worth additional noting that far from every minor accident or other hazardous occurrence (although contributing to its development) results in an emergency. As already mentioned, the latter also requires a coincidence of a certain set of conditions that happens randomly. Therefore the origin stage of emergency development may be revealed only retrospectively, that is after it actually occurs. This, of course, does not give rise to unreasonable calmness and optimism that could lead to negligence of security and safety issues, on one hand,

and to passive and waiting strategy in this area, on the other hand. If this happens, the prodromal phase would be succeeded by the next, culmination phase and pre-crisis would transfer into an acute crisis situation.

The culmination phase includes the part of the emergency development process starting from the triggering event to the effect of the hazardous impact on a social system and its ambiance (see Fig. 12; Scenario 1 marked with respective circled figure). For certain reasons hazardous agents or risk factors including social or physical and chemical energy, radioactive and toxic substances or information are released by their sources and produce dangerous impacts on the social system (people and their values) and its environment. In particular, there are 22 kinds of such agents with three of them involving the release of physical and chemical energy during dam failures, explosions at gas terminals and nuclear power plants. The remaining 19 types of risk factors involve the release of hazardous substances which happen at other high risk facilities (Hohenemser, Kates and Slovic, 1983).

Information as a risk factor or hazardous agent should especially be considered when it is intentionally used for the targeted misinformation of a decision maker, personnel or the public or accidentally diffused within the organization, community or society as a whole (rumors, gossip, leaking to mass media). In both cases, this produced a relatively rapid and disturbing effect on communities arising alarm and often panic. Thus the real events, far from being hazardous, are perceived by people as very dangerous and transfer a normal situation into emergency.

The emergency phase under discussion starts from the moment of the destructive impact on a social system or its units and its environment and terminates when the activity of the hazardous sources and risk factors expires, subsides as a result of the energy potential being exhausted or is considerably reduced or completely stopped due to the measures to localize or liquidate the emergency. The duration of this phase varies from a few hours, as it was in the cases of the Spitak and Neftegorsk earthquakes (10-12 hours), to a few days, as it was with the radiation accidents in Seversk and Chernobyl (almost a week and 15 days, respectively) and the major fire at the KamAZ truck plant (7 days). (For further details see Chapter 4).

As a rule, the culmination stage is the shortest but the affected people, who have been going through or perceived as being jeopardized by multiple dangers, very often consider it as the most lasting one. In the real world the origin and post-culmination emergency stages should be considered the longest while it is difficult to establish their exact duration. If the final point of the origin stage is more or less clear - the start of the culmination provoked a triggering event - and its starting point may be established rather tentatively, in the case of the post-culmination stage the situation is reverse.

Chronologically the post-culmination emergency phase embraces the period starting from the expiration or considerable cushioning of the impact force and its primary effect to the full alleviation and liquidation of its aftermath including secondary, tertiary and other effects.

If the respective response measures are inefficient or lacking, the acute crisis would be succeeded by a chronic crisis which involves the lasting and substantial break of the normal activities of a social system starting from people's basic needs to social and economic development (loss of working places, decrease of income and wealth level, etc.). In these circumstances the scale of human and material losses would increase, psychological stress would be aggravated with collective frustration and anxiety deepening. For the affected people all this means a reverse to the disastrous situation when they continue to be impacted by the secondary agents of the accident although its primary impact may have already been eliminated by emergency workers and volunteers.

Thus, in such a case the emergency, which has involved direct a threat to a social unit, disturbed or broken its routines for a short time that could be reestablished later, turns instead into a disaster (see Fig. 12). Its main characteristics distinguish it from an emergency on the criteria of the relative number of the people with their values involved, the degree of involvement of the population with their values within the impacted social system and the degree of social disruption or gravity of the effect within the affected communities (Britton, 1987).

As Scenario 2 (marked with the respective circled figure in the Fig. 12) shows, a disaster may arise not only from an emergency but also when a hazardous impact is protracted and the generated effects accumulate and spread within the affected social system and its environment slowly or gradually and often in a latent form. The circumstances which facilitate the release of hazardous agents or risk factors often do not serve as a catalyst or a trigger of a disaster, and its direct causes are sometimes considerably separated from the disaster itself both in time and in space. In such a case the culmination and post-culmination phases dissolute within each other thus creating a single chronic crisis stage.

Social and political disasters resulting from erroneous internal governmental policy, primarily in economic and social protection areas, provoke a deep and lasting crisis in certain regions or the country as a whole as well as the so-called environmental disasters generated by technological contamination of water, air, soils and/or by substantial destruction of the natural resources. Although in a disaster, the coming chronic crisis considerably aggravates the situation within the impacted social system, the bulk of the induced effects are not irreversible. The majority of the social units and communications between them being disturbed and broken they are however not ruptured or destroyed completely.

Therefore the situation may be turned to the better and the affected community or society may be recovered as a social system but not absolutely restored to its pre-disaster state. The latter depends decisively on the timeliness and efficiency of response and recovery actions provided by relief, social security and other organizations responsible for medical, social and psychological care and compensating the suffered economic losses as well as by the dwellers and enterprises of the affected area itself (for further discussion see Chapters 3 and 4). In this respect, the level of economic development of both the neighboring regions and the country, the type of its social and political system is really paramount.

As the experience of permanent relocation zones in the tracking areas of Chernobyl and South Urals (Cheliabinsk-65) radiation disasters, the Spitak earthquake disaster, the areas of the North Caucasus in Russia suffering from the armed regional conflicts in the republics of North Osetia, Ingoushetia and Chechnia, the areas of the so-called environmental disasters in Karabash, in the Cheliabinsk region, and Cherniye Zemli, in Kalmik Republic of Russia and others, a disaster may last from years to decades. However, if the response taken and recovery measures prove their efficiency, its duration may be substantially shortened and the chronic crisis leads to revival and rehabilitation of the normal activities of the affected social system as a whole while some families and individuals continue to suffer serious health and economic problems.

Contrarily, tardiness and inefficiency of the measures, the additional complexity generated by political instability, social and economic crisis both in the affected areas and social system in general, considerably increases the duration of the chronic crisis and the gravity of living conditions of the affected people. These circumstances provide for the pre-conditions of appearing to be new sources of hazard and conspicuously aggravate the effect of the major collective stress.

Thus, a disaster may turn into a catastrophe (see Fig. 12). This means that the bulk of the debilitating and devastating effects initially generated while the emergency and considerably worsened while it has been succeeded by a disaster, since a certain moment become irreversible. First of all, the affected social domain (community, society) looses its integrity as a system as a result of the rupture and destruction of its units, subsystems and communications and relationships between them. Therefore, as a system, it ceases its functioning and should either be succeeded by a qualitatively new social system as it was in the result of the Russian revolutions (see Sorokin, 1942), or for a long time, from years to centuries, turn into a 'desert island' as occurred in the alienated (uninhabited) zones in tracking areas of Chernobyl and the South Urals (Cheliabinsk-65) radiation disasters, in the former town of Neftegorsk which was completely destroyed by earthquake and its placed now occupied by a huge memorial complex.

Like a disaster, as Scenario No 3 (marked with a circled figure in Fig. 12) shows, a catastrophe may arise directly from the destructive impact of the hazardous agents on a social system and its ambiance at the culmination moment. This scenario is typical for warfare (wars, regional armed conflicts), in particular involving mass destruction weapons, genocidal actions and natural, technological or compound hazardous events or occasions which generate rapidly spreading impact of the dreadful quantities of energy (for example, tectonic or heat) or toxic materials, primarily radioactive and chemical substances.

CLASSIFICATION OF EMERGENCIES

The problem of emergency typology development is intrinsically bound both with the conceptualization and definition of emergency, disaster and catastrophe as research and management categories and studying of their pre-conditions and causes. For a long time this problem has been in the focus of scholars and practitioners but it is still both topical and open to discussion. Drabek, Quarantelli and some other authorities in the field of disasters reckon that the efforts undertaken from the 1950s to the mid 1980s progressed not much beyond simple and unrewarding distinctions like natural disasters versus technological disasters which represent only vague clues regarding a taxonomy of these events. Thus a typology is needed based on general dimensions that cut across not only different disaster agents but also the same agent (Drabek, 1986: 1; Quarantelli, 1987b).

I believe that this characteristic should be still valid in the late 1990s. The available experience shows evidence that the existing classifications of hazardous events and occasions have been developed for relatively narrow professional or training purposes and therefore are pragmatically-oriented. Conditionally these may be subdivided into two sets including dichotomy classifications and specialized classifications.

Within the former, the earlier-mentioned dichotomy 'natural disasters - technological disasters' has been the most widely spread. In Russia this was used as a basis for the official (state) form of statistical registration of emergencies between 1992 and 1996 which in addition to natural and technological also distinguished environmental emergencies. The subdivision of all emergencies into criminal and not criminal, which is prescriptively established by and used within the Ministry of Internal Affairs of the Russian Federation, may serve as another illustration of a dichotomy classification.

The set of specialized classifications includes various typologies of hazardous events and occasions as emergency and disaster agents. The most widely used have been classifications which involve criteria of risk and magnitude of such events, for instance ranging of earthquakes in accordance with Mercalli, MSK or Richter scales, radiation accidents on the INES scale and so forth. These type of classifications have been developed by so-called narrow or 'disciplinary' specialists representing natural and engineering sciences and knowledgeable in depth about a specific hazard provoking an emergency and/or disaster such as floods, nuclear reactors, toxic chemicals, etc.

As scholars representing comprehensive or integrated approach, primarily sociologists and systems analysts, have been pointing out for a long time, and the 'disciplinary' specialists have confessed to recently, however useful these classifications are the area of their application has been objectively limited. Thus, between 1992 and mid 1996 in the official statistical classification of emergencies in Russia mentioned above epidemic, epizootic and fires, being provoked by compound causes have been included into the column 'natural emergencies'. In the late 1996 this classification was amended by one more type of 'social emergency' and epidemic, epizootic and fires were moved there. However, this have not changed the situation much given the compound origin of these hazards, on the one hand, and the partial confusing of emergencies with their causes, on the other hand.

Indeed, in some cases such as civil disturbances, riots or forest and peat fires, the circumstances which have facilitated or provoked an emergency and/or disaster can not so easily be separated from emergencies and disasters per se. Nevertheless, given that the latter are the outcome of these circumstances, which involve the hazardous sources and their agents directly threatening the security and safety of a given social system, but are not identical with these sources and agents, the distinction between them should be considered both methodologically principal and practically important, primarily from the viewpoint of emergency management.

From the management perspective, while developing emergency classification, it is crucial to distinguish those indications or criteria and use them for making such a typology which could facilitate in the best way and increase the efficiency of the planning procedure of measures to mitigate, prepare, respond to and recover from emergencies and/or disasters. Since their prevention presumes a knowledge and deep understanding of peculiarities of the origin phase of an emergency development, and response to and recovery from this necessitate for the same requirements for specific characteristics of its culmination and post-culmination phases, respectively, so it seems reasonable that the development of a classification should involve both the typology of emergencies and typology of their pre-conditions.

The latter in turn includes the typology of direct threats to or hazardous impacts on a social system's security and the typology of these systems' vulnerability to the impact. To distinguish the types of threats I have used three basic criteria and eight additional characteristics which describe the impact's origin, intensity and degree of danger. These provide for distinguishing 23 types of hazards which, along with their brief descriptions are displayed in the Table 9.

In addition, I have used two basic criteria and two supplementary characteristics of the degree of the social systems' sensitivity to and protectability against the hazards for making the typology vulnerability of these systems. As a result, six main types of vulnerability has been distinguished and shown in the Table 10.

The development of a typology of emergencies per se as the outcome and effect of both the hazardous impact on a social system and the latter is vulnerability has been based on three main criteria and two additional characteristics which describe predictability, depth (gravity) and scale of the impact's spreading within the mentioned system. These provide for distinguishing 15 types of emergencies (including disasters and catastrophes), which together with their brief descriptions, are shown in the Table 11 while their integrated multicriteria classification is displayed in the Fig. 13.

While elaborating the proposed typologies a theoretical rather than pragmatically-oriented approach has been used. I believe that the latter requires a much more specified quantitative description or at least a qualitative formalization of the characteristics of threats to social system security both in absolute terms including interval values and relative, in particular, possibility terms. For example, such indicators as: a proportion of population involved or affected by a hazardous impact on a community, a proportion of fatalities in the total number of involved in an emergency or affected in disaster area, a proportion of direct economic damages to the GDP and some other are well applicable for description of the gravity of emergency (Britton, 1987; Quarantelli, 1991).

At the same time, the absolute figures for the number of fatalities and affected in an emergency or a disaster area and alike: for example, the earlier mentioned criterion of more than 100 killed used by the UN bodies to distinguish 'substantial natural disasters', can be applied as indicators of the scale of emergency and/or disaster. In particular, using these scale criteria for a comparative study of disasters provoked by the major earthquakes in Kobe, Japan and Neftegorsk, Russia in 1995 shows that the ratio between the number of killed and affected amount to 3:1 and 30:1, respectively while the analogous ratio in terms of the disasters gravity is just to the opposite. As a result of the earthquake, of the total population of the Kobe prefecture only 20% were affected including 0.4% killed and approximately 7% injured while the huge urbanized area as a whole preserved and kept functioning, while during the Neftegorsk earthquake almost all dwellers of the Okha region were affected, especially in the town of Neftegorsk where more than 60% of the population were killed and the town almost completely destroyed (for details see Chapter 4).

In addition to these, in order to distinguish a certain type of emergency and/or disaster other criteria shown in Table 11 and Fig. 13 as well as their normatively prescribed characteristics should also be used. The concrete quantitative values of these characteristics which are not specified at the moment vary depending on peculiarities of the national legal system or research priorities in case the specific standards are lacking. For example, Bates and Peacock, while illustrating a hypothetical disaster in a community of 10,000 people in a developing country, proposed three basic degrees of disaster magnitude involving percentage of population and material losses and duration of recovery (Bates and Peacock, 1987).

In Russia, the emergency criteria and quantitative characteristics which describe the scale of debilitating effect within the affected social system were normatively established in 1996 by the special Governmental Regulation # 1094 (*Pravitelstvo. Postanovleniye*, 1996b). Formally this classification refers to natural and technological emergencies although, as easily seen from the table, its principal restrictions can also be applied to conflict-type emergencies and/or disasters. According to the regulation these criteria are alternative and include: the number of casualties, or

Fig 13. Integral Classification of Emergencies

Gravity of impact's effect / Impact on human behavior / Predictability / Rapidness of spreading		Hardly predictable or completely unpredictable emergencies		Partly predictable emergencies		Relatively predictable emergencies	
		Rapidly spreading emergencies	Slowly spreading emergencies	Rapidly spreading emergencies	Slowly spreading emergencies	Rapidly spreading emergencies	Slowly spreading emergencies
Acute crisis situations (emergencies)	Conflict-type emergencies						
	Non-conflict type emergencies						
Chronic crisis situations (disasters)	Conflict-type emergencies						
	Non-conflict type emergencies						
Catastrophic situations (catastrophes)	Conflict-type emergencies						
	Non-conflict type emergencies						

The scale of impact's effect	Organizational	Local	Regional	National	Transboundary
	Emergencies				

Table 9. Typology of Hazards (Threats) to the Security (Safety) of a Social System

Hazards criteria and indications	Type of hazards	Characteristics of the types of hazards
(1)	(2)	(3)
1. Hazards origin 1.1 positioning of hazards towards a social system	◆ Exogenous ◆ Endogenous ◆ Compound	• Natural hazards; technological accidents, environmental contamination and social conflicts and compound hazardous occasions (epidemics, desertification, etc.) which occur in the neighboring communities (countries) or somewhere else out from a given social system but producing hazardous impact on it • Occasions and happenings originating within a given social system which include social and political conflicts (with social crimes), technological accidents and compound social and technological hazardous occasions (e.g. mass poisonings) • Compound *na-tech* (natural and technological) (e.g. landslides) and *na-soc* (natural and social) (epidemics, epizootic) hazardous occasions of combined origin

Table 9. *(Continued)*

(1)	(2)	(3)
1.2 composition (structure) of hazards sources	◆ Homogeneous	• Threats stemming from one basic hazard represented by natural, technological or social agent (e.g. earthquake, industrial accident, etc.)
	◆ Heterogeneous	• Threats stemming from simultaneous impact of various hazardous agents or impact produced by compound hazard source
1.3 reality (tangibility) of hazards (threats)	◆ Tangible (Real)	• Existing hazardous sources and factors presenting real and direct menace to the safety of a given social system and its environment (ambiance)
	◆ Intangible (Perceived)	• Threats arising from rumors, gossips spread either intentionally (misinformation) or unintentionally which refer to potentially hazardous phenomena or occasions that either not really jeopardize a given social system or their risk is over exaggerated. However, they are perceived by the people as a real danger for their lives and property that may provoke a real emergency

Table 9. *(Continued)*

(1)	(2)	(3)
1.4 purposefulness of hazards (threats)	♦ Premeditated ♦ Unpremeditated	• Social and political conflicts (including social crimes) • Natural hazards, technological accidents and compound hazardous occasions
1.5 predictability and familiarity of hazards (threats)	♦ Unfamiliar and completely not or hardly predictable ♦ Relatively familiar and predictable	• Hazardous phenomena and occasions which have unclear or understudied origin including natural hazards (e.g. earthquakes, meteorite falling, etc.) and accidents involving super modern technologies or technical (engineering) systems (e.g. biotechnological, medical, .etc.) • Other hazardous phenomena and occasions with relatively well known and studied origin (ethiology)
2. *Impact Intensiveness* 2.1 rapidity of hazard spreading	♦ Slowly spreading (Gradual)	• Latent-type social and political conflicts and crisis (e.g. increasing poverty and decreasing living standards, separate strikes and manifestations, etc.), environmental contamination and destruction caused by both technological and compound agents (e.g. "green house"

Table 9. *(Continued)*

(1)	(2)	(3)
	◆ Rapidly spreading (Rapid)	effect, ozone layer depletion, desertification, etc.) which undermine or loosen a given social system and its ambiance • Natural cataclysmic events; major fires and explosions at industrial and municipal facilities; acute-type social and political conflicts (e.g. civil disturbances, riots, etc.) and compound hazardous phenomena and occasions (e.g. epidemics, mass poisonings, etc.)
	◆ Changing (mixed)	• Hazards which may spread threats either slowly or rapidly depending on concrete circumstances (e.g. landslides, water upheaval, etc.)
2.2 recurrence (duration) of impact	◆ Single (Discrete)	• Threats provoked by a single and short-term hazardous impact on a given social system and its ambiance
	◆ Recurrent (Lasting)	• Threats caused either by recurrent or continuous impact of hazardous sources and agents which provoke lasting effect on a given social system and its ambiance

Table 9. *(Continued)*

(1)	(2)	(3)
3. *Degree of danger* 3.1 risk to lives and health (fatality of impact)	◆ Fatal	• Natural cataclysmic events; technological accidents which involve radioactive and toxic substances emission and fallout; armed social and political conflicts; mass dangerous diseases (e.g. AIDS, tuberculosis, diphtheria, etc.)
	◆ Non-fatal	• Other hazardous phenomena and occasions threatening to the safety of a given social system
3.2 domain of threat	◆ Organizational	• Hazards threatening to a given organization (e.g. facility, building, corporation, etc.)
	◆ Local	• Hazards threatening to a given community (e.g. hamlet, town, district of a city, city)
	◆ Regional	• Hazards threatening to a given region (e.g. megalopolis, province, state, republic, etc.)
	◆ National	• Hazards threatening to a group of regions or nation as a whole
	◆ International (trans-boundary)	• Hazards threatening to a group of world regions or global (international) security

Table 10. Typology of Social Systems Vulnerability

Criteria and indications	Type of systems	Characteristics of the types of systems
(1)	(2)	(3)
1. Sensitivity		
1.1 composition of the social structure	◆ Highly (especially) sensitive ◆ Sensitive	• Social systems with a high proportion of the so-called risk groups, (children, pregnant women, elderly persons), non-residents (foreigners, migrants, refugees) and invalids • Other social systems
1.2 position towards source(s) of hazard(s)	◆ Highly endangered ◆ Endangered	• Social systems located in a close proximity to the source(s) of hazard(s) • Other social systems
2. Protectability	◆ Poorly (loosely) protected ◆ Relatively well protected	• Social systems which lack necessary means and forces (including efficient forecasting and public warning and information services) and adequate level of preparedness to mitigate or cope with emergencies and/or disasters most typical for a given area • Other social systems

Table 11. Typology of Emergencies

Criteria and indications (1)	Type of emergencies (2)	Characteristics of the types of emergencies (3)
1. *Predictability*	♦ Poorly predictable or unpredictable	• Emergencies provoked by unfamiliar and hardly foreseeable or completely unforeseeable hazards and / or poor organization or malfunctioning of forecasting, warning and public information services including preparedness planning in a given social system (society, community, organization)
	♦ Partly predictable	• Emergencies provoked by unfamiliar and hardly foreseeable hazards while forecasting, warning and public information services and preparedness organization as a whole are well planned and implemented a given social system
	♦ Relatively predictable	• Other emergencies
2. *Impact on a social system (collective behavior)*	♦ Conflict	• Emergencies provoked by social and political conflicts in conditions of poor control by the social institutions responsible for conflict prevention and mitigation. These are characterized by a sharp and open confrontation between the social groups involved which aggravates the debilitating effect within a given social system

Table 11. *(Continued)*

(1)	(2)	(3)
3. *Scale of impact*	◆ Organizational	• Emergencies involving the hazardous and destructive effects spreading within a given organization
	◆ Local	• Emergencies involving the debilitating and destructive effects spreading within a given community (settlement or its district)
	◆ Regional	• Emergencies involving the debilitating and destructive effects spreading within a given region of a country
	◆ National (federal)	• Emergencies involving the debilitating and destructive effects spreading within a group of neighboring regions of a given country or country as a whole
	◆ International (trans-boundary)	• Emergencies involving the debilitating and destructive effects spreading (spilling) over the areas (countries) adjacent to a given country or more distant regions of the world

[a] For more extensive discussion of an emergency, a disaster and a catastrophe as research management categories see Chapter 1.

Table 11. *(Continued)*

(1)	(2)	(3)
	◆ Non-conflict	• Emergencies provoked both by the unintentional hazardous phenomena and occasions (natural, technological and compound agents) and vulnerability of a given social system towards their impact. These are characterized by cooperative, solidarity-type collective response behavior that alleviates the debilitating effect within the aforementioned system
2. *Degree of impact on a social system*		
2.1 rapidness of spreading	◆ Rapidly spreading	• Emergencies characterized by the accelerated and increasing involvement of a given social system into the hazardous impact's spreading
	◆ Slowly spreading	•Emergencies characterized by the gradual and slow involvement of a given social system into the hazardous impact's spreading
2.2 gravity of impact	◆ Acute crisis (emergencies *per se*)	• Emergencies *per se* which involves temporarily break of normal social routines, relatively limited number of casualties and substantial economic losses in a given social system that

Table 11. (Continued)

(1)	(2)	(3)
	◆ Chronic and grave crisis (disasters)	may be restored (compensated) to a considerable degree within a comparatively short time [a] • Occasions which involve long-term and overall break and substantial rupture of the social communications and structures within a given social system including deaths, health and / or environmental deterioration, huge material damages which may be restored, rehabilitated and compensated to a substantial degree only within a comparatively long-term perspective [a]
	◆ Catastrophic (catastrophes)	•Occasions which involve long-term, total break and rupture of the social communications and structures within a given social system including numerous deaths, mass health deterioration and morbidity, huge distress load on the affected social system and stress of the neighboring and more distant communities, enormous and practically irreversible (uncompensated) social, environmental and material damages that may be covered somewhere in a distant future only [a]

Emergency type	Number of casualties	Number of affected [a]	Material damage [b]	Emergency area
Organizational	< 10	< 100	<1	Organization
Local	10 - 50	100 - 300	1 - 5	Settlement
Regional	51 - 499	301 - 500	5 - 500	A member (a subject) of the Russian Federation [c]
Macroregional	51 - 499	501 - 1,000	500 - 5,000	2 members of the Russian Federation
National	> 500	> 1,000	> 5,000	More than 2 members of the Russian Federation
Transnational	Effects spreading beyond the territory of Russia			

[a] The people with disturbed or broken normal social routines

[b] In thousands minimal monthly salaries in Russia

[c] 89 main territorial and administrative units of the Russian Federation

Source: (Pravitelstvo. Postanovleniye, 1996b).

Table 12. Typology of Emergencies by Scale of Effect in the Russian Federation

the number of affected (with their living conditions disturbed), or the value of economic losses and the boundaries of impacted area. According to these criteria and their quantitative threshold parameters six types of emergencies have been distinguished which include: organizational (localniye), local (mestniye), regional (territorialniye), macroregional (regionalniye), national (federalniye) and transnational (transgranichniye) emergencies (see Table 12).

Unfortunately, some of the mentioned criteria are rather ambiguous: for example, it remains unclear what kind of living conditions and to what a degree should they be disturbed in order to consider the impacted people as 'affected'. Does it involve lacking or a shortage of potable water, or food, or electricity, or shelter (considering that such a category as 'homeless' is not specifically distinguished) or all of them? These and other questions need further clarification if one wants to make this classification not only methodologically correct but practically operational, in particular in terms of the emergency registration by the federal statistical service of Russia (GOSKOMSTAT).

As to concrete qualitative and quantitative criteria and characteristics of emergencies which describe the gravity of effect within the affected social system, in Russia these have been normatively established by the 1991 Natural Environment Protection Act of the Russian Federation for the so-called ecological emergency and ecological disaster areas. while the declaration of emergency areas was provided by the 1994 Federal Act of the Russian Federation on Protection of People and Territories Against Natural and Technological Emergencies. The areas should be declared as ecological emergency or ecological disaster zones in the cases can be correspond to a certain set of criteria designated in the detailed special instruction of the State Committee of the Russian Federation for Environmental Protection and Natural Resources (GOSKOMPRIRODA) (Kriterii, 1994). As far as the declaration of emergency areas is concerned, no specific criteria or characteristics have yet been normatively prescribed (for details see Chapter 3).

At the same time, anonymous interviews of some officials from regional authorities held in 1992 show too much detailed criteria for declaring an ecological emergency or ecological disaster area have diminished the value of respective instructions and considerably complicated their use in practice. In addition, the declaration of such areas as real extraordinary events or occasions is further hampered by the use of the misleading concepts of 'ecological emergency' and 'ecological disaster'.

As far as the natural environment is concerned, contrary to communities it is practically always jeopardized by the potential impact of physical agents both on inhabited or uninhabited territories. From this viewpoint any emergency or disaster can be considered as ecological because others simply do not exist. If the hazards coming from the natural environment rather than the social system or its units involved or the impact produced on them are discussed and bias is made for the fact that this impact comes from ambiance, then it is quite logical and far more preferable and clear to use the well-known term of 'natural hazard' rather than the misleading concepts.

Given this, both categories of 'ecological emergency' and 'ecological disaster' areas that are extensively used in the 1991 Natural Environment Protection Act of the Russian Federation should be considered as artificial and methodologically insolvent. As a result discrepancies and misunderstandings frequently occur both in theory and practice, in particular in normative documents including the cited act. To cope with these problems of decision-making, I believe it would be reasonable to use the emergency conceptualization and integrated classification proposed above as well as only a few simple indicators of the degree of social disorder and environmental impact as qualitative criteria which are the most convenient for decision-makers (public administrators, emergency or crisis managers and so on). This would provide for systematization of the types of crisis areas where emergency, disaster or catastrophe happened (see Table 1.11) into emergency, disaster or catastrophic areas, respectively.

As any systematization, the classification and typologies introduced are undoubtedly relative and the distinction between various types of emergencies and emergency areas in reality is not so clear-cut. For example, a set of crisis occasions labeled as a local emergency in terms of a certain criteria transform into a regional or national emergency or even a disaster since a different set of criteria is involved, in particular those associated with a perceived threat to a social system or its units. The same is also true when the differentiation of crisis areas at a given moment then changes while time passes and the social disorder and environmental degradation either increase or decrease in an affected area.

The Chernobyl disaster can serve as a good illustration of this point. Within the first months after the nuclear reactor explosion the radioactive fallout caused a disaster in the nearest (30-km radius) and a major emergency situation in the more distant areas that should have been considered as emergency or acute crisis zones, respectively. Within several months, and in some areas even after some years, inefficient deactivation of soils and buildings and relocation of residents of the affected communities have transformed these territories into chronic crisis or disaster areas. Besides other things, this means that emergency (acute crisis) and disaster (chronic crisis) areas are never synchronous, that is, do not emerge simultaneously, though they are often syntopous or coincidental, that is, occur at the same place.

Summing up the discussion on emergency classification, the specific role of those provoked by technological agents both as 'pure' impact or risk factors and a part of compound hazards should be especially stressed. Like emergencies generated by social and political conflicts, these arise or are catalyzed by the same type of endogenous threats, while like natural emergencies and disasters, they are associated with the analogous non-conflict or consensus-type crisis. Thus, technological emergencies and/or disasters are located somewhere in the focus or 'center' of the classification typologies.

This results from the intermediate or bridging function the technology plays between a social system and its ambiance, and between individuals and social units within a social system, in particular while producing goods and services. Given such a typological centrality intrinsically associated with a 'human factor', there is no wonder that in Russia technological emergencies and the bulk of compound emergencies and/or disasters which involve technological impact agents dominate statistically in terms of percentage of both the total number of emergencies and the total value of economic losses incurred by them. The peculiarities also provide for certain notable commonalties in management strategy and tactics with these and other types of emergencies and disasters.

CHAPTER 2

THE CONCEPT OF THE EMERGENCY MANAGEMENT CYCLE

An emergency or disaster always means a break of normal social routines of an affected social system and its units. Those people who happened to be directly in the center of an emergency, disaster or catastrophe area are naturally the first and most affected. Casualties and destruction undermine the very fundamental existence of families and communities making many of them homeless, refugees and so forth. Serious problems are also experienced by the rest of the regional and sometimes country's population who live outside the emergency or disaster areas but are involved in the relief to the affected communities. They do this either directly and voluntarily while providing help to the suffering relatives and friends, or indirectly while paying additional taxes to the special relief or aid funds of the local or regional budgets. The graver the emergency and/or disaster, the greater the load upon both the state and citizens. In the case of a major disaster or a catastrophe like the Chernobyl radiation disaster in the former Soviet Union, or regional armed conflicts and war in Caucasus in the contemporary Russia, this load has been felt almost by everybody for a long time.

In such a situation, the social system confronts the challenge of protection of people, their values and integrity as well as viability of the state. This naturally necessitates the development of a emergency management strategy including its reasonable conception and efficient means and methods of its implementation and control. I start first with an analysis of a mission and goals of such a strategy, then switch to the types and priorities of the strategies and finish this chapter with the phases, functions and main agents of emergency management using the former Soviet Union and contemporary Russia as illustrations.

EMERGENCY MANAGEMENT STRATEGIES: GOALS, TYPES AND PRIORITIES

MANAGEMENT GOALS: STRUCTURING AND INTERPRETATION

Goal setting is always the starting point for managing any objective including an emergency. In general with their political, social and economic activities a person, a community or a society sets two main types of goals:

Ideal or idealized goals which are considered as principally unattainable but presume approximation to them in the foreseeable or more distant future;

Real goals which principally can be realized in practice. These in turn comprise the short-term and medium-term goals which are presumed to be attained within a certain planned period, and long-term goals which are not expected to be reached but rather approximated within a certain limited time span and fully attained later on (Ackoff, 1985: 98 with the author's amendments).

As far as emergencies and/or disasters are concerned, the goal setting is methodologically predetermined by the two basic characteristics of a human society or community as an ecological and social (biosocial) system. One of these is its capability to provide its own stability and integrity, which presumes keeping the holisticity or indestructibility of the system and its capacity to self-development. These are provided by so-called negative feedback, which facilitates a community or a society like any living organism to overcome and compensate the outward hazardous impact thus diminishing the risk of rupture of the social fabric. Another characteristic presumes the capability of a social system to permanent support its own development through positive feedback, which facilitates the system's flexibility and evolution potential.

Given this, the idealized goal of emergency management can be formulated as providing absolute security for the social system development or, in other words, eliminating the risk of any emergency and/or disaster and their effects on people, their values and environment. As any ideal this goal is unattainable in principal considering that sources and agents of a hazardous impact or risk has always existed (see Chapter 1).

Nevertheless, the idealized goal has a certain practical value for management. First, it facilitates the process of real goal setting which presumes approximating the aforementioned idealized goal as close as possible with the degree of this proximity and its costs (time, material and money expenditures) being the measure of the decision making effectiveness. Secondly, it is absolutely possible to reach a zero emergency risk in relation to a given source of threat, for example the project of a facility with hazardous technology, by rejecting its construction in a certain area. At the same time, such a decision does not preclude the risk associated with the other sources and agents existing in that area.

Providing of security for both individuals, society and state should be designated as the key real goal or strategic mission of emergency management. In turn, security means protection of the aforementioned units or subsystems of a social system or security objectives against endogenous and exogenous threats which provide stability and sustainability of both the social units, the social system as a whole and its environment (see Zakon, 1992a). Therefore, the emergency management strategic mission may be conceptualized as an integral security (S_I) or a system (a tree) which comprises three main subsystems or goals including the individual security or safety (S_1), the social safety (S_2) and the state security (S_3). These in turn involve a certain number of second order subsystems or set of targets and so on.

The relationship between the main components of this system in a simplified way may be formally interpreted in the Equations (1) and (2):

$$S_I = S_1 + S_2 + S_3 \quad (1)$$
$$S_1 = f(S_2; S_3)$$
$$\{S_2 = f(S_1; S_3) \quad (2)$$
$$S_3 = f(S_1; S_2)$$

In any case S_1 S_2 while S_1 S_3 only when S_1 presumes the security of the highest state officials. Element S_1 characterizes security or safety of any individual (individual security or safety) rather then a security of a selected person (personal security) while the elements S_2 and S_3 both indicate collective security with the relationship between them being considerably predetermined by both the type of political system and social and economic development of a given nation (to be discussed further) and the type of an emergency, primarily its scale and gravity. Using the Russian official typology of emergencies by the scale of effect (Table 12), providing of the set S_1 and S_2 can be considered as the management strategic mission in organizational and local emergencies while that of S_I for such a mission in regional, macroregional and national emergencies.

In both cases, S_1 plays a key role as the key element of collective security, primarily social safety and integral security that is S_2 and S_I, respectively. The objectives of the latter include: the basic rights and freedoms of a man for life, health and so on; the material and spiritual values of a society; constitutional system, sovereignty and territorial integrity of a nation. Using these as criteria for classification, the emergency management mission of providing S_I may be subdivided into a number of goals comprising the objectives of protection, i.e., is what or who should be protected. The typology of these emergency management goals is shown in the Table 13.

Since the integral security S_I involves the protection of people and their values against certain endogenous and exogenous hazards, the latter may also be used as a criterion for decomposing the emergency management strategic mission into a number of types of goals reflecting the sources of these hazards. Using the typology of hazards (threats) to a social system security given in the Table 9 the classification of emergency management goals may be introduced as follows (Table 14).

The comparison of Tables 13 and 14 shows evidence that the content or interpretation of management goals within two typologies always differ despite the fact that sometimes their names are very much alike. For example, the concept of 'environmental' (ecological) security', which is used in both classifications, presumes principally different things: in the former case it means protection of the natural ambiance of a given social system as one of the key human values against various hazards while in the latter case it implies protection of this system against outward threats coming from the environment, that is against natural hazardous phenomena. That is why the clarity of terms and categories which designate the strategic mission, goals and targets of emergency management is needed with their definitions or conceptualizations being as clear-cut as possible.

If the hazards specified in the aforementioned tables are denominated as 'i' and the objectives of protection as 'j'" the Equation (1) may be rewritten as the Equation (3).

$$S_I = \sum_{i,j=1}^{n,m} S_{ij} \quad (3)$$

where $n, m = 1,2,3...$ are the numbers (quantities) of the sources of hazard and protection domains, respectively.

Formula (3) represents a qualitative formalized description of the structure of the emergency management strategic mission but does not reveal its content as a state of a social system being secured or protected. Using the risk category, the latter may be expressed in terms of minimization of the probability (risk) of an emergency, that is as low the number of casualties affected and the value of economic losses as achievable (see Equation (4)).

$$S_I = R_i C_{ij}^{-1} \min \quad (4)$$

Table 13. Types of Emergency Management Goals by Objective of Protection

Management goal [a]	The objective of protection
• Social safety (including individual safety)	◆ Human social rights
• Economic security (including social and economic security)	◆ Economic rights; economic (including military and economic) potential of a given social system (production units; other economic facilities and material properties)
• Environmental security	◆ Human rights for the healthy environment and favorable ecological (natural) conditions of living
• National and state security (including military security or national defense)	◆ Constitutional system; sovereignty and territorial integrity of a given country (nation)
• National (ethnic) and cultural security	◆ Cultural and historical and other values and wealth of a given country (nation)

[a] Protection of a certain domain of a social system

Table 14. Types of Emergencies Management Goals by a Source of Hazard

Management goal [a]	Hazardous source [b]
• Social safety and political security (including military and political security)	• Social and political conflicts (including international, regional and other conflicts)
• Social safety (including individual safety)	• Social crimes, epidemic, mass (collective) poisonings
• Environmental security	• Natural hazards
• Technological (including industrial) safety	• Technological accidents, including fires and explosions
• Eco-technological security (environmental security and technological) safety	• Compound na-tech hazardous occasions (desertification, landslides, induced earthquakes, etc.)
• Eco-social security (environmental security and social safety)	• Compound na-soc hazardous occasions (epidemic, epizootic, etc.)

[a] Protection against a ceratin type of hazard

[b] See also Table 9

where R_i is a probability of an emergency caused by the *i-* hazard and C_{ij} are the losses which have been incurred by the impact of *I-* hazard on *j-* unit of a social system or protection domain and directly associated with its vulnerability.

In turn the degree of vulnerability or, to the contrary, the security or safety level of people and their values are derivatives from the specific historical and cultural traditions and stereotypes, social and political conditions which considerably predetermine the availability and volume of material and financial resources, the quality of technology and equipment necessary for prevention of, preparedness, response to and recovery from emergencies and/or disasters and/or catastrophes.

These traditions and conditions substantially vary not only between different countries and regions of the world but within the same nation as well. This provides for and explains the existing discrepancies in levels of integral security, primarily social safety, which have been normatively established or perceived by people as socially acceptable thresholds of hazard or risk and should be considered as a real strategic mission of emergency management. In turn, these predetermine the pattern of tactical goals and targets of emergency management and means and methods of reaching them. At the same time, the idealized goal to protect themselves against any emergency or disaster despite the degree of real danger and available resources is not chosen by the social units and individuals, but objectively stems from their natural will for survival. Such a pattern of various goals pre-establish, first of all, the strategic management as a key type of societal policy towards emergencies and/or disasters (see Table 15).

Table 15. Management Policies Typology

Policy type	Means	Goals and targets	Mission	Ideal goal
Operative	Selected	Established	Established	Not formulated
Tactical	Selected	Selected	Established	Not formulated
Strategic	Selected	Selected	Selected	Established
Normative	Selected	Selected	Selected	Selected

Source: Based on (Ackoff, 1985: 98) with the author's amendments

TYPES AND PRIORITIES OF EMERGENCY MANAGEMENT STRATEGIES

Usually strategic management implies a set of actions which involve the development, formulation and assessment of a certain number of strategies, operational management and control for implementation of the selected strategy and tactical and operational plans. Thus it comprises two types or stages of activities: strategic planning and tactical and operational management and control of the selected strategy realization.

While planning at the highest management level, the mission, goals and targets of the organization are established and compared with the probable situations and occasions which have been forecasted as very likely to arise within a certain period. This serves as a basis for establishing priorities of goals, means and methods to reach them within a planned time span including resource assessment and the main areas of activities of organization implied in the main or strategic programs. The latter in turn are used as a basis for development of tactical and operational programs and plans including contingency plans. The management and control of all kinds of these programs and plans being carried out are conducted at the lower hierarchical levels of the organization and constitutes the content of the latter for the aforementioned two stages of strategic management activities (Antony, Dearden and Vancil, 1965: 4; Babintsev, 1988: 50-51. For further reading see: Ansoff, 1989; King and Kliland, 1982).

Strategic goal setting is both the starting point and a crucial stage of planning and management. From the emergency management perspective, it should involve a level of risk resulting from the hazard nature and degree of vulnerability, the character of risk perception and assessment by decision makers and the public, and cultural, political, social and economic conditions which provide for management priorities and resource availability. In general, two basic arguments may be used for the strategic goal setting:

(1) the risk of an emergency is completely unacceptable while the causes or emergency itself are principally preventable;

(2) the risk of an emergency is imperiously acceptable with its causes and pre-conditions being principally non-preventable, and the necessary protection measures which facilitate decreasing human and economic losses should be both timely and efficient.

These give rise to three types of strategic goals and respective management strategies which are oriented on prevention, mitigation and alleviation of emergency effects and shown in the Table 16.

Before these strategies are analyzed, it is worth noting that the strategic goals reflect the degree or levels of approximation to the idealized goal of emergency management. Within the goal-tree in the ascending order the previous goal is both the second-level goal or target in relation to the next goal and the method of reaching it. For example, the prevention of pre-conditions and causes of emergency development precludes this event or occasion itself which in turn solves the problem of reducing human and economic losses.

At the same time this serves as a preventive method for transformation of an emergency into a disaster and then into a catastrophe (see Fig. 12). Thus, goals, means and methods of emergency management strategy should be considered as the relative concepts. Their relationship is predetermined by the stage of emergency development, on one hand, and by dimensions or hierarchy of a social or organizational system involved in an emergency, on the other hand.

The *preventive strategy* is oriented towards averting the deep pre-conditions and causes of emergency origin and development and implies non-admission or banning of the actions fraught

Type of strategy	Strategic mission	Prerequisites of the strategic mission choice	Vector of the management efficiency increase
Prevention	Prevention of the causes and conditions of emergency origin	The potential hazard is great but its sources can be eliminated; the risk is unacceptable but preventable	↑
Mitigation	Prevention of an emergency *per se*	The potential hazard is great, its sources can be localized (restricted) but not fully eliminated; the risk is inevitably acceptable and partly preventable	↑
Alleviation	Cushioning and reducing the scale and gravity of the hazardous impact aftermath	The potential hazard is great and can not be eliminated; the risk is inevitably acceptable and unpreventable	↑

Table 16. Typology of Emergency Management Strategies

with a substantial threat to the integral security. In formal terms, this means that the condition R_i min should be fulfilled in order to provide S_I min requirement in formula (4).

Without going into details, the prevention strategy may be implemented by two methods. One of them involves the rejection of political, social, economic and technological decisions which create additional and considerable sources of a hazard to a social system and its units. For instance, as far as technological emergencies and/or disasters are concerned, this would imply a repudiation from diverting rivers from the North to the South, construction of various huge water reservoirs and canals and certain nuclear, chemical and paper facilities in ecologically and socially vulnerable areas which were so typical in the former Soviet Union.

If the conflict-type emergencies are taken as a case, the initial rejection of the government in early 1997 from the projected and widely criticized decision to limit pensions may serve as a good example illustrating the social policy in contemporary Russia. The project presumed paying pensions only to non-working pensioners while those who continued to work after they reached the pension age would be deprived of this right and get only wages and salaries. This governmental project arouse conspicuous public strife and if implemented could have resulted in a more serious social emergency.

In addition, given that the bulk of the working places in industries and enterprises with relatively small wage tariffs have been occupied primarily by pensioners who have agreed to work for this money with 50% and sometimes 100% of their pensions being paid, such a decision would also have lead to substantial economic losses associated with a lacking of personnel. This would mean a real disaster. However, in mid 1997 after the former cabinet was replaced, the newcomers again ear-marked this idea which means that the risk of the major social emergency or disaster had not disappeared.

As these examples show, this method of implementing prevention strategy is the most efficient at its decision making or planning stage and in respect to familiar and predictable hazards and emergencies (see Table 11). This stage is the best appropriate one to modify the private or particular interests of certain organizations, business or social groups towards more comprehensive consideration of the interests of a social unit or social system as a whole in a safer and more secure development, and choose the right option. These actions are marked with the light grey horizontal arrows in the Fig. 12.

Another method of implementing the prevention strategy implies the timely rejection or abolition of decisions which have been already taken and realized or enforced but until now have not lead to an emergency or disaster. This method should be applicable to any type of emergency although it is initially less efficient than the previous method.

The most vivid illustration in this respect has been decisions to destroy chemical weapons completely, some classes of nuclear missiles and conversion of military plants which have been enforced since late 1980s and implemented in the 1990s by United States, Russia and the other CIS countries. Such a decision is definitely comprehensive contributing to prevention of both technological accidents at military facilities (nuclear missile launch sites, chemical ammunition depot, etc.) and armed conflicts and wars which involve the mass destruction weapons.

The *mitigation strategy* is focused on averting the emergency itself. It presumes that given the existing natural, cultural, political, economic, social, organizational and technological constraints, the deep pre-conditions and causes of its origin and development can not or have not been eliminated or, in formal terms, the condition R_i min and S_I min requirement in the formula (4) are not met. Thus, if the trigger is available the 'chain reaction' of events would start and result in an emergency, disaster or a catastrophe. At the same time, it turns out to be not only necessary but principally possible to take countermeasures which would stop the aforementioned process and prevent transformation of an incident or accident into an emergency and/or disaster and/or a catastrophe by blocking the impact of the hazardous agents on a social system and reducing the vulnerability of this system and its units.

These completely refer to both conflict and non-conflict types of emergencies. For instance, the natural processes and phenomena which give rise to natural emergencies and disasters, or the combination of the former with other non-natural agents which results in compound emergencies and disasters are irremovable. It is also not possible to get rid of the sophisticated engineering systems which involve hazardous materials and technologies and objectively are the sources of high risk but have been contributing greatly to the economic development all over the world. At last, in normal everyday life although full of social problems, incidents and minor conflicts it would be unconstitutional to ban all demonstrations, manifestations and other kinds of mass movements which may transfer into or catalyze mass disturbances, riots and so forth.

Therefore, within the framework of mitigation strategy it is necessary, on the one hand, to break the earlier mentioned 'chain reaction' of events thus localizing the hazardous occasion or process and keeping it under control. In the complex engineering systems (nuclear, chemical, highly explosive and fire-prone facilities) in-built safety devices, containment, multiple redundancy and automatic safety control equipment have been used to stop reaction, fire and other hazardous processes fraught with an emergency, disaster or a catastrophe. Vaccination, early quarantine and other well-known preventive forms of mass disease control as well as preventive operations while mass movement actions (early disclosing of the probable aggressive plans, instigators and so forth) although not eliminating these hazardous occasions as such, however, considerably reduce the risk of great epidemic or pandemic and mass disturbances and riots, respectively. Using special antiseismic technologies (belts, cushions and frames), protection dams and walls and so forth also does not preclude earthquakes and floods but in many cases minimizes the risk of an emergency or disaster.

On the other hand, within the framework of mitigation strategy it is also necessary to reduce the social vulnerability by providing for preventive evacuation, sheltering, restricting the routes for mass manifestations by the less populated and open districts and so on. Thus, within the causal chain of emergency origin development, the elements 'hazardous agents (risk factors)' and 'exposition of a social system to the hazardous impact' (see Fig. 12) are blocked. In this figure the respective preventive and blocking control actions are marked with the grey horizontal arrows.

Economic effectiveness of the mitigation strategy should be especially stressed. Thus, according to the estimates of Russian specialists, each ruble of expenditures on immunization of cattle against foot-and-mouth disease saves 20 rubles. In Krasnodar region (*krai*) in 1995 alone the prevented losses from this disease accounted to 14 billion of rubles or more than US$ 3 million. To the contrary, in that year the Ramesnk district (*rayon*) of the Moscow region (*oblast*) had to pay the same sum of money to abate the foot-and-mouth epizootic because earlier it lacked only 500 million rubles to prevent this disease (Marzeeva, 1997).

The mitigation strategy also has many proved its effectiveness with earthquake emergencies and disasters, especially those with a magnitude less than 8 on the Richter scale. In the early 1980s, experts of the former Soviet Union estimated that each ruble of investment in antiseismic construction and retrofitting saved from 15 to 20 rubles in prevented losses while in California this ratio accounted to 1:6 (Kharichev, 1980).

The *alleviation strategy* is the most relevant in poorly predictable or unpredictable, rapidly spreading types of emergencies, especially those affecting poorly protected communities (see Tables 10 and 11), or in emergencies which principally could not be prevented (for example, in case of the extremely great earthquake or flood) or failed to be prevented. It is also applicable to the same types of disasters and catastrophes when scenarios 2 and 3 in the Fig. 1.12 are realized and it is principally.

It presumes maximal possible reduction of the scale and cushioning of debilitating and devastating effects including the breaks and ruptures of the social routines and communications. In a case of a gradual course of events when debilitating and devastating effects are spreading not so rapidly within an affected social system but the emergency may transition into a disaster and then even into a catastrophe (scenario 1 in Fig. 1.12), the alleviation strategy would also carry out the mitigation function of preventing these potential disasters and/or catastrophes.

The respective preventive and cushioning control actions which break the chain of events that would otherwise lead to the aforementioned types of grave crises are marked with the dark grey horizontal arrows in Fig. 12. Besides, other such actions include: timely warning, post-crisis evacuation of people and material values, effective organization of the search and rescue, medical care support and relief operations and so on.

Each of the three strategies does not exclude the other two but, to the contrary, implies their coexistence as a single set which provides for the opportunity, if necessary, to switch from one strategy to another depending on the type and phase of emergency development. As a matter of fact, this constitutes one of the main characteristics and the basic merit of strategic management which has been considering the probability of a drastic change in the conditions of organizational or social system functioning and providing for its flexible response to such a change by the immediate transition to the alternative pre-planned strategy.

These qualities are becoming more and more valuable even in everyday management of organizational and/or social systems contributing to their increased mobility and capacity to timely correct both the goals and means in correspondence with fluctuations of the situation. Each time the solving of relatively well-known and systematically recurrent or functional tasks and problems both in production and service sectors of economy, which are directly associated with the established pattern of the labor sharing in these industries including public administration, takes place in the new conditions.

This adds these functional task problem-oriented or contingent-type characteristics thus making both functionally specialized and problem-oriented (contingency planning) units necessary and organic elements of the management organization. The need to overcome discrepancies between the units and functions within line and staff organizations necessitates integration and coordination development which lessens the rigidity and centralization of the existing hierarchical organizational system making them more flexible and adding to them some characteristics of a matrix organization (Rudashevskiy, 1987: 225-226, 239; Yekaterinoslavskiy, 1988: 12).

The aforementioned merits of strategic management are even much more important and pressing in rapidly changing conditions of an emergency situation with its high degree of uncertainty which increases in direct proportion to the scale and gravity of an emergency, the rapidness of its debilitating and devastating effects spreading within a social system and in inverse proportion to its predictability (see Table 11). In addition, the search and development of flexible organizational structures and economic tools for coordination of actions of various management agents is necessary from the viewpoint that no organization, however powerful, has capacity enough to provide itself the efficient management at all the phases of all the types of emergencies.

In conditions of uncertainty, information support which provides timely and full data describing the rapidly changing situation in real time as well as pre-emergency and trans-emergency forecasting of these changes is critical for efficient decision making and implementation. Flexible organizational systems including their matrix management structures facilitate the maximal free flow of information both horizontally and vertically. Such systems are based on self-management and self-organization, use of heuristic approaches and methods of decision making and implementation based on accumulated experience rather than on command-and-order directives, instructions and clear-cut algorithms and procedures (Comfort, 1988).

These presume that the hierarchy within the organizational system is being kept and the tactical and operation management agents (operation centers, crisis commissions and committees, special focal points and so forth) would not absolutely strictly follow the directives from the command center. Instead, extensive consultation and coordination of activities based upon high competence of decision makers would be used. This type of behavior would be most typical at the origin or prodromal phase of emergency development when the necessary prevention and preparedness measures must be planned and carried out, and to a considerable extent while supporting or re-establishing social order in the case of ordinary everyday incidents and minor accidents.

However, flexible organization structures and methods of management are also becoming more and more necessary at the culmination phase of emergency development when centralization of response and partly recovery functions is objectively the most needed. The available experience shows evidence that the chiefs of operation task force have been taking decisions at the field level and implementing decisions made by chief coordinator at the tactical level with the degree of independence qualitatively incomparable with these in everyday public administration. In emergencies management is goal or function-biased rather than process-biased with the tactical goal formulated by the chief coordinator in the operation center being the single one for every management agent involved. In general, the enumerated characteristics are pertinent to emergency or operational management. (In Russia, the latter has been labeled as *situatsionnoye upravleniye* or literally 'situation management'. See, for example: Yekaterinoslavskiy, 1988).

Thus, the strategic type of management involves development and extensive use of organizational frameworks and management methods which provide both bridging and matching of the three strategies mentioned above including their mutual substitution if needed. In other words, an emergency and/or disaster calls for a set or, better, system of strategies: no one of them should be missed, otherwise the strategic mission of emergency management as a whole will fail.

Although prevention, mitigation and alleviation strategies have been used in all types of emergencies, their applicability, efficiency and effectiveness differ from one type to another (see Table 17).

In principal, prevention and mitigation strategies undoubtedly are the most efficient with their mission approximating as close as possible to the idealized goal of emergency management. In this respect, prevention strategy looks particularly attractive as it presumes the risk of emergency origin being reduced to the minimum. Nevertheless, the opportunity for this strategy to be widely used in the real life is considerably constrained. First of all, it is virtually inapplicable in hardly predictable or completely unpredictable emergencies and/or disasters, primarily natural disasters, the sources of which can not be controlled.

Substantially better prevention strategy perspectives look alike in relatively and partly predictable types of emergencies and/or disasters which involve the bulk of the non-conflict and conflict-type emergencies provoked mainly by endogenous, fatal type hazards (technological, social and political and compound accidents and crisis) (see Table 17). However, in these cases as well, its possibilities turn out to be more limited than wished, which stems primarily from a non-zero probability of an accident, emergency and so on. On the one hand, this is associated with the availability of the potential energy accumulated and biologically and chemically active elements functioning within the natural (ecological) and technological (engineering) systems and socially active or unstable units and elements ('human factor') within technological and social systems.

Type of strategy	The degree of a strategy efficiency		
	Most efficient	Efficient	Partly efficient or inefficient
Prevention	1c (En, F, I)	1b (En, F)	1a (Ex)
Mitigation	1c3b	1b/1a	None
Alleviation	1a3a (Ex, C, F)	1a/1b3b (Ex, C, N)	1b/1c2a2b (En)3b

LEGEND (see Table 11)

Types of emergencies

1a - hardly predictable and unpredictable; 1b - partly predictable; 1c - relatively predictable

2a - conflict; 2b - non-conflict

3a - rapidly spreading; 3b - slowly spreading

Types of hazards (threats)

Ex - exogenous; En - endogenous; C - combined

T - tangible (real); I - intangible (information)

F - fatal; N - non-fatal

Table 17. Efficiency of Management Strategies by Type of Emergencies

On the other hand, non-zero risk reality is predetermined by the so-called law of large numbers which postulates that a cumulative action of a great number of random factors leads to an occurrence of a result almost independent from an opportunity. Given the multiplicity of the sources and agents hazardous to human health and material values which have been existing within ecological and social systems, and even greater multiplicity and complexity of their interactions both between each other and between them and increasing number of the people exposed (see Chapter 1), an emergency, disaster or a catastrophe becomes inevitable leaving out everyday incidents or accidents.

The aforementioned is true in respect to any type of emergency. For instance, considering the safety of complex engineering systems which involve high pressure, toxic and flammable substances and so forth, the difference between them and those which do not use risky technologies is worth remembering. In the latter case the safety is primarily provided by the reliability of construction of the whole system and its units which can be relatively easy substituted if needed.

As to the safety of the complex engineering systems, it should be interpreted as the integral safety of a big system which comprises man-machine subsystems (industrial facility) and social and ecological subsystems (the neighboring communities and environment). The reliability of the former subsystem is primarily dependent on the social factors including psychological and physiological status, competence and motivation of the personnel, management organization, etc.) rather than technical parameters of the industrial facility. No less important is the its risk perception and assessment by the neighboring communities and some 'sensitive' non-governmental organizations.

All these things, along with the possibility of an industrial accident and its social and environmental impact, should be taken into account when estimating the safety status or the risk and economic effectivenessof such a facility. However negligible the probability of an accident fraught with an emergency, disaster or catastrophe is, it should by all means be considered during engineering and economic calculations. In other words, a given complex facility should meet the 'risk-effectiveness' and social acceptability criteria in order to provide integral security of a given social unit. (For more detailed discussion of these criteria applied to the radiation and nuclear hazardous facilities in Russia see: Porfiriev, 1996c).

This requirement is still more pressing given that the idea of a 'zero risk' and its variations ('may-be-it-flies-by', 'it-can't-happen-here' syndromes) have been ingrained in the consciousness of the Russian people in particular but not only there. The example of the nuclear industry fully corroborates this point.

Despite hundreds of incidents, dozens of accidents and several emergencies and disasters which happened both at military and civil nuclear facilities in the former Soviet Union, United Kingdom and United States from the late 1950s to the early 1980s, many Soviet specialists until the Chernobyl radiation disaster postulated the 'zero risk' principle in relation to national nuclear power plants. Thus, in spite of the major accidents at the nuclear power near Leningrad in 1975 and 1982, the Three Mile Island radiation emergency in the United States in 1979 until the moment of Chernobyl explosion in April 1986, in their interviews to the foreign and national mass media, top Soviet experts stressed *that* the nuclear power reactors were absolutely safe (Thournbough, 1986; *The Worst Accident*, 1986: 6-7). The same assessment was also made in respect to the nuclear heat supply plants which was constructed until the late 1980s near Nizhniy Novgorod and Voronezh.

These authoritative declarations could not but substantially influence public opinion in the former Soviet Union. The results of the joint Soviet Union-French public opinion poll in Moscow in October 1987, that is a year and a half after the Chernobyl explosion, showed that 20% of respondents considered new accidents at the Soviet nuclear power plants impossible with even a much higher proportion of those among women (Mansurov, 1987). Later on, the situation conspicuously changed both in the former Soviet Union and other countries of the world with a developed nuclear power sector (the USA, Japan, Germany) where the prevailing majority of respondents expressed much more careful opinions stressing the necessity of efficient safety measures and not increasing the existing nuclear power capacity (Naumov, 1996).

However, as early as in 1995 in Byelorus, the republic which suffered the most from the Chernobyl radioactive fallout, but lacked its own nuclear power plants, 40.4% of the respondents considered these as safe and almost the same proportion of them were in favor of construction of such a plant there. Just to compare, in the same year 44% of respondents in Japan agreed that nuclear power plants were safe although soon after the public opinion poll was conducted the serious accident occurred at the '*Monzu*' plant. As far as nuclear power specialists are concerned, the proportion of respondents from this group who were absolutely sure that the nuclear power plants were safe was much higher in almost every country (Grousha, 1996).

Although most 'green' environmental activists have often stressed this, such a perception of one of the major technological hazards can hardly be explained only by incompetence of or the wish to protect 'the honor of the regiment' by nuclear power specialists. Given that the public in Russia and other countries of the former Soviet Union has been really inadequately informed about the merits and risks associated with nuclear power however, I believe that the main reasons are those of a social, psychological and economic character.

The aforementioned technocratic style of thinking, still so typical while making and implementing decisions concerning complex engineering systems (see Chapter 1), and the deep and lasting economic crisis in the 1990s in Russia and the other CIS countries with many of them experiencing substantial shortages of energy supplies, should be especially emphasized. For example, in Byelorus the level of public anxiety associated with an expected increase of electricity prices is more than double that for the risk associated with the possible construction of a nuclear power plant there. In 1995, the respective proportions of respondents related to each other was 84.9% against 47.7% (Grousha, 1996).

In these circumstances, the 'non-zero risk' principle, even when it is perceived as trivial, gains particular importance for the conceptual framework of strategic management in emergencies. It corroborates the imperative for using a system of switching management strategies which provide an integral security of a given social system. In this connection it looks as though there is a logical discrepancy between the cited principle and the mission of preventive strategy which involves blocking the pre-conditions and elimination of risk of the emergency. However, actually there is no contradiction at all.

As discussed above, risk elimination is both possible and expedient in respect to a concrete single hazard which is directly associated with erroneous decision making. Timely refusal from or reconsideration of such a decision means an actual removal of the specific man-made potential sources of risk. But this does not touch and, therefore can not eradicate, other risk sources and agents which remain out from decision making domain thus making impossible $R_{ij} = 0$ in the formula (4). For example, a project of a certain high-risk facility construction being not carried out would not preclude the hazards associated with other functioning engineering systems leaving alone natural, social (conflict-type) and compound hazard sources and agents.

In practical terms, it is impossible to suspend or close all hazardous industrial facilities for the sake of human lives and health as some radical 'deep ecologists' in Russia and elsewhere have proposed. This would not only fail to minimize the risk but rather debilitate the integral security of a social system. It would also destroy one of the main sources which contribute to solving of emergency prevention and mitigation problems, i.e., economic and technological development, which dialectically has been carrying both the 'germ' of the future emergencies and disasters and the 'medicine' against these in terms of the new more safe engineering technologies and more effective management organization. That is why if the 'zero risk' emergency and/or disaster may be considered at least as an ideal, the apology of 'zero economic growth' to reach it should be treated as a dangerous utopia.

In addition to the circumstances mentioned above, a more wide use of a preventive emergency management strategy is deterred by some other objective, primarily economic, reasons and subjective factors including private or narrow interests of influential persons or corporations (see Chapter 1). The latter could be to a substantial extent overcome due to well-known measures like publicity, open competition, economic and technical feasibility studies and risk and environmental impact assessments by independent experts and so forth. However, no fewer multiple problems would remain thus necessitating the other two emergency management strategies, i.e., mitigation and alleviation strategies, which will be extensively discussed in the forthcoming sections of the book.

EMERGENCY MANAGEMENT MECHANISM: STAGES, FUNCTIONS AND AGENTS

The emergency management process or realization of the set of prevention, mitigation and alleviation strategies consists of a number of successive stages and phases which make up a management cycle. In addition, this process is carried out by a few key management agents (decision makers and decision executors), in Russia primarily by state legislative and especially executive authorities of various levels which perform the functions of prevention, preparedness, response to and recovery from emergencies. The type of state and political system, the competence of the public administrators and officers directly engaged in social safety and protection of people and their values during disasters to a considerable extent provide for the efficiency of emergency management.

STAGES, PHASES AND FUNCTIONS OF EMERGENCY MANAGEMENT. AN EMERGENCY MANAGEMENT CYCLE

Within any of the aforementioned emergency management strategies, two stages: the development stage and implementation stage, may be relatively clearly delineated.

The d e v e l o p m e n t   s t a g e comprises two main phases, i.e., risk assessment and risk management which provide for realization of the analytic and forecasting function of the management process (see Table 18).

Table 18. Stages, Phases, and Functions of Emergency Management Strategies

Stages		Phases	Functions
Functional approach	Strategic approach		
(1)	(2)	(3)	(4)
Prevention/mitigation	Strategy development	◆ Risk assessment ◆ Risk management (organizational, legal and economic regulation)	• Management information support (collection, processing and analysis of the data concerning hazardous sources, factors and impacts) • Forecasting (modeling of emergency origin and development scenarios) • Development of the R&D and comprehensive federal and regional emergency mitigation programs (including legal and economic regulators)

Table 18. *(Continued)*

(1)	(2)	(3)	(4)
Mitigation / alleviation	Strategy implementation (realization)		
Alleviation / cushioning of effects		◆ Emergency recovery (disaster / catastrophe mitigation)	• Caring of alive (water, food, clothes supply, etc.) and dead, (providing morgues, transportation, etc.) • Localization of secondary impacts (emergency scale and gravity restriction including epidemic and epizootic prevention) • Liquidation of the impact aftermath (removal of debris, cleaning of the affected area including deactivation and sanitary care measures) • Reconstruction, medium and long-term medical and social rehabilitation of the affected people • Investigation of the impact's aftermath and causes of the emergency, preparation of reports and recommendations to mitigate future emergencies

Table 18. *(Continued)*

(1)	(2)	(3)	(4)
Prevention / mitigation	Strategy implementation (realization)	◆ Emergency prevention and mitigation ◆ Emergency preparedness	• Emergency prevention organizational and technical support (installation of built-in safety devices, retrofitting, land planning, etc.) • Development and reconsideration of existing contingency and operation plans • Training of special cadres (search and rescue, medical, etc.) • Financial resources and material reserves accumulation • Equipment of facilities and settlements with alarm and warning systems, technical support of emergency units with special equipment • Communities and organizations warning, public information • Pre-impact evacuation and sheltering
Mitigation / alleviation		◆ Emergency response (disaster mitigation)	• Search and rescue, urgent medical care support, post-impact evacuation and sheltering

As a part of the risk assessment procedure this function presumes: identification or revelation of the sources and agents of a risk or a hazard, assessment of the degree of danger associated with each of these sources and agents to human lives and health, estimation of the geographical dimension of the expected emergency and/or disaster area and possible human and material losses. As a part of the risk management process, the aforementioned function involves the development of legal, organizational and economic means and methods designated to minimize the risk of an emergency origin and mitigate its potential (expected) effects. (I made a detailed analysis of this in: Porfiriev, 1990).

As an example of such kinds of activities, worth mentioning in particular are the development of building codes and construction standards, insurance procedures, zoning and mapping of vulnerability risk towards natural hazards, modeling and forecasting including elaboration of the scenarios of possible technological accidents and social and political conflicts, development of comprehensive and R&D programs to prevent and withstand emergencies. All these require collection, processing and analysis of the vast and reliable data which can be found both by retrospective studying of archives, statistics and so forth and current monitoring of the actual social, political, economic and environmental situation in a given social system. No less important should be the results of various 'tuning' studies including medical, psychological, microbiological, toxicological, etc. which provide the basis for establishing criteria of risk acceptability (safety and security levels) needed for a quantitative or qualitatively formal description of the strategy's mission.

The i m p l e m e n t a t i o n s t a g e of an emergency management strategy comprises a set of practical measures (administrative, organizational, economic, technological and so on) which is carried out within the well-known four phases: prevention of, preparedness and response to and recovering from an emergency and/or disaster and/or a catastrophe (see Table 18).

The *prevention and mitigation phase* involves two basic functions of monitoring / screening and correction / control. The former function includes organizational and technical measures of engineering and environmental inspections, auditing, checking and other procedures to detect the imperfections and loopholes in technological systems, buildings and construction. It also includes social monitoring, surveillance, patrol and other activities which are used to detect conflicts at their earliest, prodromal stage of development.

The correction / strengthening function presumes taking a wide gamut of practical steps to preclude the emergence of unacceptable risk sources and agents (primarily by land use planning), correct the disclosed shortcomings and strengthen communities capacity to withstand emergencies and reduce their vulnerability to hazardous impacts (retrofitting of buildings and constructions, equipment of facilities with automatic fire control systems, etc.) and retain the situation under control, i.e., not allowing it to spill over the boundaries of an everyday incident.

Within the *preparedness phase*, four key functions are realized, these are: contingency planning, training, providing facilities and settlements with alarm and warning systems and technical support of emergency units with special equipment, reserves accumulation (see Table 18). Planning implies the development of contingency plans at organizational and local management levels, coordination of these at the regional or departmental (federal) levels and using them as a basis for elaborating regional and national operational plans also considering the opportunities of international cooperation and relief.

Quite often, both in Russia and other countries of the world, the development and coordination of the aforementioned plans have been formal and sometimes even ignored. However this work should be considered as necessary and useful by saving time and resources for decision making and implementation and considerably contributing to emergency management effectiveness, primarily to reducing of the human and economic losses. According to some estimates, the post-culmination phase of an emergency occurs at organizations without a contingency or crisis management plan lasting two and a half times longer than in those that had such plans developed and enforced. Given that the time of response is inversely proportional to the scale and gravity of an emergency, it is quite natural that the bulk of administrators of state and private corporations in the West which used contingency planning, as early as at the beginning of the 1980s believed these plans worked 'very well' (Fink, 1986: 60-70).

In the former Soviet Union, and as far as I know in contemporary Russia, no extensive public surveys have been conducted among the chiefs of enterprises concerning availability and utility of contingency plans, although certain kinds of such plans, primarily evacuation planning, has been widely spread there for a long time, especially at state enterprises. My own confidential sample interviews with some of these administrators in the late 1980s and early 1990s revealed that they have overwhelmingly considered contingency plans as a formal but useless duty with a substantially higher proportion of such answers among the chief executives of private corporations.

The situation is to the contrary as far as regional operational plans are concerned: the available data shows evidence that the bulk of city and regional public administrators responsible for the social safety have agreed that these plans have been 'useful' or 'very useful'. However, given the existing incremental trend of the gravity of emergencies in Russia (see Chapter 1) and the expected subsiding of the long-term social and economic crisis by the end of the 1990s, I argue that the role of contingency planning at the organizational level should be reassessed somewhere between 2005 and 2010 at the latest.

Contingency and operation planning in emergencies differs from that used in everyday incidents and accidents. In the latter case, the unpleasant happenings have been treated as ordinary relatively well known determined-type occasions in the case of which established instructions and guides can be used. These have described step by step the necessary control actions which 'break' the causal chain of events during the development of an accident. For example, for such purposes in the nuclear industry of Russia '*General Safety Guide to Designing, Construction and Exploitation of Nuclear Power Plants*', '*Nuclear Safety Rules for Nuclear power Plants*' and technological regulations have been used. This means that in ordinary accidents, the prescriptive type of management is employed which is based upon calculation of an accident's quantitative risk involving fault tree, decision tree and other kinds of probability risk assessments.

As to extraordinary situations, when the chain of events is undetermined or probabilistic and more or less accurate risk calculations are much less reliable if possible, contingency or operation management has been efficient. This presumes the development of various kinds of solutions depending on the time, place, origin type and other characteristics of an emergency which involve using of 'what if?' or a scenario type approach. The latter and methods associated with this have been also been employed as analytic and forecasting tools not for quantitative assessment of the accident itself but rather for the modeling of the possible scenarios of unscheduled event development within an organizational or social system irrelevant to the probability of occurrence of such an event. This differentiates operation or contingency analysis from risk analysis that obligatorily requires the calculation of this probability.

The development and further implementation of contingency and operational plans is carried out by special professional cadres. Their selection, training and upgrading are another important function of the preparedness phase. In principal, no single discipline can provide the universal knowledge and skills needed by the emergency personnel thus necessitating the comprehensive, multidisciplinary approach used in the specialized institutions (academies, universities and training centers). Cooperation of these with experts from crisis consulting organizations is also useful for personnel training and as well as for emergency strategy development and planning.

The permanent emergency personnel manned by both specially trained officers, administrators and professionals (rescuers, doctors, firemen, etc.) and enlisted servicemen (military, civil defense, police and so on) are grouped into units and task forces each having its functional area of activity. The latter includes: social order and safety support, fire protection, search and rescue, medical and transportation services, debris removal, public relations and information and so on. These units are organic to chief executive bodies (commissions, committees, staffs), means and forces which function both at organizational and all-authority levels. In Russia, these are labeled as regular forces (literally as 'permanent readiness forces').

These very forces and services organize and coordinate all activities during a response to an emergency. Therefore at the preparedness phase, the staff of operational services organize special exercises both in the training operation center and in the field. They simulate and practically verify the possible scenarios of emergency development and respective response actions of the regular emergency forces, attached units, communities and others. The results of these exercises are used for the development and correction of existing contingency and operational plans.

In Russia at the local, regional and federal levels, regular emergency units have been conducting regular field and class exercises which proved their efficiency during real emergencies and disasters, in particular during the KamAZ big fire and Neftegorsk major earthquake in Sakhalin (see Chapter 4). Unfortunately, at the organizational level, i.e., at facilities, enterprises, companies, schools, etc., despite the obvious necessity of pre-crisis training, such exercises have been rarely carried out by the respective emergency units which lack funds and often the will of their chief executives and adequate supervision from responsible authorities.

The reasons for this vary. For example, in the former Soviet Union in the mid 1980s, many chief executives and administrators in the hazardous industries who were motivated by the economic system to produce more and more, underestimated the role of simulators, test benches and models which had been not directly involved in production but required additional expenditures (Paton, 1986).

In Russia in the mid 1990s, the deep and lasting economic depression was accompanied by huge indebtedness of the state enterprises leading to a shortage of funds needed for industrial safety policy. In addition, given the accelerated rates of crimes against property and its owners, which have been closely associated with economic crisis, the chief executives and administrators of many companies were forced to spend much of the 'safety' money on numerous guards and alarm systems instead of investing it in technological safety, in particular, fire safety. As a result, fires became one of the most debilitating hazardous agents for private companies.

The equipment of facilities and settlements with alarm and early warning systems, safety shelters, vehicles for evacuation and so forth and technical support of emergency units with special equipment (fire extinguishers, water pumps, rescue instruments, etc.) which are employed during an emergency response constitute one more important functions of the preparedness phase.

The last, but not the least, function of this phase involves accumulation of financial resources and material reserves used both in response to and recovery from an emergency. In the former Soviet Union and contemporary Russia this has been carried out, first, through compulsory state insurance of lives of personnel and material properties of the enterprises and organizations and voluntary insurance of the citizens' lives and property against risks. Private insurance although existing in the country only since the late 1980s, is still playing a minor role. Secondly, the centralized federal system of the state material reserves headed by GOSKOMREZERV (the former State Committee for Material and Technical Reserves or currently the State Committee of the

Russian Federation for State Reserves) has been employed to accumulate and distribute reserves of food, medical, shelter and other items.

At the *response phase*, both the 'theater' and the gravity of an emergency, its debilitating and destructive effects within a social system should be restricted. This has been attained by implementing four functions including: warning, localization and rescue and evacuation (see Table 18)

The first function involves two groups of measures, those activated immediately prior to (warning) and immediately following disaster impact (early notification). Timely implementation of warning systems provides both community organizations as well as individuals the opportunity to use shelters and evacuation and some other pre-impact measures. It also provides 'supracommunity' and community organizations starting early preparations for search and rescue and relief operations thus reducing the devastating potential of a disaster. The latter is also facilitated by post-impact early notification of the respective authorities and emergency organizations and public information about the tentative damage assessments.

The core of the localization function is the isolation of an emergency or disaster area and protection of its dwellers and their property against threats of secondary impacts. The respective measures include imposing sanitary and police cordons, blocking and control posts in case of both conflict type emergencies and/or disasters and some non-conflict type compound emergencies, in particular epidemic and epizootic. At the same time, the measures which are designated to preclude secondary impact (fires, inundation, epidemic and alike in affected and the neighboring communities) and include disconnection of electricity, water, gas and other supplies, urgent contouring of the affected areas (making cuttings in the burning forests, erection of ramparts and coffer-dams and so on) have proved their efficiency in non-conflict type emergencies and/or disasters provoked by natural hazards and technological accidents.

As an example of the aforementioned response actions during the latter type of disasters, the heroic and successful efforts of firemen to stop the fire at the block # 4 and prevent its spreading over to the adjacent blocks of the Chernobyl nuclear power plant during the first hours after the explosion occurred in April 1986, should be cited first and foremost. If the fire had spread over to block # 3, the scale and gravity of the world is worst radiation disaster would have been considerably increased. Such a tactic of localization and cutting off the neighboring areas has been also regularly used in Russia and other countries of the world in case of forest and peat fires (see Mikeev, 1994, 1996).

The case of terrorist acts in Budennovsk and Kizliar which occurred in Russia in 1995 and 1996 during the regional war in Chechnia, may serve as an illustration of the negative experience of carrying out a localization function during a conflict-type emergency. These acts were substantially facilitated by the inefficient organization of and loopholes in the cordon system which comprised a certain number of blocking and control posts manned by policemen and servicemen of internal troops (somewhat analogous to the National Guard in the United States) that circled the combat area in the Chechen Republic. As a result, one emergency (the regional war) not only gave rise to other emergencies (terrorist acts) which lead to almost 100 fatalities among the dwellers, policemen and servicemen but also increased its own geographical dimensions by spilling over the borders of the Caucasus region. Since that time, the terrorist acts have been happening on the territory of the 'core' Russia (in Moscow, Volgograd, Armavir and Piatigorsk).

Carrying out the rescue and evacuation functions imply shelter in the specially equipped or improvised accommodations, caring for casualties and survivors. It includes: providing potable water, meals and clothes, emergency medical care, sheltering and evacuation of those alive along with activities to restore minimum community services. It also involves providing morgues and funeral facilities for the dead, registration of both alive, dead and missing persons as well as an inventory of their property and documents. In some cases like compound emergencies or disasters (epidemic, epizootic) or conflict-type emergencies and disasters followed by imposing martial law in the affected areas, early evacuation measures are further supplemented by restrictions for leaving the emergency or disaster area through imposing a quarantine or curfew.

Given a certain logical consequence of the enumerated measures that sometimes are actually carried out one after another, in most practice they overlap in time and space within two kinds of community processes. One of these is accentuated by group and organizational activities for maintaining the community order, motivation and morale. The other one generated by the aforementioned activities manifests itself in collecting and transmitting information, controlling activities and coordinating involvement (Drabek, 1986; Dynes, 1974).

Communication serves as a key element and basis for emergency response both at pre-impact and post-impact phases. Lacking accurate and timely information delivered in a useful format through a right channel to the right person substantially decreases or voids the effectiveness of the measures taken to minimize the damage. At the same time, there are difficulties dealing with the tremendous increase in the volume of information and transmission speed of both upward and downward communication though the latter have not always found empirical support (see: Rosenthal et al, 1989). Considering the possible loopholes in or ruptures of existing communication systems, these prove the urgency to maintain the functioning and provide alternative information flow channels.

US scholars have presumed that a decentralized response is more frequent in disasters, both in developed and developing countries, while some crisis experts, represented mainly by European specialists, consider a more balanced model to be a typical one (see, for instance: Rosenthal et al, 1989: 457-458; t'Hart et al, 1993). As to Russia, despite the important changes which occurred since the mid-1980s towards increasing the role of regions in social and economic life, the centralized response is still prevailing. However, the decentralized approach keeps its significance at the prevention and mitigation and preparedness phases as well as at the recovery phase, given that these phases have been most capital intensive and federal authorities have always wished to shift both the financial load and social and political responsibility to the regional and municipal levels. The pattern of the personnel and goods used by the organizations involved in response activities reveals that the problems have been mainly in the quick and integrated utilization of the available items rather than obtaining new ones (Drabek, 1986; Quarantelli and Dynes, 1977; Quarantelli, 1992a).

The *recovery phase* implies carrying out two main functions, i.e., alleviation of social, economic and environmental effects of the emergency and prevention and mitigation of its transformation into a disaster and further into a catastrophe. These involve two sets of the cushioning measures including short-term and medium- and long-term actions.

Urgent (extraordinary) short-term actions bridge response and recovery phases and are usually associated with emergencies and emergency areas. However in cases of abnormally great and discrete or permanent impact of the highly dangerous agents (for example, radiation, toxic chemicals, mass disease vectors or mass destruction weapons) when an emergency practically immediately becomes a disaster or chronic and grave crisis, these measures are also applicable in the disaster areas. With the latter medium-term and long-term actions are normally associated when alleviation of the gravity of and immediate or at least soonest recovery from the emergency has been impossible or failed.

These sets of actions presume taking a wide gamut of administrative, organizational and engineering measures, in particular carrying out of primary rehabilitation and maintenance work in order to resume the functioning of the critical minimum of the lifelines and supplies (debris removal, construction of temporal shelters and lifelines and so on). These should be carried out either within an emergency or disaster area, or in the especially designated and delineated site away from this area if within the latter during the post-culmination stage of emergency development the impact of the aforementioned highly dangerous agents on a social system and its ambiance continues. Such works last until the moment of social rehabilitation of the affected area with its temporarily relocated dwellers coming back there. For example, this may occur in case of reestablishing social order and social safety in the areas which have been affected by the conflict-type emergencies or successful recovery and providing of normal living conditions in the areas subjected to natural or technological disasters.

In catastrophes the restoration of the normal social routines and living conditions is impossible either due to the complete destruction of a settlement as it was in the case of the town of Neftegorsk demolished by a major earthquake in 1995 at Sakhalin Island, or the long-term and fatal impact of the risk agents, as in the cases of the catastrophe areas or alienation zones (as they have been labeled in Russian law), which were established within the territory affected by the radioactive fallout of the South Urals (Cheliabinsk-65) and Chernobyl radiation disasters. In such circumstances the recovery works must last until the time when the state of 'green lawn' (vacant site) is provided for the most affected area like the memorial complex which has been built at the place of former Neftegorsk, or until complete isolation of this area from the neighboring communities (10 km-radius zone around the Chernobyl nuclear power plant) is achieved.

Given this and depending on the efficiency of recovery actions, two possible scenarios may take place in an affected area at the post-culmination stage:

• effective recovery work leading to emergency area status is deferred upon the decision of respective authorities;

• complexity and gravity of a situation is keep for a long time thus necessitating for a change in the existing status of the affected area and declaring it as a disaster area or/and further as a catastrophic area by the respective authorities. The latter also develop a mid- and long-term a rehabilitation program that prescribe successive alleviation measures and the elimination of a hazardous impact effects, or analogous protection or conservation program for the catastrophe area. The status of the affected area which determines its utility regime, social protection measures, environmental rehabilitation or, vice versa, closing (classifying or alienation) of this area with its former dwellers being permanently relocated, should be normatively established.

Section 2 of the 1992 Federal Act for Social Protection of the Persons Affected by Radiation as a Result of the Chernobyl Catastrophe As Amended in 1995 may serve as a good illustration of the point. It established the following four categories of the aforementioned area zones:

• alienation zone (abandoned by people for many decades, may be for centuries);

• resettling zone or the zone of resettlement;

• zone of living with a right to leave with certain monetary compensation;

• zone with privileged social and economic status providing its dwellers with special donations from the federal budget (*Federalnii Zakon*, 1995g).

Following the emergency typology presented in the Table 9, the latter category should be denoted as a crisis area, two intermediate categories as disaster areas and the first one as a catastrophe area. Within the catastrophe area the sites which have been contaminated by Cs^{137} at a density over 40 Curies (Ci) / km^2 or by Sr^{90} at a density over 3 Ci / km^2 in particular in mitigation, warning and mobilization of human and resources both in the first critical hours of emergency response and later on while carrying out the bulk of recovery activities or by Pt^{239} and

Pt^{240} over 0,1 Ci / km^2 and provided for individual irradiation dose exceeding 5 millisievert (mSv) per year, people have been prohibited to live and the former permanent residents should have been evacuated and relocated and economic activities strongly restricted.

In the zones of resettlement with a density of contamination of Cs^{137} between 15-40 Ci / km^2 or respectively limited densities of contamination by Sr^{90} and Pt^{239} and Pt^{240}, people have been permitted to live permanently after being regularly screened, tested and medically treated by radiobiologists and doctors, respectively. Rigid protection measures to decrease irradiation loads must be undertaken by the local and regional authorities. Communities as well as individuals should be informed about these measures and activities via mass media. The citizens right-to-know about what has been happening made by the responsible bodies in the areas affected by the radiation impact has been also provided for by the federal act cited earlier (see *Federalnii Zakon*, 1995g: Section 46).

The sequence of the aforementioned stages and phases of the emergency management strategy reflect the logic of the proactive management process, when control actions start from the detection of hazardous sources and agents which may provoke an emergency, then are followed by elimination or mitigation of impact of these agents on a social system and its ambiance and finally imply response to and alleviation of the emergency effect. However, in real life these phases overlap or impose each on the other which stems from the continuity of the management process itself which in turn has been predetermined by the continuity and cycling pattern of the emergency development. In particular, if the response and recovery efforts in a given emergency have been erroneous or inefficient, in the depths of its post-culmination phase the seeds of a new emergency may appear.

For example, ineffective deactivation measures taken in the areas affected by the Chernobyl radioactive fallout between 1986 and 1989 did not decrease conspicuously the irradiation levels there thus keeping the risk for the health of the residents, especially children, as well as the level of collective stress relatively high. Moreover, the hiding of information and misinforming of the local people by authorities increased the anxiety and psychological tension in these areas and in 1989 and 1990 resulted in crowded meetings and manifestations organized by the villagers of Narovlia and Bragin (Byelorus) and Narodichi (Ukraine) in the capitals of these republics of the former Soviet Union. That meant a hazard of a new conflict-type emergency.

Later on, in the 1990s poor enforcement of the acts for social protection of the people affected by this radiation disaster which had been adopted in the former Soviet Union in 1991 and then in contemporary Russia, in particular substantial delays of allowance payments, often lacking special medical treatment and so on, provoked mass hunger-strikes and manifestations in Russia. In some areas, for instance in the Tula region (*oblast*) in 1996, people were on the edge of a riot.

In order to prevent such a boomerang effect, all phases should be tied into a single management cycle. In a given emergency the aforementioned phases are combined into the following three stages: prevention stage which comprises the development of an emergency management strategy and the first two phases of its implementation, and the response and recovery stages which would include the respective phases of the same name. It is reasonable to consider the recovery stage as a prevention stage in relation to both possible subsequent disaster and catastrophe (see Fig. 12) and a new emergency.

The relationship between the emergency management stages, phases and functions is presented in Table 18. As to the relationship between the management functions and measures being carried out within these phases and stages, on one hand, and the emergency strategies discussed earlier, on the other hand, the prevention strategy presumes implementation of the whole the set of monitoring / screening functions and a part of the correction / control functions associated with risk elimination which should be realized at the prevention and mitigation phase. In turn, the mitigation strategy implies implementation of the rest of the correction / control functions associated with reducing risk, as well as the whole gamut of measures and functions which should be taken within preparedness and response phases. The alleviation strategy involves carrying out all the measures and functions to be implemented while the recovery phase of the emergency management cycle.

In this connotation the difference in means and methods of motivation of emergency personnel working at various phases and stages of emergency management is worth noting. Those who are responsible for monitoring, correction and control functions at the prevention and mitigation phase should be encouraged and given incentives for the safe functioning of the organization or social unit while in the former Soviet Union and to a considerable extent in present-day Russia, these have been paid premiums for production increases regardless of the safety status of the facility.

At the same time, those who are responsible for carrying out the whole gamut of the functions within the preparedness and response phases of the emergency management cycle should be encouraged and given incentives if urgent measures to save lives, health, properties and values, including environmental values, prove to be successful. Lastly, those engaged in recovery work should receive their premium on the same grounds as people working everyday in extreme environments (too cold or too hot climatic conditions, in desert areas and so forth).

THE EMERGENCY POLICY AND MANAGEMENT AGENTS

As mentioned above, both the development and implementation of emergency management strategies are carried out within a given social and/or organizational system which is characterized by a specific set of natural, historical, cultural, political, social and economic conditions. In any case emergency management constitutes an organic part of the national policy which is pursued by different social and political agents (individuals, social, political and business groups, political and industrial organizations) with different and often opposing interests and motivations.

This means that the mission, goals and tasks of a given emergency management strategy as well as the means and methods of implementing them are derived from the national policy pursued by the state, which is a special organization which created by human civilization to regulate conflicting interests within society in a way that would be most suitable for a social system as a whole. As Engels put it:

"The state is a product of a society at a certain development stage: the state is evidence that this society has become entangled in an insoluble contradiction with itself, split into a irreconcilable opposites which it cannot get rid of. And to prevent these opposites, classes with discrepant interests, from devouring each other and the society during a vain struggle, a force becomes necessary which should be over society, cushion the collision and retain it within the limits of 'order'. And this force, which originated from society, puts itself over and more and more alienating itself from it [society] state' (Marx and Engels, 1961: 169-170).

By establishing the goals, tasks and main directions of national policy, the state which comprises all levels and branches of authority at the same time predetermines the basic characteristics of emergency management as an intrinsic component of this policy. Given this fact and considering in addition that the authorities are the organizer and administrator of the training and employment of the emergency units which implement this important direction of national policy, the state has logically turned into the key subject (agent) of emergency management.

Non-state organizations, including private enterprises and public (non-governmental) organizations and action groups, and individuals are the other important agents of emergency management. However, in Russia they are not as active and influential as in the most developed countries of the world and the role of the state and state bodies has been absolutely dominating. Like the latter, the non-state organizations and individuals represent both the object (goal) and subject (agents) of integral security (S_I) the providing of which constitutes the mission of an emergency management strategy (see Chapter 1). With this the capabilities of these management agents considerably differ. Individuals and their families objectively can, but far from always provide, their own safety and protection of their property (S_1) in emergencies while organizations and collectivities can afford collective security for its members and their material values (S_2).

As to the state which comprises local, regional and federal authorities, these should not only integrate the earlier mentioned efforts of individuals and social units, but also provide both the integral (S_I) and its own state security S_3. They should extensively involve the available means and forces which many times exceed those of the aforementioned management agents (see Table 19).

Domain of protection (security / safety goal [a]) Management agent	S_3 and S_s	S_2	S_1
The state (federal, regional and local authorities, primarily the especially designated executive bodies: emergency or urgent response services)	*	*	*
Social organizations (communities, enterprises, institutions, etc.)		*	*
Individuals (and their families)			*

[a] S_1, S_2, S_3 and S_s are the indicators of individual, social (group or collective), state and integral security and safety, respectively. For discussion see Chapter 2.

Table 19. Fields of Responsibility of the Main Emergency Management Agents

Being the representative of economically and politically dominating social groups and strata and their interests in a given social system, the state in this or that way reflects these in the area of national security including emergency management during the development of strategies and setting of priorities. Given the integral security S_I being the common goal of these groups and strata, it is no wonder that in general their interests in this area of national policy coincide and S_1, S_2 and S_3 as the key subsystems of the S_I are congruent.

Each of them and together the emergency management agents (or in a broader perspective the national security agents) are objectively interested in a sustainable development with a minimal risk of emergencies, disasters and catastrophes. Using this and the legal and economic standards being developed within the legislative process the state, primarily the regional and federal authorities, establish the safety/protection or socially acceptable risk levels within given communities and society as a whole. These serve as a formal description of the mission of emergency management strategy both at the regional and national levels.

However, this does not completely eliminate the differences existing between the interests of various social strata. For example, at the prevention and recovery stages of the emergency management cycle as the most resource intensive these are manifested in the competition between the distributors and recipients of resources. In conditions of resource shortage and multiple demand for them from organizations which carry out mitigation and alleviation functions, the responsible bureaucrats and experts in the federal government may considerably influence the pattern of resource sharing between various recipients.

The respective preferences may be stipulated by professional, psychological and other personal reasons leaving out bribery and corruption and display itself during the priorities setting of the development policy (including the social safety policy and emergency management) than during the process of distributing resources as such. This calls for the transparent and multifaceted decision making on both priorities setting during the development of an emergency management strategy and resource distribution during its implementation which should be rather a compromise than a bureaucratic procedure of a selected group of the top decision makers.

In democratic-type social systems the state, first of all the federal government, has been doing everything to keep the differences and discrepancies mentioned above within certain acceptable limits precluding an antagonistic confrontation between the social groups for the sake of social safety including individual safety, that is S_1 and S_2 This implies meeting the basic rights for life and health which are intrinsic to both the existence and development of any person and human community.

To the contrary, in undemocratic-types or underdemocratized social systems, in particular under authoritative and dictatorship regimes, the priorities setting of the national security policy and emergency management as its organic part is substantially biased on providing state security S_3, primarily of the high officials and bureaucrats and selected social groups and individuals, in particular servicemen. At the same time the bulk of the population remain underprotected and vulnerable against the major hazards. This is vividly illustrated by the numerous natural disasters and armed conflicts and regional wars when the poor, without rights and least socially secured, have been the most affected (see Chapter 1).

While stressing the important role of the type of social system, in particular the degree of democratization and the pattern of political and social interests of prevailing social groups and strata, the professional composition of the groups is worth noting. Some of them represent the big resource intensive industrial companies including the powerful energy and military and industrial corporations which for decades have been producing considerable influence on national policy of the former Soviet Union, contemporary Russia and many other countries. These groups and individuals have always been interested in obtaining more and more profits by increasing the capacity and complexity of the respective facilities which have been associated with higher technological and environmental risk. Those producing weapons have been closely entangled with the risk of armed conflicts.

It is time that the policy of industrial conversion which was promulgated in the former Soviet Union in the late 1980s provided an impetus for such enterprises to invest money in the development of high technologies including environmentally and risk-free equipment and facilities. Although some positive results have been attained, the inconsistency of this policy, aggravated by the deep economic and social crisis in the 1990s, has considerably restrained the opportunities provided thus maintaining the relatively high level of risk typical for the aforementioned industries.

To the contrary, business and social interests of some other social groups and strata which have been relatively weak in Russia until the end of the 1990s are associated with the maximal reduction of the technological, environmental and other risks to human lives and health. These are represented by research and information intensive corporations including agricultural, medical companies, companies producing many consumer goods and services, pollution treatment equipment and so on. In this respect their interests are opposite to those of the resource intensive corporations.

Despite the discrepancy between the two social groups mentioned above, which exists not only in Russia but in some industrialized countries of the West including the United States, Germany and Great Britain as well, it is in their common interest to provide social safety and integral (national) security. In democratic-type social systems and societies in transition, this decisively contributes to government strengthening the policies and measures to provide normal routines including social order, technological safety and environmental protection.

Moreover, in conditions of increasing complexity of global problems (climate change, alimentation, terrorism and extremism and others) in these societies the state still being the proponent of the interests of the dominating social groups has been forced to consider seriously the interests of the general public including the opposite nongovernmental organizations. It also can not ignore the needs of the low-income strata. Being supported by the mass media, the role of which in Russia has tremendously grown since the mid 1980s, these groups produce substantial influence on the political establishment's setting of policy priorities, primarily in the national security area, and in particular on emergency management policy.

The nuclear power industry of the former Soviet Union may serve as a vivid illustration of this point. Since 1986, after the Chernobyl radiation disaster, construction work has been suspended at 40 sites in Russia and Byelorus. In addition the moratorium on construction of new nuclear power plants was imposed in Ukraine and the unit # 2 of the single nuclear power plant in Armenia in Metzamor was closed. Undoubtedly, the latter actions by the national governments resulted not only from antinuclear public movements and action group activities but were also dictated by economic considerations, in particular huge expenditures on response to and recovery from the major radiation emergencies and disasters. Nevertheless, it is important to underline the increasing role of the general public and nongovernmental organizations in the national policy in many countries including the former Soviet Union in the 1980s.

In the 1990s notable changes occurred in these countries in terms of the government and public perception and assessment and mass media coverage of safety issues in the nuclear power industry mainly due to economic reasons. In Russia and the other CIS countries the deep and lasting social and economic crisis in the last decade of the 20th century has been accompanied by a painful energy crisis. As a result the problem of electricity and heat supplies both to industrial and residential consumers in cold winters remain pressing. In these circumstances the risk associated with potential radiation accidents at nuclear facilities has been substantially surpassed by mass social protests including civil strife and disturbances against disconnection from key lifelines.

In particular, the latter forced the government of Armenia to resume the exploitation of unit # 2 of the nuclear power plant in Metzamor after it was closed for six years. The government of Ukraine had to continue exploitation of the Chernobyl nuclear power plant and those in Byelorus and Kazakhstan declared their readiness to construct such plants on their territory. At the same time, economic reasons along with environmental protection arguments, were used by the special parliamentary commission in Sweden which in 1995 argued the impossibility of a complete halt to nuclear power plants by 2010 (Gagarinskiy and Gagarinskaia, 1996; Commission, 1995).

However, the shift of nuclear safety issues to the periphery of public attention could hardly last too long. A few examples from different world regions corroborate the point that in general in the West the public perception of the nuclear industry tends to be watchful and its anxiety substantially high. In Russia, where public participation and mass media support conspicuously contributed to the increasing safety of the nuclear power plans after Chernobyl, the opposition to these facilities to be constructed is still very strong in Kostroma, Rostov regions, in the Urals and East Siberia. In addition, nuclear power proponents have been increasingly opposed by the competing non-nuclear energy companies, in particular the *Gasprom* corporation which actively supports the opinion of the high risk and economic inefficiency associated with nuclear power plants.

At this time the role of various subjects (agents), primarily the state in the development of emergency management strategies has been discussed and accentuated. No less important are the functions exercised by the state while implementation of these strategies, resources mobilization and supply in particular. Concentrating political, legal and administrative power and huge economic potential the federal, regional and local authorities constitute a unique force which has a capacity to mobilize the necessary funds, means and forces within a short period of emergency response and coordinate and integrate the efforts of the different management agents involved. With this the budget funds and materiel reserves including strategic reserves are actively supplemented and reinforced by the so-called redistribution mechanism (monetary, credit, tax, amortization and other economic instruments).

This point is crucial considering that the emergency management are very resource intensive. Leaving out disaster and catastrophe, the emergency demands not only considerable financial and material resources but human resources, trained professional cadres in particular, as well. This is typical for the whole emergency management cycle: starting from the prevention stage which involves expenditures on the monitoring, control, mitigation and training and finishing by the recovery stage which necessitates huge expenditures on alleviation and elimination of destructive and debilitating effects (medical and psychological rehabilitation of the affected dwellers and emergency personnel, restoration of destroyed buildings and constructions, re-establishing of the broken communications and so on).

The following figures concerning non-conflict emergencies offer some idea about the volume of the funds required. In the United States the annual investments and expenditures on prevention, mitigation and recovery from major technological accidents and disasters account to an estimated US$ 220 billion or vary from 5% to 7% of the GNP. Deactivation work alone at the malfunctioned unit of the TMI nuclear power plant cost more than US$ 1 billion (Hohenemser, Kasperson and Kates, 1985: 171). The recovery from the Kobe earthquake disaster in Japan would cost no less than US$ 100 billion.

Russia spends annually from 1.5% to 2% of the GNP on recovery work alone while in certain years these figures have been much greater. According to some estimates, the total economic losses and response and recovery expenditures associated with the Chernobyl radiation disaster in the countries of the former Soviet Union including Russia by the year 2000 will soar to US$ 80 billion at least leaving out the compensation and expenditures on medical treatment to the affected. Economic losses alone incurred by the Neftegorsk earthquake in 1995 amounted to from US$ 300 million to US$ 400 million (see Chapter 1).

Using political, administrative and economic powers, the authorities coordinate the activities on implementation of the operational plans at every management level and exercise control over the realization of the respective programs and efficiencyof emergency management strategy as a whole. In contrast to the development stage where the mission, goals and means of a strategy are elaborated and then established by professional experts and politicians, at the implementation stage the state carries out its emergency management functions through the especially authorized or representative bodies and organizations.

At the prevention stage these include social, technological and environmental monitoring and control, exercise licensing, supervision and auditing of the hazardous facilities and especially vulnerable social units, raise funds and material reserves and so forth. At the response and recovery stages the respective authorized state bodies and organizations coordinate and directly participate in search and rescue, medical care support, fire extinguishing, reestablishing social order and safety, emergency engineering and reconstruction work and so on.

These bodies and organizations provide assistance and directly cooperate with high public administrators (mayors, governors) and chief executives and administrators of the enterprises (companies) in conjunction with the developed emergency management strategies and transform them into detailed tactical programs and operational plans. These activities are supported by nongovernmental professional institutions (universities, consulting companies, foundations, etc.) and individual experts who participate in such a work either on a contractual basis which is more widespread in Russia or receiving grants from the government which is more typical in the West.

The development and implementation of regional and local operational plans involve the development and implementation of organizational contingency plans which also serve as a basis for further specification of operational plans. The latter are developed by professional planners and officersof the especially authorized bodies which in Russia are represented by the regional and local (district or municipal) emergency commissions or committees that since 1997 have been substituting for the former civil defense and emergency staffs. Contingency plans are developed within organizations (enterprises and institutions) by the especially authorized units or responsible administrators. In Russia these are represented by the civil defense and emergency units or officers, respectively in the state enterprises and chief executives and security administrators in the private companies (like crisis managers or managing units in Western corporations). The latter are controlled by inspector and supervision services which are either organic to the local (district and municipal) authorities or are the part of respective professional associations and by public (nongovernmental) organizations.

Organizations including enterprises and institutions and local and regional authorities are the main agents at the prevention and recovery stages of the emergency management cycle. They have to transform the normative prescriptions and safety standards into concrete administrative and technical decisions which would mitigate the possible hazardous impact and provide adequate protection both for personnel and local people. In addition, they are responsible for the development and implementation of the rehabilitation plans and programs and carrying out alleviation measures in the post-culmination period. In case of major disasters and catastrophes, these are supplemented by special large scale federal aid programs.

Emergency units and services (fire, medical care, rescue, transportation and so forth) either municipal, district or regional are the key management agents which are responsible for saving lives and material values in the affectedcommunities at the response stage of the emergency management cycle. In the case of a major disaster (like the Chernobyl radiation disaster or the earthquake disaster in Kobe and Neftegorsk) these are supplemented by federal aid, primarily by the army units, especially chemical, engineer, signal and some other special troops. In Russia, such aid would be provided first of all by the special rescue units of the Ministry of the Russian Federation for Civil Defense, Emergencies and Natural Disaster Response (MES) which has been specially authorized by the president of Russia and the government as the chief federal body responsible for planning and conducting emergency operations (see Chapter 3).

The role of the voluntary organizations is of particular importance in the course of the whole emergency management cycle. In normal social routines, such organizations have been purposefully formed at the grass-roots level in order to prepare for possible emergencies and disasters. The volunteers train in advance to abate fire, provide emergency medical care, remove heaps and debris and so forth to save the lives and property of the community dwellers, in particular to help handicapped persons and invalids during emergencies and disasters. These kinds of organizations were created and working for decades in many countries of the world including pre-Revolutionary Russia and the former Soviet Union. In contemporary Russia, they are functioning under the aegis of the MES.

In addition to these, in an emergency most active community dwellers unite their efforts to facilitate, accelerate and increase the efficiency of response activities thus making up another type of voluntary organizations. Quarantelli and Dynes, prominent US disaster sociologists, have characterized these as emergent groups and in addition proposed distinguishing three more types of organizations specified on the basis of reconciliation of the organization and collective behavior approaches (Quarantelli, 1966; Dynes and Quarantelli, 1968).

One of these are established organizations with traditional structures engaged in their regular tasks represented usually by emergency services like police, fire departments, etc. The next are expanding organizations like Red Cross, some social welfare agencies and other voluntary associations that perform designated regular tasks while their structures are being changed (expanded). Contrary to that, extending organizations that are probably the most numerous of all key response actors maintain their traditional structures while undertaking irregular or non-institutionalized tasks during an emergency or disaster. For example, a mining company or an army unit may become involved in debris clearance, infrastructure repair and so forth. Finally, the emergent groups mentioned above are non-existent in pre-emergency period organizations performing new tasks through a newly developed structures, e.g. informal search and rescue or medical care teams. They tend to people disaster situations, especially the more severe ones, and although having only transitory existence, their functioning may be crucial to the whole trans- and post-emergency response. (Dynes, 1974; Quarantelli, 1966, 1992a; Quarantelli and Dynes, 1977).

Quarantelli and Dynes consider that these four institutionalized and new groups are normally sequentially involved in community stress situations during its scope changes (increases) from localized community emergency to disaster and then to major community disaster. It is believed that:

'established organizations tend to be the first to respond in disasters. They are followed in their response by the involvement of expanding, and then extending, organizations. Only after when these more traditional organizations are participating it is likely that there will be involvement of emergent organizations or groups. More important, it is the very involvement of the more established and traditional organizations in the disaster response that creates the conditions of the generation and emergence of new groups' (Quarantelli and Dynes, 1977: 33-34).

Given the principle of continuity they also argue that the pattern of the aforementioned organizations functioning and coordinating their activities during the culmination phase of emergency development to a substantial degree consistent with their everyday functions with the notable exception of emergent groups that simply do not exist before a disaster. Traditional organization activities are normally based on contingency and operation emergency planning. But even in its absence or the event of weak planning their key organizational personnel do their jobs without any substantial behavioral role conflict while emergent organizations act with a high degree of improvisation. However, in Russia, as will be discussed later, notable deviations from this pattern and peculiarities manifest themselves during emergencies and disasters (see Chapter 4).

Federal authorities have been dominating in the field of emergency management, primarily in terms of fund raising during the major emergencies and disasters. On one hand, this objectively stems from the scale and gravity of such great mishaps which necessitate enormous expenditures on response and recovery and is typical for most countries of the world. On the other hand, it is a legacy of the overcentralized public administration and economic policy model in the former Soviet Union which was vividly manifested while emergencies. Having concentrated economic and political powers, the federal government provided practically all financial, material and a considerable part of the human resources needed to cope with an emergency or disaster. The free labor of the army units and young people, members of the All-Union Young Communist League of the Soviet Union (*komsomol*), and sometimes of prisoners was widely used.

Since the mid 1980s, the situation has been gradually but notably changing in favor of regional, local authorities and nongovernmental organizations increased participation and influence both in the everyday life in the former Soviet Union and contemporary Russia and emergency management, in particular in mitigation, warning and mobilization of human and resources both in the first critical hours of emergency response and later on while carrying out the bulk of recovery activities.

This was stipulated by the historical coincidence of the drastic political changes in the country started by *perestroika* and followed by the dissolution of the Soviet Union and the Chernobyl radiation disaster, the worst industrial accident in the world so far. Perhaps, for the first time since World War II, voluntary donations from citizens constituted a substantial part of the relief funds for those affected in this disaster. The citizens of the former Soviet Union transferred to the special 'Chernobyl' account # 904 almost 540 million rubles or nearly 60% of the total sum of compensation and allowances paid to the affected people in 1986 and 1987.

The discussion of the main phases, stages and functions of the emergency management cycle and the key management agents given above provide no more than a general outline. We have stressed the commonalties of these during development and implementation of an emergency management strategy which have been stipulated by the essence of an emergency and/or disaster as an extraordinary occasion and are therefore independent or only slightly dependent on the type of social system. At the same time, the crucial peculiarities of the emergency management mechanism resulting from the principal differences between various types of social systems which predetermine both the degree of their vulnerability and the efficiency of their protection against the major hazards have only been touched upon here. The following chapters will provide much more detailed analysis of these peculiarities in Russia.

CHAPTER 3

THE STATE EMERGENCY MANAGEMENT POLICY IN RUSSIA: LEGAL BASIS AND ORGANIZATIONAL ISSUES

Implementation of strategies and models of emergency management considered in the preceding chapter has both commonalties and peculiarities of form and content. These are determined by natural, cultural and historic, political, economic and social country-specific environments, Russia in particular (See Chapter 1), as well as by the circumstances of specific emergencies, disasters and catastrophes. For decades, both in Russia and other countries, the protection of people and national wealth in emergencies have been the responsibility of the state. The legislative and executive activities of the federal, regional and local authorities have specified these responsibilities.

Hereinafter I will describe common and specific features of the legal regulation of emergencies in Russia within the context of the key world trends in this field as well as organization and development of the Unified State System for Emergency Prevention and Response of the Russian Federation (RUSPRE). The peculiarities of organizational preparedness and response of the local, regional and federal authorities, the emergency services, administrators and personnel of the affected facilities and dwellers of the affected communities during concrete emergencies and/or disasters are considered in Chapter 4.

THE LEGAL BASIS OF EMERGENCY AND DISASTER POLICY: TRENDS IN THE WORLD AND RUSSIA

PECULIARITIES OF THE DEVELOPMENT OF EMERGENCY AND DISASTER LEGISLATION

Legal (normative) regulation of executive authorities and community activities for the prevention of, preparedness and response to and recovery from emergencies, disasters and catastrophes has been considered paramount since the early days when the state first appeared in the world. Up to the late 19th century, legal regulation of the above activities had been almost totally reduced to protecting and providing relief aid to those affected in natural calamities, fires or epidemics. Early in the 20th century, some countries enforced the first national laws concerning industrial personnel safety. In 1925, the first international conventions in this area were adopted (*Konventsii I Recomendatsii*, 1991: 101,113,116).

The foundation of modern legislation relating to technological emergencies and disasters was developed only after World War II. Since its ending, powerful facilities which involve high risk technologies and products (chemical, nuclear and so on), transportation of huge volumes of hazardous cargoes (oil, liquefied gas and so forth) by sea and land and were associated primarily with the military and industrial complex appeared and began to develop rapidly as a result of the start of the 'Cold War' and crucial technological change. The scale and gravity of the effects of emergencies and disasters which accompanied this process were comparable with and even exceeded those inflicted not only by natural calamities but by wars as well. This naturally called for development and enforcement of special legal regulations on the part of the national state and the world community as a whole.

At that stage, the bias of development of the laws and regulations of emergencies and disasters started to be changed gradually in favor of mitigation strategy prevention, and to a substantially lesser extent to prevention strategy while the alleviation strategy still undoubtedly prevailed. Thus, along with civil defense laws which were adopted and enforced in the United States, Western Europe and Japan between the late 1940s and the early 1960s, the statutes and laws with respect to nuclear and radiation safety including personnel protection against irradiation became operative in these and some developing countries (for example, in Argentine and India) in about the same period (See Ioyrish and Choporniak, 1990: 11-13). In the former Soviet Union, where industrial and energy power plants were not only among the most economically powerful but being 'socialist enterprises' were unequivocally labeled by the top Communist Party and state officials as absolutely safe, the development and enforcement of these laws have been delayed for decades.

The sharp increase of technological load on a natural environment and that of the frequency and scale of emergencies and disasters between the 1960s and 1980s contributed to a drastic change in both the essence of the problems associated with socioeconomic and environmental losses incurred by those adverse events and occasions and their perception by the public. National governments and the international community have been more and more regarding these problems as a national security issue (See Chapters 1 and 2). That logically found reflection in the respective national and international legislation, primarily since the late 1960s - much more active development and enforcement of laws and regulations for emergency management in the leading countries of the world which earlier than others confronted the serious threats and experienced the debilitating and devastating social and environmental effect associated with the impact of modern high risk technologies. I believe that between the 1970s and 1980s the total number of various normative acts (laws, regulations with amendments) dealing with emergency and disaster management in the United States alone increased threefold.

BASIC TRENDS IN LEGISLATION DEVELOPMENT

In addition to this quantitative growth within the designated period, substantial changes have begun and being continued in the enforcement of laws and regulations concerning the area of development. In this respect, the following three basic trends should be distinguished.

The first is *diversification of legislation regulating emergency management policy* which has been associated with the appearance of new kinds of hazards, primarily of a compound nature and a sharp increase of the degree of their danger for communities and the environment. In particular, in the countries of the West and Japan a new branch of environmental law oriented on preventing and abating ambient contamination including that by hazardous and toxic substances has emerged and begun to develop very fast.

The next has been the tendency of *integration and unification of the emergency management legislation*. This has been and is now manifested in seeking a better harmonization of all the basic emergency management strategies mentioned earlier within a national emergency management policy, on the one hand, and development and adoption of the principles of creating an efficient legal basis in this field which would be common for different communities and societies using the framework of existing regional and international organizations (EC, IAEA, OECD, UN, UNEP, WHO, etc.), on the other hand.

This point may be corroborated, in particular, by the laws and amendments thereto concerning different types of hazards (floods, earthquakes, accidents at chemical and nuclear power plants and so on) which were adopted and enforced in the 1970s and 1980s in the United States, Japan, Western European countries and the European Community as a whole, including the so-called Seveso Directive of 1982, conventions for transboundary pollution by hazardous and toxic substances, early warning and notification in radiation emergencies and some others. The former Soviet Union (USSR) and then Russia joined a number of these international agreements later, whereas the respective national legislation either has been developed and enforced with a much more pronounced delay or is even still lacking in some important areas.

Given the undoubted general progress in the field of emergency and disaster legislation, both nationally and internationally, noteworthy is a certain partition existing between the normative acts which regulate the legal relationships in the field as well as the lack of some key federal normative acts concerning emergency management both in Russia and a number of other countries. The fragmentary character of emergency and disaster legislation results from the complexity and heterogeneity of the objects of emergency management (that is different types of emergencies, disasters and catastrophes). At the same time it is rooted in the past emergency policy which was developed and promoted during decades of open military confrontation which implied organization of an efficient national civil defense system to save people and protect material values from the probable enemy's nuclear or other mass destructive strike. This means that the military dimension of national security has been dominating both in political thinking and public perception of the main threats and logically should prevail and really has been prevailing in the national and international legislation in the area of security and safety.

Lastly, one more general trend involves the tendency of *conspicuously increasing the role and priority of prevention and mitigation strategies* within the legal framework of emergency and disaster policies. It also implies a change in the type of emergency management from predominantly reactive and adaptive to proactive (anticipatory) and flexible. For example, in Russia it manifests itself in a striving for changing the proportion of the federal budget expenditures on federal mitigation and response and recovery programs and projects in favor of the former. In fiscal year 1996, such a proportion between the ear-marked mitigation allocations, including the resources of the special governmental fund for emergency response and those for recovery and rehabilitation, were almost equal.

However, it is important to note that despite the fact that the process was gaining impetus in a number of developed countries of the world in the last 10 to 15 years, it would hardly be erroneous to consider that in general in the late 1990s emergency and disaster legislation (primarily, on a highest government level) has been oriented largely towards preparedness, response and recovery. Prevention and mitigation issues have been receiving lower priority and are underdeveloped. prioritized. One of the reasons for this is closely associated with the relatively short duration of the striving of national legislative systems for a creating integrated legal basis which would involve all possible hazardous sources and agents as well as stages of an emergency development.

Another reason deals with the actual pressing needs and existing stereotypes in decision making while sharing resources for emergency management when the funds necessary for coping with the consequences of the accidents have been provided more eagerly and in greater volume than for prevention and mitigation. Thus, in the above example with the Russian federal budget, the proportion of actual expenditures on prevention / mitigation and recovery / rehabilitation was 1 : 1.5 in favor of the latter measures. This is partly explained by a well-justified wish of financial managers to reduce where possible expenditures on prevention measures that may well turn out useless (if there is no emergency). At the same time such decisions are forced by a strong public demand from the affectedcommunities to spend more and without delay on their own needs in case an emergency and/or disaster really strikes.

The aforesaid substantial changes in emergency and disaster legislation have been carried out in two main directions. One of these implies the development of new laws and normative acts which regulate activities to lower or eliminate new risk sources and agents threatening social and environmental safety or enforcing new legal means and methods to solve the well known typical problems associated with emergencies and disasters. Another direction involves more efficient harmonization and specification of the existing normative acts by developing and adopting amendments to the existing laws as well as regulations, instructions and comments for better distinguishing of areas of responsibility and coordination of the key bodies and services engaged in emergency management. In practice, both directions are closely intertwined thus making a more or less holistic legal basis for regulating prevention of, preparedness and response to and recovery from emergencies, disasters and catastrophes on regional, national and international levels.

By the late 1990s, the above-mentioned legal basis of emergency management policy which use a solid foundation of both federal and regional laws and regulations had been built in the most developed countries of the world with many of these normative acts effectively functioning for decades. Contrary to that, in Russia this kind of national legislation has been at a stage of active development and enforcement and has relied on a limited number of federal laws while much more should be done as early as the nearest decade. At the same time, in both cases, there has been a constant though irregular development and renewal of emergency and disaster legislation thus representing a functioning feedback within the state system of emergency management.

The latter includes as an organic component or subsystem the emergency and disaster legislation which, in turn, embrace the normative (laws, regulations, decrees) and prescriptive acts (directives, instructions) which regulate the activities of various subjects (agents) of law while prevention and coping with specific types of emergencies and their functions at concrete stages and phases of the emergency management cycle. In fact, both types of acts are widely applied separately whereas their combination occurs less frequently substantially depending on a legislative traditions and preferences while creating a system of legislation in the designated area of public administration and state policy.

Two main approaches to this procedure may be distinguished in world practice. One of them which has been employed in many European countries, such as Great Britain and Sweden, proceeds from the assumption that legal relation between community members while emergency management area taken as a whole the does not constitute an independent special set which is principally different from the similar set of relationships existing in the non-emergency environment. Thus, these should be managed by the laws and regulations which are common for such kinds of relations, for example health care, environmental law and so forth and do not need any single act which would integrate all emergency related normative and prescriptive documents.

Another legislative approach involves his recognition that emergency management is a relatively independent area of legal regulation. This logically requires the development and adoption of a single comprehensive normative act (or a compact group thereof as a code) which would cover the total field of emergency management and integrate into a unified system all the laws and regulations in force in this field. In particular, such a policy has been employed in the United States where the Disaster Relief Act has been enforced as early as 1950. In the subsequent decades, it was amended and supplemented and nowadays is functioning as the Robert T. Stafford Disaster Relief and Emergency Assistance Act.

A similar approach was followed by the Netherlands where a single Disaster Management Plans Act was enforced in 1981 and in 1985 was substituted by the currently functioning Disasters Act. Canada passed two basic laws in 1988, the Emergency Preparedness Act and Emergencies Act, while Russia developed and in 1994 enforced the Federal Act of the Russian Federation for Communities and Regional Protection in Natural and Technological Emergencies (hereafter referred as Federal Emergency Act) later on supplemented by the respective governmental regulations (see *Federalnii Zakon*, 1994; *Pravitelstvo. Postanovleniye*, 1995d, 1995e, 1996a, 1996b, 1997).

The above mentioned approaches are not absolutely separate from each other. First of all, quite recently, as late as the beginning of the 1980s or even later, the countries with a functioning single comprehensive emergency and/or disaster act followed the previous approach which implied several laws providing for prevention of and response to specific types of emergencies (for example, landslides or toxic spills). The civil defense or war acts were the only integral instrument of regulating federal government activities in the emergency management area (Summary, 1995: 3).

In addition, the basic integrated emergency and/or disaster acts enforced in this group of countries have been and still are not always comprehensive. Quite often they regulate the relationships between different legal agents only at the specific stage (phase) or while carrying out a specific management function within the emergency management cycle, for instance risk insurance, resource mobilization, rescue of the victims and so on. Even the most comprehensive acts passed in the Netherlands and Russia have substantial lacunas. For example, the Federal Emergency Act in Russia regulates community protection only against natural and technological hazards and does not involve conflict type emergencies. At the same time, both legislative approaches cited earlier and those who have been following them do not preclude special regulation of concrete types of emergencies and/or disasters (earthquakes, floods, radiation, etc.) which are also available in these countries.

Moreover, the selection of a legal regulation model to prevent and cope with emergencies, disasters and catastrophes which relies on a single integrated act as a basis of a respective branch of the law, has been not always accompanied by a similar approach to organization of the emergency management system. For instance, the United States and Russia have established special state bodies responsible for emergency policy: the Federal Emergency Management Agency (FEMA) and the Ministry of the Russian Federation for Civil Defense, Emergencies and Natural Disaster Response (MES or EMERCOM), respectively. At the same time, in Canada, similar functions have been carried out by Emergency Preparedness Canada, an independent organization affiliated with the national Department of Defense whereas in Great Britain and the Netherlands, these have been the prerogative of the Department of the Interior as well as in a number of other countries which have also been relying upon the emergency and disaster law that involves a system of normative acts rather than a single integrated act.

Finally, given that the availability of such an act is not an absolute necessity. It should not be considered as a sufficient condition for building up an integrated *system* of law regulating the legal relationship within an emergency management area. To create such a system, one needs a comprehensive 'package' of interrelated acts providing regulation either for specific functions of communities and society protection in emergencies or a whole set of such functions with respect to a specific emergency type and integration (incorporation or codification) of the acts mentioned above.

Considering the absence of a single integrated emergency and/or disaster act, the integration of specific acts should create and often does create a self-sufficient legal basis for emergency management. In case a system ('umbrella') act is enforced, this would provide for its specification in relation to individual means and methods as well as stages and phases of emergency management. In addition, in certain cases the role of the missing integrated emergency act is successfully substituted by the other key federal acts, primarily civil defense acts.

As known, almost all countries have been using gradual incorporation as the main integration method of emergency related acts although the fragmentary character of respective legislation mentioned earlier has not yet been overcome. Given this fact the emergency management legislation has all grounds to be considered as a developing regulation system in these countries including Russia with the rate and form of this process varies from one nation or world region to another. The latter, while following one of the two earlier specified approaches to develop emergency and disaster legislation, has been providing for building up one of the two respective legal systems which may be conditionally labeled as 'centralized' and 'decentralized'. The decentralized systems involve only one whereas the centralized systems incorporate both of the following basic sets of normative acts, these are:

- system acts which embrace the whole gamut of functions of communities and societal protection against any hazard or threat and in any type of emergency and/or disaster;
- specific acts which regulate either a specific function within an emergency management cycle or the whole set of functions in relation to a specific type of an emergency and/or disaster.

Further, I shall consider the peculiarities of the centralized system being built up in Russia and compare it, where possible, with those of the leading countries of the world which employ the same kind of emergency legislation model.

LEGAL REGULATION OF PREVENTION AND RESPONSE TO EMERGENCIES IN RUSSIA

Unlike most developed countries of the world, and even in socioeconomic policy of Russia itself (for example, in the field of property relations, privatization of enterprises, taxation) the development of emergency and disaster legislation by the members (subjects) of the Russian Federation, that is in the regions of Russia, by the late 1990s has been in the cradle. This stems from the objective need for a relatively higher degree of centralization of emergency management than that in the area of economic and social policy in general which means a respective legislative reinforcement by federal law. In addition, this is also the result of the Russia's regional authorities still lagging substantially behind the federal government in development and enforcement of laws although the situation is different in terms of other normative and prescriptive acts (regulations, orders, instructions and so forth). Therefore, emergency and disaster legislation in Russia has remained dominated by federal laws and regulations of both systems and specific types.

THE SYSTEMS ACTS

These comprehensive acts which serve as the key subsystems within the emergency legislation system being developed in Russia provide a description of the basic conceptual framework, principles, goals and tasks of the state emergency management policy. In Russia these acts include primarily:
- Constitution of the Russian Federation with Paragraphs 20, 35, 41 and 42 establishing the right of the Russian citizens for life, health and property. The protection of these rights is the key objective of state policy in the emergency management area. The Constitution also specifies possible restriction of these rights and freedoms of people to ensure their safety in emergencies and/or disasters when the President of Russia declares a state of emergency (Paragraph 56). It also designates the areas of responsibility and competence of both federal and regional authorities of the Russian Federation in prevention of, preparedness and response to and recovery from emergencies, disasters and catastrophes (Paragraph 71).
- Security and Safety Act of the Russian Federation (*Zakon*, 1992a) which provide a formulation of the basic concepts associated with the mission and goals of emergency management strategy including 'security', 'safety', 'security and safety system'. It also establishes the principles and describes the main components and functions of a security and safety system in emergencies (Paragraphs 1, 5, 8 and 9). Paragraph 10 of this act distinguishes the powers of the federal legislative, executive and judicial bodies within the national security and safety system. While a similar distinction between the federal and regional authorities is also mentioned in this act (Paragraph 11) it is more clearly formulated in the above mentioned paragraphs of the Constitution of the Russian Federation which was adopted one year after the act. An inventory of the basic forces and means to ensure state security and safety policy implementation is specified in Paragraph 12 of the act which was later on supplemented by the subsequent decrees and regulations by the President and government of Russia, respectively.

In particular, the Decree of the President of Russia of 27 May, 1996 No. 784 'On Civil Defense' enforced the Rules and Regulations for Civil Defense Troops, designated the structure and composition of the bodies especially authorized for planning and implementation of civil defense and emergency management policies including the employment of civil defense troops in peacetime emergencies, disasters and catastrophes. This decree will be valid until a federal civil defense law is adopted.
- Fundamentals of the Health Law of the Russian Federation (*Osnovi*, 1993) which imply medical, sanitary and epidemiological safety and welfare of the Russian people. These should be provided both in everyday activities to prevent and mitigate such an emergency or disaster as epidemics, pandemics or epizootic and in conditions of emergency and/or disaster as well as environmentally unhealthy areas (Paragraph 28) to efficiently alleviate the debilitating and devastating effects of the crisis occasions for human health..
- Insurance Act of the Russian Federation (*Zakon*, 1992d) which establishes the goals, tasks and mechanism of life, health and property protection of the insured individuals and organizations in the events or occasions involving the specified kinds of risk including emergencies, disasters and catastrophes. The insurance clauses which are described in Paragraphs 16-18 and 20-21 and demand from the insurant to keep with existing safety norms and standards are oriented towards

minimization of risk associated with the insured event and its effect for insured health and material values thus contributing to prevention and mitigation of possible emergencies. If these norms and standards are followed the law provides for respective insurance compensation and/or coverage to the insurant to cope with direct or indirect damages incurred during an emergency, disaster or catastrophe.

- State of Emergency Act of the Russian Soviet Federative Socialist Republic adopted in 1991 in the former Soviet Union but is still in force in contemporary Russia (see *Zakon*, 1991a). Paragraphs 3-14 of this act establish the legitimate possibility, clauses and conditions, basis, duration and space limits and the procedure for imposing a special legal regime which is specified in the above-mentioned Paragraph 56 of the Russian Constitution. In particular, Paragraph 4(b) of the act provides for a state of emergency being imposed in case of non-conflict type (natural and technological) emergency and/or disaster while Paragraph 4(a) applies during conflict-type emergencies (civil strife, mass disturbances, riots, etc.). The special form of public administration, means and methods used to protect rights and freedoms of Russian citizens in such circumstances are prescribed by Paragraphs 15-36 of the given act.
- the earlier mentioned Federal Act of the Russian Federation for Communities and Regional Protection in Natural and Technological Emergencies (or Federal Emergency Act) (*Federalnii Zakon*, 1994) which later on has been supplemented and specified by governmental regulation No. 738 'Procedure for Community Preparedness to Emergencies and Disasters' and No 1113 'Unified State System for Prevention and Response to Emergencies in the Russian Federation (RUSPRE)' which were passed in 1995 (*Pravitelstvo. Postanovleniye*, 1995d, 1995e) and regulations No 924 'Forces and means of the Unified State System for Prevention and Response to Emergencies in the Russian Federation (RUSPRE)' and No 1094 'Classification of Natural and Technological Emergencies and Disasters in the Russian Federation' adopted and enforced in 1996 (*Pravitelstvo. Postanovleniye*, 1996a, 1996b).

According to Paragraph 2 of the Federal Emergency Act it should carry out (and to a great extent, it does so) of a key integrating component within the evolving system of the federal emergency and disaster legislation. It defines the basic concepts in this area including 'emergency', 'emergency prevention', 'emergency liquidation', 'emergency area') (Paragraph 1) and formulates the basic principles of communities and regional protection in emergencies, disasters and catastrophes (Paragraphs 6 and 7) which will be especially considered further on in this chapter.

These in turn serve as a basis for distinguishing the powers of the responsible authorities including the President of Russia, the Federal Assembly (the Duma and the Federation Council) and the Government of the Russian Federation and public administration bodies in the regions and municipalities of the Russian Federation members (subjects) which are specified in Paragraphs 8-11 of the Federal Emergency Act. Its next eight paragraphs, which were later supplemented by the above said government regulations No 1113 and No 924 provide for delineation of areas of competence, tasks and functions of administration and management organizations and individuals involved in the RUSPRE including volunteers and their associations during prevention of, preparedness and response to and recovery from emergencies, disasters and catastrophes.

The Federal Emergency Act embraces practically all stages and phases of the emergency management cycle, levels of public administration and management. However, this law, as mentioned above regulates issues concerning communities and regional protection in emergencies provoked by natural and technological hazards alone and does not refer to the conflict-type and some kinds of compound emergencies and disasters. In particular, it does not cover emergencies caused by civil strife, mass disturbances and disorders, ethnic conflicts, terrorist acts, including technological terrorism. In this connection, it is noteworthy that this act does not mention emergencies, disasters or catastrophes caused by a possible enemy's attack with modern weapons of mass destruction which were especially indicated in the governmental regulation of 18 April 1992, No 261 that preceded the Federal Emergency Act and gave initial impetus to the RUSPRE development (see *Pravitelstvo. Postanovleniye*, 1992)

In a certain sense, such a legislative approach has its own logic that presumes the Federal Emergency Act should supplement and specify the more general Security and Safety Act of the Russian Federation with respect to ensuring the community and regional safety in specific non-conflict type emergencies resulting from natural and technological hazardous impacts. As to the legal regulation of the conflict type emergencies and/or disasters, these are specified in other federal laws which establish the goal, tasks and objectives and functions of respective state security departments including the Ministry of the Internal Affairs (MIA), the Federal Security Service (FSS), the Federal Frontier Service (FFS) and others.

At the same time, the approach restrains and debilitates the systems potential of the Federal Emergency Act and reduces it to a specific act. For example, this breaks an organic link existing between the given act and the State of Emergency Act of 1991 on emergency, primarily Paragraph 4(a). Even more important is that this version of the Federal Emergency Act narrows the scope and comprehensiveness of the RUSPRE which use this act as a legal basis and, judging by its inner logic and title, should provide individual and collective security and protection against all possible kinds of threats.

Just for comparison, unlike this act, the two system emergency acts enforced in Canada in 1988 and the US Presidential Decree which established FEMA in 1978 (see US Congress, 1978: 5-6) are practically free of this shortcoming. They use the coverage of all kinds of hazards and threats to social and environmental safety as one of the key requirements along with some other principles. In particular, in Canadian emergency legislation these principles include: the lowest level competent to respond (also stressed in the Federal Emergency Act of Russia), all-hazard approach to planning, emergency plans and arrangements based on existing organizational structures and procedures, combination of the centralized direction and coordination with decentralized implementation and response. The emergencies, which involve threats to public order and safety, social welfare as well as territorial integrity and sovereignty, in particular interior armed conflicts and regional wars and those on allies territory, are regarded as a national emergency (disaster) (Summary, 1995: 4).

THE SPECIFIC ACTS

The so-called specific acts make up another subsystem of the emergency legislation system being built in Russia. These acts may be subdivided into two groups conditionally labeled as specific and functional.

The *specific acts group* incorporates laws and regulations covering specific types of emergencies including technological disasters. For example, federal acts for social protection of persons affected by impact of the South Urals (Cheliabinsk-65) and Chernobyl radiation disasters, these for using atomic energy and radiation safety of the people (see *Federalnii Zakon*, 1993b, 1995c, 1995e, 1995g) concern nuclear and radiation emergencies and/or disasters while the Road

Safety Act (*Federalnii Zakon*, 1995b) deals with transportation accidents and Environmental Protection Act and Ecological Expertise Act (*Zakon*, 1992b) refer to the hazardous and toxic contamination of the environment.

In addition, this group also includes acts which regulate prevention and response to emergencies caused by natural and compound hazards, for example, epidemics, epizootic, epiphytotic (*Zakon*, 1991c). As to those provoked by geophysical hazardous phenomena, these acts lack respective federal laws which especially regulate communities and regional protection in specific natural calamities like the laws that have been enforced in the United States for a long time (Flood Insurance Act of 1968, Earthquake Hazards Reduction Act of 1977 as amended and so forth).

In Russia these issues are regulated either by the respective paragraphs (sections) of the systems laws or more widely by presidential decrees and governmental regulations. Undoubtedly, these are insufficient and besides, until recently, have tackled only separate large scale natural disasters. As late as in 1993, the government of the Russian Federation passed the comprehensive regulation No. 444 concerning earthquake emergencies and disasters which has covered the issues of forecasting and preparedness while the flood disasters remained untouched by the federal emergency legislation. Although the latter (floods) have been the most dangerous geophysical hazard in Russia (see Chapter 1) these were especially mentioned among other natural threats to communities and regions only in the governmental regulation of 1992 No 1011 which described the goals, tasks and functions of the Federal Hydrometeorology and Environmental Monitoring Service of the Russian Federation (ROSGIDROMET).

As to the group of specific acts related to the conflict-type emergencies these also almost totally lack specific federal laws which especially regulate the issues dealing with communities and regional protection in specific types or kinds of emergencies. The Defense Act of the Russian Federation of 1992, which covers civil protection issues arising during armed conflicts, wars and terrorist attacks may be cited as a unique exception in this respect. Other pressing issues of the conflict type emergencies are handled only by presidential decrees and governmental regulations which refer to specific sociopolitical conflicts (for example, in Northern Osetia, Ingoushetia, Chechnia). The situation is further complicated by the earlier mentioned Federal Emergency Act excluding this type of emergencies and disasters from its area of responsibility thereby leaving it out not only from the RUSPRE organizational system but emergency legislation system as well. Recognizing the integrity of the latter I, however, consider it both methodologically and practically necessary to keep the acts which regulate conflict type emergencies within this legislation system as its intrinsic component.

Another set of emergency and/or disaster acts or *functional acts group* includes laws and regulations which govern or manage concrete functions or activities of specific emergency services associated with prevention and coping with multifaceted emergencies. In particular, this group involves the federal Militia (Police) Act of 1991, Penitentiary Criminal Institutions Act of 1993, Fire Safety Act of 1994, Emergency and Rescue Service and Rescuer Status Act of 1994, the Russian Federation Federal Security Service Act of 1995, Internal Troops Act of 1997 and more numerous presidential decrees and governmental regulations (see *Zakon*, 1991b; *Federalnii Zakon*, 1995a, 1995d, 1997).

The above classification of specific acts is convenient for further systematization. Nevertheless, to a great extent it is conditional. In fact, many of the enforced laws and regulations marry both specific and functional characteristics covering certain types of emergencies and/ or disasters as well as concrete functions and actions of a given public administration body to prevent, prepare, respond to and recover from a crisis. However, these are integrated within specific acts to a substantially lower degree than those of the systems acts. For example, the Fire Safety Act of 1994 and the Sanitary and Epidemiological Welfare of People Act of 1991 regulate prevention of and response to fires and epidemics as specific kinds of an emergency and/or disaster and at the same time they provide for carrying out the functions of fire and medical control in all types and kinds of emergencies.

Practically every system and specific act contains multiple paragraphs and sections which regulate emergency prevention and mitigation and provide motivation to develop and implement measures facilitating early detection and mitigation of the risks and threats to human lives and health, social and economic welfare, national integrity and constitutional order. This must be achieved through the legally demanded procedure of expert examination of the drafts and auditing of the decisions being implemented which filter out those considered unacceptable by safety (risk) criteria. The law also prescribes preventive measures to ensure integral security and safety while carrying out routine monitoring, control and supervision functions provided by responsible state, public and private organizations.

However, in Russia the inventory nomenclature of respective emergency acts and their degree of detail, in particular, the accuracy and comprehensiveness of safety criteria, can hardly be considered exhaustive. The bulk of these acts incorporate no more than a general list of requirements and not always provide for a specific mechanism of respective sanctions for non-compliance. In addition, the standards which should serve as a main calibration instrument for specialists have been and are often reconsidered, sometimes to loosen them. For example, this has happened in the case of the maximum permissible concentration of nitrates in food products and radionucleids in the milk (see Porfiriev, 1993a).

Industrial personnel safety and industrial production safety acts occupy a special place among the laws and regulations related to prevention and mitigation of technological emergencies. In the former Soviet Union and contemporary Russia, these are known as the Fundamentals of Labor Security Law of the Russian Federation (as amended in 1993) with the basic concept 'labor security' being, in my opinion, linguistically incorrect and misleading in substantive terms.

Although the above-mentioned act is directly and indirectly associated with prevention of technological accidents and emergencies, it tends to be excessively biased towards passive means and methods of personnel protection within a given facility against industrial hazards including compensation payments for post-impact health effects. Accident and emergency prevention and mitigation issues, in particular by using modern information intensive technologies and sociologically and psychologically adjusted management organizations, and the interrelationship between the personnel and technological safety and safety of the neighboring communities are only briefly mentioned. This is unlike analogous personnel health and industrial safety acts which have been enforced in the United States, Japan, Great Britain and other countries several decades ago (Porfiriev, 1991a, 1991b).

Among the laws and regulations oriented to emergency prevention and mitigation no less an important role is played by the land use planning acts, construction standards and operational licenses. Sanitary and environmental constraints on design of and building up within the settlements prohibit the construction of hazardous industrial, energy power, transport and other facilities in dangerous proximity to residential districts and force making the buffer sanitary and protection belts around such facilities.

These constraints, along with the operational license requirements, are established in paragraphs 11 and 38 of the above mentioned Sanitary and Epidemiological Welfare of People Act, Environmental Protection Act of 1991 (Sections V-VII), Environmental Impact Assessment Act of 1995 (Paragraphs 11,12) as well as in construction standards developed and enforced by respective construction departments in Russia. The latter also provide regulation of planning and construction of settlements, industrial and other facilities within hazard prone areas vulnerable to landslides, floods, earthquakes, etc. It is worth mentioning that abroad these standards have a higher status, being usually codified and enforced by regional and federal laws, such as the Urban and Rural Planning Law of 1971 in Great Britain.

Industrial safety declarations for hazardous facilities is another means and method of legal prevention and mitigation of possible technological accidents and emergencies. Although it is well known and has been long used in the West, this regulation instrument is relatively new in Russia. Governmental regulation No 765, which enforced the legal demand for the bulk of industrial facilities to declare its safety status in a special document, was passed as late as 1995. In 1996 the Ministry of the Russian Federation for Civil Defense, Emergencies and Natural Disaster Response (MES or EMERCOM) and the Federal Mining and Industrial Supervision of Russia (GOSGORTECHNADZOR) approved the procedure of its preparation and assessment which prescribed that to get an operational license the declaration should be obligatorily submitted to GOSGORTECHNADZOR with its contents being the responsibility of the owner or operating manager of a respective facility. In its turn, GOSGORTECHNADZOR and MES judge the sufficiency and effectiveness of an accident and emergency prevention and mitigation measures, and provide monitoring and supervision over their implementation while exploitation (Shoigu, 1996).

In addition to prevention and mitigation issues, almost all of the above-mentioned specific acts also contain paragraphs and sections which regulate emergency preparedness activities of individuals, organizations, communities and regional of Russia. Contingency planning, training and upgrading of emergency workers (fire, militia, rescue, medical care and other personnel), public information and training, funds raising, reserve accumulation and resource mobilization constitute the basics of such activities prescribed by the respective acts. For example, the procedure for accumulating the state emergency material and technical reserves is determined by the State Reserves Development Act of the Russian Federation of 1992.

As a rule, Russian law distinguishes, albeit not always consistently and completely, the responsibilities and functions of the public administration bodies involved in emergency management. The notable exception is the federal Emergency and Rescue Service and Rescuer Status Act of 1994 which regulates emergency personnel training (see *Federalnii Zakon*, 1995a) while specific requirements for and the very procedures of planning, personnel teaching and training are described in detail in numerous orders and manuals of the respective federal departments. For example, in the order of the Ministry of Internal Affairs of the Russian Federation (MIA) dated 12 January 1996 which concerned improvement of emergency training for militia (police) and internal troops (somewhat analogous to the National Guard in the United States) of the MIA these requirements and implementation procedures are extensively prescribed in relation to the content of a 'model' operation plan, calculation of forces and means patterns in conditions of criminal and non-criminal (natural and technological) emergencies and/or disasters. Such orders, instructions and also personnel manuals are used by other federal departments engaged in emergency prevention and response, first of all in the MES of Russia. The hazardous industries and facilities use respective production and technological manuals.

However, in particular, the experience of response to earthquakes in Spitak in 1988 and in Neftegorsk in 1995 (in relation to non-conflict type disaster) and terrorist attacks in Budennovsk in 1995 and Kizliar and Pervomaiskoye in 1996 (in respect to a conflict type disaster) show evidence that such orders, instructions and manuals are insufficient to cope with the crisis the if respective specific acts (laws) or special paragraphs which regulate preparedness (especially, the interaction of responsible state departments in an emergency) are lacking. Among these missing laws are federal constitutional and federal acts for civil defense, chemical safety, transportation of toxic and highly hazardous materials, earthquake and flood hazard reduction and so on.

Some of these were developed long ago but still have been not adopted and enforced or have been adopted quite recently and applied on a limited scale, as for example the Radiation Safety Act and Atomic Energy Use Act of 1995. Some of them have not even been ear-marked by legislators as projected for the nearest future. Meanwhile, in the countries of the West and Japan such acts have been functioning for a long time, in particular the Atomic Energy Act and the Civil Defense Act in the United States since 1946 and 1950, respectively; atomic energy acts in Switzerland and Germany since 1959 and in France since 1963 and so on.

Finally, the specific acts under discussion also include paragraphs and sections which provide regulation for response to and recovery from an emergency and/or disaster and catastrophes. This regulation implies both legal sanctions and motivation to eliminate or alleviate immediate and remote social and environmental effects of a crisis irrespective of emergency type, including search and rescue operations, trans-emergency and post-emergency evacuation of, medical care support, relief and compensation to the affected people, rehabilitation and reconstruction of destroyed facilities and buildings. In the former Soviet Union until the late 1980s in the absence of federal laws these activities were carried out within the legal framework of governmental regulations with the respective federal laws lacking whereas abroad these existed for many years. For example, in United States the Disaster Relief Act has been effective since 1950 while the Flood Insurance Act and the Comprehensive Environmental Regulation, Compensation and Liability Act (CERCLA) since 1956 and 1980, respectively.

The acts which ensure legal support for carrying out some of the above-mentioned actions to recover from emergencies, disasters and catastrophes were developed and enforced in the former Soviet Union as late as in the late 1980s. In particular, Paragraph 34 of the former USSR Enterprise Act of 1987 compelled the enterprise to compensate any damage which was incurred as a result of non-compliance with technological, environmental, sanitary, medical and safety standards and make respective payments to the affected neighboring communities and consumers of its products as well as fines to the responsible environmental supervision agencies. These sanctions have been kept in the Russian federal law, in particular the Russian Federation Environmental Protection Act of 1991, Consumer Rights Protection Act of 1992 and Environmental Impact Assessment Act of 1995. However, given the negligible fine tariffs and the majority of enterprises being on the edge of bankruptcy in the 1990s, the demanded compliance to the standards seems either ineffective or unrealistic.

Among the acts which regulate the response to and recovery from emergencies in Russia, insurance legislation plays a somewhat unique role. As is well known, this kind of legislation is of a systems or comprehensive character almost everywhere in the West, providing expected loss reduction at every stage and phase of the emergency management cycle: from prevention to recovery and is not constrained by compensation to the victims. Moreover, it carries out primarily the mitigation function which stimulates the insurant to keep within established standards and recommendations to provide safety for him and his business and minimize the risk. At the same time, in the former Soviet Union this function was reduced to routine compensation with the notable peculiarities of the payment procedure.

The point is that in conditions of absolute state ownership of enterprises and a centralized economy which existed in the country until the mid 1980s, the insurance of life and property, including that against natural and industrial hazards, was monopolized by an All-Union organization named GOSSTRAKH (the Russian acronym for State Insurance Company). It was empowered to collect insurance premiums from all Soviet citizens and enterprises while the insurance itself was compulsory. Part of the acquired premiums were transferred to a special reserve fund which was used to pay to the victims or their families not as insurance obligations but as allowances for the loss of a breadwinner as well as disability, funerals, etc. thus somewhat alleviating the emergency and/or disaster effect. The procedure and amount of such allowances were specified by the governmental regulations of the former Soviet Union while both the All-Union and republican insurance laws were lacking. Such a procedure, along with negligible amounts of allowances, could not but impede the progress of national insurance and predetermined its inefficiency and low priority within emergency management policy.

In contemporary Russia, the situation has somewhat improved with the federal laws crucial for insurance development being adopted and enforced in the 1990s. These include primarily the Medical Insurance of the Russian Federation Citizens Act of 1991 and Insurance Act of 1992 (see *Zakon*, 1992d). The insurance related norms were also established by Environment Protection Act (Paragraphs 11 and 23), Militia (Police) Act of 1991(Paragraph 29) and Military Servicemen Status Act of 1993 (Paragraphs 16 and 18). Closely related to these acts and paragraphs are the federal laws which provide additional guarantees and compensation to servicemen operating in conditions of a state of emergency and armed conflicts and were signed by the President of Russia adopted in 1993 and 1995 in connection with the regional armed conflicts in the Northern Caucasus and other hotbeds (see *Federalnii Zakon* 1993a, 1995f). Nevertheless, given that the insurance market and policy in Russia is still in the cradle and in respect to emergency management still perform a predominantly compensation function, the Insurance Act may be referred the as a systems one only with substantial reservations.

Within the Russian emergency related legislation there are laws and regulations which directly refer to the state bodies and services for urgent response including fire, militia, rescue, medical care and some others. Thus, in the Militia Act (as amended in 1993) Paragraph 29 prescribes for compulsory personal insurance of the militia (police) officers at the expense of the special foundations which are supported by budget resources. In case a militiaman is killed in action, Sections 2 and 3 of this paragraph provide for his family a compensation in a lump-sum allowance equal to his 10-year salary while if he is wounded or disabled and his further service is ruled out the allowance would be equal to his 5-year salary.

Despite the above-mentioned positive changes in Russian insurance policy and legislation in the 1990s, these areas still lack a number of important specific acts which would regulate property and other liabilities of individuals and organizations during emergencies, disasters and catastrophes. This lacuna is especially vivid if a cross-national comparison is involved. For example, in the United States the laws and regulations for flood insurance have been in force since 1956, those dealing with nuclear and radiation risks function there since 1957 (Anderson - Price Act with subsequent amendments) while those relating to the hazardous materials railway transportation have been effective since 1970 (since 1975 these have been substituted by a more comprehensive Transportation Safety Act).

As a result, in Russia such widely applied kinds of insurance as damage risk insurance, insurance for hazardous facilities liability for risks associated with the possible effect of accidents or emergencies are still missing. Given this and poor development of the private insurance companies in the 1990s, one should not wonder at the low compensation tariffs established and implemented by the state insurance organizations to affected people (victims for more detail see Chapter 4).

Laws and regulations which establish the status of and designate the schedule and regime of activities within the specific emergency and/or disaster areas, should be also distinguished in emergency legislation, primarily specific acts. In Russia there are a few dozen such areas which have existed for many years leaving out a substantial greater number of those 'short-lived' (see

Chapter 1). However, a comprehensive federal law which would both provide clear-cut criteria for distinguishing and establishing the status of such types of areas and serve as a 'legal umbrella' for already exiting specific acts and governmental regulations that cover specific cases is lacking. It is notable that even the systems' Federal Emergency Act provides the definition of these areas (Paragraph 2) but only mentions a procedure for establishing of their boundaries by field emergency coordinators in Paragraph 5. The only exception is the Environmental Protection Act of 1991 which determines the status of and the schedule for activities within an environmental emergency and disaster area (Paragraphs 58 and 59).

At the same time, although with a considerable delay, Russia has developed and enforced federal laws which regulate the status and economic activities within specific radiation disaster areas including those in the European part of the country which resulted from the Chernobyl tragedy and the Urals region which is a legacy of the South Urals (Cheliabinsk-65) major accident as well as in Altai region which was caused by the effect of nuclear testing near Semipalatinsk (Kazakhstan). However, similar disaster areas which appeared in Kemerovo region (South Siberia), Tatarstan, Bashkortastan, Kalmik republics and other regions of Russia as a result of multiyear and environmental contamination and degradation, lack such specific laws and thus involve the above- mentioned general clauses of the Environmental Protection Act. In addition, the legal status of these areas and natural disaster areas as well as the respective kinds of economic activities within them in Russia are designated in specific government regulations (for details see Chapter 4). In other countries of the world it is normal practice to base response and recovery operations in a specific large-scale emergency or disaster on a specific federal or regional being especially developed and enforced immediately after the crisis occurs. Directive No 501 of 1982, adopted by the European Community after a well-known major chemical accident in the town of Seveso in Italy, respective acts on recovery from emergencies and disasters resulting from the San Fernando earthquake in 1971, Hurricane Hugo in 1991 and the "Exxon Valdez" oil spill tanker accident in 1989 in the United States may serve as a good illustrations of this point.

Finally, emergency legislation also called for regulation of the emergency and disaster relief to the affected communities, in particular to the refugees, and the issues which involve investigation and research of the preconditions and causes of these crisis situations. This is so that they can be prevented in the future while responsible officials considered guilty can be legally prosecuted. In Russia, federal emergency and disaster relief laws and refugees acts have not yet been developed and enforced although actually there are more than 700,000 refugees (see Chapter 1).

The situation looks substantially better in respect to the federal laws which regulate investigation of the pre-conditions and causes of the accidents, emergencies, disasters and catastrophes. Some of such acts which had been effective in the former Soviet Union still continue to be used in contemporary Russia (although with new titles and amendments). Suffice it to cite the Criminal Code (its substantively new version in Russia has been in force since 1 January 1997), the Code of Administrative Offenses (Tort Law) with the paragraphs concerning carelessness, non-compliance to industrial and technological safety rules, etc. as well numerous regulations and orders of the Russian government and instructions of federal ministries (departments).

In 1995 alone, these were supplemented by the Russian Federation Operation Search and Investigation Act and the Federal Security Service Act which provided regulation for early detection, revelation and prevention of as well as counter operations against terrorist attacks, hostage seizure and other criminal conflict-type emergencies. However, either the nomenclature or the content of the federal acts effective in the discussed field of emergency legislation could hardly be considered exhaustive.

The State Emergency and Disaster Policy and Organization of Emergency Management in Russia

The elaboration and enforcement of the above-mentioned systems and specific acts is an organic and important component of the process of development of state emergency and disaster policy. At the same time these constitute the legal basis of the actual state unified emergency management system (RUSPRE) the building of which was started in the former Soviet Union and contemporary Russia in the late 1980s - early 1990s. In the mid-1990s the RUSPRE entered a qualitatively new phase of its development.

State Policy and Organization of a Unified System for Emergency Prevention and Response in the Russian Federation (RUSPRE)

Until the late 1980s the protection communities and regions against various hazards in the former Soviet Union as in the majority of the countries of the West was carried out within the framework of a national civil defense system. In full accordance with political and ideological priorities of the "Cold War" epoch, its mission was to provide and guarantee security of the civil population and strategic facilities of a national economy against military threats, primarily nuclear attack. Therefore, it was quite natural that civil defense in the former Soviet Union was made an organic component or subsystem within the national defense system and was organized, like the latter, in accordance with a geographical or spatial criterion being subdivided into a number of special districts. Accordingly, the Civil Soviet was headed by the Deputy Minister of Defense while those who served in the civil defense system were military servicemen.

The radical political changes in the former Soviet Union in the second half of the 1980s, which coincided in time with a set of the major emergencies, disasters and catastrophes with the Chernobyl radiation disaster being the most devastating. This facilitated and accelerated substitution of the past civil defense paradigm by a new one which implied the priority of peacetime protection of communities and regions against natural, technological and compound threats and a respective radical organizational change in the national defense system.

In 1989, the State Emergency Committee of the Soviet Union was established by special governmental regulation while approximately a year later an analogous committee was set up in the Russian Federation as a part of its Council of Ministers (the Government of Russia). Soon it was moved to the Administration of the President of Russia and renamed as the State Committee of the Russian Federation for Civil Defense, Emergencies and Natural Disaster Response or EMERCOM. This symbolized and officially constituted the communities and regional protection in both peacetime and wartime emergencies as a relatively independent and important area of Russian state policy.

The dissolution of the Soviet Union in 1991 led to the closure of the State Emergency Committee of the Soviet Union and thus strengthened the role of the Russian EMERCOM which was vested with the responsibility to develop and enforce an effective national state system for prevention of and responding to emergencies, disasters and catastrophes. Officially the development of such a system in Russia was initiated by the Governmental Regulation of 18 April 1992, No 261 which stressed the necessity of building up the Russian System for Prevention of and Actions in Emergencies. It also provided for enforcing its Rules and Regulations which designated the system's goal, tasks and operational schedule.

At the same time, the crucial issues of emergency protection or management strategy as a part of national security policy are determined by President of Russia. During decision making, he relies upon the comprehensive analysis and consultations provided by the Security Council which was organized in 1992 as a part of the President's Administration and is officially headed by the president himself. Besides the President of Russia, the Chairman of the Security Council and the Commander-in-Chief of the Armed Forces, the members of this council include: the Prime Minister (who is officially the Chief of Civil Defense of the Russian Federation), the chairmen of both Houses of the Russian Federation Federal Assembly, the heads of the ministries for emergencies, internal affairs, foreign affairs, finance, justice and the Federal Security Service as well as the Security Council Secretary.

In 1994, enforcement of the Federal Emergency Act, EMERCOM of Russia was transformed into the Russian Federation Ministry for Civil Defense, Emergencies and Natural Disaster Response (MES) and governmental regulation No. 261 was nullified. By the same act and supplementing governmental regulation of 1995 (*Postanovleniye. Pravitelstvo*, 1995d) the Russian System for Prevention of and Actions in Emergencies was reorganized into the Russian Federation United State System of Prevention which has kept its abbreviation (RUSPRE).

These legislative and organizational changes in the mid-1990s have contributed to an increase of the number of the RUSPRE member organizations and organizational subsystems as compared to 1992 and which in 1996 amounted to 31 (see Annex 2) and respective widening of the system's operational range. Accordingly, federal budget expenditures on RUSPRE have also been conspicuously augmented. In fiscal year 1997, these exceeded 8,000 million rubles or 2.1% of the total budget expenditures leaving out those for the special government emergency fund.

The changes mentioned above also marked the beginning of the next qualitative new stage of development of Russian state emergency and disaster policy. This was especially noted in the 1996 annual message of the President of Russia to the Federal Assembly which was dedicated to national defense issues and distinguished the protection of individual and societal interests in emergencies caused by natural, technological and other hazards as one of the key areas of the state security and safety policy with RUSPRE being responsible for its implementation (see Shoigu, 1996).

In spite of crucial changes in the federal emergency legislation and reorganization of RUSPRE into a formally more comprehensive system, its operation area in terms of the variety of types of emergencies being covered has not been broadened and is still constrained by those provoked by natural and technological hazards. Although in accordance with its name and declared goal and functions, the RUSPRE should be an integrated system which provides security and safety for communities and regions of Russia against any major hazard and in any emergency including conflict-type and compound crisis, the latter are excluded from the scope of the RUSPRE activities.

This predetermined a certain internal ambiguity of the RUSPRE as in the late 1990s. On the one hand, it covers the entire territory of Russia and all management stages, phases, functions and authority levels mentioned earlier and in this respect satisfies one of the main criteria of systems approach, that is integrity or comprehensiveness. On the other hand, the existing RUSPRE does not fit the indicated criterion being a specific rather than an integrated and comprehensive organizational system in terms of the 'subject' indicator, that is involving the strictly limited range of emergencies. For this reason it neither fully corresponds to the concept of a 'unified system' in name since the latter, besides other things, presumes the completeness of a variety of emergencies being managed by the system. Such an internal discrepancy within the RUSPRE contradict its intrinsic logic which initially implies integrity and harmonization of the functions related to communities and regional protection against any major threat both in times of peace and war.

In this connection, the obvious discrepancy between the legislative constraints imposed on the operational area of the RUSPRE and the considerably more extensive competence and prerogatives of its chief manager and operator, that is MES. In accordance with the respective Rules and Regulations established by the Russian government, the MES should provide protection and assistance to communities and regions not only in non-conflict type mass emergencies provoked by natural and technological hazards (as the RUSPRE does) but in the conflict type large scale emergencies as well. In particular, its functions embrace: civil defense planning and implementation, search and rescue, urgent evacuation of and medical care, sheltering and other relief support to the affected people in Russia and abroad if requested, including delivery of relief aid to the areas seized by regional and international ethnic conflicts.

BASICS OF ORGANIZATION AND STRUCTURE AND COMPOSITION OF THE RUSPRE

I start the discussion of the specifics of the RUSPRE organization I start with an analysis of its key functions and principles, then pass to its structure and composition considering the key subsystems, components and their functions. The main accent will be on the federal level of emergency policy and management which remains very important in emergency prevention and still plays a decisive role in large scale emergencies, disasters and catastrophes.

FUNCTIONS AND PRINCIPLES OF THE RUSPRE ORGANIZATION

As any organizational system, RUSPRE carries out three general functions which are closely intertwined. These include: goal setting, goal implementation by selection and activating of the means and methods best suited to reach it, and timely correction of both the selected goal and implementation mechanism using feedback relationships within a given system.

To execute the first of the enumerated functions and give a clear description of the established goal, Paragraph 4 of the Federal Emergency Act stipulates the development and implementation of the legal and economic standards to provide efficient and effective protection of communities and regions in emergencies. Some kinds of these standards (construction, industrial safety and so forth) have been already discussed above.

Goal implementation and feedback functions involve a set of various measures. Specifically at the prevention and preparedness phases of emergency management cycle these include: emergency risk forecasting and assessment of its socio-economic effect;

carrying out specific federal state R&D programs for emergency prevention and mitigation and increasing the sustainability and reliability for functioning of organizations irrespective of the type of ownership and property;

ensuring emergency preparedness of communities and authorities, in particular the services specially designated to respond to and recover from emergencies and/or disasters including training of both professionals and the public;
- creating emergency reserve funds and accumulation of financial and material resources;
- providing supervision, inspections and control of hazard prone facilities and areas by the responsible state agencies.

Especially during the response and recovery phases, the respective measures imply:
- alleviation and elimination of emergency social and environmental effects;
- relief aid to and social security support of the affectedcommunities and regions including compensation and humanitarian actions;
- social security support including privileges and compensation to those injured while carrying out rescue, evacuation and relief operations (both volunteers and professionals).

Throughout the entire management cycle with all the phases being involved, the following measures should be undertaken to follow the requirements of the law:
- collection, processing and exchange of data related to emergencies and/or disasters and catastrophes;
- promotion of international cooperation in the field of protection of communities and regions in emergencies (see *Federalnii Zakon*, 1994, Paragraph 4).

To implement these functions, the RUSPRE has been following a number of the principles which are also specified in the Federal Emergency Act and include:
- free access to the relevant information or the public right-to-know (except cases especially reserved in the Russian law in force);
- timely and precise preparedness measures with due consideration of the regional peculiarities and degree of risk hazard;
- contingency planning based on the requirements (needed) sufficiency and maximum utilization of the available forces and means;
- priority of the forces and means for emergency services of organizations, municipalities and regions of the Russian Federation affected by any of the crisis. The emergency forces and means of the federal level are involved only if the efforts already undertaken turn to be insufficient (lowest level involvement principle).

ORGANIZATIONAL STRUCTURE AND COMPOSITION OF RUSPRE

These principles in turn provide for two basic requirements to the RUSPRE organization and composition. One of these implies complete coverage of the operational area, functions and authority and management levels involved. Given the reservations made above, coverage thus may be considered as a comprehensiveness requirement. Another basic requirement calls for the organizational system hierarchy which should combine the centralized coordination of contingency and operational planning with the 'from bottom to top' efforts to implement these plans along with grass-roots initiatives while responding to emergencies and/or disasters.

In accordance with the former requirement, RUSPRE is organized along spatial (geographical) and functional criteria and includes two key subsystems of the same name (see Fig. 14)

The *spatial or territorial subsystems* are organized by executive authorities of the Russian regions, that is the entities (members) of the Russian Federation, and local authorities in accordance with the administrative and spatial division of the national territory established by the Constitution of the Russian Federation. These subsystems include: management bodies, public

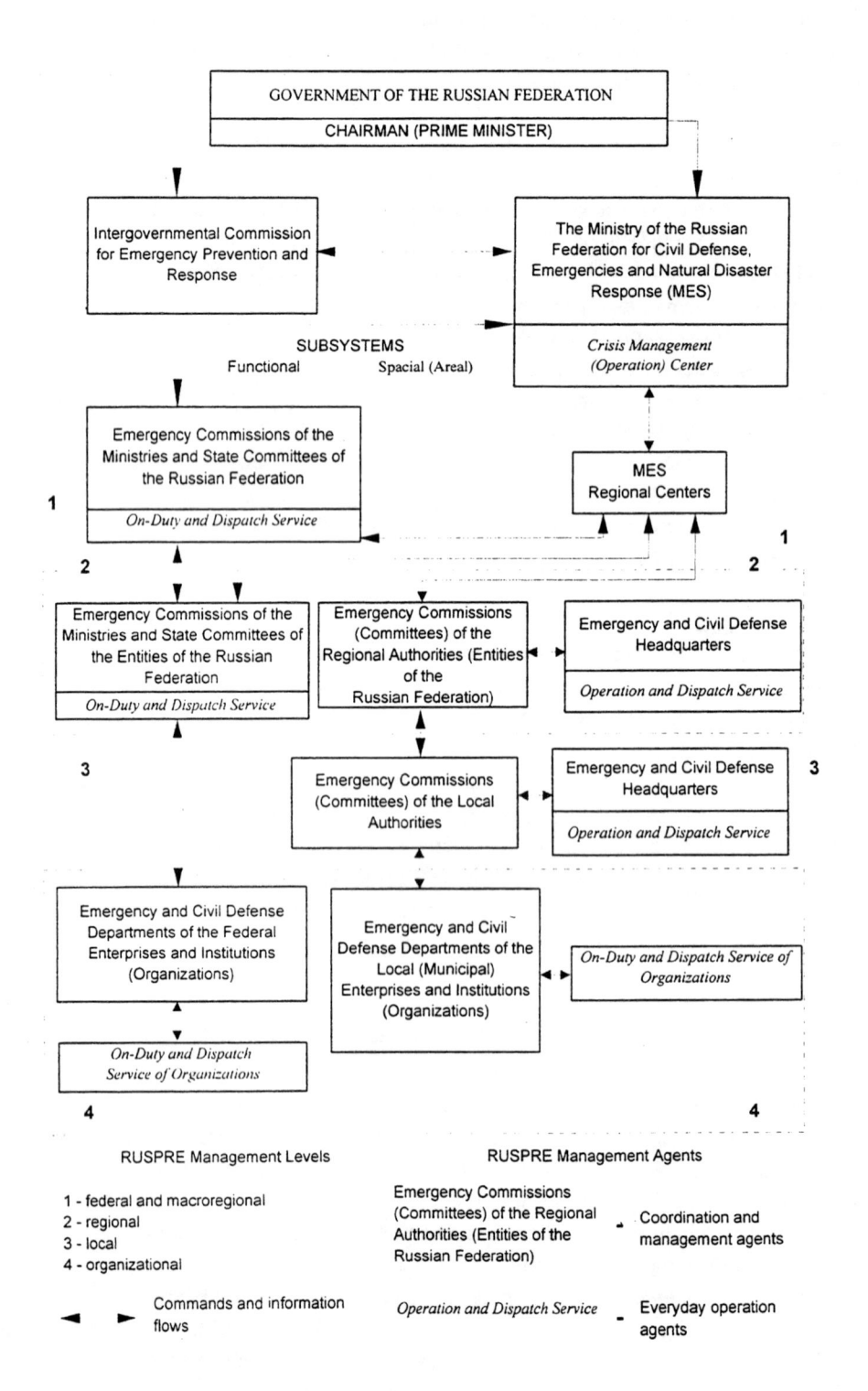

Fig 14. Organizational Structure of the RUSPRE

administration, forces and means of the executive authorities of the Russian Federation entities, local authorities and organizations responsible for communities and regional protection against natural and technological hazards. My estimate shows that RUSPRE should embrace more than 5,000 spatial subsystems including those in 89 entities (members) of the Russian Federation subjects, over 1,000 in urbanized areas and big cities and more than 2,200 in towns, hamlets and villages in the rural areas.

The *functional subsystems* are organized by the federal executive authorities and consist of the federal government, forces and means of the federal ministries and departments responsible for emergency prevention and response in the areas and industries of their competence and prerogatives. The list of federal organizations included in RUSPRE is shown in Annex 2. These amount to 31 and are responsible for creating and managing the activities of the same number of functional subsystems which should carry out almost 20 various functions. Both the functional subsystems and functions being implemented may be united into the following three main types:
- monitoring (observation and control);
- operational management (emergency preparedness, response and recovery);
- logistical support (material, technical, financial, etc.).

The respective distribution of the subsystems and their key functional types is shown in the Fig. 15a and 15b).

These pictures demonstrate the pronounced superiority of operational emergency management functions which account for almost half of the total number of the RUSPRE functional subsystems and their functions. The analogous proportion of the monitoring and logistics support subsystems are almost equal amounting to approximately 23% and 26%, respectively. As to their functions, the monitoring and control conspicuously prevail over logistics support.

A more detailed analysis of the functions being carried out by each of the three functional subsystems reveals that the monitoring and operational management subsystems are primarily focused on prevention of and response to emergencies and/or disasters provoked by technological accidents. These account for more than 70% of the total number of the functional subsystems which are specialized in monitoring and control within the RUSPRE framework with the rest of them handling natural emergencies and/or disasters.

Among the operational management subsystems the proportion of those related to technological emergencies occurring at the facilities of the "secondary" sector of the national economy (that is industry, energy power, construction) amounts to 45% whereas those associated with the "primary" (agriculture, forestry, fisheries) and the "tertiary" (transport, communications, informatics, communal services, etc.) sectors account to 27% each. At the same time, among the logistics support subsystems those providing material and technical supplies and financial aid from the federal reserve funds dominate. These account for 37% and 25%, respectively of the total number of subsystems of a given type while the proportion of the subsystems which provide emergency information, organizational and transportation support amounts to 12% each.

Such a structure and composition of the RUSPRE functional subsystems and their functions corresponds to the pattern of emergencies and disasters social and environmental effect existing in the country in the 1990s. As it has been shown above (see Chapter 1), the bulk of both the number of emergencies and disasters, and the casualties and value of economic losses incurred by these in Russia have been caused by industrial and other technological accidents. However, this can be treated as the functional structure and composition of the RUSPRE meeting the existing needs in communities and regional security and safety only if the conflict type emergencies (which are excluded from the RUSPRE by law) are not considered.

In addition, the existing structure and composition of RUSPRE reflects the adaptive and reflexive

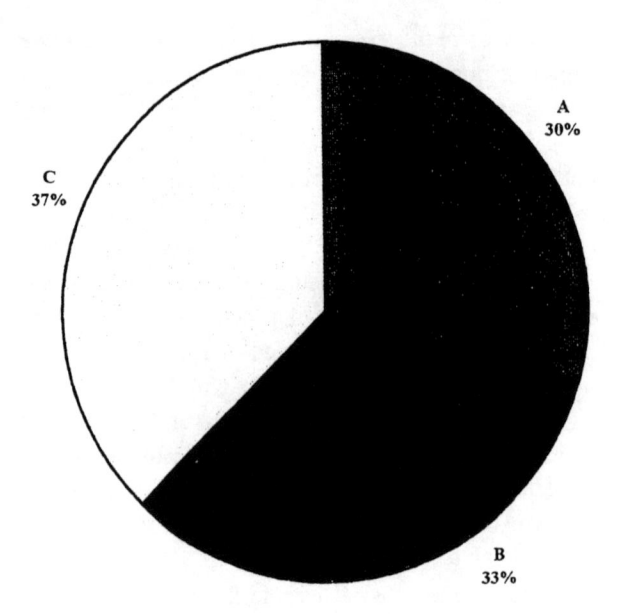

Fig 15a. The Structure of the Functions Carried Out by the Federal Government Bodies Within the RUSPRE

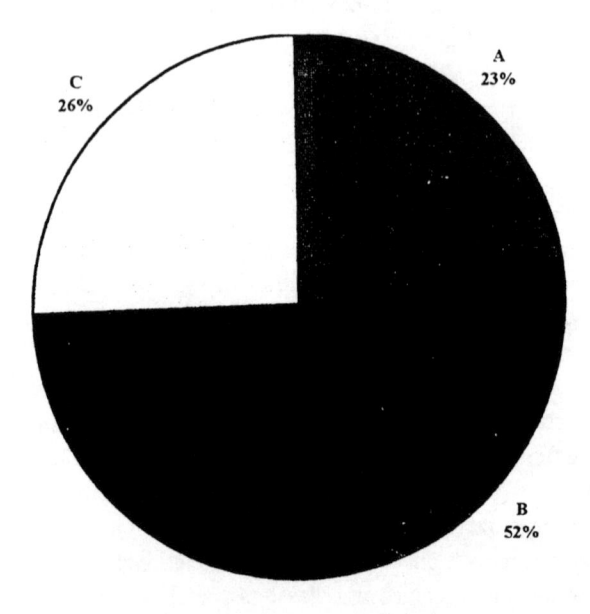

Fig 15b. The Structure of the Functions Carried Out by the Key Subsystems of the RUSPRE

A - Monitoring (observation and control)
B - Operative (preparedness, response, recovery)
C - Logistics and support

or *reactive* (see Ackoff, 1985: 84) type of emergency policy and management being preserved by the RUSPRE which is still biased toward response and recovery functions and measures. I believe it to be a natural and logical stage in the history of RUSPRE development in circumstances when in the former Soviet Union the federal and regional emergency services have not existed for decades being substituted by the army. In recent years the situation has been changing, although too slowly, towards a more pronounced accent on anticipatory or *proactive* and flexible system of RUSPRE organization and operation.

In accordance with another requirement of the RUSPRE organization which implies its hierarchy, this system is subdivided into five basic levels which correspond to the levels making and implementing decisions related to emergencies with special respect to the scale and gravity of their effect (see Chapter 1). These include:

- organizational level (*localnii uroven*) which provides emergency protection of a facility or institution;
- local level (*mestnii uroven*) which implies emergency protection of a town or city district, or a town and a city themselves;
- regional level (*territorialnii uroven*) which provides emergency protection of the area of an entity (member) of the Russian Federation;
- macroregional level (*regionalnii uroven*) which implies emergency protection of the area of the two entities (members) of the Russian Federation;
- federal level (*federalnii uroven*) which provides emergency protection of the area of more than two entities (members) of the Russian Federation and the national territory as a whole.

In an emergency or disaster which involves an area or facility owned by the federal government, for example, the nuclear power plants, boundary coastal sea waters and so forth, the respective decisions are the competence of the federal and to a minor extent regional levels.

Each of the above-mentioned management levels of the RUSPRE has a similar composition of operation and control bodies which include:

- coordination bodies;
- permanent operation and control bodies especially authorized to provide communities and regional protection in emergencies;
- everyday operation and control bodies;
- forces and means, financial, material and technical reserves, communication, warning and information support systems (see: *Federalnii Zakon*, 1994; *Pravitelstvo. Postanovleniye*, 1995d).

The coordination bodies of the RUSPRE carry out the functions of strategic and tactical planning which are primarily associated with prevention and response preparedness by taking an active part in the development of the specific emergency related federal and regional programs. They also provide operational management for the implementation of these programs being in charge of preparedness projects to insure the availability, reliability and effectiveness of the departmental (industrial) and regional warning and response systems, and coordinating the recovery activities. Nine federal and regional programs for prevention and mitigation of major emergencies and disasters alone were carried out in Russia between 1995 and 1997(Shoigu, 1996).

At the federal level, RUSPRE coordinating bodies are represented, first, by the Interdepartmental Commission for Emergency Prevention and Response which was organized in February 1995 and includes 38 members, mainly deputy ministers and chairmen of the respective ministries and state committees (agencies) (see Annex 2; *Pravitelstvo. Postanovleniye*, 1997). The emergency commissions of these ministries and state committees are also a part the federal coordinating bodies. At the macroregional level, these are represented by the MES nine regional centers whereas at the regional, local and organizational levels the coordination bodies involve emergency commissions (committees) of the executive authorities of the entities (members) of the Russian Federation, local authorities and organizations respectively (see Fig. 14 and 16).

The permanent operational and control bodies of the RUSPRE especially authorized to provide communities and regional protection in emergencies carry out the functions of operational planning and management by preparing contingency and operation plans and exercising administration and control of their implementation, in particular emergency preparedness and response. At the federal level, MES is the chief state body of this category within RUSPRE while at the macroregional level this role is played by the nine regional centers of the ministry. At the regional and local levels, permanent operation and control is provided by the defense and emergency headquarters or centers which are operational branches of the earlier mentioned emergency commissions of the executive authorities in the entities (members) of the Russian Federation and local authorities. At the organizational level, these functions are exercised by the civil defense and emergency departments or specially authorized persons.

Presidential Decree No. 784 and the Rules and Regulations for Civil Defense of the Russian Federation established by respective order of the Prime Minister of the Government of the Russian Federation (the chief of the Civil Defense of Russia or CDR) and enforced in 1996, provided a plan and schedule for reorganization of the civil defense system as a whole and the RUSPRE, in particular. MES together with the executive authorities in the Russian regions which were established as responsible state bodies for implementing this plan, have started its execution at the regional and local levels by reorganizing the existent civil defense and emergency headquarters (centers) into civil defense and emergency committees and offices. This should provide more flexibility to RUSPRE by bridging the current gaps between its spatial and functional subsystems (see Shoigu, 1996).

Lastly, the everyday operation and control bodies of RUSPRE provide monitoring and information support to the responsible agencies throughout the whole emergency management cycle and operational response during the culmination or emergency stage. These bodies include the crisis operation centers as well as operation and dispatch services within the especially authorized permanent operation and control bodies at all levels of the RUSPRE management bodies. In addition, they also involve on-duty and dispatch services and special units of the federal executive authorities (that is the ministries and state committees of Russia) and organizations (facilities and institutions) (see Fig. 14).

Among the basic RUSPRE functional subsystems discussed above, the main burden for both development and implementation of emergency prevention, mitigation and alleviation measures is laid on the permanent operation and control bodies especially authorized to provide protection to communities and regions. From these, the role of the Russian Federation Ministry for Civil Defense, Emergencies and Natural Disaster Response or MES should be especially pinpointed as a key coordinator in major emergencies.

Moreover, given its impressive concentration of forces and means, primarily at the federal level, the ministry should be considered as a powerful operational force as well, particularly while the largest emergencies and disasters. The latter is reinforced, first, by the incompleteness of RUSPRE functional subsystems development by the late 1990s with only a few of these including energy power, food, and transport subsystems should have been fully shaped by the end of 1997. Secondly, this stems from a shortage of trained emergency personnel and resources at the regional and local levels of the spatial subsystems of the RUSPRE.

MES is a part of the federal government of Russia. Its minister who is also the first deputy chief of Civil Defense of Russian Federation (CDR) and commander of the national Civil Defense Troops is directly subordinated to the Chairman of the Government of the Russian Federation as his chief both in the Cabinet and the CDR. As a member of the Security Council at the President's Administration, the MES minister directly reports to the President of Russia. He also heads the Interdepartmental Commission for Emergency Prevention and Response which, as already mentioned, serves as a chief federal governmental coordinator within the RUSPRE (see Fig. 14).

The structure and composition of the MES of Russia has been regularly varying in correlation with changes in goal setting predetermined by the Russian government and the president and associated with important changes in the political and social situation and sometimes with reorganizations in the Government of Russia. As of mid-1997, the ministry was composed of a central office with eight departments, a number of boards and offices and nine regional centers (see Fig. 17). In addition, it included a number of R&D and training organizations as well excluding the so-called permanent readiness forces. The latter involve a set of special organizations and units especially authorized by the government and designated to provide 24-hour monitoring, environmental, health and technological risk assessment and early response to major emergencies and/or disasters within the RUSPRE which are manned and equipped for working autonomously for 72 hours or more. The total number of employees equals 5,000 (see Vorobyev, 1996).

As mentioned earlier, coordination, especially authorized permanent operational and control bodies and everyday operational and control bodies as command and control posts at each of the basic levels of the RUSPRE are supplemented by respective forces and means which execute their commands and directives. These include forces and means which provide two main set of functions, including everyday monitoring and operational control, and emergency response.

The forces and means providing monitoring and operational control incorporate primarily the services (institutions) and organizations of the federal ministries and state committees which are responsible for and conduct environmental and medical monitoring, screening and control of hazardous facilities and adjacent areas, and risk assessment for human health both at these facilities, and neighboring and remote communities. In particular, these services and organizations include: the State Sanitation and Epidemiological Supervision Service affiliated with the Russian Federation Ministry of Public Health (MOP), Veterinary Service and institutions for supervision and laboratory control of food and food product quality which are a part the Russian Federation Ministry of Food and Agriculture (MINSELKHOZPROD of Russia); the State Fire Supervision Service of the State Fire Service (SFS) of the Ministry of Internal Affairs of the Russian Federation (MIA), permanent readiness units of the Federal Hydrometeorology and Environmental Monitoring Service of the Russian Federation (ROSGIDROMET), institutions of the Federal Mining and Industrial Supervision of Russia (GOSGORTECHNADZOR) and the Federal Supervision of Russia for Nuclear and Radiation Safety (GOSATOMNADZOR) and others.

In addition, the forces and means for monitoring and operational control of the RUSPRE involve interdepartmental organizations and services including those that are not the part of the federal government (Geophysical Service of the Russian Academy of Sciences (RAS), institutions for monitoring and laboratory control network of the CDR and some others). In recent years there has been a conspicuous trend to consolidate these forces and means under the auspices of MES. In particular, following governmental resolution No. 444 of 1993, the geophysical services of both RAS and the six federal ministries (defense, construction and others) have been integrated into the Federal Seismological Monitoring and Forecasting Service being coordinated and directed by MES.

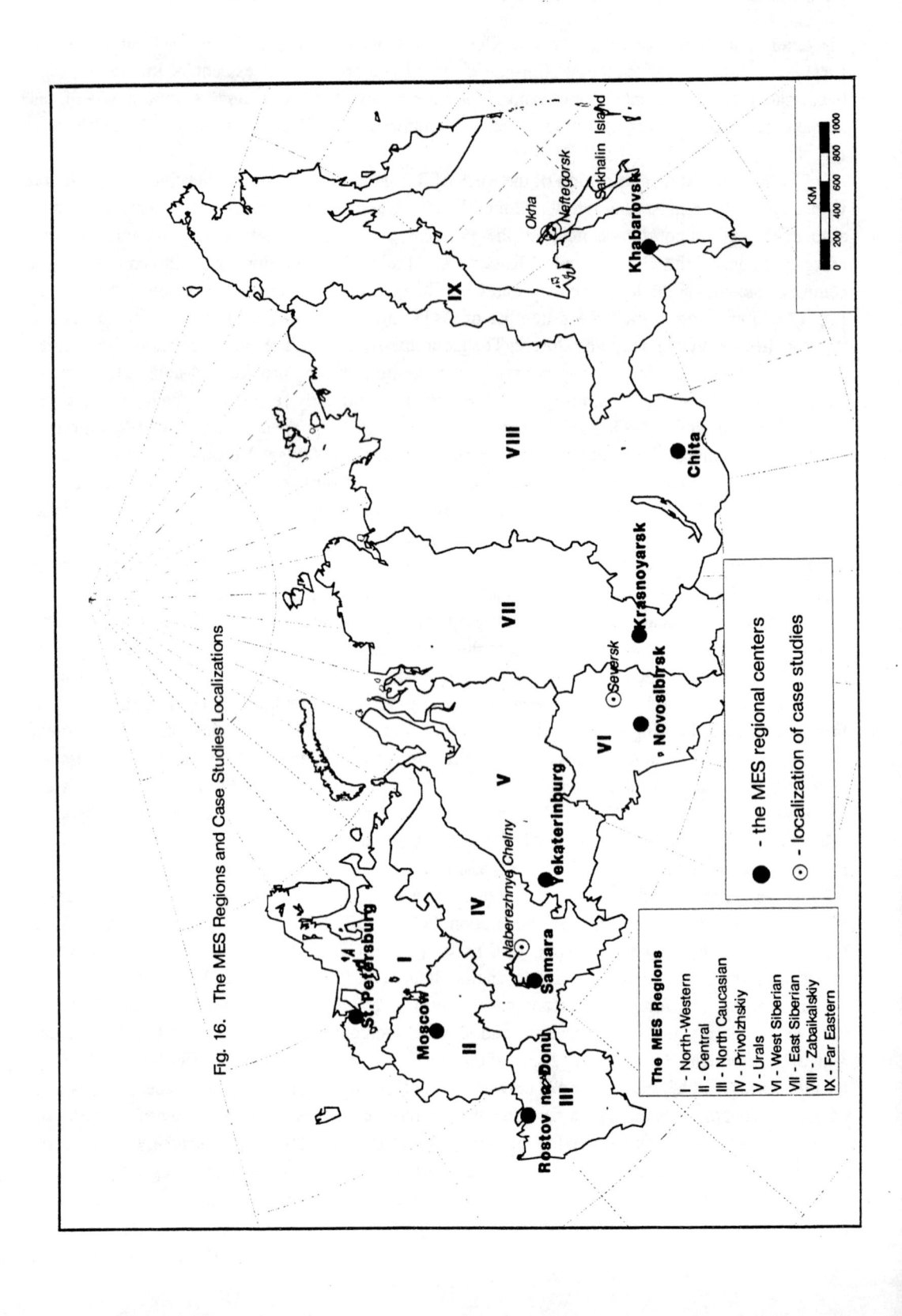

Fig. 16. The MES Regions and Case Studies Localizations

The MES Regions
I - North-Western
II - Central
III - North Caucasian
IV - Privolzhskiy
V - Urals
VI - West Siberian
VII - East Siberian
VIII - Zabaikalskiy
IX - Far Eastern

● - the MES regional centers
⊙ - localization of case studies

The forces and means for emergency response involve fire, search and rescue, emergency and rescue, emergency technical support and emergency recovery units of the federal executive authorities. These include: the combat SFS units, emergency technical centers of the Ministry of the Russian Federation for Nuclear Energy (MINATOM), emergency and rescue services and units including rescue-coordination centers of the navy, the search and emergency rescue of civil aviation flight support services of the Russian Federation Ministry of Transportation (MINTRANS); units and institutions of the All-Russia Disaster Medical Service of MOP, the Veterinary Service and Plant Protection Service of the MINSELKHOZPROD, special troops of the Russian Federation Ministry of Defense (MOD) and others.

Organic to the forces and means for emergency response are also fire, emergency technical support, emergency medical care, militia (police), civil defense units of the regional and local (including municipal) authorities, as well as construction and transportation companies and so on.

Among the forces and means of the RUSPRE, a key place is occupied by the permanent preparedness forces at the federal level which involves emergency (crisis) operation centers and operational units of the 13 federal ministries and services, these are: MES, MIA, MOP, MINATOM, MINSELKHOZPROD, MINSTROY, MINTRANS, ROSGIDROMET as well as the ministries of economy, fuel and energy power, railways, the Federal Forestry Service of Russia and the State Committee for Environmental Protection of the Russian Federation (GOSKOMPRIRODA) (see Annexes 2 and 3).

Of these, the permanent readiness forces of MES play the leading role in large scale emergencies and/or disasters. These forces include: the Central Airmobile Rescue Team or CENTROSPAS equipped with transport (IL-76) and other planes and helicopters located near the town of Zhukovskiy of the Moscow region, 58 search and rescue services and helicopter units in the four largest MES regional centers (Krasnoyarsk, Khabarovsk Moscow and Yekaterinburg) (see the map in Fig. 16) as well as the Russian Relief Operations Response Corps and the Agency for the Russia Participation Support and Coordination in International Relief Operations. The operational control of these forces and means is provided by the Crisis Operation Center in the central office of MES in Moscow and headquarters of the MES regional centers. (Vorobyev, 1996)

Within the structure of the permanent readiness forces of MES, the most manned are the combined mobile units of the Civil Defense Troop regiments, brigades and large units which in total concentrate almost 30,000 servicemen. The general leadership for these forces is provided by the President of Russia through the CDR Chief (the Prime Minister) who determines the procedure of the troops being involved while direct operational control is vested on and executed by the MES Minister who is practically a commander of these troops in time of peace. As to the units, large units of the Civil Defense Troops and CDR organizations located in the respective MES regions of the Russian Federation, these are controlled by the headquarters of the MES regional centers whereas the regionally based units subordinated to the MES central office are operated directly by the MES Minister or his deputies.

Fig 17. Organizational Structure of the MES

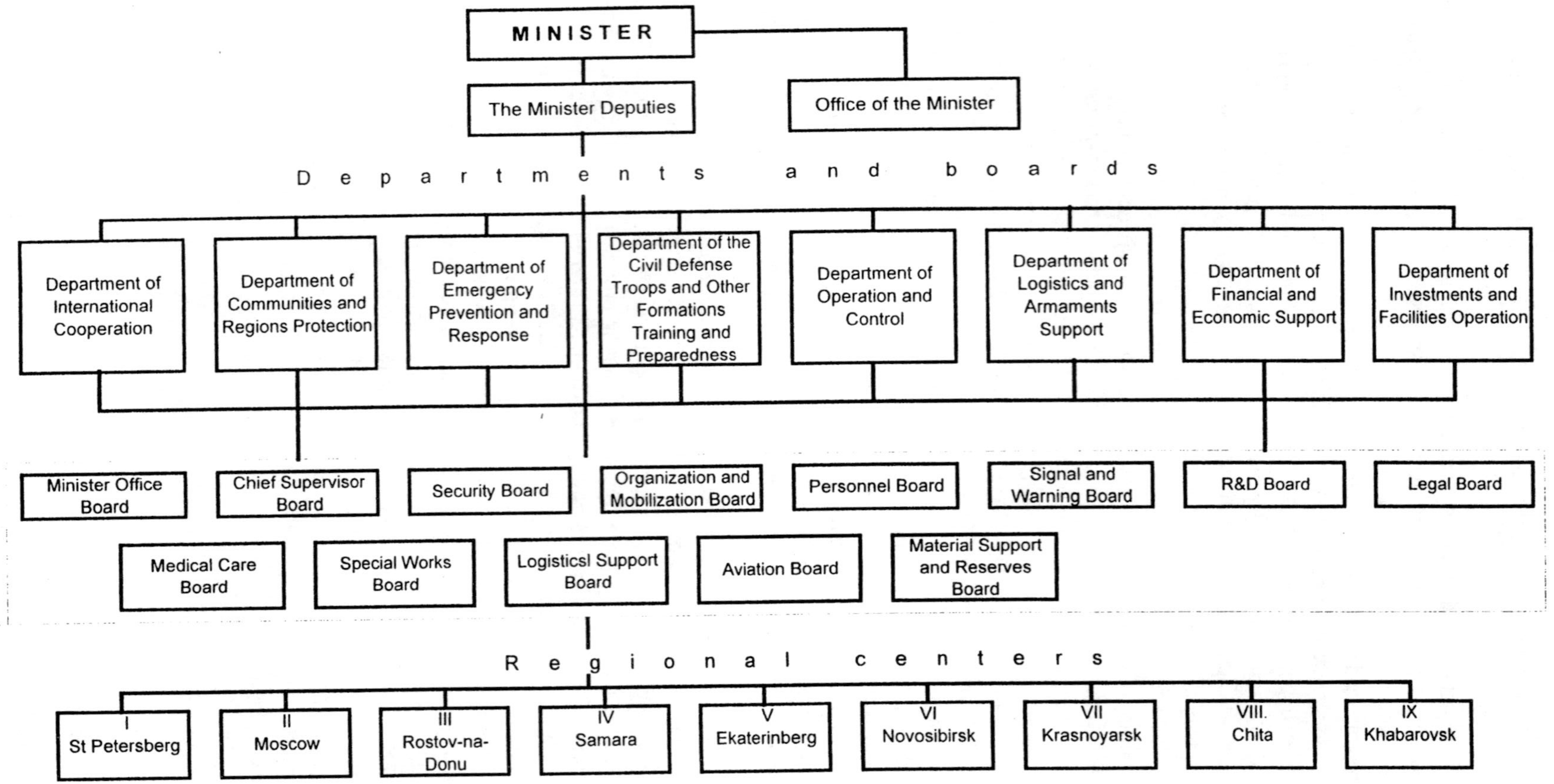

Departments and boards

- MINISTER
  - Office of the Minister
  - The Minister Deputies
    - Department of International Cooperation
    - Department of Communities and Regions Protection
    - Department of Emergency Prevention and Response
    - Department of the Civil Defense Troops and Other Formations Training and Preparedness
    - Department of Operation and Control
    - Department of Logistics and Armaments Support
    - Department of Financial and Economic Support
    - Department of Investments and Facilities Operation

Boards:
- Minister Office Board
- Chief Supervisor Board
- Security Board
- Organization and Mobilization Board
- Personnel Board
- Signal and Warning Board
- R&D Board
- Legal Board
- Medical Care Board
- Special Works Board
- Logistical Support Board
- Aviation Board
- Material Support and Reserves Board

Regional centers

I	II	III	IV	V	VI	VII	VIII	IX
St Petersberg	Moscow	Rostov-na-Donu	Samara	Ekaterinberg	Novosibirsk	Krasnoyarsk	Chita	Khabarovsk

RUSPRE OPERATIONAL ROUTINE AND CAPACITY

Depending on the situation and the scale of the expected actual emergency, a decision maker at the respective level of the RUSPRE selects one of the following three basic types of routines:
- everyday (ordinary) routines;
- alert (increased readiness) routines;
- emergency (extraordinary) routines.

The everyday routine implies the peacetime established day-to-day way of living of communities with only minor incidents and disturbances without breaking and rupturing communications and the fabric of a social system which predetermines the normal functioning of RUSPRE. The basic measures being implemented while this type of routine are those already enumerated above include a list of the RUSPRE functions and tasks except emergency response and recovery operations including relief aid. Among these, worth special note are: environmental monitoring and monitoring of the hazardous facilities carried out by the forces and means for monitoring and operational control, contingency planning, setting up and supplementing of emergency reserve funds, emergency personnel training and the public information support.

Contingency planning within the RUSPRE framework is provided on a basis of national (federal) operational response and mobilization plans, respective plans of the federal ministries, services and state committees and those of the regional authorities of the entities (members) of the Russian Federation. It also involves operational response plans of the local authorities and organizations and regional plans of emergency coordination between the RUSPRE components (participants) being developed by MES. While developing such plans, the administration of organizations and facilities including their owners and operators are vested with responsibility to assure technological and personnel safety and production continuity. The contingency plan per se should be developed by emergency and civil defense department within a given organization or facility.

Similar responsibility for contingency planning, adequate preparedness of the forces and means to stipulate efficient protection of communities and regions in Russia as well as public information support and training is laid out by the law on local and regional authorities in the entities (members) of the Russian Federation. The plans are prepared at the emergency and civil defense headquarters (centers) and then scrutinized and approved by local and regional emergency and civil defense committees or commissions. Along with the MES regional centers these also organize training, field exercises in order to check the degree of preparedness of both communities and the RUSPRE subsystems with methodological guidance and organizational leadership over the planning process as a whole being provided by MES.

Although peculiarities associated with each facility and region require for specific contingency and operational plans, all of them should necessarily contain the following elements :
- description of the composition of an operational command center and procedure (schedule) for its staff involvement in an emergency;
- list and localization of organizational, local and regional crisis or operation centers (civil defense and emergency headquarters);
- characteristics of the forces and means involved in emergency response including their special equipment, means of communication, transportation and logistic support;
- description of a warning procedure and means and response preparedness of the respective forces and means;

- characteristics of boarding places and the available routes of the forces and means transportation to an emergency area, including calculations of various options of this transportation by different means and methods ;
- list of tasks and functions of specific units and description of a procedure for their interaction during emergency response;
- characteristics of the security and safety measures.

This information should be presented both as a text and graphics (maps, diagrams) and supplemented by a comprehensive presentation of the operation or served area with distinct administrative borders, natural, demographic and socioeconomic specifics including hazardous facilities and hazard prone areas.

The everyday routine of RUSPRE activities also involves organization of and providing additional supplies to emergency funds and material and technical reserves. These reserves are accumulated by the federal ministries and regional and local authorities at the expense of the corresponding budgets and by organizations at their own expense. In addition, the State Reserve Fund and Federal Emergency Fund are organized by the Government of Russia at the expense of the federal budget to provide material and financial resources to compensate the affected people (injured, homeless and others) and support the most urgent recovery works, respectively. In 1997, the budget of the Federal Emergency Fund amounted to 1,300 billion rubles or almost US$ 250 million..

The alert (increased readiness) routine implies the RUSPRE components functioning in the perceived or actual worsening of geophysical, radiation, chemical, biological and other conditions which have been forecasted and/or assessed as early indicators of the forthcoming emergency and/or disaster. The basic measures implemented while this type of routine include:
- taking responsibility for direct operational control over the RUSPRE subsystems and units by the operational centers which are organized by the emergency and civil defense commissions, and, if necessary, organization operational reconnaissance and express assessment units to reveal the reasons for a situation being deteriorated and provide recommendations for its normalization;
- intensification of the on-duty and dispatch services operation;
- intensification of environmental monitoring and operational control and that at the hazardous facilities and adjacent areas, short-term emergency forecasting;
- carrying out social and environmental protection measures and those contributing to the reduction of risk associated with the hazardous facilities;
- providing adequate alert preparedness of the forces and means designated for emergency response, specification of their operational plans of action and, if necessary, their advancement (transportation) to an area of the expected emergency.

The extraordinary routine implies that the RUSPRE components operate in conditions of an actual emergency and strive for alleviation and elimination of its social and environmental effects. At this phase of response, the necessary measures involve:
- organization of community protection (evacuation, timely sheltering, etc.);
- preventive boundary delineation of an emergency area;
- advancement (transportation) of the operational response units within the permanent readiness forces to an emergency area and its cordoning;
- conducting response operations including search and rescue, fire extinguishing, urgent medical care support to and evacuation of the affected people and so forth:
- organization of temporary shelters and supplies of water, food, clothing and so on, immediate restoration of electricity, gas, communication and other life lines, resuming the functioning of industrial facilities and business organizations;

- providing 24-hour environmental and social monitoring and operational control in the emergency area, especially at the hazardous facilities and adjacent zones.

The procedure of response (including immediate recovery measures) to an emergency and sequential involvement of the RUSPRE forces and means, is much similar to that existing in many developed countries of the world and corresponds to the requirement of enough sufficiency and maximum utilization of the available resources for saving people, rescuing material values and protecting the environment. This presumes a gradual increase of the forces and means being involved in response and then recovery activities along with reconsideration of the degree of social and environmental risk or danger. The more the situation in the emergency area turns to the worse and transforms into a major disaster or a catastrophe, the higher is the RUSPRE level and its capabilities involved.

The organization of recovery from an emergency or disaster has been traditionally the prerogative of local authorities and organizations which use the available forces and means located in the affected area, primarily fire, police, medical care and other emergency services. If the scale and gravity of an emergency are beyond their capabilities, the local administration applies for external help. More frequently this appeal goes to the federal government rather than to the authorities of the neighboring and more distant regions of Russia given the preserved 'centrality syndrome' of the local and regional administrators with concentration of economic and administrative powers remaining in the hands of the federal authorities.

At the response phase, the mayors and governors of the affected regions apply to forces and means of the regional MES operation centers. If the situation is too complicated to be handled by them, the latter immediately call for the help of CENTROSPAS and the civil defense units of the neighboring regions. forces. In case of a macroregional or national (federal) emergencies (see Table 12) upon the inquiry of the MES minister and/or in view of an utmost need for imposing the state of emergency, the President of the Russian Federation may take a decision to use the army units of MOD and other units and troops to cope with an emergency as soon and efficient as possible.

The national and international emergency and disaster legislation, and the principles, goal, functions and organizational structure and composition of the RUSPRE discussed above provide a general picture of the emergency and disaster policy and emergency management in Russia. However, its real capability to effectively prevent, respond and alleviate an emergency and/or disaster is far from being decisively determined by the logical and organizational design merits or, vice versa, shortcomings of this general framework. Given the inseparable interrelationship between the political and economic system and conditions, on one hand, and emergency and disaster policy, on the other hand, the efficiency of the latter policy as a whole and RUSPRE, in particular, are dependent on the socioeconomic policy and influenced by peculiarities of the social space and time of a specific emergency or disaster and concrete decisions made during it.

In this connection, an evaluation of both the RUSPRE system and its operational environment in the 1990s would be somewhat ambiguous. The relatively prompt organization and progressive development of this system are obviously a substantial achievement. Its other merits involve the coverage of all main functions and levels of the authorities, and compatibility of the RUSPRE organizational pattern with a number of important peculiarities of the Russian environment. In particular, it implies the system's bias towards mitigation of and response to major technological accidents in the big cities and industrial centers as well as organizational and local scale emergencies which like the technological accidents, prevail within the total number and social and environmental effects of non-conflict type emergencies in the 1990s.

All this has contributed to the success of the response operations in the five-year period of the RUSPRE existence (from 1992 to 1997). The most important of these include: prevention of large-scale accidents at the Ufa oil refinery, and the localization of a large epizootic in the Sayan Mountains in 1992, localization of the environmental effect associated with the major accident at a nuclear-powered submarine *'Komsomolets'* in the Norwegian Sea, and rescue of many people while responding to the Kuril and Neftegorsk earthquake disasters in 1994 and 1995, respectively. The evacuation and relief aid to tens of thousands of civilians in the Chechen Republic during the regional war in 1994-1996 should be added to this list. It also includes the immediate response to and recovery from emergencies provoked by explosions of residential buildings in the towns of Svetogorsk and Priozersk in the St. Petersburg region, and that in the town of Kaspiisk in the Republic of Daghestan being a result of a terrorist act in 1996. Worth special note are MES relief operations abroad: between 1993 and 1996 alone, their total number exceeded 20 covering the affected regions in Africa, Asia, Central America and Europe (see Annex 3)

This substantial contribution to communities and regional protection in non-conflict type emergencies (leaving out the conflict type crisis) has been provided by not only by MES units but by forces and means of other executive authority bodies as well. These forces and means for decades were used almost exclusively within the framework of their own organizational systems and actually are a part the developing RUSPRE system. At organizational and local levels and often at a regional level the key preparedness, response and partially recovery efforts are undertaken by the fire, militia (police) and medical units which are mostly involved in coping with the bulk of both conflict and non-conflict emergencies and disasters.

At the same time, an analysis of the RUSPRE organizational structure, in particular the spatial distribution and operational composition of its forces and means, as well as its information, technical and logistics support, reveals serious shortcomings and certain non-compliance of the system's capacity to the actual and perspective needs of communities and regional protection in emergencies. These primarily involve inadequate strength of the local and regional search and rescue units and those of the civil defense troops. In particular they involve the shortage of the clearing units which provide obstacle and debris removal to allow the rescue units and medical teams access to the affected area. There is also a lack of sanitary care and especially relief units to provide sanitation, water, meals, clothes and sheltering to the affected people. and primary life-support to the victims. For example, even the densely populated and industrially developed regions in the European part and North Caucasus of Russia dispose only of 20% of the needed civil defense forces and means that restrain the volume of the basic rescue operations being carried out there by 60% only (See Yarigin, 1996).

In addition, the existing organization and technical support of the RUSPRE, including the quality of information and communication systems, still preclude efficient and rapid mobilization of response forces and means under conditions of emergency. The alert preparedness time-span of response units in the mid 1990s varied from one and a half hours to 10 days, i.e., far from requirements for a modern response organization. Lastly, given the existing transportation problems, especially the shortage of transportation means, the concentration of the RUSPRE forces and means in big cities, primarily MES regional centers, limits the response capabilities of the rescue and other units in remote and difficult-to-reach areas of Russia. This reduces the total volume of the rescue and technical support works to be done to approximately 20% being carried out primarily during organizational and local emergencies.

The main reasons for this are rooted in the organizational loopholes of the RUSPRE, in particular, incompleteness and insufficient flexibility of its structure and lack of important units within its staff, as well as a comparatively short time of the system's operation. Even more important is the impact being produced on the RUSPRE by the lasting and deep socioeconomic crisis in Russia which resulted in a shortage of emergency funds and material supplies in the

1990s. For example, the federal budget expenditures for the civil defense troop modernization and reorganization program in 1996-2000, which should provide for reducing the time for search and rescue by three or four times, and the number of casualties and material losses by 1.5-2-fold, respectively should amount to 3,663 billion rubles (Yarigin, 1996: 9). Even if this indicator is successfully achieved, I seriously doubt whether the real needs of the RUSPRE in this respect would be covered by one third.

As to the impact of the socioeconomic and environmental peculiarities and specific circumstances of a concrete emergency on response and recovery efficiency of RUSPRE units, I shall discuss these in the next chapter while studying certain cases which involve various non-conflict type emergencies. Primarily considered are the basic functional subsystems of the RUSPRE: accident prevention and response at nuclear power plants, fire and rescue and militia (police) units, as well as its spatial subsystems in three entities of the Russian Federation (the Republic of Tatarstan, and the Tomsk and Sakhalin regions) and the RUSPRE system as a whole.

CHAPTER 4

EMERGENCY MANAGEMENT IN RUSSIA IN PRACTICE: CASE STUDIES OF THE 1990S

This chapter involves ramifications of both the theoretical and applied issues of emergency and disaster policy and emergency management in Russia discussed above. It deals with three case studies of the most hazardous and devastating natural and technological emergencies which occurred in the main regions of the country, namely: the European part, Siberia and the Far East, in the 1990s. Their localization is shown on map in the Fig. 16.

In some respect these events, including a serious radiation accident and major fire and earthquake disasters, have turned out to be the worst in the Russia and even in modern world history of catastrophes. However, the gravity of the aftermath, whatever worth considering, is not the only criterion for the cases have been selected. Even more important are the commonalties and peculiarities of the management practice to prevent and cope with these tragic events, especially those of public administration that plays a key role in mitigating and alleviating of accidents and disasters in Russia. Given the specific characteristics of and availability of data on each case selected, I had to attribute different priorities and accents to various aspects and phases of the management cycle, while scrutinizing the degree and pattern of involvement of local, regional and federal authorities and emergency services (fire, medical and so on). At the same time, the precondition deep fact and triggering events in each case studied are treated with more 'equal' profundity.

THE AFTERMATH AND RESPONSE TO THE RADIATION ACCIDENT AT THE SIBERIAN CHEMICAL COMPLEX: REMINISCENT OF CHERNOBYL?

INTRODUCTION

The town of Tomsk-7 (also known as Seversk) is situated on the bank of the Tom River, 15 km to the northwest of Tomsk, an administrative center of the West Siberian region (*oblast*) with 500,000 citizens. The population of Seversk, about 150,000, mainly consists of people who work at the Siberian Chemical Complex (SCC) and members of their families. The emergence of this town in the late 1940s was directly correlated with the erecting of a special military-industrial

enriched uranium and plutonium for nuclear warheads. Analogous enterprises were constructed nearly at the same time in the shadow town of Cheliabinsk-65 (now called Ozersk) in the Urals region and the shadow town of Krasnoiarsk-26 or Zheleznogorsk in the East Siberia region. At a later date industrial functions of these facilities and the SCC were supplemented with the recycling of the processed reactor fuel for nuclear power plants (Illesh and Kostyukovskiy, 1993b).

The military profile of the main industrial complex of the town that existed for more than 40 years naturally predetermined the secret status of Seversk. Up to the late 1980s, the public knew nothing about the existence and functions of this town which did not even appear in USSR maps. At present, the status of the town has been somewhat softened but the bulk of the earlier restrictions, primarily regarding the SCC, still exist.

The first nuclear reactor was put into action in 1951, and later was supplemented with four other uranium and graphite channel reactors (or Chernobyl-type) reactors. Following the recent industrial conversion strategy, three of them which once enriched uranium and plutonium for nuclear warheads, have had their operations suspended. The other two have kept their recycling operations and produce electricity and heat for Seversk and Tomsk, covering 100% and 40%, respectively, of the needs of these towns (Illesh and Kostyukovskiy, 1993a; Illesh and Kostyukovskiy, 1993b). However M. Wald from the *New York Times* suggests that only a quarter of Tomsk electricity needs are met by the two reactors (Wald, 1994).

The start of conversion also led to initiatives to deploy a depository for dismantled nuclear warheads in Seversk, thus objectively increasing both nuclear and radiation risks. Besides recycled uranium and plutonium for foreign and federal nuclear power plants and electricity and heat for adjacent communities, both consumer goods and special chemicals with unique characteristics have also been supplied by the SCC's factories (Tsarev, 1993).

At one of those factories - the radiochemical plant, located 15 km from Seversk and 28 km from Tomsk (see Fig. 16) - on April 6, 1993 at 12:58 a.m. (local time) an explosion of an extractor filled with a radioactive solution resulted in destruction of the apparatus and the containment building and emission of radionucleides into the environment, where they were deposited mainly on uninhabited territory. The radiation emitted and doses absorbed outside the site of the plant site and its protection zone in general were well below standard safety levels.

This motivated the officials and federal departments involved to assess the situation in April 1993 as:

> medically non-hazardous but still requiring control and certain technical and organizational countermeasures to reduce the potential irradiation of the population (Akt, 1993).

They also widely stressed that according to the International Atomic Energy Agency (IAEA) scale, the situation should be treated as a serious incident (level III) that was in no way comparable with Chernobyl and thus it was not regarded as a significant industrial crisis. Even more, next month, in May 1993 another official report came to the conclusion on

> inexpediency of undertaking urgent measures to protect the local population and environment (Tomsk-7, 1993).

However, as early as in July 1993 the Supreme Soviet (parliament) of the Russian Federation issued a special regulation followed by the governmental order that treated the accident as a rather serious occurrence requiring both federal and regional authorities taking substantial measures to mitigate the consequences of the accident and compensate the inflicted damage including providing medical care support to the suffered SCC personnel and local communities of the Tomsk *oblast* and environmental safety for this region (see: *Verkhovnii Sovet. Postanovleniye*, 1993; *Pravitelstvo. Rasporiazheniye*, 1993). Moreover these official documents viewed the accident as a precedent necessitating substantial changes in issuance of operational licenses to nuclear energy and industrial facilities as well as development of the federal "targeted" program on radiation safety of those facilities.

The following analysis of the causes and consequences as well as preparedness, response to and recovery from the radiation accident at the SCC corroborates its seriousness and proves that although the scales are really incomparable, some parallels between this accident and Chernobyl disaster important from the viewpoint of disaster and emergency management can be and should be drawn.

A SYSTEM ANALYSIS OF THE CAUSES

The accident at the SCC resulted from a complex of both political and socioeconomic conditions that may be treated as a set of *external* factors, and interdependent human, organizational and technological errors and flaws within the SCC that can be viewed as *internal* factors. Earlier studies by other researchers suggest that such factors are practically organic to every industrial crisis (see Kates, Hohenemser and Kasperson, 1985; Kasperson and Kasperson, 1988; Mitroff, Pauchant and Shrivastava, 1988; Lagadec, 1990; Meshkati, 1991; Quarantelli, 1992; Clarke and Short, 1993). To show how the whole cluster of factors developed and resulted in an explosion and to make the system analysis dynamic, I will add to it a time dimension thus converting and at the same time amending the dichotomy of external and internal factors with another dual framework involving *deep* or antecedent and *direct* or immediate prerequisites and causes of the accident.

The links in the causal chain of events that led to the accident are undoubtedly related with the latter and lie within the organization, i.e. inside the SCC, that failed to provide adequate personnel training, technological auditing and operations control, etc. for preventing the explosion. Meanwhile, the initial and perhaps key elements of that chain should be looked for outside the SCC and Seversk. We believe that the roots of not only the accident, but also antecedent radiation emergencies--including the worst and most famous cases of Cheliabinsk-40 (now the town of Ozersk) in 1957 and Chernobyl in 1986 as well--are deep and intrinsically rooted in the specific historical development of the Soviet and Russian nuclear complex systems (Porfiriev et al, 1993).

DEEP OR EXTERNAL PREREQUISITES: MILITARY-POLITICAL CAUSES

The international situation in the mid 1940s, the race for leadership in getting an atomic bomb between Germany, the USA and the USSR, predetermined for decades ahead the basic direction of research and development (R & D) in the nuclear field. Since that very time, in the peripheral, practically non-populated areas of the Soviet Union, a process was initiated of erecting ten "shadow" (i.e. not public) towns, led by Cheliabinsk-40 and Seversk, within which were secret facilities for producing uranium for nuclear warheads. The present day population of these towns totals one million. The same or nearly the same process of building secret nuclear plants took place in the USA and the United Kingdom thus insuring many common problems in the development of all nuclear complexes.

Among the most important has been the nuclear and radiation safety of the personnel of the plants, the neighboring communities, and the environment. On the other hand, the nearly exclusive orientation towards the urgent development of new weapons set back attempts at solutions of critical R & D issues, e.g., how low radiation doses impacted human health was replaced by studying the effects of large doses that are typical for nuclear warfare radiation. Also other practical issues, including human, technological and organizational aspects of nuclear and radiation safety were often neglected.

That could not but increase the risk in functioning nuclear facilities. It was quite natural that the first accidents in 1957 occurred just at those military nuclear plants in Windscale in the UK, and Cheliabinsk-40 in the USSR. Nearly at the same time the first though less serious accidents started to occur at the SCC nuclear facilities in Seversk. In total, for more than a 40 year period from 1951 on, there occurred 23 accidents that were never publicly reported (Biychaninova and Nekrasov, 1993; Gordon, 1994; Kostyukovskiy, 1993; Tchernikh, 1993a).

TOTAL SECRECY AND WEAKNESS OF LEGAL REGULATION

A veil of secrecy covered not only the Soviet military nuclear programs and facilities, but those in other countries as well, in the UK in particular. For example, detailed information concerning the earlier mentioned radiation accident at Windscale was declassified by the British government only in 1988 or more than 30 years later (Liutiy, 1988). But in the former Soviet Union the problem was somewhat different. Until the late 1980s the increasing number of classified military nuclear facilities preserved a policy of total secrecy. This restricted the access of even local personnel to routine information concerning radiation impacts on human health, let alone local communities. Scientists and engineers working at those top secret complexes could get only limited data relevant to their specific professional rank or orientation, and never got information on closely related issues.

As a result, serious problems in dealing with early warning and safety system development and for the learning of lessons from previous shortcomings in the design and construction of nuclear industrial plants, were never comprehensively addressed. This contributed to the recurrence of incidents and accidents at those plants including the SCC where emergencies actually occurred about once every two years.

In recent years, secrecy about the shadow towns was somewhat lessened, most of all because of the enactment of the 1992 Federal Act on Classified Administrative and Territorial Formations. But it is still not easy for plant personnel and especially local communities to get any important information (see Kariakina, 1993). Moreover the majority of the local population of the shadow towns voted in favor of keeping the numerous restrictions while referenda in early 1990s (Kostyukovskiy and Perepletkin 1991) and still support this policy.

The secrecy factor has been especially responsible for weakness in legal regulation of the nuclear complexes for many decades. In a closed organizational and information system there was no need and possibility for the development and enactment of laws that could guarantee persons or communities legal protection against nuclear and radiation hazards. As to nuclear plant personnel, their status was tightly regulated by instructions regarding their obligations and limitations but with little legal support for their rights.

As was mentioned earlier (see Chapter 3) despite substantial sociopolitical changes in Russia and other former Soviet republics since the late 1980s, the situation about nuclear legal regulations still remains complicated. On one hand Federal Act for the Social Protection of Citizens Who Suffered from the Chernobyl Disaster was enforced in 1991 providing important community rights, including right-to-know information on radiation accident consequences, and also some compensation and preferences(i.e., privileges), etc. to victims and their families. As late as 1995 two paramount and long expected laws - Nuclear Energy Act and Radiation Safety of the Population Act - were enforced though in the USA and Europe those have been used for several decades.

On other hand no less important laws like the Nuclear Damage Compensation and Insurance Act (analogous to Anderson-Price Act in the USA), Radioactive Wastes Storage and Handling Act, Communities Right to Know Act although drafts of some of them had been developed as early as 1991 and having analogues elsewhere in the world, have not yet been adopted. Unfortunately contradictions between presidential and parliament branches of state power as well as federal and regional authorities among other reasons delayed and keep impeding the enactment of a number of the key laws and regulations thus limiting both the right of communities for protection against risks connected with nuclear plants, and the obligatory responsibility of owners to provide this protection for plant personnel (see Kariakina, 1993).

NEGLECTING THE PRIORITY OF HUMAN FACTORS

Among the deep or antecedent prerequisites and causes of the SCC accident, one should especially emphasize the multiyear trend of declining attention by Soviet and Russian top rank party and state officials responsible for economic progress in general and the military and industrial complex development in particular, towards so-called human factors in nuclear and radiation safety. This trend began in the mid 1950s and affected both the nuclear scientists and engineers and the operating personnel of the nuclear facilities.

Academician Valeriy Legasov, well known to the world thanks to his outstanding activities during Chernobyl crisis, made the following comment on the situation in Soviet nuclear science in the 1960-mid 1980s:

> Research organizations once powerful in the country were losing having the most modern equipment, were confronted with aging personnel and restrictions on new methods and approaches...There has grown a generation of engineers well trained in their specific areas of activities, but not treating critically the reactors and safety systems (Legasov, 1988)

Since the mid 1950s salaries in R & D sector had been decreasing although within 1940-1970 they still exceeded those paid in other branches of the national economy. Starting from 1970 the situation had been changing to the worse and the level of salaries in the R & D sector including nuclear research was less than in industry and construction as a whole. As far as operating personnel of the nuclear plants is concerned, an effective economic system for labor motivation based on paying substantial bonuses for good safety records since late 1950s had been substituted step by step by a considerable increase in salaries and a conspicuous cutting of those bonuses. In the following decades this naturally led to negative qualitative changes among personnel, and helped augment the number of incidents and accidents at the nuclear plants.

THE ROLE OF SOCIOPOLITICAL AND ECONOMIC CHANGES IN THE LATE 1980S AND IN THE 1990S

Since the latter half of the 1980s the situation in Soviet nuclear science and industry has become even more complicated. Perestroika, which encompassed both the Chernobyl disaster and the further dissolution of the Soviet Union, was accompanied by a drastic decrease in sociopolitical priority of and financial support for relevant R & D activities for functioning nuclear plants and constructing new facilities. As a result the most dramatic negative changes in financing nuclear R & D and research sector in general occurred in early 1990s. In 1992, a year before the SCC accident, the average salary paid there was only 70.9.8% of that in the national economy and 59.9% in industry. In 1995 these figures were slightly better 75% and 65%, respectively (Burtseva and Motova, 1996). This forced many talented and highly qualified nuclear specialists in Russia to leave their laboratories and plants for business or emigrate overseas.

In addition deep economic crisis started in the early 1990s, primarily tardiness or complete lacking of consumers' payments transfers to electricity producers and substantial delays in paying salaries to the personnel of nuclear power plants considerably worsened the situation in the shadow towns and nuclear industry that could not but impact negatively on the integral safety of the nuclear facilities prior the SCC accident. As a result, nuclear plants in Russia continue to suffer from numerous malfunctions, incidents and sometime accidents. For example, even after the Chernobyl disaster, in 1987-1991, former Soviet plants suffered about 30 fires and in 1993 alone, two serious incidents occurred at the earlier mentioned nuclear complex in Snezhinsk (Cheliabinsk-40), resulting from the poor quality of the equipment and shortcomings in the training and performance of operators and managers. These very factors served as the direct or internal ones for causing the SCC accident.

THE DIRECT CAUSES AND DEVELOPMENT OF THE ACCIDENT

In May, 1993, the special governmental commission including representatives from responsible governmental departments and services such as the Ministry for Nuclear Energy--that is MINATOM; the Nuclear Regulatory Committee--that is GOSATOMNADZOR; and the State Committee for Civil Defense, Emergencies and Natural Disaster Response - that is EMERCOM (since 1994 the Ministry of the Russian Federation for Civil Defense, Emergencies and Natural Disaster Response or MES) presented an official report with an agreed upon version of the case (Akt, 1993; Biychaninova and Nekrasov, 1993). However as shown further even several years after the explosion there has been no consensus shared by all experts and the public on details of what were the causes of the accident.

THE SITUATION PRIOR TO THE ACCIDENT

Early on the morning of April 6, 1993, routine quarterly operations were initiated at the extractor of uranium and plutonium. The latter represented a 34.1 m^3 vessel made from stainless steel and located underground at a depth of 10.4 m. About 4 m^3 of nitrogen acid solution of uranium derived from an extraction of uranium, plutonium, neptunium and thorium was put into the apparatus. At that time it contained a total of 8,773 kg of uranium, 310 g of plutonium, 248 g of neptunium and 142 g of thorium and some organic fractions from a solution that had not been adequately purified at previous technological processing stages.

A few hours later, at approximately at 11:00 a.m., one more portion of the analogous solution of nitrogen acid was added. In total, directly before the accident, the vessel contained about 21 m^3 of nitrogen acid solution of uranium with an activity of 537 Ci of alpha- and 22 Ci of beta-radiation respectively, which could be explained by the earlier removal of the most hazardous nuclei including plutonium (Arutiunian et al, 1993; Illesh and Kostyukovskiy, 1993a; Illesh, 1993b; Kunitsina, 1993; Tchernikh, 1993b).

THE TRIGGERING EVENT

Inadequate purging of organic matter from the solution and excessive concentration of nitrogen acid should be considered as the initial prerequisites or causes of the accident, which were later greatly aggravated by operator's manipulations. Operator F, performed the last manipulation with an improper mixing and managed it poorly, thus inaugurating a catalytic dissolution process that facilitated the creation of an organic solution which further reacted with nitrogen acid. This reaction, characterized by a chain effect and the creation of large volumes of vapor and gases prone to explosion, predetermined a chemical rather than nuclear origin of the accident that followed. There were no existing conditions for a nuclear chain reaction at all.

Having detected the increased pressure in the vessel, the operator opened the valve to cut the pressure down, but loosened it only partially, thus violating the standard procedure for removing gases from the apparatus and starting the sequence of events. Moreover, operators were too late in switching on the special pressure safety system, which was not foolproof, and in six minutes the pressure reach 17 atmospheres or 3.5 times the standard for reliability. Given that the reliability coefficient in this apparatus was only two (against an international standard for such a device of five), the critical pressure level was naturally surpassed (Illesh and Kostyukovskiy, 1993b; Illesh, 1993b; Kostyukovskiy, 1993; Biychaninova and Nekrasov, 1993).

HUMAN, ORGANIZATIONAL AND TECHNOLOGICAL FACTORS AND THEIR CULMINATION

The vessel cracked and gases leaked into the protection chamber where they were ignited by a spark and exploded. The upper cover of the extractor was torn away and the walls of the chamber were destroyed, thus very much resembling the situation in the Chernobyl disaster case. The radioactive gases start to flow into the environment through the big hole made by the explosion, but they were blocked by a northwesterly wind, which blew into the hole at a speed of 9-12 m / s. That is why the main outflow from the ruined vessel was coming from the ventilation system equipped with filters that were not designed for such emergency emissions. The explosion also resulted in ignition of technical garbage inside the building and of a small part of the 11-meter-high roof which was made from combustible materials.

Outside the building the temperature was 3.2 Centigrade and between 3:00 p.m. and up to 1:00 a.m. of the next day the wet snowfall facilitated the accelerated fallout (mainly on the surface inside the safety protective zone around the plant) from the radionuclide cloud as it moved to the north east. The emergency situation forced technological processes to be suspended and about three hours after the explosion, at approximately 4:00 p.m., the aerosol emission ceased (Akt, 1993; Biychaninova and Nekrasov, 1993; Semenchenko, 1993; Tchernikh, 1993a; Tchernikh, 1993b).

When they assessed the input of each of the human, technological and organizational factors to the development of the accident, all commissions that participated in the official investigation laid particular stress upon the role of operator errors and insufficiency in automatic control system. However, a few experts who scrutinized the direct causes of the accident gave priority to design shortcomings of the apparatus.

The latter point is argued particularly by N. Guriev (Guriev, 1993), a specialist working at the afflicted plant He cited extensively the results of US and British research work on analogous explosions in those countries as well as the previous accidents at the SCC more than a 30 years before. These research works found that explosions stem from the inappropriateness of extraction technology *per se*, which under certain conditions might cause a expansive effect that could not be contained. That is why Guriev argued that the responsibility for the SCC accident should be shared not only by the plant operators, but also by the design engineers and the examining commission that licensed the plant to operate.

Other experts noted that the radioactive components processed in the plant's extractor came from France and believed that the very origin of the raw materials played a key role in starting the accident. The French processed uranium, which is more or less close to its Russian analog in some respects, contains a higher concentration of a few uranium isotopes that favor additional radiation and heat emission. This determines the difference in technology for processing Russian and French uranium, and if it was a mix of those two types of uranium inside the extractor, the lack of a respective separation scheme would lead to an overheating, resulting in an explosion (Belianinov, 1993).

All versions, mentioned above, of the causes of the SCC accident were made public in mid 1993 and by now have still not been officially rejected. Thus every version can be treated as equally possible. Summing them up, one may conclude that the loopholes or shortcomings in the apparatus design, its technology control and safety systems, should be considered as the main culprits of this serious accident, while operator errors served as a trigger. Combustible materials used in the chamber roof was an aggravating factor, the mitigating factors of the accident were its timing and prevailing meteorological conditions, which favored containment.

Even in retrospect it is hard to be completely sure about the nature of the mentioned human shortcomings, but at least two circumstances should be stressed. First, poor training, upgrading and supervising of technical personnel and the administrative discipline and performance were marked in particular by a sharp decrease in the number of plant inspections and a weaknesses in internal safety organization and in planning procedures.

Secondly, psychological aspects of the safe management of complex technological systems like the extractor in the SCC were ignored or neglected. A few years previously, this point had been particularly stressed by the experts studying the causes of the Chernobyl disaster. In particular, they underlined the negative impact of an unfavorable geomagnetic situation on the personnel performing experiments at the Chernobyl nuclear power plant at night on April 25, 1986. Regarding the SCC accident, the same causes of high explosion risk at aging nuclear plants were pointed out as early as January and March 1993 by I. Gavrilin, a research fellow of the Biological Institute of the Siberian Chapter of the Russian Academy of Sciences (Vzriv, 1993). He warned first the federal government and later the regional authorities about the hazard and recommended the suspension of the operation of nuclear reactors. Although it would be unrealistic to follow that advice fully sense was unrealistic, such warnings should have been taken seriously and in a timely way in order to strengthen supervision and control over both the nuclear devices and the personnel.

THE CONSEQUENCES OF THE ACCIDENT AND ITS ASSESSMENT

The Scale of Radioactive Contamination of the Environment

The main and direct result of the explosion was the radioactive contamination of the surrounding territory. According to an estimate of ROSGIDROMET (The Federal Hydrometeorology and Environmental Monitoring Service of the Russian Federation), the total emission volume varied from 40 to 400 Ci for beta- and 0.2-0.6 for alpha (Pt^{239}) isotope activity. Thus, the maximum emission values for both isotopes did not exceed 20% and 3.1%, respectively, of the activity in the apparatus before the accident (Arutiunian et al, 1993) and at the same time were 50-100 thousand times less than activity of the emissions which followed the Southern Urals (Cheliabinsk-65) and Chernobyl radiation disasters in 1957 and 1986, respectively.

In general, the radioactive contamination of the land resulting from the SCC accident resembles that from Chernobyl in the sense that it was uneven and spotty, and thus caused substantial spatial differencein radiation levels and densities. This makes it difficult to estimate accurately the area of the polluted territory. There has been a rather wide spectrum of the contamination scale assessments, including those for the site of the plant where the fallout was greatest. L. Khasanov, the head of the technology department of the plant, believed the plant's roof, where the gamma radiation exposure dose rate equaled 2 mR / h, was the most irradiated place, while the EMERCOM experts argued that the radiation value here was 300 times greater, reaching 650 mR / h (Akt, 1993; Kunitsina, 1993).

According to experts' preliminary data for the day after the SCC accident (7 April), the radiation exposure dose level "at the explosion site" was 30 mR / h (Illesh and Kostyukovskiy, 1993a) or 200 times more than the natural radiation level and 50 times above the health protection standard. A week later, the EMERCOM experts specified that the radiation exposure dose level reached 5 R / h at a distance of 1.5 m from the extractor, or nearly 170 times greater than the figure mentioned earlier, while 15-20 m away from the plant's walls it varied from 0.25 to 45 mR / h (Akt, 1993).

Alternative information sources argued that measuring radiation exposure dose levels directly at the explosion's epicenter, even in May, after intensive deactivation, showed that level skyrocketed to 10-15 R / h (Kostyukovskiy, 1993) or twice as large as the EMERCOM and MINATOM reported. It is of note in any case that the last two assessment values exceed natural radiation exposure levels by three orders of magnitude! In June 1993, supposedly due to effective deactivation countermeasures, the dose level substantially decreased to 0.1-0.2 mR / h. At the site of the plant, within the 100 µR / h isoline, the contaminated area equaled 7 km^2 (Akt, 1993; Kostyukovskiy, 1993).

An equally strong contrast in radiation level and area assessments exist for the land area outside the plant. The discrepancy in official data of the responsible federal bodies in some cases exceeded one order of magnitude: in fact, assessments for the area contaminated varied from 10 to 200 km^2. This is illustrated in the Table 20, which is based on mass media information containing references to the mentioned official data sources, starting with MINATOM.

According to these sources, outside the plant the highest radiation exposure dose level (400-450 μR / h) was registered in the forest area and four km to the north from the village Chernaia Rechka (Illesh and Kostyukovskiy, 1993b; Tomsk-7, 1993). A few unofficial or independent experts and journalists consider the forest to be the most hazardous place, as animals and birds could carry and spread radioactive particles. No pollution was detected in the air and rivers. As to soils outside the forested area, contamination affected about 1,130 hectares of agricultural lands including 743 hectares of arable lands, 248 hectares of hayfields and 139 hectares of pastures.

The MINATOM specialists also pointed out one other small contaminated area about 300-800 m long at the part of the Tomsk-Samus road. At the same time, the EMERCOM experts supported by ROSGIDROMET and ROSGEOKOM (the State Geological Committee of the Russian Federation) argued that this part of the road was at least five times as affected as pointed earlier and hence it turned to be the most contaminated place. The radiation exposure dose levels there, which on April 7 reached the maximum registered outside of the plant, varied from 250 to 480 μR / h (see Table 20) while the radioactive contamination density was within 23-27 Ci / km^2 interval (Tomsk-7, 1993).

The official sources reported that the most distant polluted point was the village of Georgievka, 22 km from the site of explosion. The radiation exposure dose level there was 21-42 μR / h, which twice exceeded the natural radiation level but still is considered not hazardous for human health (Illesh and Yakov, 1933; Tomsk-7 Schitaet, 1993). However, measurements made by independent researchers from Tomsk showed that the radiation exposure dose level in that village varied from 70 to 100 μR / h and at some spots, primarily in orchards, it reached 2 mR / h while the radioactive contamination density varied from six to 12 Ci / km^2 (Boltachev, 1993; Tchernikh, 1993b; Tomsk-7, 1993).

According to the ROSGIDROMET and EMERCOM reconnaissance data for the territory within a 60 kilometer radius from the explosion epicenter, the maximum length and area of the contamination plume's track with levels more than 15 μR / h for gamma radiation was 28 km and 123 km^2 respectively. The figures for the territory with contamination levels that surpassed those of natural radiation were greater, i.e. more than 30 km and were about 200 km^2, respectively (see Table 20).

Those figures confirm in particular that the village of Chernaia Rechka, 34 km from the explosion site, was within the contamination track zone. The federal bodies mentioned above also believed that the radiation exposure doses at some spots were up to 50 μR / h. Moreover the specialists from MINPRIRODA (the Ministry of Environmental Protection and Natural Resources of the Russian Federation) found several spots of up to 160 m^2 each where radiation exposure doses exceeded that figure by five to six times (Akt, 1993; Arutiunian et al, 1993; Illesh, 1993c).

Even the most conservative and careful approach to summing up the figures cited makes the following conclusions inevitable. The accident caused substantial radioactive contamination of lands adjacent to the SCC reaching 0.03 Ci / km^2 for Pt^{239} (Galushkin et al, 1993). The real scale of the accident's aftermath considerably exceeded both the initial assessments made by responsible government bodies and the federal radiation safety standards for urban and sanitary protective zones, i.e., 20 and 60 μR / h, respectively. It spread outside the plant and the SCC area at a distance of more than 30 km and covered a substantial part of the surrounding territory. Considering the woodlands impacted by the radioactive fallout alone constituted 200 km^2 and the

Date	Information source[a]	Distance from epicenter of explosion (km)	Radiation exposure dose (μR/h)	Contaminated area (km^2)
04/07/93	MINATOM (ITAR-TASS)	-	From a few mR/h to a few R/h	A few hundreds of m^2
04/07/93	EMERCOM	19	40	10
04/08/93	EMERCOM	<15	400 - 250	-
04/08/93	EMERCOM	15 - 18	250 - 120	-
04/08/93	EMERCOM	18 - 22	120 - 35	-
04/08/93	EMERCOM	-	<400	200
04/08/93	Seversk CC[b]	-	300	-
04/08/93	Seversk COME[c]	22	70 - 102	-
04/08/93	Seversk COME	3	25 - 100	-
04/09/93	MINATOM	10	30	<90
04/12/93	MINATOM			35
04/15/93	MINATOM			120
04/15/93	EMERCOM	-	>60	30 - 35
04/15/93	EMERCOM	-	>15	123

Table 20. Radiation Dosage and Area Contaminated by the SCC Accident

04/16/93	ROSGIDROMET ROSGEOKOM	-	-	100
04/16/93	ROSGIDROMET ROSGEOKOM	-	30	50
04/16/93	ROSGIDROMET ROSGEOKOM	-	240 - 480	-
04/19/93	IGCE[d]	-	-	100
04/21/93	Anonymous	-	>20	250
04/93	RNC[e]	<0.5	500	-
05/93	"ERAECOS"[f]	-	-	800
05/93	MINATOM	-	-	123

[a] For acronyms see Annex 1 and footnotes below

[b] Seversk CC - the City Council of Seversk;

[c] Seversk COME - the City Committee for Ecology of Seversk;

[d] IGCE - Institute for Global Climate and Ecology of ROSGIDROMET;

[e] RNC - Russian Nuclear Center "Kurchatovskiy Institute" of the Russian Academy of Sciences;

[f] ERAECOS - Ecological Association "ERAECOS".

Source: compiled from reports of the aforementioned governmental and nongovernmental organizations both original and cited in the Russian newspapers

Table 20. *(Continued)*

possibility that radionucleides would spread due to forest fires, windstorms and so on, proved to be real as the post-Chernobyl experience, this shows that it should have been stated that the whole area suffered from the accident and radiation levels conspicuously exceed the earlier figures.

THE PATTERN OF RADIOACTIVE CONTAMINATION OF THE ENVIRONMENT

Assessments of the radioactive contamination structure or isotope composition of the fallout do not differ as much as those of its scale. According to the official data, supported by the data of detailed survey by joint EMERCOM and Russian Academy of Sciences task force as well as by the data of several "green" organizations, in mid 1993 the isotope composition of the fallout in the area adjacent to the plant was represented primarily by heavy metals. These include isotopes with half lives from 35 days to one year, namely: niobium-95, zirconium-95, ruthenium-103, ruthenium-106 (Galushkin et al, 1993; Illesh and Yakov, 1993). Such a composition which is obviously less hazardous than that of Chernobyl, was strongly predetermined by the time the SCC accident occurred, i.e. at the end of the technological cycle, when the bulk of Cs^{137} and nearly all Sr^{90} with a half-life of about 30 years had been removed at previous stages (Tchernikh, 1993c).

Initially, the experts failed to detect Pt^{239}, a considerably more dangerous isotope having a half-life of about 20,000 years, in the environment, and sometimes even denied the possibility of such a radionuclide being incorporated into emissions. However, as early as a week after the explosion some experts from MINATOM confirmed the negligible value of 8 $\mu Ci/km^2$ of fallout of Pt^{239}, in particular in Georgievka (see Shoigu, 1993). In May and June 1993 specialists from the EMERCOM Institute and Institute for Geochemistry of the Russian Academy of Sciences conducted more thorough joint radiation survey of lands that revealed considerably more hazardous contamination by Pt^{239} reaching as much as 30 mCi / km^2 (Galushkin et al, 1993). This means that the earlier assessments were exceeded by more than an order of three in magnitude!

Some data have not been widely released to the public and some even are lacking in the official reports of the responsible governmental bodies. For example, the specialists from the Russian Research Center "Kurchatovskiy Institute" found intensive radiation of Cs^{137} isotopes at a distance of 2 km from the explosion's epicenter which proved the presence of cesium in the fallout products (Borisov, Buturlin and Maleev, 1993). Those specialists as well as experts from ROSGEOKOM have detected isotopes of antimony (sibium)-125 having half-life of about three years, while a group from the Tomsk Polytechnic University headed by Prof. L. Rikhvanov discovered two hot particles with a size of 8-10 μM and radiation exposure doses of 5 and 22 mR / h respectively. The great danger of such particles is well known both to specialists and the public as a result of Chernobyl disaster (Arutiunian et al, 1933; Borisov, Buturlin and Maleev, 1993; Illesh, 1993a).

IMPACT ON HUMAN HEALTH

At the same time, bearing in mind that the fallout was deposited primarily on the industrial and health (sanitary) protection zones of the plant's site and the adjacent uninhabited woodland area, one may argue that the exposure of both personnel and local communities was rather limited.

My guess is that the maximum number of persons immediately affected by the accident did not exceed 200, mainly plant personnel and firefighters, the figure which is incomparably less than the Chernobyl's impact upon millions of people.

For this reason the SCC accident's impact on human health and safety, in terms of killed, wounded and evacuated persons, was fortunately not so conspicuous as it might have been had the accident not occurred in a part of the plant with few personnel, at lunch time, at a late stage of technological process and with winds that favored containment. At the same time its ecological consequences should be considered notable bearing in mind that according to law persons who lived in the areas with 5-15 and 1-5 Ci / km^2 have the right to be relocated or to get compensation, respectively (Federalnii Zakon, 1995: para 10 and 11). However these consequences should not be overestimated being considerably less than those of the Chernobyl disaster. Also, in contrast to the accident that had taken place at SCC more than 40 years before which resulted in two deaths, the explosion of the extractor at the complex in April 1993 did not lead to immediate human losses or lethal irradiation of any human being.

At the moment of explosion there were about 160 people inside the plant. About 30 emergency medical personnel and firefighting worked on countermeasures in the immediate vicinity of the explosion just after the accident. The EMERCOM reported the maximum individual radiation equivalent dose registered for two persons was 7 mSv, which constituted 14% of the annual permissible limit for personnel and other category "A" persons at a normal functioning of the plant and less than 3% of that for once-only emergency irradiation. Besides that, one more person received 6 mSv. Thus, a total of four persons who stayed close to the ruined apparatus got more than 5-mSv dose considered as annual permissible irradiation limit for individuals or category "B" persons (see Table 21).

Regarding the people affected outside the plant, official sources indicated only two communities, the village of Georgievka (30 inhabitants) and to a lesser extent the village of Chernaia Rechka, turned out to be within the radioactive plume's track. These sources stressed the doses there to be substantially lower than the permissible limits and thus not hazardous to human health. The total beta-activity of the fallout did not exceed in those localities 50 Ci, while the overall dose of internal and external irradiation was less than 5 mSv for forecasted life expectancy equal to 70 years while the permissible indicator is 7 mSv.

The latter figure is endorsed by some independent experts, especially those from the RNC "Kurchatovskiy Institute". They argued that with an average radioactive contamination density of 2 Ci / km^2 the additional external radiation dose for the first post-accident year would not surpass 0.4 mSv, whereas for the next year it would be about 0.08 mSv which is well below the 1 mSv considered as a starting threshold for federal nuclear hazard regulation (Borisov, Buturlin and Maleev, 1993; Romanov, 1993).

However, the earlier mentioned value of activity released due to the accident into the environment is disputed by these experts, who considered activity to be 6-11 times greater (Kostyukovskiy, 1994). It is also worth remembering about the contaminated spots in Georgievka and Chernaia Rechka with radiation levels substantially exceeding those mentioned above and requiring, at least according to the law, measures to mitigate the negative impact of the accident.

In addition, noting the important fact that the radioactive cloud generally missed both Seversk and Tomsk, thus making the radiation situation in these cities relatively safe, experts nevertheless pointed out local contamination spots within those areas as well. For instance, such a spot was detected at one of the bus stops where the radiation exposure dose levels varied from 50 to 90 μR / h. Besides, danger may stem from hot particles, two of which were found by Tomsk researchers as mentioned above. These particles have great energy potential and may be easily transported

Dose (mSv)	Number of Persons Irradiated	% of Total
0.0 - 0.2	8	26.6
0.2 - 0.3	2	6.7
0.3 - 0.4	2	6.7
0.4 - 0.5	2	6.7
0.5 - 1.0	1	3.3
1.0 - 2.0	5	16.7
2.0 - 3.0	3	10.0
3.0 - 4.0	3	10.0
4.0 - 6.0	3	10.0
6.0 - 7.0	1	3.3
> 7.0	2	6.7
TOTAL	30	100

Source: (Arutiunian et al, 1993)

Table 21. Radiation Dose and Number of Persons Irradiated While the SCC Accident

long distances, inflicting damage to human health through inhalation, eating meals or drinking water (Tarasov, 1993).

Although the SCC accident did not create serious problems in terms of somatic and genetic health, the data cited here and other assessments give no incontrovertible grounds for saying that the consequences for human health are absolutely negligible. One should take into account the effects of low radiation doses, and the accumulation of additional emergency doses, with those produced by natural potassium-40, uranium and thorium radionucleides as well as by radioactive contamination caused by prolonged exposure to the SCC nuclear reactors and to global radioactive fallout.

An official from the medical administration of the Tomsk region, S. Khlinin, pointed out that when they were compared with the so-called control areas, the lands located to the northeast of the SCC, i.e. along the plume's path, demonstrated a sharp increase both in teenage morbidity and cancer and blood sickness. Although it was later followed by a decrease, an analogous increase within a half a year of the explosion occurred in genetically hurt cells of the inhabitants of Samus village as well as of several other communities at Tomsk, Chainskii and Pervomaiskii districts (*rayons*) that are also located within the plume path. The frequency of these aberrations for schoolchildren in that community is more than twice as much as their neighbors living close to Semipalatinsk nuclear testing field. Professor V. Klimov discovered that immunological irregularities in children living at the community of Georgievka and neighboring community of Naumovka considerably surpassed those recorded at the village of Loskutovo, which was chosen as a control area (Kostyukovskiy, 1994).

Besides somatic effects, lessons of the 1979 Three Mile Island accident in the USA and the 1986 Chernobyl disaster in the former Soviet Union also teach everybody to pay special attention to the social and psychological repercussions of an accident and the psychic or mental health effects on the neighboring communities. On 8 April 1993, two days after the explosion, residents of the village of Naumovka, especially women, who are known to exhibit anxiety and fear at lower levels than men (see Drabek, 1986), expressed alarm for their own health as well as that of their children in the light of rumors about special tablets to be issued to the residents of Seversk. The women complained about tiredness, headaches and general malaise. A similar alarm level was registered in the neighboring village of Malinovka, where a few local people confessed to panic and buying all iodine stock in the nearest village drug stores, a situation that recalled the grim days of Chernobyl (Kondratiev, 1993),. Analogous reports were also recorded in Seversk and discussed in particular by Dr. Masliuk, the chief of the town's sanitary and epidemiological service (Kunitsina, 1993).

At the same time, data concerning the fallout composition and radiation exposure doses in the villages showed that there were no objective reasons for such a response. On the other hand, the lack of necessary and true information made that type of human stress behavior quite expected.

RESPONSE TO AND RECOVERY FROM THE ACCIDENT

The explosion at the plant and the consequent dispersion of a radioactive cloud beyond the SCC boundaries required an immediate response by the local and regional authorities, neighboring communities, and the special services designated to manage emergencies including their localization and alleviation of the aftermath.

WARNING AND EARLY NOTIFICATION

Timely warning of the people about the risks and hazards expected or emerged serve as the first necessary action that predetermine the effectiveness of these response operations. The available data reveals substantial tardiness in warning chief managers and responsible services both of the plant, EMERCOM and MINATOM.

The chief of the Civil Defense Service of Seversk received the information about the explosion occurred at 12:58 p.m. on April 6 only 17 minutes later, i.e. at 1:19 p.m., while the SCC chief engineer and the chief of the town's chapter of the Ministry of Security (now the Federal Security Service of the Russian Federation) received it even later, at 1:20 and 1:55 p.m. or 22 and 55 minutes after the explosion, respectively. The warning reached the town, regional and federal authorities with a more pronounced delay. For instance, the head of the Tomsk regional administration was informed about the accident only at 2:30 p. m., while residents of Seversk and Tomsk heard about it by radio an hour and more than an hour later (Arutiunian et al, 1993; Khronika, 1993; Pereubedit, 1993; Zakharov, 1993).

Soon after the accident the chief of EMERCOM passed a special memorandum to the Russian parliament confessing that:

> as it was in Chernobyl the information concerning the accident both at local and federal levels was communicated by MINATOM with a considerable delay that could have resulted in tragic consequences (Illesh, 1993c)

Although, as discussed earlier, the actual medical and radioecological effects of the accident were not too conspicuous, the delay in warning that varied from 17 minutes to nearly five hours meant that the radioactive cloud moved a distance of from nine to 60 km, thus substantially increasing the contaminated area and response and recovery costs. Regular public information flow was provided by local, regional and federal mass media only since the evening of April 6.

In part, the reason for such a substantial tardiness of the warning is related to technological factors. In particular, the EMERCOM memorandum mentioned above stated a lack of automatic radiation control system and local emergency warning system within a 30-km zone around the SCC (Illesh, 1993c). In addition, the chief of the town council of Seversk stressed the unsatisfactory functioning of existing communication lines and the lack of reserve ones (Illesh, 1993c; Pereubedit, 1993). The quality of the equipment for public communication and warning should be considered even worse. For example, the residents of the village of Chernaia Rechka lacked any warning about the explosion at the SCC simply because the only telephone apparatus in the local school was not functioning (Malash, 1993).

However, untimely or lack of warning of the population in the South of the Tomsk region, which is highly saturated with hazardous industries, was primarily linked with socioeconomic and organizational reasons, including human factor. The loopholes and technical shortcomings of the local and regional warning as well as public communication systems, which had been and still do exist despite the grim lessons of Chernobyl and recurrent accidents at the SCC *per se*, stem from both undervalue of and resources shortage for organizing and functioning of comprehensive protection system both for the personnel of hazardous nuclear and chemical plants and local communities. The lack of funding, in particular in 1990s, result from the deep socioeconomic crisis in Russia and the Tomsk region, in particular, while the country's transition to the so-called "free market" society. The repercussions of this process have been numerous including those affecting the social security and public safety. Suffice it to note that the reason for the malfunction of the telephone apparatus in Chernaia Rechka was its disconnection by the local telephone service since the school simply had no money to pay for it (Malash, 1933; Zakharov, 1993).

Passiveness and incompetence of local and regional authorities were the other key factors contributed to the pronounced delay in warning local people and the federal government. To illustrate the point I would cite the fact that on the day of the accident, 6 April 1993, nearly all key officials of Tomsk region participated at the big conference organized by regional council from 10 a.m. to 7 p.m. Until the end of the meeting none of the participants was aware about the explosion at the SCC while the head of the council, who had received confidential information about the accident from the chief of the regional administration as early as 3:00 p.m. made no attempt to share it with his colleagues. Thus, the members of the regional administration learned about what had happened together with the public only when they went back home and switched on their TV sets (Khronika, 1993).

RESPONSE MEANS, FORCES AND OPERATIONS

Notable shortcomings in organization and functioning of the warning system were further aggravated by loopholes in planning, preparedness for and operative response to the accident by the plant staff as well as by local and regional authorities and responsible bodies including the civil defense service. In particular, the contingency planning did not provide for alternative or redundant emergency information sources. For example, the information from the SCC operation manager was the unique source of data for both the Seversk and regional civil defense services. Coordination procedures between the SCC, town of Seversk and Tomsk regional authorities and their services were not delineated clearly and in advance (Pereubedit, 1993). Even given the complexity of the situation in Russia in early 1990s the technical and logistics support preparedness to respond and alleviate the accident's aftermath should be considered as insufficient. As V. Kishkurko, the chief of the Special Department of the State (Federal) Fire Service (SFS), put it:

> Seversk is the least equipped in terms of fire protection among all so-called closed towns. For example, Cheliabinsk-65 (former Cheliabinsk-40 and actually Ozersk) has developed an excellent fire protection and response system and there it is considered criminal to economize on relevant costs (see Semenchenko, 1993).

Mr. V. Kress, the governor of the Tomsk *oblast*, addressed the same issue at his press conference on 9 April 1993 in a more complex and critical way confessing that:

> the accident revealed extremely low preparedness of the civil defense, State Sanitary and Epidemiological Inspection, hydrometeorological, nature protection services to such kind of situations (see Tchernikh, 1993b).

The shortcomings in organizational preparedness predetermined delays in making crucial decisions and lowered the efficiency of the decisions implemented, in particular establishing regional emergency operation center immediately after the accident. In its turn, this disturbed and postponed organization of timely reconnaissance, mobilization of necessary means and forces, warning and informing the local people as well as starting recovery activities, e.g. deactivation of the contaminated areas.

However, later on the SCC personnel and responsible organizations of the Tomsk region supported by highly qualified experts from various regions, who came to provide necessary operative assistance, succeeded in taking the situation under control. The key role was undoubtedly played by the accident's culprit, i.e. the *specialists and services of the SCC*. Three stationary air monitoring posts, which have been subordinated to the environmental safety bureau of the SCC and located within the control area, were switched to a 24-hour schedule of taking samples for ruthenium-103, ruthenium-106, zirconium-95 and niobium-95. The specialists from the mentioned SCC bureau also took samples of the waste waters of the complex, as well as from the waters of the Samuska and Tom rivers.

The SCC special group along with the sanitary and epidemiological service and emergency commissions of the complex and of the town of Seversk, town's Committee for Environment and Natural Resources supported by the emergency commission of the Tomsk *oblast* and the medical unit of the Federal Department of Biomedical and Emergency Issues of the Ministry of Health (MOH) of the Russian Federation, also conducted monitoring of the areas of possible radioactive fallout and measurements of radiation doses absorbed in order to assess external irradiation potential. In addition, experts from the Tomsk Polytechnic University actively participated in laboratory activities while attached armed forces elements, including aviation and signal service units, provided support for route reconnaissance and monitoring. Material support for the aforementioned activities included Helicopter Mi-8 with dosimeters, one radiological and three agrochemical laboratories together with three hydrometeorological posts (Arutiunian et al, 1933; Tchernykh, 1993b).

Given all means and forces involved in response activities, the *fire and rescue service* of the town of Seversk, as it was in Chernobyl, demonstrated high preparedness for and effectiveness of response to the accident. Immediately after the explosion 53 firefighters and nine pieces of special firefighting equipment were delivered to the plant's site. A search for hotbeds of fires and radioactively contaminated spots was immediately initiated and in less than ten minutes the fire inside the building and on its roof was extinguished. The active search for injured and lost persons by firemen and rescue personnel revealed that there was none. After these operations some firemen needed special medical care while their equipment needed irradiation treatment (Kishkurko, 1993; Semenchenko, 1993).

No less effective were actions carried out by *militia (police) and medical care service*, although those were objectively involved at a less degree than in Chernobyl taking into account incomparably minor consequences of the SCC accident. The chief of the Department of Internal Affairs (DIA) of the Tomsk *oblast* (or regional police department) as soon as he received the message about the explosion issued an order to deploy 24-hour control posts at the road Tomsk-Samus to prevent spreading of radioactive contamination by cars and to mobilize the chemical units of the town police to provide urgent assistance to all other means and forces involved in radiation reconnaissance within the urban area.

The medical care service of both the SCC, the town of Seversk and Tomsk city provided radiation dose screening of the personnel directly involved in response and recovery activities as well as intensive selective screening of the people in the communities reported to be within the radioactive plume's track. Physicians insisted on temporary evacuation of the children from these communities while adults continued to live and work there. Within the two days, on 6-8 April, 65 persons, including workers, firefighters, service personnel, and physicians who worked in the affected building and participated in the mentioned activities were examined at the SCC medical center. No irradiation was found, however since 12 April 1993 additional biophysical investigations have been undertaken but their results remained unknown to the public (Arutiunian et al, 1993).

As to the *federal authorities*, the response of several responsible governmental bodies and services to the accident was timely enough, being initiated almost immediately after getting a warning from the site. In organizational terms, the responsible departments included MINATOM, EMERCOM, the Ministry of Health, among others as well as various interdepartmental task forces which created commissions for assessing the causes and consequences of the accident and for making decisions on recovery and reconstruction activities.

As early as the evening of 6 April, a special team headed by V. Vladimirov, the deputy chief of EMERCOM, was established and on the next day it left Moscow for Seversk. This team together with experts from the other responsible organizations conducted radiation reconnaissance at the accident's site and assessed the gravity of the aftermath until 13 April. On this date S. Shoigu, the Chairman of EMERCOM (now the minister of MES) arrived to Seversk where he analyzed the results of the team's work and on 15 April signed the official report often cited here.

A little bit later, on 8 April 1993, the Joint Commission, including representatives from MINATOM, the Russian Academy of Sciences, the Ministry of Defense, the Ministry of Health, started its work under the chair of a person from the former department. This commission worked at the SCC for ten days, up to April 17 being supervised directly by V. Mikhailov, the minister of MINATOM himself, who came to Seversk on 15-17 April. Three days later, on 20 April, he signed the commission's official report to the Russian government. Another report was prepared by GOSATOMNADZOR which received a directive from the Russian government to conduct independent investigation of what had happened at the SCC.

The Ministry of Foreign Affairs and MINATOM sent a joint invitation to the IAEA to visit the site of the accident. The commission headed by A. Gonzales, the deputy director of the nuclear safety department of the IAEA, and including B. Bennet from the United Nations Scientific Committee for Effects of Atomic Radiation and J. Webb, the Secretary of the National Radiological Protection Council of Great Britain, visited Seversk on 15-16 April and examined the site and adjacent territory. It assessed the radioecological situation both at the plant's site and the village of Georgievka and inspected the radiological protection laboratory of the SCC. As a preliminary result of that work the commission's chairman denoted in particular the inadequacy of technical and material support and the obsolesce of the SCC equipment used and that there would be a special official report by the IAEA on the accident.

In *legal and organizational terms*, the response of the federal authorities to the Seversk accident involved the preparation and enforcement of three regulative documents by the President, the Supreme Soviet (parliament) and by the Council of Ministers (government) of the Russian Federation, respectively. On 9 April the President of Russia issued special Executive Order # 224 prescribing carrying out urgent and comprehensive measures on establishing governmental as well as nongovernmental control over the safety of civil and military nuclear facilities, as well as accelerating the development and implementing a concept for population protection and economic activities in the territories suffered from radioactive contamination.

That Executive Order provided directives to responsible departments, including MINATOM, MINPRIRODA, etc. and to the Tomsk regional administration to promote necessary recovery measures for the areas contaminated by the radioactive fallout, to assess losses and to calculate and pay compensation to the suffered population. This document also served as a basis for enactment of Executive Order #636 issued in October, 1993 that strengthened the power of

GOSATOMNADZOR as the main institutional body regulating the safety of the nuclear facilities in Russia (Rogozhin, 1993b).

In mid-April 1993, the Committee for Environmental and Natural Resources of the Supreme Soviet of the Russian Federation set up a special task force to analyze the causes and consequences of the SCC accident. On 23 July 1993 it passed the aforementioned regulation on eliminating the SCC accident's consequences in Tomsk *oblast* (region) (see Verkhovnii Sovet. Postanovleniye, 1993). On 7 October 1993 this was followed and supplemented by the Council of Minister's Executive Order #1770-p requiring the respective federal and regional administrative bodies to develop more effective measures to liquidate the consequences of the SCC accident, in particular providing compensation and medical care support to the SCC personnel and suffered local and regional communities (Pravitelstvo. Rasporiazheniye, 1993). Moreover, this Executive Order serve as a catalyst for the development of a special federal program on nuclear which considered the long-term radiation impact of the SCC and other nuclear facilities. Unfortunately, it took more than two years to prepare and adopt this program in the Fall 1995 and even after that its implementation has been substantially limited by scarce budget funding resulting from continuos and deep social and economic crisis in Russia.

The loopholes and shortcomings in warning, preparedness and response to the SCC accident primarily at the local and regional authority levels as well as contradictions and discrepancy in providing data on gravity and scale of the accident's aftermath could not but impact the character of *response of involved communities*. Many people felt unrest and alarm listening to the too brief TV message made by the regional emergency commission on 6 April 1993 considering that more extensive and detailed data usually published in the newspapers was not available. Logically, as early as the next morning, on 7 April, this provoked numerous rumors that quickly spread among the affected communities and disturbed seriously a considerable part of the population of the Tomsk region. The publication of official data concerning the accident in the newspapers could not stop the gossips given these data were either out of date or incomplete (Kunitsina, 1993; Vigon, 1993).

Many people also demonstrated partial or very often complete distrust to both the description and interpretation of what had happened by the SCC administration and MINATOM as well as by local and regional authorities. As Yefrosinya Grikova, 84, who was born in the village of Georgievka, pinpointed, these declarations said everything to be fine but the local people were not told the truth and knew nothing (Gordon, 1994). Although even now I have no idea about any public opinion survey conducted in the affected communities, which could disclose to what degree the official information on the case had been considered as incomplete or even false, the analysis of analogous situations, e.g., those connected with the nuclear testing in 1940-1970s near Semipalatinsk and its long term effects on the population of the Altai region that borders the Tomsk region in the southwest (see Popov, Sazonov and Farberov, 1993; Zakharov, 1993), gives me substantial grounds to reckon such a perception mode as dominant.

The reasons for that are deeply rooted in the specificity of the social space of the SCC accident discussed earlier. Firstly, in the multiyear secrecy veil over the very existence of shadow towns not to mention malfunctioning and accidents at the plants located there. But spurred by the SCC near-disaster and increasing burden of the lasting economic and social crisis long-silent villagers and citizens as well as authorities in the nearby city of Tomsk are now speaking out about the problems in the nuclear complex. Secondly, in what might be labeled as a 'historic memory' of people, i.e. experience from the previous accidents that occurred to be publicized, especially

Chernobyl disaster, but were elucidated and treated by the former USSR authorities in a false and incompetent ways.

These factors were further aggravated by the incompleteness and ambiguity of the official information, delay of warning and early notification of the neighboring communities stemming from the authorities' wish to disregard the responsibility for inadequate preparedness and response to the accident. Incompatible declarations like "the powerful explosion ruined the apparatus containment" and "radioactive products left inside the containment", or about deactivation works in the village of Georgievka where the radiation exposure level was reported to be as low as 30 μR / h may serve as an illustration of the point why people do not trust the data and their interpretation by authorities and other official sources of information.

In addition, a substantial segment of the population feel doubts or distrust not only towards these sources, but also to mass media comments on the scale and gravity of accidents, including the one occurred at the SCC, considering that newspapers and TV are inclined to overdramatize or mythologize the real events. As disaster and emergency research literature shows, the latter phenomenon is typical for mass media all over the world (see, for instance Walters, Wilkins and Walters, 1989; Quarantelli, 1993). In this situation many residents of the Tomsk region like the many Russians preferred to reply upon the opinions and judgments of their friends, relatives, neighbors or simply acquaintances or even fortuitous others. However, a lot of people lacking other trustworthy information sources preferred to rely upon mass media messages. Such a controversial situation easily provoked fear followed by overactive hasty behavior of some groups.

For example, having heard the first radio messages concerning the SCC accident a team of the US specialists from an international financial corporation, who happened to be assisting colleagues in Tomsk in a privatization effort, hastily left the city by taxicab. They were soon followed by other foreign businesspersons and specialists. Some families in Tomsk took their children out of the city, and some left by airplane. Many persons remembering Chernobyl started to save vodka and iodine although there was no medical need for such behavior. In some kindergartens and schools in the first two days after the accident, iodine tablets were distributed by personnel with the best of intention to the children. But they got a reverse effect in some instances as a few children were poisoned by the iodine. Despite this and explanations by members of the regional emergency commission in the following several days, the demand for iodine tablets in the region surpassed all reasonable limits. A similar alarm and anxiety, especially in the first days, was also felt by residents of the communities located within the track of the radioactive fallout (see Kishkurko, 1993; Kunitsina, 1993; Zakharov, 1993).

As to the recovery from the accident, the "culprit" of the accident, i.e., the SCC, was assigned by the federal government to play the key role in practical implementation of deactivation and compensation although its financing should come and really came from the federal budget. Deactivation of the affected areas, extraction of unreacted and unexploded part of the radioactive solution containing uranium and plutonium from the exploded apparatus (that could not be repaired) and examination of its residues followed by burial in a concrete containment structure were among the most important recovery steps some of which were not finished even in early 1997. However, due to the measures undertaken during the accident's aftermath, radiation exposure doses in the contaminated areas of the Tomsk region were cut by 25-30% as early as by June 1993 while the further countermeasures helped decrease these levels even more, i.e. by more than 70% in 1994 and by more than 90% in 1996.

Within the recovery phase the federal government also prescribed to the SCC as well as local and regional administrations to introduce substantial changes in safety control and emergency preparedness systems in order to prevent or minimize the risk of a new accident. In particular, the

EMERCOM special commission necessitated the SCC director, the emergency commissions of Seversk and Tomsk to:

> revise contingency plans, insert corrections in time schedules and warning procedures in case of an emergency, improve the organization of radiation monitoring and control and the composition of means and forces designated for alleviation and recovery activities (Akt, 1993).

In addition, as mentioned earlier, MINATOM proposed and the federal government approved a special program for upgrading the safety level of all nuclear power and industrial facilities in Russia in 1996-2000 with a total financing of nearly 4,000 billion rubles or about US$ 1.2-1.3 billion.

The Tomsk region administration assessed the losses due to the SCC accident as surpassing 200 billion rubles (using June 1993 prices) or about US$ 200 million. In their turn, the chiefs of both the SCC and MINATOM argued that this figure is an overestimation of the real damage by at least one order of magnitude and I share this view. Indeed, in Chernobyl total costs including direct and indirect losses and expenditures on relocation and rehabilitation were believed to be about 220-250 billion rubles in 1988 prices or about US$ 200 billion while direct losses, urgent evacuation and (primary) recovery expenditures were officially assessed as 10 billion rubles in 1988 prices or about US$ 10 billion. The latter figure exceeds that of the assessment of the losses of the SCC accident by only 50 times while the medical, ecological and socioeconomic consequences Chernobyl disaster were incomparably greater than that of Seversk. However 5 billion rubles (in 1993 prices) or about US$ 1 million, that the federal government could afford to allocate from its budget to the SCC administration for recovery purposes within 1993-1995 (see Ioyrish and Rogozhin, 1995), should be considered as unquestionably insufficient and this partly explains why the recovery program for the SCC was not fully implemented even by early 1997.

PREPAREDNESS, RESPONSE TO AND RECOVERY FROM THE MAJOR FIRE AT THE KAMSKI CAR PLANT

INTRODUCTION

The Kamski car plant (KamAZ) with its 100,000 employees and production capacity of 150,000 trucks per year, primarily for the army and agriculture, is considered the largest truck assembling complex in Europe. In 1987 it manufactured about 120,000 trucks although in 1990-1992, i.e. on the eve and just after the dissolution of the Soviet Union this number dropped to 90-100,000 (Evseev, 1994).

KamAZ is located in the city of Naberezhniye Chelni on the banks of the Kama River, a tributary of the Volga River, 125 miles east of Kazan, the capital of the Tatarstan Republic within the Russian Federation (see Fig. 16). Before 1930 it was a small community, and then received the status of a town and later that of a city where there now live more than 500,000 people. The truck manufacturing complex, which includes many units in the city of Naberezhniye Chelni as well as in other regions and towns of Russia (Bolshoi Entsiklopedicheskiy Slovar, 1991), provides the bulk of the working places and infrastructure services in this city. Thus the existence and efficiency of functioning of KamAZ complex predetermined in a crucial way the development of the city of Naberezhniye Chelni both currently and in the foreseeable future.

The engine assembly plant which before the fire had employed about 19,000 workers and produced 600 truck engines every day was one of the most important units of KamAZ. It consisted of a one story building that was 1,152 m long, 363 m wide and up to 14 m high with a steel roof covered by a sandwich like heating layer composed of foamed polystyrene 50 mm thick and four layers of ruberiod-bitumen mix. In the basement of the building, 9 m underground, there was a complex of tunnels used for assembly operations as well as for storing a metal shavings conveyor, as well as oil, lubricant and coolant tanks. The plant was equipped with hydrants mounted on 300 and 400-800 mm. fire prevention water pipes; automatic sprinkler and drenches systems for water and foam fire extinguishing purposes; and had a special para-military unit of 67 firemen. The total number of fire fighting personnel at the KamAZ complex consisted of 424 persons (Pozhar, 1993b).

On April 14, 1993 the engine assembly plant of KamAZ complex was ceased by a major fire that was contained only after a week of intensive and heroic response efforts. Although it caused no fatalities this fire incurred enormous economic damage involving direct losses of constructions, equipment and raw materials and indirect costs resulting from breaking normal functioning of both suppliers and customers of KamAZ. It This has turned this emergency situation into one of the most serious industrial crisis in Russia in the 1990s. Specialists are practically unanimous in considering this fire to be the worst in the history of car industry both in the former Soviet Union and the CIS (Commonwealth of Independent States).

Within the week during extinguishing and other response operations were under way and afterwards both KamAZ administration and chiefs of the responsible governmental bodies, the State Fire Service (SFS) in particular, as well as independent experts and journalists made numerous comments on the causes and damage incurred by the fire. A few surveys providing details of what had happened were also published (see Pozhar, 1993b). However, all of them lacked comprehensive analysis of the aforementioned major fire as an industrial crisis requiring long-term cooperative recovery efforts. This makes the following case study from the viewpoint of an emergency management necessary and interesting both theoretically and practically.

DEEP AND DIRECT CAUSES OF THE FIRE

The analysis of its prehistory shows that the fire was a logical and in certain respect inevitable result of a continuous causal chain of events involving a mixture of socioeconomic and political (external) factors as well as interdependent human, organizational and technological loopholes (internal factors) within both the KamAZ complex and its engine assembly plant. As mentioned earlier in this chapter, disaster and crisis theories and scholars justly argue for this set of factors to be organic to nearly every technological incident or accident. At the same time another typology of factors subdividing them into deep or antecedent, and direct or immediate prerequisites and causes should be considered as no less applicable.

The final links of the aforementioned causal chain are undoubtedly embedded within the organization, i.e. both the KamAZ complex as a whole and its engine assembly plant, in particular. Their chief executives should be considered as primarily responsible for what had happened as they failed to provide supervision and control over:

(a) adequate fireproof design and construction by using incombustible or fire-resistant materials (given that polystyrene burns very fast and emits large quantities of thermal energy and toxic substances);

(b) effective fire prevention and extinguishing measures including technological auditing, control and early notification (alarm) system.

These predetermined the plant's continual vulnerability to fire and eventually turned out to be the main direct prerequisites of the April 1993 accident.

DEEP OR EXTERNAL PREREQUISITES: POLITICAL, ECONOMIC, ORGANIZATIONAL AND LEGAL ASPECTS

However, the initial and perhaps the key elements of the causal chain of KamAZ major fire should be looked for far away from the city of Naberezhniye Chelni and the car complex itself. I believe that the causes of this fire and many other major accidents have been deeply rooted, firstly, in erroneous, long-term social and economic policy in the former Soviet Union that have not been overcome completely in Russia in the 1990s. These involved the mentality and way of actions of policy creators and executors, including the chiefs of industrial ministries, departments and major state enterprises which for decades had been oriented to a short term financial and production benefits at the expense of the long term social interests. The latter include besides other sustainability and safety, in particular fire safety, of development of both local and regional communities and the nation as a whole (see Chapter 1).

Secondly, deep or antecedent prerequisites under discussion have been catalyzed by the loopholes and serious shortcomings of the reforms recently and currently realized in Russia. These involve the reform's leaders ambitious strive to accelerate the process of transition to a new type of society, underestimation of inertia of the national social psychology oriented on people's trust in the state's support and full responsibility nearly for everything (i.e. in state's paternalism) and of the complexity of the problems inherited from the previous Soviet times.

Both important observations may be vividly illustrated by the history of using foamed polystyrene (or more briefly, polystyrene) as a construction material that served a crucial aggravating factor of a number of large industrial accidents including the major fire at KamAZ. In the former Soviet Union in the early 1960s production of polystyrene was initiated as a response to demands of the rapidly developing massive construction of large plants which needed new light and relatively cheap heating. Given that no other type of ownership had been existing for decades in the Soviet industry, all those plants were built by the state owned construction companies which had been prescribed by the GOSPLAN (the State Planning Committee) to increase volume and decrease costs of production at all expenses. In the 1970s this principal was embodied in a dismally famous directive "Economy must be economical".

Therefore, until as late as the early 1990s erection of those plants was considered as very efficient and was set as one of the priorities of the national industrial and construction development. Polystyrene began to be widely used due to its low specific gravity and thermal conductivity, durability, and convenience for operations. While applicated with steel elements it considerably decreases the total mass of buildings (e.g., compared to ferro-concrete) thus providing savings through substituting much more expensive steel constructions and cutting down building costs (see Pozhar, 1993b). These characteristics of polystyrene played a key role in 1962 when the responsible governmental bodies, primarily the USSR State Construction Committee (GOSSTROY) and the USSR State Technological Supervision for Mining and Industry (GOSGORTECHNADZOR) issued the permission to use this material as a construction component.

The permission was amended with an important reservation that polystyrene could be used in practice only after consultations with the local and regional supervision branches of the Chief Board of Fire Protection (CBFP) of the Ministry of Internal Affairs (MIA) that had a right to discuss but lacked the power of establishing fire prevention standards. Naturally, the construction companies ignored consultations with either foreign or Soviet chemists who might have noted that polystyrene was substantially hazardous, given its combustibility and toxicity. Moreover, in 1969 the GOSSTROY itself neglected the warning of the CBFP and issued permission for the use of polystyrene in metal fencing panels.

Two years later, in 1971, it removed all restrictions and limits on using polystyrene in construction works. The CBFP tried to block that decision, appealing to the Cabinet of Ministers and some other governmental bodies to substitute for polystyrene by producing fireproofmaterials. In 1971-1972 only a dozen of such appeals were issued (Pozhar, 1993b). But all those efforts failed given the loose legal basis and the lack of a fire prevention act which could provide broad power to the CBFP inspectors in supervising the process of fire standards development and execution. They were ignored by influential industrial ministries, GOSSTROY being the first, that had superior status within the executive state power of the former Soviet Union than had the fire prevention service represented only by the CBFP.

Currently the fire and industrial safety is still inadequate despite the serious changes occurred in this field in Russia in recent years. The Federal Fire Safety Act adopted in December 1994 which put much more power, particularly in terms of developing and supervision of the federal fire safety standards, in the hands of the State Fire Service (SFS) of MIA, should be considered as the most important. The SFS succeeded the Fire Prevention and Rescue Service (FIPRES) that in its turn earlier replaced the CBFP. However, the lasting and deep economic crisis along with erroneous tax policy in the 1990s has resulted in funds shortage of industrial companies and facilities thus forcing many of them to cut the number of fire teams and firemen and keep using obsolete prevention and extinguishing equipment. The same process has been typical for municipal fire services in many Russian towns and cities with a few exceptions only. In this respect the situation in Russia in mid 1990s could not and did not change much to the better being compared to that in the former Soviet Union in early 1970s.

Therefore the lessons from the past major fires involving polystyrene have not been drawn completely both at KamAZ and other facilities. The most devastating were the fire at the metal structures plant in Zhitomir, the Ukraine, in 1972 which led to the collapse of 17,800 m^2 of roofing; the fire at the Bukhar cotton plant in Uzbekistan in 1973 which resulted in the complete burning of more than 40,000 square feet of roofing. In spite of those accidents, in the same year 1973 GOSSTROY developed and enforced the code CH 454-73 for designing light metal structures for buildings which made legal massive use of polystyrene while construction of the key industrial facilities in the former Soviet Union in 1970-1980s. Besides others, these facilities included nearly all nuclear power plants, 19 thermal power and heating stations, about 70 industrial giants like '*Atommash*', '*Rostselmash*', 'ZIL', etc. (Nazarov, 1993; Pozhar, 1993b).

The KamAZ complex was also among the aforementioned facilities. While its construction which started in 1973 the CBFP several times initiated discussions with GOSSTROY, the Ministry of Car Production and the Cabinet of Ministers on substituting for the polystyrene in roofing of the large industrial units. But as usual, the decisions made were palliative. In particular, instead of the recommended substitution for polystyrene by incombustible material, GOSSTROY prescribed to administration of the complex to divide the roofing with polystyrene with fire bars 6 m wide thus segmenting them into a few sections of 10,000-12,000 m^2 each. That order referred to KamAZ engine assembly plant which had been under construction at that moment but involved only its units without roofs. However, at that time the nearly 80% of the plant's covering had already been mantled and combustible materials had been kept within all its main structures (Pozhar, 1993b).

This palliative and highly dubious decision in the 1970s was stipulated by the thrust of the industrial ministries and the KamAZ chiefs to be "economical" and gain short term profits through cutting "non-productive" costs. It was also supported by the self-protection and ambiguous policy of the regional fire bureau which was much interested in maintaining the number of personnel in the fire units and thus agreed to compromise with influential car and construction bosses. As Ye. Kiriukhantsev, the former chief of the State Fire Inspection Department of the CBFP, pinpointed:

> It (this policy) was mainly oriented on keeping the number of the fire units that provided safety to KamAZ and contributed decisively to organization of fire extinguishing in the city ofNaberezhniye Chelni. The discrepancy that emerged between the need to keep those fire units and imperative for providing effective state fire supervision at this facility (KamAZ) has beenovercome through compromise (Pozhar, 1993b).

In the next decade of the 1980s no substantial positive changes in solving or at least mitigating the polystyrene problem at KamAZ occurred. As a result, more than 40% of the fire prevention measures prescribed to the plant by fire inspectors were ignored and thus the fire safety problem has been transferred to later years. In particular, within 1987-1992 the regional fire supervision service of the CBFP sued administratively 711 chiefs and other responsible persons of the engine assembly plant for breaking fire rules and regulations and suspended partially or entirely the work of 67 production and supplementary units which broke the fire standards or were considered as fire prone or hazardous.

It is worth mentioning that KamAZ was in no way unique in this respect and close picture existed at the other major facilities using polystyrene in their building structures. In particular, this led to the complete burning off 26,000 m^2 at the Kapchagai china plant in Khazakhstan in 1981, and destruction of a considerable part of the roofing of the nuclear power plant in Zaporozhye in Ukraine in 1984. As to the engine assembly plant of KamAZ itself, in 1978-1992 57 fires occurred there while in 1987-1993 alone 32 incidents and accidents (i.e., breaks, burning, etc.) were registered (Pozhar, 1993b).

DIRECT CAUSES: TECHNOLOGICAL AND ORGANIZATIONAL FAILURES

As mentioned earlier, those deep or external factors were further aggravated by the serious technological and organizational shortcomings within KamAZ itself including loopholes in electrical supply system, organization of technological supervision and inspection checks as well as control and early notification (alarm) system. The latter substantially weakened the effectivenessof fire prevention and extinguishing measures when an electric fault burned through the weak protective armor of the cables, igniting them and thus triggering the fire at the engine assembly plant.

This occurred at 6.41 p.m. on April 14, 1993 and provoked the flames starting to spread along cables which lacked fire protection partitions and moving towards the main control panel. It caught the flame within 14-16 minutes. From 6:55 p.m. on, within two or three minutes, faults were affecting several cables which caused an explosion of the transformer thus shutting off the plant's electricity supply and consequently suspending the main and then the reserve lighting and functioning of equipment. At 6:58 p.m. the fire left the surface (zero level) and ignited overpass structures. At that time about 20 m^2 of the plant's structure were affected by the fire.

There was no automatic alarm system so the workers began to understand what was happening only when the lights in their units went off. One worker was alerted by the smell of burning insulation from the electric substation, and while approaching it he noticed thick fumes coming from the door. In a minute, i.e., at 7:00 p.m., he called the operator of the plant's electric supply division and told him about the fire. Later on, the investigation discovered that the first indications of the fire including claps, crashes, etc., had been noticed as early as around 6:45 p.m., but the workers thought those were routine industrial noises.

Meanwhile, within only three or four minutes, i.e., at 7:01-7:03 p.m. the flames enveloping the overoiled structures and pipes, reached the roof and melted the polystyrene and bitumen mixture. At that time, since there were no fire protection belts or any other obstacles, it spread quickly and freely at a speed of 6-8 m per minute and affected about 600 m^2 of the roof. By 7:20 p.m. the affected area reached 8,000 m^2 and in 32 minutes when the first burnt parts of the roof structure collapsed, skyrocketed to nearly 10,000 m^2. By 8:19 p.m., this figure grew more than 10-fold reaching 103,000 m^2. By 9:31 p.m. or lees than three hours after the fire started it increased to approximately 420,000 m^2 or 700-fold!

Next day, on April 15, by 11 a.m. the fire on the roof and on the surface (zero level) had been extinguished. However at 5:05 p.m. that day the situation worsened due to the fires started in the huge tunnels under the plant. These tunnels 9 m deep, 6.8 km long with a total volume reaching 344,000 m^3 contained the tanks filled with oil which had been enflamed by the burning mass of polystyrene and bitumen flowed there from the roof. This considerably complicated the situation and the work of firemen making the struggle against the underground fire lasted until 21 April 1993 (Pozhar, 1993b).

THE FIRE'S AFTERMATH AND ITS ASSESSMENT

Surprisingly, the fire resulted in no deaths or seriously injured among the plant's personnel or the firefighters. Only two persons with light burns had to get medical treatment. This was primarily due to the time of the incident which occurred when the second shift of the plant's personnel had have their lunch and there was nobody in the plant's shops. High level training and effective extinguishing operations of the fire officers were other important contributing factors that cushioned the accident's consequences.

Therefore, the main result of the massive fire was the enormous economic damage that involved both direct losses of valuable equipment and indirect losses incurred by prolonged suspension of the normal functioning of the KamAZ technological and marketing networks where supplies from the engine assembly plant played a crucial role. The production volume decreased by 38% being compared to 1992 and reached only 62,100 trucks by the end of 1993 (Evseev, 1994). Tens of thousands of workers both from the engine assembly plant and some other KamAZ units and cooperating facilities in other towns and cities had to break their normal work and either participate in recovery activities or perform other duties that had been not entirely adapted for. Given the crucial role of KamAZ in the life of Naberezhniye Chelni, this could not but impact negatively the normal routine life of the whole city thus threatening some basic structures both of the industrial complex and the city necessitating their chiefs and administrations to make critical and urgent response and then recovery decisions.

The fire's aftermath overlapped on the existing unfavorable market situation when the shortage of funds of the main consumers of trucks (especially, the army and to lesser extent agriculture) provoked considerable decrease of demand thus aggravating the situation in the national truck industry. As a result the number of trucks supplied by KamAZ dropped from 62,100 in 1993 to about 35,000 in 1994 and less than 21,000 in 1996 (Evseev, 1994; Pavlov, 1996b; Suverov, 1997). All these give substantial grounds to consider the KamAZ fire as a real industrial crisis (see Rosenthal et al, 1989: 10; Shrivastava, 1992: 5).

Nobody calculated the exact figures of the damage while existing official estimates substantially differed ranging from tens of billions of rubles or tens of millions of US dollars (Bronshtein, 1993a; Grigoriev, 1993) to hundreds of millions of US dollars (Mitin, 1993) with little explanation being provided for this gap of an order of magnitude. To assess the direct losses of the fire, we have started from the value of the plant. While converting KamAZ from the state owned enterprise into a corporation both the auditors and stockholders estimated the value of the engine assembly plant as 109 billion rubles or about US$ 200 million. This figure that essentially included the plant's basic value, primarily its expensive imported equipment, its buildings and other constructions now is considered by many Russian economists as too low. However we share the aforementioned assessment, in particular taking into account that the liquidation value of KamAZ as a whole in 1996 was about US$ 1.4 billion while its real value was less than 50% of that (Pavlov, 1996).

The value of the raw materials and components lost in the fire had not been incorporated in the assessment value mentioned above. Consequently, we assume that US$ 220 million could be considered as the least figure of total value of the plant prior to the fire. Taking into account that the fire completely destroyed all metal structures and cables, and from 50% (Pozhar, 1993b) to nearly 70% (Nazarov, 1993) of the equipment and supposing that unburned materials were somehow involved in reconstruction and other useful purposes, we believe that the minimum value of direct damage should be estimated in the order of 190 billion of rubles or about US$ 170 million (given April-May 1993 dollar-ruble ratios). However, the KamAZ administration assures this figure to be more than twice as large reaching US$ 370 million (Roubtsov, 1994) that may be considered as maximum assessment (rather an overvaluation) of direct economic damage.

To obtain a figure for total damage one should also add the costs of response operations including those of extinguishing the fire, search and rescue as well the value of the indirect losses and costs caused by the fire. These losses and costs involve expenditures on importing truck engines from abroad, adaptation of consumers of the original KamAZ engines traditional to the engines of other suppliers including changes in transportation schedules, retraining of the plant's personnel who lost their jobs. To have some idea about the scale of all those things, it is sufficeto note that the burnt plant supplied engines not only for KamAZ trucks but also for the Ural car factory, ZIL, some bus assemblies and some military plants. A few sources within the car industry have believed only the net profit lost by KamAZ due to the fire should be within the order of hundreds of millions of rubles or hundreds of thousands of US dollars.

Having no statistics on specific consumers, plants and operations, it is not possible to calculate the earlier mentioned costs though there is still a room for an expert assessment. If one takes the average proportion between direct and indirect losses typical for aftermath of fires in Russia and equal to 1:5 as a starting point for further calculations, the indirect and total costs and losses incurred by the KamAZ fire can be estimated as about US$ 850 million and US$ 1,000 million respectively. The latter indicator does not incorporate costs for the reconstruction, or to be more precise, the construction of the new engine assembly plant that we discuss later. Even this reservation considered, in terms of the inflicted damage the major fire at KamAZ turns out to be the one of the worst industrial accident in the former Soviet Union and Russia.

Both the cost of the fire and the recovery could have been much less if the plant had been insured. In the mid-1970s when the plant and the KamAZ complex as a whole was ready to start functioning, their chief executives studied the prospects of insurance. According to experts from "*Ingosstrakh*", the organization which insure facilities involving foreign investments, the insurance premium for the plant at that time could have reached 0.5-1.0% of insured property, i.e. around one billion rubles or US$ 2 million (Mitin, 1993). But at that time only state property and the unique state insurance company, *Gosstrakh*, existed and in such circumstances the federal government considered it unreasonable to pay such a premium to and put such an overburden in terms of insurance liabilities on its own (state) company. This made KamAZ chief executives to approach some US insurance companies who asked for a premium of US$ 150 million per year, though for the whole KamAZ complex. That figure seemed to be unreasonable and the contract was not made. However, as it turned out in April 1993, the fire was worse than the worst insurance risk forecasts (Bronshtein, 1993a: Nazarov, 1993).

RESPONSE TO THE FIRE:
CHRONOLOGY AND EFFICIENCY OF OPERATIONS

The starting and rapid spreading of the fire over the whole plant served as a catalyst for response activities, primarily the KamAZ fire service responsible for detecting, localizing, extinguishing of fires and mitigating the aftermath of any incident. In general, the activities of the fire service should be considered as fairly effective. However some important issues, primarily operative response and reliability of the warning as well as the automated fire control systems, draw our attention while studying the efficiency of preparedness and response to the accident.

The analysis reveals that those systems failed to function as they should have. In particular, the automated fire control system did not work lacking necessary redundancy and because of the failure of both the main electricity supply at 6:57 p.m. and the reserve supply seven minutes later. That was one reason why the warning about the explosion of the electric transformer and the news of the fire itself reached the plant's fire unit only at 7:00 p.m., that is, with a 19 minute delay, and why 11 fire section units came to the scene four minutes later, i.e. at 7:04 p.m. Given a strong wind blowing at the moment of development of the fire, that 23 minute delay provided time enough to increase the burning area 30 fold (Pozhar, 1993b).

As to organizational response, N. Tsigankov, the duty fire officer immediately after his unit's arrival to the scene at 7:04 p.m. and assessment of the seriousness of the situation gave a signal for full mobilization of firefighting means and forces of the city while the plant's fire unit on duty organized evacuation of personnel from the plant and the plugging in of tank trucks into hydrants. When A. Volkov, the chief of the KamAZ fire service, arrived at the scene at 7:20 p.m. the situation turned to the worse both due to the wind increased from 6-8 to 10 m / s and insufficiency of the means and forces involved. Therefore he enacted the special contingency plan providing for attachment of supplementary fire equipment and personnel units from Republic Tatarstan (within Russia) and organized the operation center to coordinate and control all firefighting activities. Meanwhile, by 7:25 p.m. all firemen and equipment involved including reserves were activated but failed even to localize the fire given that the water supply which was only 600 liters per second or 30% of the needed volume. As a result, by 7:52 p.m., more than a quarter of the roofing was on fire, some metal structures had crashed and collapsed, and flames were encroaching yet unaffected areas and sometime enveloping fire officers on the scene.

By 8:19 p.m. the operation center with attached engineers from the plant, finished deploying the means and forces that arrived from the city of Naberezhniye Chelni. The fire scene was segmented into nine combat sectors and all the fire personnel was respectively grouped into nine combat units equipped with about 30 stationary and moveable pipes. Later on, when the burning area had already exceeded 100,000 m^2 and following the contingency plan the attached fire units, reinforced with civil defense units, came to the scene from the neighboring cities of Nizhnekamsk, Almetievsk and Elabuga. However, they still failed to contain the fire and by 9:31 p.m. the entire roof of the plant more than one kilometer long was on fire.

Early next day, at 00:47 a.m., I. Nizamutdinov and N. Lobov, the deputy chiefs of the FIPRES of the Tatarstan MIA together with an operation task force came to the fire scene followed two hours later (at 2:50 a.m.) by general N. Krasko, the chief of the FIPRES of the Tatarstan MIA, escorted by another operation task force. These commanders re-deployed means and forces and attached to them fire units from the neighboring communities. They also organized a reconnaissance in the plant's tunnels where the level of water had already reached one meter. At last, at 5:05 a.m., general V. Dedikov, the chief of the FIPRES of the MIA of the Russian Federation at that time came from Moscow to the scene and headed the operation center thus coordinating all firefighting activities.

Due to those tremendous efforts, that in particular provided for an increase of the rate of the water supply to 720 liters per second, by 11:00 a.m. on 15 April the situation at the surface level had been taken under control. However, the situation in the plant's underground tunnels was getting worse given that the fire approached directly to the oil tanks. The access of the fire units to them was considerably limited by thick smoke and high temperature (500-600 C) as well as the narrowness and limited number of entries into those tunnels (Pozhar, 1993b). Given such a complexity, the operation center took a decision to re-deploy the means and forces involved into four combat groups acting within new four combat sectors. Within next 26 hours these groups pumped the foam from 45 generators through the main entries to the tunnels and isolated other holes with mineralized wadding, thus inhibiting the fire intensiveness and limiting the access of oxygen to the fire zone. These measures provided for decreasing of the temperature in the tunnels from 500-600 C to 120-140 C and more effective use of the foam generators.

On the fourth day of the fire, on 17 April, the situation was suddenly complicated by spreading of the fire to the oil and diesel fuel tanks in the engines' testing station located 5.2 m beneath the surface. The operation center ordered to isolate the station by using bricks and gravel to block the tunnel between it and the main basement. The station was saved and on 21 April the major fire at KamAZ engine assembly plant was at last contained.

While response the operation center staff has been changed every day to facilitate the work and involve new specialists. Those included personnel from such unit as signal; information and documentation support; safety; material supply; repair and technical support; rear support divisions headed by officials from the plant's administration; the city fire protective service, the FIPRES of Tatarstan and Russia, among others. Since his arrival to the operation center it was headed by the chief of the FIPRES of the Russian Federation. In total, 560 firemen and 54 civil defense servicemen (not considering a medical emergency teams), from the city of Naberezhniye Chelni and adjacent Nizhnekamsk, Almetievsk, Elabuga along with those from more distant areas such as the city of Kazan, the Udmurt and Bahskortastan Republics, as well as Samara and the Nizhniy Novgorod *oblasts* of Russia were fighting the major fire at KamAZ. They were equipped with 64 pieces of fire fighting equipment, 236 various kinds of machines and gears and used more than 2,400 tons of foam generator and 110 tons of foam powder (Pozhar, 1993b).

The main results of the fire fighting efforts were no casualties and saving of up to 50% of the production equipment, 85% of the building columns, and 40% of the walls, although in general the functioning of the plant had to be suspended and the workers could not do their work. Despite that, there were no massive discharge of personnel. Within the following six months, only 33 persons or less than 2% of the plant's staff were fired, included those 21 who were retired on pension (later eight persons from this group were re-employed at KamAZ). Part of the plant's personnel got temporary retraining to become construction workers and took part in reconstruction of the ruined plant thus constituting the bulk of the personnel of the recovery teams involved in this process. There were also no suspension of social security and support measures, pensions, cultural and other development programs of KamAZ (Bronshtein, 1993b; Grigoriev, 1993).

As to the legal response to the fire, the Council of Ministers (government) of Russia passed regulations and a few orders to stipulate reconstruction of the suffered plant and recovery process as a whole. On 21 April 1993 it also issued an order creating a special commission to investigate the circumstances facilitated both the start and development of the fire at the plant. The commission's report confirmed that the plant's light and unprotected metal structures covered with polystyrene made it fireproof and substantially complicated firefighting operations thus decreasing the capability of the firemen to respond effectively to the destruction of the plant. The governmental commission also formulated technical and organizational recommendations to change the situation in the area of the national fire safety. These was followed by the governmental regulation, passed on 23 August 1993 and establishing the State Fire Service (SFS) instead of the FIPRES of the Russian Federation with power to set fire standards and control responsibilities. However all these had limited value since the status of the fire service in Russia remained the same for some time. Only the Federal Fire Safety Act adopted in December 1994 considerably improved the legal basis of fire prevention and protection in the country although, as mentioned before, this have not changed the overall situation in this area in the 1990s much to the better due to the lasting social and economic crisis.

RECOVERY FROM THE FIRE'S AFTERMATH: RECONSTRUCTION AND COPING WITH A CRISIS

The specific characteristic of recovery from the major KamAZ fire, however typical for the situation in many developing countries, has been that substantial damage inflicted by the fire overlapped upon and aggravated the social and economic crisis existing both in the city of Naberezhniye Chelni, Tatarstan Republic and Russian Federation. This dramatic coincidence in social time and space predetermined both complexity and the large scale of the recovery activities.

THE VOLUME OF RECOVERY EXPENDITURES

Soon after the accident N. Bekh, the former president of the KamAZ company, believed that the initial phase only, including the purchasing, construction and fitting of 100,000 tons of metal structures, 1,260 km of electric cables as well as the purchasing and mounting of hundreds of tools, would require 150 billion rubles or more than US$ 150 million. Taking these figures as a basis, some experts reckoned that the total expenditures on the plant's reconstruction would skyrocket from US$ 140 to US$ 400 million (Mitin, 1993; Nazarov, 1993; Pertsevaia, 1993; Vishnevskiy, 1993b) or, in other words, from 1 / 7 to 2 / 5 of the aforementioned sum of the total losses.

If US$ 300 million are considered a right guess, the fire's total costs covering the sum of the total losses (both of KamAZ, the city of Naberezhniye Chelni and the national truck industry), response expenditures, and reconstruction costs would reach US$ 1.2-1.25 billion. Some experts cited the figure of US$ 1 billion and felt pessimistic about the possibility of the full recovery of the plant at all or within short or medium perspective, at least (Yudin, 1995). Despite this the plant's board of directors believed in April 1993 that 1,700 trucks would be assembled as early as October 1993 while 3,000 and 4,000 pieces could be produced by November and December 1993 respectively. By January 1994 they claimed to reach the level of 100,000 trucks yearly (Bronshtein, 1993b; Morozov, 1993a, 1993b; Ukhov, 1993a; Vishnevskiy, 1993a).

Indeed, more than 250 billion rubles and US$ 150 million (or totally about US$ 280 million) were actually invested by mid-1994 (Bronshtein, 1994). These along with some typically Soviet (Russian) organizational and technological decisions and well known management instruments of reconstruction contributed decisively to accelerated reconstruction of the burnt plant and recovery process of KamAZ as a whole. In particular, the unburned equipment was retrieved from the ruins and put into the spare sections of the neighboring plants of the KamAZ complex where it was immediately used, like in the times of World War II.

THE MAIN SOURCES AND AGENTS OF RECOVERY AND ITS PROGRESS

Invaluable help and assistance were provided by business partners of KamAZ (i.e., component suppliers and truck engine consumers) and 11,000 volunteers, including construction and assembly workers, from Donetsk in the Ukraine, Akmola in Khazakhstan, Ufa in Bashkortastan, and other cities and regions of Russia and the CIS countries. They came to KamAZ and by working 12 hours a day within May-September 1993 erected the roof over the unaffected part of the plant. Considering the lessons drawn from the major fire, the new roof has been equipped with fire belts that previously were lacking.

Substantial support for accelerating recovery was provided through direct and indirect credits. The latter involved the stockholders of the KamAZ company refusing the 1993 dividends and the government of the Republic of Tatarstan introducing temporary tax discounts. In 1993 the complex also got a commercial credit of 18 billion rubles (about US$ 18 million) at 170% per annum and an equal sum of donation from the federal government. Later on it also loaned 253,9 billion rubles (about US$ 120 million) as a public loan until the year 2000 while another steady flow of credits have come through the US investment company KKR (Kohlberg Kravis Roberts), the main financial partner of KamAZ. In 1995 only it facilitated providing US$ 300 million of credit to KamAZ while the names of the creditors remained unknown (Yudin, 1995).

However, the bulk of the efforts needed for recovery in 1993 were invested by KamAZ itself. Many specialists were surprised and pessimistic to the idea to continue to produce and sell trucks without engines. But this turned to be paid off for several months considering that a lot of customers, following Soviet traditions, kept spare engines at their stocks while some others bought them from the truck service companies. In addition, small scale production of engines had been continued at the aforementioned reestablished units within KamAZ and at its plants outside

Naberezhniye Chelni. Suffice it to note, that as early as the end of April 1993 250 pieces were produced. Due to this the complex succeeded to get 50 billion rubles (about US$ 50 million) as a monthly income that partially was invested in plant's reconstruction.

These and some other extraordinary measures resulted in the daily assembling of 100-150 trucks or 1500-2000 per month within April 1994 - April 1995 while in May 1995 this number reached 3,000 This was followed by nearly double increase of the KamAZ stock prices from 2,800 rubles in March to 5,200 rubles in May 1995 and stable demand for them at the national and European stock market within that year (Bronshtein, 1994; Yudin, 1995).

However, It is easily seen that these figures are much inferior to those cited above and initially planned for December 1994. There are two main factors that hampered the recovery of KamAZ and reconstruction of its engine assembling plant, in particular. Firstly, the continuing economic crisis in Russia that manifested itself in particular in shrinking demand for capital goods by majority of consumers. Given that 30% of production capacity of KamAZ had been oriented to manufacturing of special trucks, the most crucial for the complex was the sharp drop of demand from the army.

Secondly, organizational loopholes in the federal government also contributed negatively to the rate of recovery. In 1993 in spite of several governmental prescriptions adopted, by September that year nothing had been loaned from the ear-marked 30 billion rubles of urgent assistance. The same thing occurred to the preferential (low interest) credit of 45 billion rubles (earlier ear-marked as 75 billion rubles) to be loaned from the federal budget. As mentioned earlier, 18 billion rubles out from 50 billion rubles or only 36% of the federal donation authorized for KamAZ by the special order of the Supreme Council of the Russian Federation (the parliament) reached KamAZ by the end of 1993.

In addition, the KamAZ administration also had to obtain resources to compensate to the personnel of the burnt engine assembly plant for several months at least. Those funds were initially requested from commercial banks which agreed to provide up to 500 billion rubles for the plant's reconstruction as a commercial high-interest credit but therefore were rejected by KamAZ board of directors preferring getting assistance from the federal budget. However, as mentioned before, it turned out to be not much reliable. Just to pay the commercial credits back, the KamAZ administration was forced to sell part of its hard currency reserves accumulated through export operations, cut the speed of residential building construction and take some other restrictive measures to save necessary resources but succeeded only in cushioning the situation (Bronshtein, 1993b; Ukhov, 1993b; Vishnevskiy, 1993a). All these consequently led to the KamAZ company's 90 billion rubles (about US$ 80 million) indebtedness to suppliers and construction firms only as early as June 1993 (Bronshtein, 1993b; Vishnevskiy, 1993a Vishnevskiy, 1993b).

ECONOMIC CRISIS, RECOVERY EFFICIENCY AND DEVELOPMENT PERSPECTIVES: HOPES AND DISILLUSIONS

To cope with these problems and to overcome economic crisis through diversification of production in 1994 the KamAZ joint-stock company elaborated and started implementing the strategic development program for the years 1995-2002. It included modernization of the whole complex including the new engine assembly plant, manufacturing of a new truck model as well as cars and buses, and reestablishing the total volume of production to the level of early 1990s, i.e. 80,000-90,000 trucks plus 50,000 cars and 10,000 buses yearly. The considerable investments necessary for this program should come both from federal budget and commercial sources, including foreign ones. To attract the latter the KamAZ company succeeded to get the insurance policy amounted to US$ 4.5 billion provided by a consortium of five Russian and 47 foreign insurance companies in 1994. In case of an insurance risk case this policy should make available for insurant up to US$ 500 million of compensation (Roubtsov, 1994).

This facilitated KamAZ receiving by the end of 1995 the first US$ 150 million from US$ 3,500 million of investments that should be provided for the company's implementing its strategic development program within 1995-2002 according to the agreement signed with the aforementioned KKR corporation. This huge investment project was followed by the US$ 100 million of credit received from the European Bank for Reconstruction and Development (EBRD) also in late 1995 for KamAZ stabilization and development. Even more important for KamAZ were 253.9 billion rubles (more than US$ 60 million) supplied by the federal government in budget loans and 1,280 billion rubles (about US$ 300 million) of credits from Russian commercial banks (Bronshtein, 1994; Gapeevtsev, 1995; Roubtsov, 1994; Yudin, 1995).

The presidential decree "On State Support for Restructuring and Development of the Enterprises of KamAZ Joint Stock Company" signed on 19 December 1995 and followed by the governmental regulation dated 12 February 1996 provided for crucial and considerable indirect credit both for the plant's reconstruction from the fire, diversification and modernization of the KamAZ corporation. This made possible to postpone not only the payments for the aforementioned federal loans to the year 2000 but debts of KamAZ to commercial banks as well considering that those debts were converted into debts to the federal budget. Commercial banks received the bills of the Ministry of Finance of Russia that should be repaid within one year at the interest rate of one third of that of the Central Bank while KamAZ should repay all debts within 1998-2002. KamAZ also received 100 billion rubles of credit from the Naberezhniye Chelni city budget (Pavlov, 1996a).

In addition, KamAZ succeeded in realizing the agreement signed as early as in 1993 between the KamAZ stock company and Cummins Engine Corporation, the US producer of truck engines, that provided an opportunity to mantle these engines from 250 to 430 horsepower on KamAZ trucks. In 1995 such trucks that cost 25% more than "pure" Russian were available in market (Yudin, 1995). All these provided for decrease of prices by 10% on average and stabilize the demand for and production of the trucks that again reached 23,000 in 1996. The share of KamAZ in the CIS truck market respectively grew from 25% in 1994 to 36% in 1996. However, KamAZ complex still have not overcome entirely the problems of its recovery from the major fire and the lasting economic crisis and kept confronting problems of sales (as low as 20,737 trucks in 1996) and credit indebtedness skyrocketing to more than 2,000 billion rubles (about US$ 360 million) (Suverov, 1997).

THE FIRE IN THE MIRROR OF PUBLIC OPINION AND THE MASS MEDIA

In general the reaction of the Russian population, especially the residents of Naberezhniye Chelni and neighboring communities, towards the fire was a typical disaster (major emergency or crisis) response. The accident and its aftermath arouse in people feelings of empathy and an eagerness to help that for centuries has been typical towards those who lost their possessions in a fire in Russia. Just in the first dreadful night, while the fire was raging at the plant, many of its workers and citizens of Naberezhniye Chelni started to collect money for its reconstruction. Some sacrificed their savings, some gave part of their salaries to a special reconstruction fund established in April 1993 (Ukhov, 1993a). As mentioned earlier, many volunteers from different regions of

Russia and the CIS countries came to help and provided assistance, several for months. While conducting firefighting operations until the moment when the fire was contained the KamAZ administration got moral support from the city's religious communities of different faiths (Vishnevskiy, 1993a).

However, as far as the causes of the fire are concerned, the city was full of rumors some of them treating the accident as revenge by racketeers that had been refused payment, or by some other offended persons. Interestingly, the director of the plant himself has been continuing to support a version of arson, while local nationalists accused him in the latter in favor of shifting the KamAZ main property from Tatarstan to Russia. They proposed that the public prosecutor to start a law suit and nationalize the entire complex. Other persons saw the fire as resulting from the heavy drinking of plant personnel after getting paid. There were also many rumors concerning the gravity of the fire's aftermath and response effectiveness. Some people said that eight firemen had perished in the plant's ruins while the local newspaper, '*Meschanka*', reported three workers had been killed by the fire although giving no evidence to support this information which was actually false (Bronshtein, 1993a; Bronshtein, 1993b; Morozov, 1993b).

Lacking any opinion polls or surveys reflecting public perception of both the fire and firefighting operations and thus lacking any representative data, it is only possible to make general observation that the response of the local communities to the accident may be characterized as calm and rational. People did not waste much time discussing the situation but instead started actively to restore and construct the facilities so the plant could function again. This was facilitated by the constructive policy of the KamAZ administration as well as the generally moderate tone of communication messages and publications in mass media.

Here it is worth remembering that in the former Soviet Union information on emergencies and disasters for decades had been limited to an only brief and dubious message that something had happened but "there have been no victims and no damage" and "the situation is under control and active measures are being taken". Only since Chernobyl disaster and starting of *glasnost* policy in the second half of 1980s the data concerning accidents and catastrophes published or demonstrated in Soviet and Russian mass media became more extensive and trustworthy. For the first time in the Soviet history the official data on causes and consequences of emergencies and disasters had been openly criticized and the figures on hundreds of thousands suffered from Chernobyl nuclear disaster in 1986, thousands killed by the earthquake in Armenia in 1988, hundreds of victims of the Ufa tragedy in 1989 and so on were made in mass media. At that time as well the Soviet TV, radio and newspapers published data on the major disasters and accidents previously unknown to the public (for example, earthquake in Ashkhabad, Turkmenia in 1948, radiation disaster in the South Urals in 1957, etc.)

The mass media response to the major fire at KamAZ in 1993 was practically immediate. The first reports were broadcast exactly on the day of the fire, on April 14, in the evening and night news of local TV and radio and in the main federal TV channels ("*Ostankino*" and "*Russian TV*"). Next day, reports were published in the newspapers which turned to be the most informative sources among the whole mass media. This conclusion stems from the analysis of the KamAZ fire's coverage by the five newspapers including four dailies (*Izvestiya, Komsomolskaia Pravda, Pravda,* and *Trud*) and one weekly (*Moscow News*). Given that these newspapers have been issued from hundreds of thousands to several million of copies and distributed throughout Russia, in the CIS, and even some Western countries, their illumination of any substantial event, emergencies and disasters in particular, attracts attention of many people and has considerable impact on the Russian audience.

While covering the major fire at KamAZ the aforementioned newspapers followed the typical pattern of disaster media news reporting known as "better than reported but worse than necessary" (Scanlon, Luukko and Morton, 1978). Both the frequency and depth of reporting were uneven. Within nearly six months after the fire had been contained the newspapers published no more than one article or comment per day. During that time span, 15 stories amounting to 2,369 lines were published about the KamAZ fire in these newspapers or, in other words, one article or comment was published each 11-12 days (see Fig. 18 and 19).

If these figures are compared with those for the SCC radiation accident in Seversk in the same year, the ratio of coverage, number and frequency of reporting would be 1.3:1, 1.6:1 and 3:1 respective in favor of the latter case while contrary to that duration of reporting would be 3:1 in favor of the KamAZ fire story.

A more detailed analysis of frequency and contents of the publications on KamAZ major fire reveals that these fit the general trends typical of the media coverage of unexpected occurrences, at least in relation to federal-level newspapers. Within the reporting process four main phases should be specified including :

1) official brief information (message) about an emergency or disaster in all or at least the bulk of the federal-level mass media, in particular newspapers;

2) much more detailed elucidation of the case in most of these sources of information while the information flow dramatically increases;

3) detailed characteristic of selected issues of the case while the information flow sharply decreases;

4) incidental messages and publications in a limited number of mass media.

The analysis shows that brief official comments in the aforementioned newspapers during the first three days of the fire were replaced by substantially more detailed information. The coverage increased exponentially from an average 19 lines per article in 15-17 April to 349 lines in 18-20 April or was 18-fold. If recalculated for an average daily reporting, the increase would not be so I mpressive, although it would be still considerable reaching from 19 to 64 lines, respectively or 3.5-fold.

Later on, a week after the fire had been contained, the volume and frequency of reporting demonstrated a typical declining trend reflecting the diminished acuteness of the situation, tension and anxiety of authorities and people, on one hand, and decreasing interest of the mass media towards the fire given their permanent seeking primarily for sensations, on other hand. The decline n intensiveness of reporting lasted until mid-May. The average volume of the newspapers during 29 April - 13 May went down to 73 lines per article or to 15 lines per day that means a more than 4-fold decrease (see Fig. 18).

The following week, from 14 May to 21 May, a new wave of public and mass media interest to the major fire at KamAZ arouse, perhaps as a result of the governmental special commission finished its preliminary investigation and the SFS officials made public fairly exhaustive data about the accident. The frequency and volume of reporting respectively increased 2.5-fold and 6.6-fold in comparison with the previous period. The articles devoted directly to the fire's causes and aftermath and recovery from the accident were sporadic and published within May - October 1993. The most detailed and relatively more regular were the publications in *Izvestiya*, *Trud* and *Komsomolskaia Pravda* (see Fig. 20). Since November 1993 until March 1997 these newspapers along with *Pravda* and *Moscow News* also published about 30 articles on KamAZ although

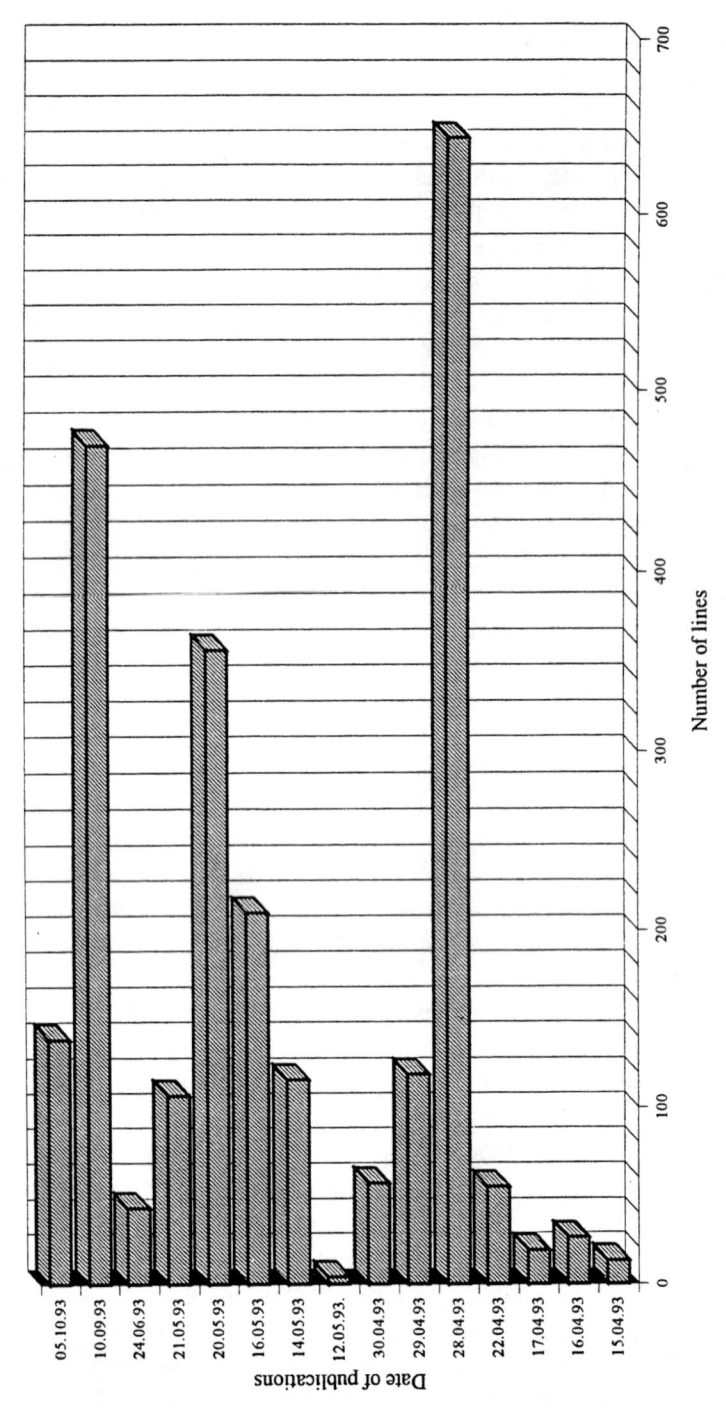

Fig. 18 The Total Number of Lines in the Stories on KamAZ Big Fire Published in the Russia Most Circulated Newspapers From 15 April to 5 October, 1993

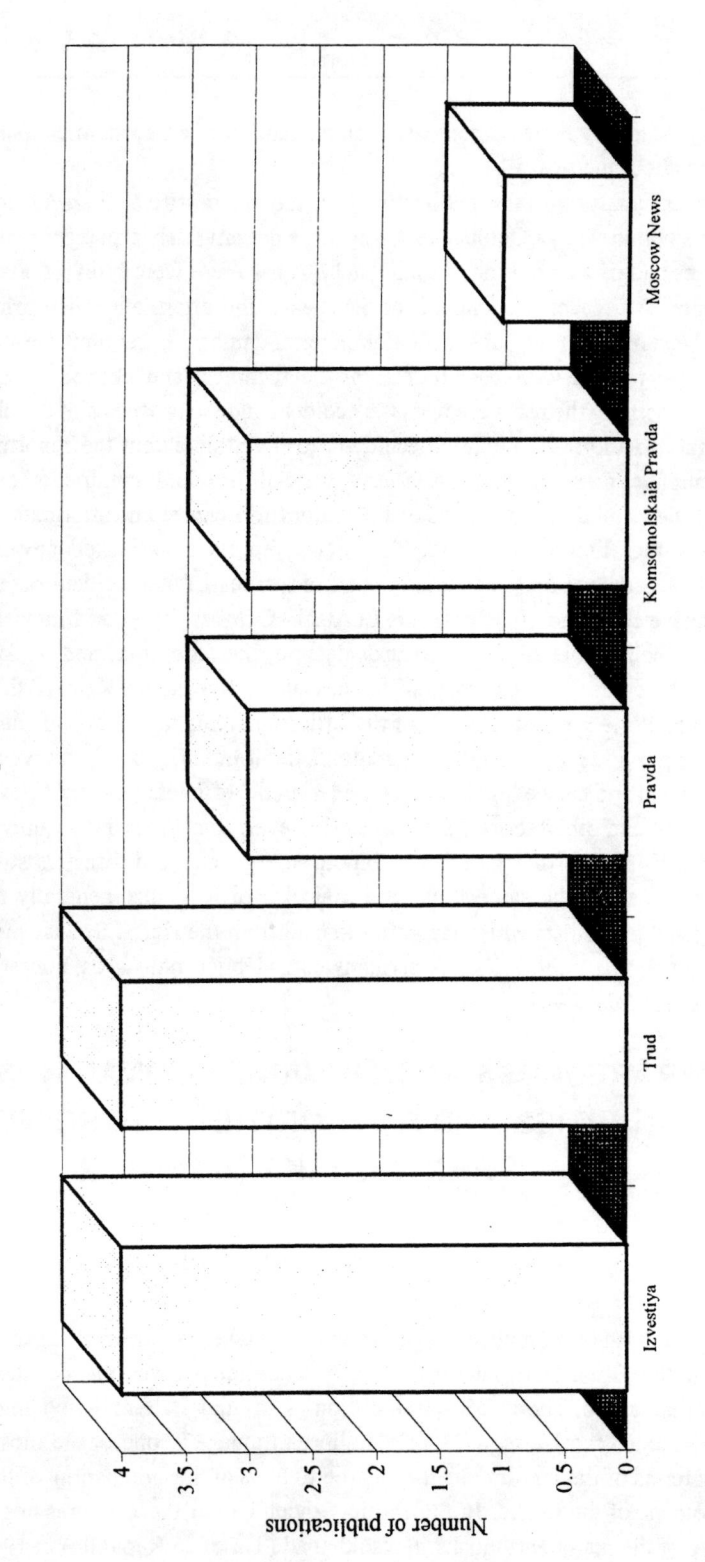

Fig. 19. The Number of the Stories on KamAZ Big Fire Published in the Russian Most Circulated Newspapers from 15 April to 5 October, 1993

considering primarily development issues in a situation of an economic crisis and only incidentally mentioning about the fire.

A content analysis of the publications on the major fire at KamAZ in the selected leading newspapers within April - October 1993 reveals a pattern fairly typical for mass media reporting of emergencies and disasters. First, during 15-17 April there were brief reports on the fact of the fire supplemented with laconic comments on its causes and aftermath which primarily pinpointed that there had been no fatalities but substantial material damage. Later on these were followed by much more detailed reports with descriptions of the technical and economic aspects of the fire and forecasts concerning the recovery from the accident and the prospects of the plant's reconstruction.

Contrary to the SCC radiation accident, to a certain extent the reporting kept following the Soviet template presenting primarily the official data and comments on the case while the alternative views of different experts on the major fire's causes and aftermath as well as "unofficial" data were rather limited and rare. The news reports also lacked any serious discussion of organizational or legal and social and economic issues of the accident both within the period of more intensive coverage of the case (i.e. in April - October 1993) and incidental mentioning about the fire in their publications afterwards despite the adoption and enforcement of important governmental regulations and orders which directly referred to the KamAZ fire.

In general, the content-analysis of the articles reveals reporters and mass media trust to the information provided by the SFS, the major federal authority in fire prevention and containment. This has logical and easy explanations considering the efficiency of the fire service operations both in the KamAZ and other serious accidents. However, this looks rather untypical for Russia given doubts and distrust to official information on emergencies and disasters still prevailing in public perception mode. At the same time, the majority of Russians generally trust the comments of "independent" journalists while according to data from the Harris Service public opinion survey in the USA in 1996, only 7% of Americans consider journalists as honest and their reports as trustworthy (Sturua, 1996).

PREPAREDNESS AND ORGANIZATIONAL RESPONSE OF COMMUNITIES AND AUTHORITIES TO THE NEFTEGORSK EARTHQUAKE DISASTER

INTRODUCTION

In the mid-1990s a number of disastrous earthquakes occurred in Japan, Russia and the USA. Given that the Great Hanshin-Awaji or Kobe earthquake was the costliest disaster ever, with economic damage of about US$ 100 billion - around half of Kobe region's normal annual economic output, the Neftegorsk or Sakhalin earthquake is one of the most tragic in the world history in terms of the fatality rate that soared to 62% of the population of the town of Neftegorsk at the moment of the quake. In the former Soviet Union these figures might be compared only with those of the major earthquake in Ashkhabad (Turkmen Republic) in 1948 and major tsunami disaster in Severo-Kurilsk (Russia) in 1952 that surpassed 80% and also resulted in complete destruction of the cities (Sasayama, 1996; Vikulin, 1996).

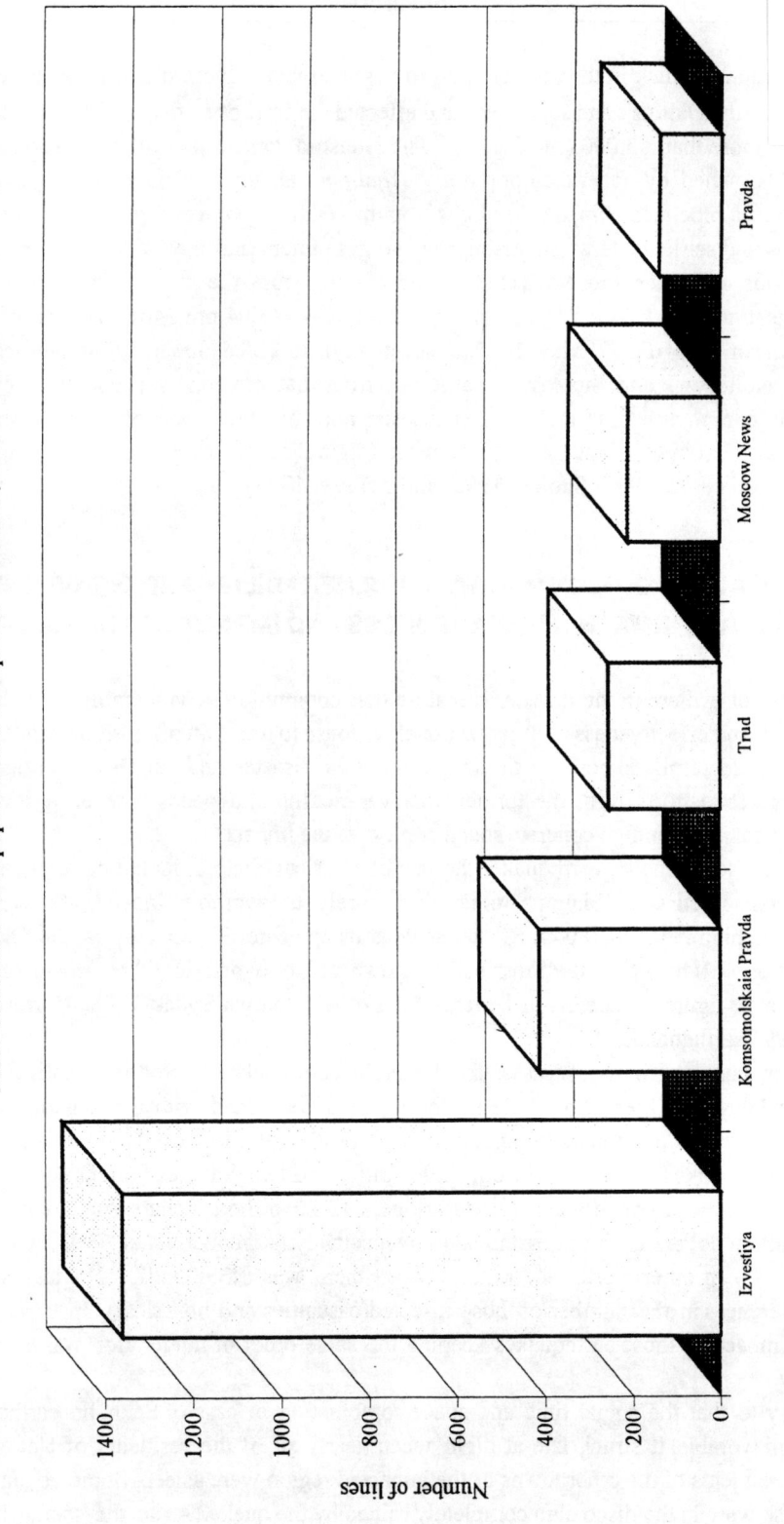

Fig. 20. The Number of Lines in the Stories on KamAZ Big Fire Published in the Russian Most Circulated Newspapers From 15 April to 5 October, 1993

The earthquake struck in the northern part of Sakhalin Island located in the far eastern area of Russia between the Okhotsk and Japan seas and affected the territory of about 15,000 km^2 with a population of more than 55,000 (see Fig. 16). The industrial landscape of this area consists of oil and gas fields owned by federal corporation *Sakhalinmorneftegaz*. This company extracts and through undersea pipelines pumps oil and gas from the Okha *rayon* (or regional district) that has several towns and settlements where mainly oil and gas miners and their families live. This very area turned out to be the most affected by and suffered from the devastating earthquake that occurred late at night at 1:04 am local time on 28 May 1995 (5:04 pm Moscow time or 1:04 pm Greenwich mean time on 27 May 1995, respectively). It killed about 2,000 out from 3,200 residents of Neftegorsk and those who came out from that city on weekends and completely destroyed the community thus making this disaster not only the worst of its kind in Russian history but, as mentioned earlier, one of the most tragic disasters ever (the statistics cited come from: Ostrovskaia et al, 1995; Shoigu, 1995; and Zaitsev, 1995).

THE CAUSES OF COMMUNITIES' VULNERABILITY AND GRAVITY OF DISASTER'S AFTERMATH: PREPAREDNESS AND IMPACT OF THE EARTHQUAKE

It is noted elsewhere in the disaster literature that communities' vulnerability, on one hand, and the pattern and effectiveness of organizational response to a certain disaster, on other hand, are substantially predetermined both by the magnitude of a disaster and success of mitigation and preparedness efforts. In its turn, the former whatever measured, depends both on a severity of a specific physical agent and on concrete social context of the impact.

In case of the Sakhalin earthquake, the set of physical factors, including time and space, should be considered as ambiguous rather than purely unfavorable. Indeed, the earthquake's magnitude was high reaching 9.0 on Richter scale at its epicenter 33 km deep in the Okhotsk sea and varied from 7.1 to 7.6 at the most suffered town of Neftegorsk in Okha *rayon* of Sakhalin Island. The latter figures are nearly as large as those of well known Spitak 1988, Northridge 1994 and Kobe 1995 earthquakes.

However, contrary to those cases, the Sakhalin earthquake affected the relatively scarcely populated and developed territory of the northern part of the island with a population density of less than four persons per square kilometer. This substantially decreased its overall destructive force of the earthquake that resulted in only $0.5 billion of US dollars of direct economic losses compared to $13-20 billion dollars for Northridge, $15-20 billion dollars for Spitak and more than $100 billion dollars for Kobe earthquakes, respectively (Aizenberg et al, 1995; Arnold, 1995; Comfort, 1994). In other words, the ratio between them was 1:33:35:200. No less spectacular were the differences in the number of those affected (casualties and homeless). In these terms the ratio of the impacts of those earthquakes keeping the same order of numeration was 1:16:43:170, respectively.

Contrary to that the social time and space combination in case of Sakhalin earthquake was definitely unfavorable. It struck late at night when nearly all of the residents of Neftegorsk and most of the residents of the other towns of the impacted region were asleep. Some young residents of Neftegorsk were in the disco club completely ruined by the quake. As to the social time of the earthquake, it occurred on weekends when many workers from neighboring oil fields had come back home from their weekly shifts. In addition, it struck at the beginning of school summer vacations when children visit their relatives and friends. According to some estimates, dozens of them came to Neftegorsk just before the tragedy. Besides that, the earthquake occurred in late Spring when the night temperature in the affected area is often less than $0°$ C. That considerably worsened the situation of trapped persons trying to survive the cold and exposure for several nights.. (the statistics cited come from: Ostrovskaia et al, 1995; Shoigu and Vorobyov, 1995; Zaitsev, 1995).

These negative characteristics of the social time were further aggravated by the vulnerability of the social and economic space impacted, stemming from erroneous fundamentals of the economic policy in the former Soviet Union (see the discussion earlier) that was especially adverse in the remote regions including the Far East. Excessive militarization and centralization of the Soviet economy for decades deterred financing and development of the civil industries in those areas involving cost-saving approach to construction of civil objectives including residential buildings. This facilitated the accumulation of resources for development of the military and industrial complex while the number of cheap municipal apartments and infrastructure units increased at the expense of safety and comfort. The deep economic crisis resulting from the dissolution of the Soviet Union and defective and inconsistent economic reforms in early 1990s, further increased vulnerability of the social and economic space. In particular, this substantially narrowed the financial and material basis of implementing mitigation and preparedness measures in the disaster prone areas, including those subjected to earthquakes.

All these had at least two important implications for the disaster under discussion. One of these relate to the quality of construction at Sakhalin Island that immediately arise recollections of Spitak earthquake aftermath in Armenia in 1988 (see: Wyllie and Filson, 1989; Porfiriev, 1993b). Cheap and weak construction materials and technologies, which had been widely used in the construction of buildings and social infrastructure, along with the poor quality of the construction work as a result of low labor discipline, morale and supervision of the workers could not but decisively decrease the sustainability of the structures and augment vulnerability of the affected communities. Obviously, these explanations for the poor quality of construction differ from those often cited in disaster literature and related to poverty or lower income groups, especially in developing countries that simply can not afford construction of housing in safe locations and to adequate structural standards. Nevertheless, the consequences are similar: the increased vulnerability of the exposed communities.

Another implication, mentioned earlier, deals with preparedness including forecasting and warning that preclude and considerably presuppose the success or failure of response operations. From 22 seismological stations that existed in the Far East as late as in 1994, including the one close to Neftegorsk (in Okha City), 19 or 86%, including that in Okha City, had become inoperative because of a lack of budget funds. Similarly, three months before the earthquake the only fire station at Neftegorsk was closed and its team dismissed (Riabchikov, 1995; Tsarev and Zolotov, 1995a). This intensified the deleterious impact stemming from the loopholes in the perspective seismological zoning of the former Soviet Union's territory, which had been conducted in late 1960s and served as a basis for the building codes existed at that moment. Those substantially underestimated the seismicity of the area of Sakhalin Island thus providing an opportunity to build cheaper houses without special protection measures (Ulomov, 1995).

In addition, the regional warning system of the Sakhalin *oblast* which was constructed in 1980 and incorporated 242 electric sirens, 38 broadcasting stations, 34 circular warning consoles and radio and TV networks designated for centralized warning of 75% of the population within 2 minutes and of 85% of that within 5 minutes, covered totally about 95% of the region's residents. Unfortunately, the small town of Neftegorsk was not included in that system and lacked any centralized warning. Given that there was no local warning system in the region, which had 26 hazardous chemical facilities and 7 areas of potential catastrophic flooding, the residents of the affected areas, including Neftegorsk, could only rely upon the telephone early notification, but all automatic telephone stations in the affectedarea and the only telephone cable in Neftegorsk were destroyed by the earthquake (Kaznacheev, 1995; Komandirov, 1995).

These unfavorable conditions, resulting from the shortcomings of previous and current policy at the national level, were further aggravated at the local level by the specific features of the industrial landscape of the impacted territory cited earlier. As the world experience shows, and this study confirms, numerous pipelines and infrastructure facilities (electric grids, roads and so on) providing supplies to an oil and gas complex and neighboring towns and settlements, are prone to the impact of a disaster's agent and often involve substantial economic losses. Moreover, many seismologists believe that the development of oil and gas deposits itself contributed to the initiation of the earthquake. As professor A. Nikolayev, an authority in the Russian and world seismological science, pit it:

Obviously, according to all criteria enumerated earlier the Sakhalin earthquake fits to the hypothesis about potentially substantial impact of oil extraction on the earthquake's preparedness. Essentially, there is not doubt in that the development of the oil fields affected both the process of creating earthquake's center and its scenario (Nikolayev, 1995).

As a result of the Sakhalin earthquake, 17 large residential buildings with 80 apartments in each, the buildings of the local hospital, school, boiler, bakery as well as the officeof the local Department of Internal Affairs(DIA) and the town club were totally destroyed while the other facilities were only partially or slightly destroyed. Between 2,500 to 3,000 persons were entrapped. According to estimates of the Ministry of the Russian Federation for Civil Defense, Emergencies and Natural Disaster Response (MES), the total number of fatalities was 1958 which includes those who died in the hospitals; in addition another 386 persons who survived were hospitalized (Goncharov and Melnikov, 1995; Shoigu and Vorobyev, 1995; Treschina, 1995; Zaitsev, 1995).

The impact of the earthquake also lead to the collapse of all bridges on Neftegorsk-Okha road, the multiple and serious raptures of communication, electrical grid lines and oil and gas pipelines. In Neftegorsk alone the direct economic loss from damages to residential and infrastructure buildings exceeded $100 million dollars while the total economic losses and rehabilitation costs incurred by the earthquake to the Northern Sakhalin soared up to $1.0 billion dollars (Aizenberg et al, 1995; Koff, 1995) (see Table 22).

Stressing the key role of the specific features of the social and economic space in the former Soviet Union and contemporary Russia as a whole, and in the Northern Sakhalin, in particular, as vulnerability factors, of course, does not mean that some common problems of preparedness have not been important. One of these is the well known issue of possibility and accuracy of seismological forecasting, especially for short-term perspective.

This is tightly linked with another crucial problem of preparedness, involving emergency and disaster planning. In case of the Sakhalin earthquake, the contingency plan had been developed jointly by the MES headquarters and its Far East and Siberian regional centers not long before it occurred. The plan relied upon the experience of the field training in April 1995 to respond major earthquakes at Kamchatka peninsular which had been initiated after the seismological forecast of a major earthquake to strike this area in the Fall 1995. These forecasts were immediately followed by the MES order necessitating urgent preparedness measures to effectively respond and alleviate the aftermath of a possible earthquake at the specified area. The field exercises were attended by the high officials from the federal government (Shoigu and Vorobyov, 1995). However, given the real events occurred at another place and with different scenario, the aforementioned contingency plan was to be substantially changed.

Another commonality deals with the so-called structural preparedness and involves the sustainability of the buildings. Like in many other natural disasters, in Neftegorsk the lifelines and older houses erected according to the outdated building codes, poorly withstood the quake's impact while the newer buildings proved to be much safer. All 17 large panel 'old' houses completely destroyed by the earthquake were built in Neftegorsk in 1969-1970 according to the former USSR building codes that tended to underestimate the seismicity of the area while a few 'new' houses constructed within 1979-1983, in accordance with revised codes, were only slightly damaged. These data is comparable with those of Kobe earthquake where totally destroyed were 66% of the 'old' and only 3% of the 'new' buildings (Great, 1995; Koff, 1995; Sasayama, 1996). But even in these common circumstances one could find the impact of the aforementioned specific features of the social space. Suffice it to note that the 'old' buildings in Neftegorsk had been represented the large panel constructions which, while collapsed totally, produced very massive piles of rubble with only few empty spaces within which victims might survive and which may have eased the operations of search and rescue teams. In contrast, both the Mexico 1985 and Kobe 1995 earthquakes featured the flat-slab design and more accurate construction of buildings, thus providing many empty spaces within the rubble and hence greater opportunity for possible survivors and rescue teams.

ORGANIZATIONAL RESPONSE TO DISASTER

The analyzed commonalties and peculiarities of the social context of and preparedness to the Sakhalin earthquake substantially predetermined not only the vulnerability of communities and pattern of its catastrophic aftermath, but on the pattern and efficiency of organizational responses as well.

WARNING AND EARLY NOTIFICATION OF COMMUNITIES AND AUTHORITIES

As well known, implementing warning and early notification systems is the cornerstone of immediate pre-disaster preparedness or early response activities. This requirement failed to be followed in the initial stage of the organizational response to the Sakhalin earthquake, creating a substantial and dangerous delay in providing important information about the coming disaster. The same occurred to early notification of the respective authorities, emergency organizations and public about the scale of the disaster, thus drastically reducing their potential to provide

Category of impact and damage	Indicator
The number of casualties	
Killed	1,989
Missing	150
Injured	375
The number of damaged facilities	
Houses[a]	26
Totally destroyed	17
Severely destroyed	0
Partially destroyed	9
Buildings	9
Lifeline and industrial utilities	
Water supply suspended (duration, hours)	24
Electrical grid lines destroyed (length, km)	200
Telephone lines ruptured (length, km)	300
Oil and gas pipelines ruptured (length, km)	375
Oil and gas terminals suspended (number)	3

[a] Municipal houses only. The data on 1,500 private houses are lacking.

Sources: (Goncharov and Melnikov, 1995; Koff, 1995; Treschina, 1995b; Shoigu and Vorobyov, 1995; Yermolayev, 1996; Zaitsev, 1995).

Table 22. The Neftegorsk Earthquake Disaster Effect

evacuation opportunities and prepare effectively for search and rescue operations. Undoubtedly, a disastrous nature of the earthquake was substantially responsible for that failure and provoked the disruption of communication lines, complete destruction of buildings, including 'command and communication posts' (police department, emergency medical department and so on), deaths and entrapping of the people, including emergency organizations personnel (for example, nearly two thirds of police officers and medical personnel in Neftegorsk were killed, while many others were injured). The lack of short-term seismological forecasting along with the warning system's obsolescence also contributed to that failure.

However, more deeply, as the history of accidents and disasters in the former Soviet Union and modern Russia shows, the lack of warning and early notification (information dissemination) while immediate pre-impact and post-impact response stages, respectively, is rooted in the structural vulnerabilities of the social and economic space in Russia that are especially notable in remote areas. Communication probably may serve the best illustration of the point.

A number of small hamlets and villages in those areas are still lacking telephone lines, let alone more sophisticated communication systems, especially mobile ones. In those settlements, where telephone service exists, it is of poor quality and often is represented by the only telephone apparatus being somewhere at school or local authority. If disconnected due to a rupture or as a telephone company's sanction for delays in payment, it leaves the whole community or even several communities without communication. In an emergency or crisis situation, as some case studies, including the SCC accident (see above), corroborate, it may lead to a disaster.

As to the warning systems in the remote areas of Russia, including the one existing at Sakhalin Island, regardless technological obsolescence and vulnerability to disaster impacts, often such systems do not include small settlements; the aforementioned exclusion of Neftegorsk from the regional warning network in no way is an exception. Moreover, even limited opportunities provided by the existing warning systems are sometimes missed as in case of Sakhalin, where the regional warning system failed to be used "due to the unexpectedness of the earthquake" (Komandirov, 1995). In these circumstances collective and individual initiatives start to play a decisive role in initial response behavior.

The first information about the scale of the disaster came from a police officer who was fortunate to survive after his apartment and the whole building were completely destroyed. Although injured he managed to find an undamaged police car and used it both for reconnaissance of the suffered settlement and to reach the closest settlement. Though the latter was only 20 km away from Neftegorsk, it took him plenty of time to complete the journey due to the destruction of roads. The telephone there was functioning and he informed the rayon authorities in the Okha City about the tragedy.

At that moment the administration and the Civil Defense Service (CDS) staff of Okha City were trying to help 37,000 of their own citizens who had experienced quakes of 4.0 to 5.0 degrees on the Richter scale which fortunately only created cracks and breaks in some buildings. Having received the message from the policeman about the situation in Neftegorsk and not being prepared enough to cope simultaneously with multiple emergencies, the City Mayor and Chief of Staff of the Okha CDS sent helicopter and mobile ground reconnaissance groups to specify the picture of damage (Kozlova, 1995; Ostrovskaia et al, 1995).

The field reports were received and the message was transmitted to the MES, Moscow only by 1:50 am (hereupon Moscow time) on 28 May 1995. Thus, regional and federal authorities had been unaware about the magnitude of disaster for nearly eight and nine hours, respectively after the earthquake struck That does not mean, of course, that until that moment both regional and federal emergency organizations and authorities did not know about the earthquake as such. Its geological characteristics were transmitted through the communication circuits of the Ministry of Defense of the Russian Federation and received at the Far East Regional Center of the MES in Khabarovsk and the MES Emergency Operation Center in Moscow much earlier, at 5:46 pm on the previous day, 27 May. Yet even in this case, the delay in the information exchange exceeded 40 minutes (Dibskiy and Trofimov, 1995).

Given the lack of warning and early notification, the substantial tardiness in getting the necessary information about the magnitude of disaster and consequently in assessing the volume, structure and schedule of the delivery of means and forces required for effective response, and considering the remoteness of the affected area, the emergency operations there were delayed by as much as 17 hours. In sake of justice, it is worth noting that such a pronounced delay could hardly be considered as a unique, especially given the remoteness of the affected area and the state of communication there. For example, there was no immediate response in Japan when the Great Hanshin-Awaji earthquake subsided in 1995. Four hours passed before the governor of the Hyogo prefecture asked for help from the Japanese Defense Forces which were mobilized only within another five hours and arrived in Kobe City as late as two days after the earthquake. Japanese prime minister T. Murayama confessed that a lack of preparedness and bureaucratic bungling significantly delayed response efforts (Arnold, 1995; Sasayama, 1996). This is also true for the Sakhalin disaster where considerable delay had paramount and adverse implications for the pattern of organizational response as well as for the effectiveness of the search and rescue and emergency medical care operations.

SEARCH AND RESCUE OPERATIONS, FIRE EXTINGUISHING AND PREVENTION ACTIVITIES

According to the generic organizational response model (see: Quarantelli, 1966; Quarantelli and Dynes, 1977; Drabek, 1986) established organizations represented by police, emergency medical and professional search and rescue units should be the first to appear and act at Neftegorsk later followed by expanding, extending and at last emergent organizations. However, the severity of disaster, loopholes in preparedness and warning as well as the conspicuous delay in communication and decision making reversed this sequence of involvement.

Emergent groups created by those few who had been not seriously injured and able to get from the rubble themselves, were the primary response force immediately after the earthquake. Less than a hundred persons united in small collectives, which with bare hands only tried to find and help relatives and neighbors buried under the ruins, while some survivors were paralyzed by shock and could not move. Their search activities resulted in localizing several places within the ruins where the suffered persons had been still alive. However, the effectiveness of their rescue actions was very low, with just a few persons saved.

These emergent groups were soon followed by extending organizations represented mainly by the personnel of the *Sakhalinmorneftegaz* oil and gas extracting corporation. Miners, operators and others left their work and hurried to their homes and families immediately after the impact. Confronted with the emerging tragedy, they brought in mining equipment (bulldozers, car cranes and so on), whilst some tried to assist the emerging collectives, joining them and forming what may be labeled as mixed or a combined groups. The other volunteers from the *Sakhalinmorneftegaz* personnel used the construction and transport equipment to repair roads so as to facilitate the transportation of professional emergency means and forces.

The administration of that corporation in Okha City after getting the information from Neftegorsk formed and dispatched two mechanized columns with special equipment from that place and Nogliki Town to Neftegorsk. By 2:00 am, on May 28, the group from Okha City, comprising more than 390 workers, reached Neftegorsk. Some of them joined their colleagues repairing the roads; the others, using 120 pieces of equipment including welders units and chisels, joined rescue operations. Later that day, they successfully worked on restoring minimum community services, repairing the phone system and setting up temporary camps and kitchens to provide hot meals for the affected persons. The professional rescuers who arrived later also used these facilities (Yurin, 1995). Unfortunately, the search and especially rescue activities of those extending groups together with emergent and mixed groups continued to be inefficient. The cranes they used to remove the rubble were not powerful enough to lift the heavy plates. They only moved plates, thus sometimes reducing the existing empty space within the debris and even worsening the situation for entrapped persons.

Only then, after emergent and extending groups started initial search and rescue operations, were the established and expanding organizations involved both in these tasks and fire extinguishing and preventing activities. The first established organizations involved were emergency organizations (police and fire units) from the Okha *rayon* and Sakhalin *oblast*, representing local and regional executive authorities, respectively. Around 3:00 am, on 28 May, the joint special unit of 368 police and internal forces servicemen organized by the specially created Operation Center of the Sakhalin DIA department, arrived in Neftegorsk to maintain security, performing patrol, corps identification and documentation duties in the affected area. Despite the complete damage of the DIA building and the death of 70% of the police officers in Neftegorsk, social order and security were effectively maintained throughout the crisis.

As early as the first day, these teams stopped seven looting attempts in Neftegorsk (Ostrovskaia et al, 1995). That not only corroborates the point but also serves as one more illustration of the peculiarities of the social space in Russia during disasters. Given that disaster sociologists usually and justly believe looting to be untypical while natural calamities (Dynes and Quarantelli, 1968; Quarantelli, 1992b; 1992c), with Mexico and Kobe earthquakes with no looting completely supports this observation, one could not but consider Russia, and the Sakhalin disaster in particular, as an interesting case for further study.

Besides police units, the established organizations involved from the local and regional levels were well represented by the fire service. Its units were active not only in containing fires and preventing fire breaks out at the base camp, but in extrication of the victims from the rubble and debris removal. Due to the aforementioned reasons, the extinguishing of local fires in Neftegorsk started as late at 5:00 am, on May 28, when the three squads from the fire depot of the Sakhalin oblast DIA arrived. On the next day, those operations were intensified by the special team of 12 fire-fighters who came with rescue equipment from the Sakhalin *oblast* State Fire Service (SFS). From 28 May to 9 June, the elements of the SFS of the Russian Ministry of Internal Affairs (MIA) only extinguished 13 fires in the rubble and in the base camp, extricated 92 persons including 17 living, while directly participating in rescue operations at one of the demolished buildings (Mikeev, 1996).

Although the established local and partially regional emergency organizations involved increased the scale and effectiveness of search and rescue operations, the latter continued to be dominated by local emergent and extending groups with no or little experience and lacking special equipment both for rescue and medical treatment and evacuation of the mass casualties. The situation called for more active participation of regional authorities and emergency

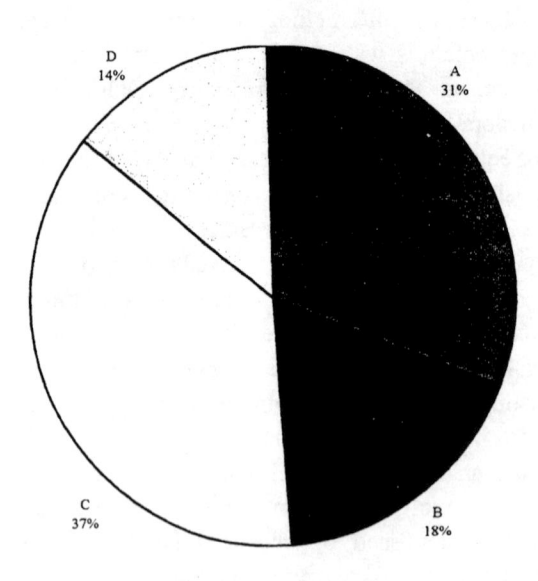

A - Volonteers (local and regional)
B - Workers and employees of industrial and municipal facilities (local and regional)
C - Personnel of the MES of Russia (federal and regional)
D - Personnal of the MOD of Russia (regional)

A - 31%
B - 18%
C - 37%
D - 14%

Fig 21. The Structure of Search and Rescue Personnel Involved in Response to the Neftegorsk Earthquake.

organizations (both from Sakhalin and the neighboring big regions, Khabarovsk and Primorsk *krayas*) and urgent involvement of the federal government, especially the MES and its regional branches as well as some key ministries (health, transport, finance) coordinated by the permanent Intergovernmental Commission for Emergency Prevention and Liquidation headed by the MES Minister. The response activities of these and the Far East and Siberian regional centers of the MES to a certain extent relied upon the aforementioned contingency plan developed just before the earthquake for Kamchatka peninsula.

After clarifying the situation, the MES Crisis Management Center in Moscow and its Far Eastern Regional Center in Khabarovsk from 12:40 pm, on 28 May, functioned on an emergency basis. On the same day, the Operation Center in Moscow, the operation task forces of the MES Far Eastern Regional Center in Khabarovsk, Okha, Neftegorsk and that of the regional (*oblast*) CDS staff in the city of Yuzhno-Sakhalinsk, were organized and actively started to work.. At 6:00 am, the Governor and the Chief of Staff of the CDS of Sakhalin oblast together with 5 rescuers from the Sakhalin Search and Rescue Service and eight physicians left from Yuzhno-Sakhalinsk for Okha. At 6:50 am, a group including eight rescuers, six surgeons, and 13 servicemen of the Central Airmobile Team of the MES (CENTROSPAS) special brigade, also left Moscow for Okha City. At 8:15 am, the MES helicopter with a special team left from the Khabarovsk area directly for Neftegorsk. At 8:45 am, the MES Operation Task Force headed by the MES minister himself and including 23 CENTROSPAS rescuers left Moscow for the disaster area. There they joined the group of 59 rescuers from Kamchatka, Khabarovsk and Sakhalin regions and two mobile units of the MES regional center already working in Neftegorsk (Dibskiy and Trofimov, 1995; Koff, 1995; Shoigu and Vorobyov, 1995).

Later there was a considerable and sharp increase in efforts to transport deliveries into the disaster area, as well as the means and forces of the regional and federal centers of the MES. Within 24 hours only, on May 28-29, the number of rescue personnel and equipment pieces was augmented by a factor of four and two, respectively. After May 30, the operation group, although the strength of its personnel varied through time, numbered up to 1,600 persons, including more than 600 professional rescuers, about 190 pieces of equipment, 20 aircraft and 15 helicopters (Shoigu and Vorobyov, 1995). Not only the rapidity but the degree of the emergency personnel and equipment concentration in Neftegorsk should be especially stressed. Calculations show that the number of personnel involved there in search and rescue operations per 1,000 of the population affected reached 500 as opposed to 19 in Kobe City and the ratio between these figures was as large as 26:1. The analogous ratio for doctors and nurses soared to 56:1 while for policemen it was also in favor of Neftegorsk although less spectacular (Table 23).

The means and forces of the MES, both from federal headquarters and regional centers, served as a nucleus for the search and rescue and emergency medical care operations in the disaster area. Together with firefighting units of the DIA of the Sakhalin *oblast* and municipal teams of professional rescuers they represented 42% of the total personnel involved thus making established organizations the dominant actors in the mentioned activities. The next key actors were emergent and mixed organizations (the first ones obviously prevailed) jointly accounting for 31%. Extending organizations were composed of the groups of industrial workers of *Sakhalinmorneftegaz* and units of the Far Eastern military district of the Russian Ministry of Defense in fairly equal proportions, and jointly accounted for the remaining 27% of the personnel involved.

If viewed from another perspective, the latter was dominated by local and regional organizations, contributing more than 70% of the people responding to disaster directly in Neftegorsk (Fig. 21).

Given this observation, however, it would erroneous and premature to conclude decentralization to be the key characteristic of disaster response, considering that the management of this process had been administered by the representatives of the federal government of Russia, mainly the MES. So, it would be more reasonable to view the pattern of the Sakhalin disaster response as a balanced one. For example, in contrast to the Spitak earthquake in 1988, when fire fighting activities were managed in the field (Wyllie and Filson, 1989), in Neftegorsk, since May 30, all fire fighting activities in disaster area were commanded by regional and federal coordinating officers, who had in particular come from regional SFS in Yuzhno-Sakhalinsk and federal SFS in Moscow.

The extensive transportation provided, and the concentration of all means and forces and their coordination by the MES Operation Task Force, facilitated intensive and effective search and rescue activities performed in extremely complex environment. During the first day, May 28, 150 victims were extricated from the rubble. The next day this figure increased by 30%. In two days it doubled with more than 300 persons being found, more than half of them alive. Unfortunately, the time factor mentioned earlier worked against the rescuers and from 4 June only dead bodies were extricated from the ruins. By 10 June, when rescue operations were stopped, the total number of those extricated from the rubble had soared to 2,364 including 1,958 dead (268 of which were children) and 406 alive. Later, 31 persons of those rescued alive died in hospitals, increasing the number of fatalities up to 1,989 (Fig. 22).

Professional category	The number of personnel per 1,000 of the population[a]		Ratio (2) : (3)
	Town of Neftegorsk	Kobe City	
(1)	(2)	(3)	(4)
Search and rescue personnel	500.0	19.8	25.2 : 1
Doctors and nurses	33.7	0.6	56.2 : 1
Policemen	22.8	18.4	1.2 : 1

[a] According to the sources cited below the number of population before the earthquake in Neftegorsk was 3,200 while those in Kobe City reached 1,468,000.

Sources: (Goncharov and Melnikov, 1995; Shoigu and Vorobyov, 1995; Great, 1995)

Table 23. Professionals Involved in Response to the Earthquake Disasters in Kobe and Neftegorsk

MEDICAL AND HEALTH CARE, HOSPITALIZATION AND EVACUATION OF VICTIMS.

As mentioned earlier, the earthquake damaged medical facilities and killed most of the medical personnel in Neftegorsk, thus considerably complicating urgent medical and health care activities during the first hours of disaster. The pattern of medical and health care organizational response differed from that of search and rescue operations and fire fighting activities. If the latter were initiated by emergent and extending groups and their mixture followed then by established ones, expanding organizations dominated medical and health care activities during the whole trans-disaster period. The key role was played by units of the All-Russia Emergency Medical Care Service (Goncharov and Melnikov, 1995).

As early as morning of 28 May, 'assembled' medical teams from hospitals of Okha *rayon* and Yuzhno-Sakhalinsk started providing treatment to those who were successful in getting out from under the debris. More than 100 patients received emergency medical care before the main means and forces from Moscow and the Far East region arrived. By the end of that day the number of physicians working in the disaster area reached 40, thanks to the arrival from Khabarovsk the personnel from the Far Eastern Emergency Medical Regional Center. The number of those who received medical care thus increased to more than 120, including 107 who had been seriously injured and who were then evacuated to Okha City.

Starting 29 May, the brigade from All-Russia Emergency Medical Care Center *Zaschita*, including well-equipped specialists with much experience of work in conditions of mass casualties, started providing high-level professional assistance. In addition, about 28 tons of medical supplies arrived from Surgut, Ufa, Perm, Khabarovsk, Vladivostok and other cities and places of Russia while foreign countries and international organizations provided more than 342 tons (Goncharov and Melnikov, 1995; Shoigu and Vorobyov, 1995). Two mobile medical posts with six changing medical teams functioned directly on-site in Neftegorsk, while in Okha City another mobile facility with 40 physicians and 28 nurses was activated (Gvozdikov, Litovkin and Ostrovskaia, 1995). In total, medical care was given to 510 victims including 180 children. The field hospital deployed by *Zaschita* as close as 20 m to ruins, undertook 42 urgent amputation operations, including 15 to children (Goncharov and Melnikov, 1995).

Additionally, the Sakhalin as well as the Khabarovsk and Primorsk regional administrations substantially contributed to an organized evacuation and hospitalization of 203 patients in clinics of Okha City, as well as 98 to Khabarovsk, 43 to Vladivostok, 40 to Yuzhno-Sakhalinsk and one to Nogliki town. A very seriously injured person was hospitalized in Moscow. The regional authorities also took active measures to provide assistance to the homeless; 72 persons were relocated to Okha City and 51 to Yuzhno-Sakhalinsk (Shoigu and Vorobyov, 1995).

Because of damages to and breaks in lifelines, primarily water and sewage systems, many human and animal corpses complicated the epidemiological situation at the disaster area. On 29 May, a special team of 14 specialists organized by the State Sanitation and Epidemiological Inspection Service of the Sakhalin *oblast* started its work in Neftegorsk. Carefully surveying and testing water sources and food, carrying out disinfection and sanitation control at burial places they succeeded in maintaining epidemiological safety in the disaster area (Goncharov and Melnikov, 1995).

Fig 22. The Efficiency of Search and Rescue Operations During the Neftegorsk Earthquake Disaster

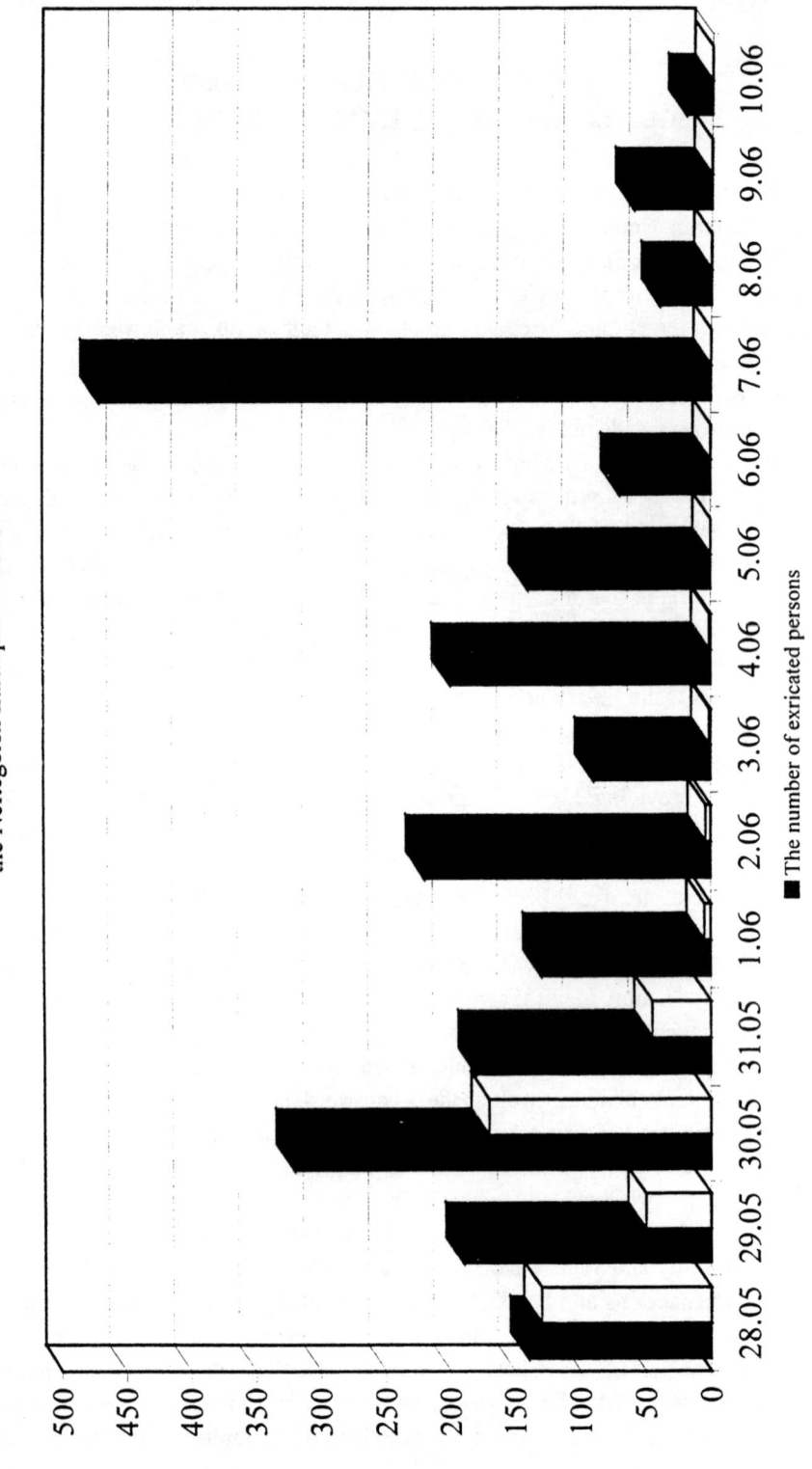

FEDERAL AND INTERNATIONAL RELIEF

The major earthquake disaster at Neftegorsk drew the special attention of the federal administration of Russia and international community. Since he received the first message about the earthquake from the MES at 8:06 am, on 28 May, the president of Russia was permanently provided with the new data on casualties, losses and rescue operations progress. On 30 May, the president appeared on television to express condolences for the families of victims families and to declare the next day as national day of mourning.

The federal government was the key agent in organization and providing federal disaster relief to the suffered people. The Council of Ministers of the Russian Federation after the receiving the aforementioned message early in the morning of May 28, immediately issued the executive order which established the Inter-organizational Governmental Commission for Emergency Prevention and Liquidation headed by the MES minister, S. Shoigu. The responsibility of the Commission was to serve as the principal coordinator for the federal, regional and local executive bodies involved, to estimate the scope of the relief needed, and to develop measures necessary to alleviate the aftermath of the earthquake in the Okha *rayon* of the Sakhalin *oblast*, including coordination of both federal and international relief aid. The latter was of a particular concern of the commission, given that by 13 July 1995 about 441 tons of humanitarian aid came from the Russian regions and from abroad. The bulk of this or 77% was provided by more than 100 foreign countries and international organizations, including 118 tons of equipment and materials, 114 tons of medical supplies, 76 tons of food items and 35 tons of clothes (Shoigu and Vorobyov, 1995).

This executive governmental order also entrusted the Ministry of Finance to allocate to the MES an additional 30 billion rubles (about US$ 7.5 million) to support urgent search and rescue operations and medical care while GOSKOMREZERV (the State Committee for Material and Technical Reserves), the Ministry of Transport and the Railway Ministry were responsible for providing and transportation of rescuers and equipment. Due to these prescriptions, the federal relief aid of 1.0 million rubles (approximately US$ 250) was provided to each affected person in a lump sum, with the first 93 men and women received it as early as 1 June (Pravitelstvo. Rasporiazheniye, 1995a; Neftegorsk, 1995b).

Just after the order was signed, the Federal Governmental Commission, including the chiefs of the ministries and state committees of health, transport, railways and construction and headed by the First Deputy Chairman of the Council of Ministers, left for Sakhalin soon after the MES Operation Task Force. The results of the on-site surveillance and consultative activities of this commission served as a basis for five governmental directives (regulations and executive orders) which should have guided federal relief to and recovery of Neftegorsk. Just to compare, in Japan the federal authorities passed 16 federal laws (acts) regulating relief to and recovery of the Kobe City area (Agafonov, 1996).

As to relief aid to Sakhalin, the government of Russia issued two regulations and one more executive order dated 2 and 3 June 1995, respectively which channeled the flow of financial aid, 107 billion rubles (about US$ 27 million), ear-marked for the impacted area (Pravitelstvo. Postanovleniye, 1995a; 1995b; Pravitelstvo. Rasporiazheniye, 1995b). In addition to the earlier mentioned individual aid of 1.0 million rubles (US$ 250), these documents prescribed providing each family the relief aid, also in a lump sum, of 5.0 million rubles (about US$ 1,200) for burial expenses, 50 million rubles (about US$ 12,000) as compensation for house and property losses and a compensation for a dead family member equal to 200 minimal monthly salaries or about 10 million rubles (US$ 2,400). By 6 June, these allowances and compensation, although incomplete in terms of volume (less than 2.5 million rubles to each) had been issued to 889 victims (Gvozdikov, 1995a).

The federal relief aid activities were tightly linked with the governmental efforts for recovery from the disaster, which also involved adoption and implementation of the two documents both dated 5 June 1995. Those included the regulation on liquidation of the Sakhalin earthquake's aftermath and the executive order concerning financing of search and rescue and rehabilitation works at the oil and gas facilities in the affected area. The documents called for respective federal and regional executive bodies to invest efforts into assessment of the damage and scale of rehabilitation efforts, reinforcement of the ruptured structures in Okha City and some smaller towns in Sakhalin Island to provide room for relocated residents from Neftegorsk, reconstruction of transportation infrastructure and industrial facilities of *Sakhalinmorneftegaz,* and development and carrying out the federal mitigation program including reestablishing of the closed seismological stations, more accurate and detailed seismological zoning of Sakhalin Island (Pravitelstvo. Postanovleniye, 1995c). Besides the direct financial aid to the suffered area, the Russian government provided tax and some other privileges totaled to 465 billion rubles (over US$ 100 million) to *Sakhalinmorneftegaz* to compensate its expenditures on rescue and rehabilitation of the damaged oil and gas mines that surpassed 100 billion rubles in 1995 only and should have reached nearly 1,000 billion (about $210 million) within two years, 1995-1996 (Baskaev, 1996).

Given the complete destruction of Neftegorsk *per se*, the Russian government decided that the town would not be rebuilt and its surviving residents should be relocated within the Sakhalin *oblast,* namely to the cities of Okha and Yuzhno-Sakhalinsk and the town of Nogliki (Tsarev, 1995b). For that the Sakhalin *oblast* and Okha City administrations along with *Sakhalinmorneftegaz* provided funds for building 71 and 12 apartments, respectively, although it would be undoubtedly insufficient for the 500 affected families. Financial support was also earmarked to relocate another 183 families who wished to move to the mainland.

However, as in cases of the SCC radiation accident and KamAZ major fire in 1993, the implementation of these intentions and declarations was considerably limited by red tape and corruption of the bureaucrats and the lack of funds resulting from a lasting economic crisis in Russia in the 1990s. Suffice it to note, that as late as two months after the earthquake, in July 1995, full compensation had been received only by half of the victims while from the earmarked federal relief aid of 107 billion rubles by that time only 10% was received (Gvozdikov, 1995b; Drouzhinin, 1995).

The situation worsened and became dramatic in January 1996 when another earthquake reaching 6.1 on a Richter scale struck in the northern Sakhalin and severely destroyed 14 houses, leaving 800 families homeless (Ostrovskaia, 1996). Given that the Federal 1996 Federal Budget Act lacked mentioning expenditures for recovery from the Sakhalin 1995 earthquake disaster for the fiscal year 1996, the new disaster aggravated even more the problem of funds for the main actors of recovery process including regional authorities and *Sakhalinmorneftegaz* state corporation. In early 1996 its indebtedness to the federal budget increased to more than 135 billion rubles (US$ 30 million), while the overall demand for funds needed for recovery only from the 1995 disaster (not considering the aftermath of the 1996 earthquake) in that year soared to 458 billion rubles (about US$ 90 million) (Baskaev, 1996).

SUMMARY OF THE CASE STUDIES

The above detailed discussion of all three cases shows evidence that in the 1990s Russia has been keeping high degree of social and environmental vulnerability to the major hazards with the SCC radiation accident being the most serious in the world after Chernobyl, KamAZ big fire one of the largest accident in the whole history of the Soviet and Russian industry and Neftegorsk earthquake disaster being the worst event of this kind in Russia ever. Even leaving alone casualties and environmental damage which sometimes were fortunately negligible these adverse happenings inflicted considerable economic losses and provoked or increased social and psychological tension and anxiety in tens of thousands of people in the affected areas reinforced by their permanent distrust to the information from official sources. These transform these accidents into real mass emergencies (the KamAZ case) and disasters (the SCC and Neftegorsk crisis).

Although the direct causes, pattern of the effect and the character of emergency preparedness, response and recovery in the aforementioned cases substantially differed from each other and turned out to be greatly inferior to that in Chernobyl disaster, some important parallels between them should be worthwhile. First of all, they have much in common in respect to the pre-conditions and triggering events involved, prevention and preparedness issues given their resulting from a set of poor standards, loopholes in design and construction defects of both industrial facilities and residential buildings, serious shortcomings in the safety control systems, improper training of the industrial personnel, operators in particular, and human irresponsibility.

These stemmed from and was facilitated by the loopholes in production management organization and emergency prevention and mitigation, primarily defects in contingency planning and emergency communication, the lack of efficient legal regulation of industrial and construction safety in general. They in turn have been deeply rooted in history of the social and economic policy in Russia, mainly its ideologization, excessive militarization and centralization in the times of the former Soviet Union and the lasting deep economic crisis in Russia in the 1990s.

All these reflect the commonalties in the social space where emergencies and disasters analyzed in this chapter occurred and which provided for increased vulnerability of the affected communities. In addition, some essential characteristics of the social time and environmental conditions of these emergencies are also comparable. Some of them have contributed to or aggravated while the other cushioned debilitating and devastating effects of emergencies and disasters (for example, meteorological and geological factors which favored the mostly densely populated towns and cities). The peculiarities of the social and economic space also substantially predetermine both similarities and differences between the organizational response in Russia which has been highlighted above, on one hand, and that overseas which has been reflected in the generic model elaborated by the Western scholars and accumulating the experience of the past disaster research, on other hand. While the key elements and links within the model were found to be the same in the above case studies, the lack of some important components and activities (for example, warning) and availability of those believed atypical (for example, looting during natural disasters) as well as the reverse sequence of response involvement of the main types of emergency organizations should be considered notable. Further systematic and truly cross-societal studies which are still lacking should contribute to the better explanation and modeling of organizational response to disasters.

The similarities in response to and recovery from the Russian emergencies and disasters under discussion are of special interest also from another viewpoint. These reveal a more effective organizational response than in the former Soviet Union in the previous decades, especially while

Chernobyl and Spitak disasters when the system analogous to RUSPRE did not exist at all, although it bears remembering that the scale and gravity of the disasters were incomparably greater than those of the above studied cases.

In particular, the fire, medical and police (militia) services of the affected facilities and communities as well as their colleagues from the neighboring and more distant towns, cities and regions demonstrated their high mobilization and preparedness potential. Despite the obsolesce of the special equipment and sometimes transportation problems they acted effectively thus substantially decreasing the possible afflicted damage. All of this proves that the experience of Chernobyl and other major emergencies and disasters has been not in vain.

However, the efficiency of organizational response to and recovery from the aforementioned emergencies and disasters should be considered as only partially successful. The reasons for this have been inefficiency, unreliability or even lacking of forecasting, warning and communication systems, shortage of the respective specialists and equipment and inadequate public information policy in the affected communities and regions, loopholes in cooperation of all means and forces involved in response operations.

These shortcomings in preparedness have lead to pronounced delays in early notification of the people and authorities, search and rescue operations, sometimes confusion, misunderstanding and misinterpretation between the various levels of authorities, emergency services and volunteers involved in initial stages of response, distortions in informing the public all over the country. This also made inevitable to activate the federal level of the RUSPRE although the effect of the hazardous impact was not always a disaster. experts and services from the federal bodies.

The enumerated problems contributed to the decrease of both efficiency and effectiveness of response and then recovery efforts in terms of additional casualties and economic losses and costs, and the increase of uncertainty and anxiety of the affected people for their children, their own lives and health. The regional and federal executive governmental bodies' efforts to provide relief aid and compensation to the most affected communities and industries, necessary funds for rehabilitation and reconstruction of the destroyed facilities and buildings should be also considered far from excellent.

It is especially vivid if compared with the results of analogous efforts undertaken in the aftermath of the major emergencies overseas, in particular after the devastating earthquake disaster in 1995 in the Kobe prefecture of Japan. Its government not only succeeded in rehabilitation of the world largest trade sea port of Kobe and the city itself by Fall 1997 but developed and started implementing the 10-year program "Phoenix" (1996-2006) of restructuring and radical restructuring of the affected area. This involves improvement of seismic resistance of existing buildings, fire fighting capability, protection of lifelines, community preparedness, but also the measures making the recovery from disaster economically efficient and thus profitable (Agafonov, 1996; Sasayama, 1996).

All these are worth special consideration by respective authorities and decision makers while elaborating the national development and security strategy with emergency management policy as its organic component for the rest of the 1990s and coming decades of the 21st century given the intrinsic interlacing between development and disasters in general, and the lasting social and economic crisis in Russia in particular. The latter has been loosening the integral security, industrial and social safety including that of the nuclear installations.

The latest event, illustrating this and directly involving the SCC, was the emergency suspension of its nuclear reactor on 18 January 1997 which facilitated prevention of a serious radiation accidents (Siniavskiy, 1997). These increasing radiation risks are stemming not only from technological shortcomings and 'human factor' as such but also from decreasing support from the federal government, primarily in terms of timely and adequate payments to the personnel of the nuclear plants.

This process has even reached the point where the chief executives of the nuclear plants took unprecedented measures such as decreasing the capacity of the plants to self-supporting levels as occurred in October, 1993 at the Kola nuclear power plant and sometimes are even at the edge of strikes which are forbidden by the law and the participants may be prosecuted. One can easily explain this paradox taking into account, for example, that during 10 months of the year 1996 personnel of the Smolensk nuclear power plant got no payments at all while the debt in salaries to the personnel of this plant including specialists providing nuclear safety surpassed 16 billion rubles (about US$ 3 million) (Rabotnikov, 1996). In July 1997 the operators of this plant supported by those from the other Russian nuclear power plants undertook a successful march to Moscow and forced the federal government a written promise for soonest compensation.

Thus, lessons should be drawn, conclusions made and stipulation provided for development and implementation of politically realistic and economically viable mitigation strategies including necessary but nowadays missing laws and regulations, flexible social and organizational frameworks, more safe standards and technologies, especially information intensive, and production and emergency personnel retraining and upgrading. In spite of the hard times currently being suffered by Russia, the necessary prerequisites and opportunities always exist for those who possess goodwill, industriousness and readiness to act but not to wait.

AFTERWORD

The above systems analysis of both theoretical and empirical issues of emergencies and disasters and emergency management policy in Russia provides for a number of general conclusions. These refer to the fundamental relationship between emergencies and/or disasters, on one hand, and national and social development, on other hand.

In the recent decades there has been a worldwide trend of increasing the number and complexity of hazards to integral security and safety of communities and societies that have not existed in the past. These have been associated with accelerated industrialization, primarily new technologies and their mixture with natural and social risk sources thus creating specific and escalating kinds of complex hazards. The latter have finally lead to and will increasingly result in compound accidents which produce more debilitating and devastating effect within an affected social system.

However, the rates of this increase and more important the gravity of the effect on communities that would transfer an accident into an emergency, or a disaster or a catastrophe have varied and will vary considerably depending on the degree of social vulnerability of communities which in turn are determined by pattern of economic and social development and national security policy including public protection priorities within a given social system. The societies in transition from industrial to the R&D and information intensive economic systems, from underdemocratized to democratic type social and national development have turned to be the most affected by compound emergencies and disasters, first of all in terms of the absolute number casualties and proportion of economic damage to their GDP. These societies have attained a considerable degree of industrialization being escorted by increasing involvement of high risk modern technologies, but have been still lagging substantially in area of development and application of the information intensive technologies which are effective both in economic (production) terms and providing public and social safety and, most important, have not reached the phase of cultural and social development where the value and protection of a human life are considered as a key priority of a national public policy.

In particular, the experience of the former Soviet Union corroborates this point by a number of the largest accidents in chemical and pipeline industries and, of course, by Chernobyl, the worst peacetime disaster in the world ever. In contemporary Russia although fortunately there has been no reiteration of such a tragedy the case studies of the major emergencies and disasters which occurred there in the 1990s show that in certain respects those have some important parallels with Chernobyl, primarily in terms of its deep pre-conditions and emergency management issues. This may serve as a early warning of the future disasters with the same or even greater magnitude of devastating impact on the society if the necessary lessons are not drawn and the national security and social safety policy including public protection against emergencies and disasters are not radically changed.

In the 1990s the bad news have been the dissolution of the former Soviet Union, the preserving legacy of organic drawbacks and subjective mistakes of the past political and economic policy mixed with the serious loopholes in the current socioeconomic policy. These have resulted in the long lasting and deep economic and social crisis that has considerably narrowed the material and financial basis for reforms, in particular in the emergency management policy area, especially in prevention and mitigation and recovery. At the same time, the good news have been that during this decade the key emergency units (fire, police, medical care) of the former Soviet Union have been preserved in Russia and started to be transformed into a national integrated system for emergency prevention and response (RUSPRE). Although it was still in its infancy in mid 1990s this system already helped Russia to avoid much worse emergencies and disasters that really occurred there contributing between 1992 and 1996 alone to saving of more than 5,000 people and material values worth more than 1,000 billion rubles (almost US$ 250 million).

Nevertheless, RUSPRE could not save much more people while the major emergencies and disasters which have struck Russia in the 1990s and would hardly do this in the nearest future given the incompleteness of this civil protection system and substantial time needed for its full deployment with available resources being scarce in conditions of the lasting deep economic crisis. May be even more important would be the keeping bias on technical capacity of this organizational system which implies the increase of availability and efficiency of its information collection and processing, search and rescue and relief capabilities. Although these would definitely contribute positively to preparedness and response and help to reduce substantially the number of casualties in the affected areas it would most unlikely decrease both the frequency of emergencies and/or disasters, the absolute number and proportion of people involved and therefore the overall gravity of the crisis if social dimension is still neglected.

As the voluminous disaster research literature in the West shows and the above comprehensive discussion of theoretical and empirical issues of emergency management policy in Russia proves, emergencies, disasters and catastrophes are social phenomena being deeply rooted in the nature of human behavior and social organization and decision making and implementation, and intrinsically associated with the impact on communities and societies. It means that whatever sophisticated are information and other modern technologies involved in these would be insufficient for organization of an efficient and effective system of protection people against multiple threats.

Such an organizational system should no less but even more require for social solutions of emergency problems, especially in terms of their prevention and mitigation. These imply proactive emergency management policy including planning as a main component which should be an organic but specific part of national development and security policies responsible for reducing social and environmental vulnerability of communities and society as a whole. This in turn presumes the emphasis on endogenous rather than exogenous causes and agents of emergencies, disasters and catastrophes and much better understanding of collective and organizational behavior in diverse cultural domains, in particular during warning, trans-emergency communication and relief.

Unfortunately, for many decades in the former Soviet Union and to a substantial extent in contemporary Russia these issues have been ignored by ideological reasons and then undervalued due to considerations of momentary political and research advantages. As a result there is still a considerable discrepancy between what should be studied and implemented as a priority task of the national emergency management strategy and policy, on one hand, and what has been done in theory and practice in this field, on other hand. It means that the conspicuously increasing proportion of research and management efforts should be invested in overcoming this gap in order to prevent and cope efficiently with even more debilitating and devastating emergencies, disasters and catastrophes. In particular, these should give impetus to studying both positive and negative experience of Russia itself and the societies and nations more advanced in the area under discussion.

In this study I have tried to make a feasible contribution to this research agenda and a better understanding of the most important and pressing issues of emergency and disaster policy in Russia by international research and management communities and general interested public. If this succeeds even partially I would consider the main task of this book fulfilled.

ANNEX 1

LIST OF ABBREVIATIONS AND ACRONYMS
1. UNITS, MEASURES AND SYMBOLS
1.1 Linear, Square and Volume Measures

m	meter(s)
m^2	square meter(s)
m^3	cubic meter(s)
km	kilometer(s)
km^2	square kilometer(s)
1.2	Time Measure
s	second(s)
h	hour(s)
1.3	Temperature Measure
C	centigrade (Celsius)
1.4	Radiation Measures
Ci	curies
mCi	millicuries
μCi	microcuries
R	roentgen
mR	milliroentgen
μR	microroentgen
1.5	Mathematical Symbols
$+$	addition
x	multiplication
$:$	division
f	function
min	minimum
$\rightarrow$	approaches to
Σ	algebraic sum
$\subset$	is contained in

2. ORGANIZATIONS

Abbreviations and acronyms of the Russian federal executive bodies and governmental organizations most frequently cited are presented below. The names of these are given in accordance with the latest Presidential Decree No 1177 approved on 14 August 1996 except the cases especially specified. In the text they are also marked with capitals and the meaning of each abbreviation (acronym) used for the first time in each chapter is given there. As to specific terms' abbreviations and acronyms, they are commented directly in the text of the book and marked there with capital letters.

CBFP - Chief Board of Fire Protection in the Ministry of Internal Affairs of the Russian Federation (since 1994 the FIPRES)
CENTROSPAS - Central Airmobile Rescue Team of the MES
CDR - Civil Defense of the Russian Federation
CIS - Commonwealth of Independent States
DIA - Department of Internal Affairs (in the regions and cities of Russia)

EMERCOM - State Committee of the Russian Federation for Civil Defense, Emergencies and Natural Disaster Response (since 1994 the MES which also preserved this acronym, EMERCOM)

FIPRES - Fire Prevention and Rescue Service in the Ministry of Internal Affairs of the Russian Federation (since 1995 the SFS)

FSS - Federal Security Service of the Russian Federation

GOSATOMNADZOR - Nuclear Regulatory Committee of the Russian Federation (since August 1996 the Federal Supervision of Russia for Nuclear and Radiation Safety)

GOSKOMPRIRODA - State Committee for Environmental Protection and Natural Resources (both in the former USSR and Russia till 1993 when replaced by MINPRIRODA) and the State Committee of the Russian Federation for Environmental Protection (since August 1996 when MINPRIRODA Russia was dismissed)

GOSKOMREZERV - State Committee for Material and Technical Reserves of the Russian Federation (since August 1996 the State Committee of the Russian Federation for State Reserves)

GOSKOMSTAT - State Statistical Committee of the Russian Federation

GOSGORTECHNADZOR - State Technological Supervision for Mining and Industry in Russia (since August 1996 the Federal Mining and Industrial Supervision of Russia)

GOSSTRAKH - State Insurance Company of the USSR

GOSSTROY - USSR (or the Russian Federation) State Construction Committee (since August 1996 the MINSTROY)

IAEA - International Atomic Energy Agency

MES (EMERCOM) - Ministry of the Russian Federation for Civil Defense Emergencies and Natural Disaster Response

MIA - Ministry of Internal Affairs of the Russian Federation

MINATOM - Ministry of the Russian Federation for Nuclear Energy;

MINPRIRODA - Ministry of Environmental Protection and Natural Resources of the Russian Federation (since August 1996 the State Committee of the Russian Federation for Environmental Protection)

MINSTROY - Ministry of Construction of the Russian Federation

MINTRANS - Ministry of Transportation of the Russian Federation

MOD - Ministry of Defense of the Russian Federation

MOP - Ministry of Public Health of the Russian Federation

REST - Regional Special Team (of firefighters)

ROSGEOKOM - State Geological Committee of the Russian Federation (in August 1996 transformed into a department within the new Ministry of Natural Resources of the Russian Federation)

ROSGIDROMET - Federal Hydrometeorology and Environmental Monitoring Service of the Russian Federation (in August 1996 transformed into a department within the new Ministry of Natural Resources of the Russian Federation)

RUSPRE - Unified State System for Emergency Prevention and Response of the Russian Federation

SERES - Search and Rescue Service Units of the MES

SFS - State Fire Service of the Ministry of Internal Affairs of the Russian Federation

ANNEX 2

FEDERAL EXECUTIVE BODIES INCORPORATED WITHIN THE UNIFIED STATE SYSTEM FOR EMERGENCY PREVENTION AND RESPONSE IN THE RUSSIAN FEDERATION (RUSPRE)

(as approved by the Governmental Regulation of 5 November 1995 No. 1113 and amended by the Presidential Decrees of 14 August 1996 No 1177 and of 17 March 1997 No 249)

1. Federal ministries
The Ministry of Agriculture and Food of the Russian Federation
The Ministry of Communications the Russian Federation
The Ministry of Construction of the Russian Federation
The Ministry of Defense of the Russian Federation
The Ministry of Economy of the Russian Federation
The Ministry of Finance of the Russian Federation
The Ministry of Foreign Affairs of the Russian Federation
The Ministry of Fuel and Energy of the Russian Federation
The Ministry of General and Professional Education of the Russian Federation
The Ministry of Health of the Russian Federation
The Ministry of Internal Affairs of the Russian Federation
The Ministry of Labor and Social Development of the Russian Federation
The Ministry of Natural Resources of the Russian Federation
The Ministry of Railways of the Russian Federation
The Ministry of the Russian Federation for Civil Defence, Emergencies and Liquidation of the Consequences of Natural Disasters
The Ministry of the Russian Federation for Cooperation With the Countries - Members of the Commonwealth of Independent States (CIS)
The Ministry of the Russian Federation for Nationalities and Federative Relations
The Ministry of Transport the Russian Federation

2. Other federal executive bodies

State Committees of the Russian Federation
The State Committee of the Russian Federation for Communication and Information
The State Committee of the Russian Federation for Environmental Protection
The State Committee of the Russian Federation for Science and Technology
The State Committee of the Russian Federation for Standards, Metrology and Certification
The State Committee of the Russian Federation for State Reserves

Federal Services
The Federal Forest Service of Russia
The Federal Migration Service of Russia
The Federal Security Service of Russia
The Federal Service of Russia for Hydrometeorology and Environmental Monitoring
Russian agencies
The Federal Agency for Governmental Communication and Information at the President's Office

Federal Supervisions of Russia
The Federal Mining and Industrial Supervision of Russia
The Federal Supervision of Russia for Nuclear and Radiation Safety

ANNEX 3

OVERSEAS HUMANITARIAN RELIEF OPERATIONS OF THE MINISTRY OF THE RUSSIAN FEDERATION FOR CIVIL DEFENSE, EMERGENCIES AND NATURAL DISASTER RESPONSE (MES)
(by March 1997)

Year (1)	Country (2)	Type of emergency (3)	Type of relief (4)
1993	Yugoslavia	international conflict	food and medical relief
	Albania	floods	delivery of blankets
	Cuba	natural disaster	medical relief
1994	Yugoslavia, Bosnia and Hersegovina	international conflict	child food and medical relief
	Madagascar	hurricane	financial aid
	Tansania	international conflict	food relief
1994	Zaire	international conflict	food relief
	Egypt	floods	delivery of tents, medicine and water vessels
	Japan	earthquake	delivery of clothes and sleeping bags
1995	Afghanistan	armed conflict	food relief
	Congo	epidemics	medical relief
	China	floods	delivery of tents and blankets
	Yugoslavia	international conflict	delivery of food, medicine and clothes
	Korea	floods	food and medical relief
1996	Zaire	international conflict	financial aid
	Iraq	natural disaster	food and medical relief
	Yugoslavia	international conflict	diesel heating fuel

(Continued)

(1)	(2)	(3)	(4)
1996	China	natural disaster	food and medical relief
	Uganda, Mali, Ethiopia, Rwanda		food, medical and agricultural stock relief
	Livan	natural disaster	delivery of tents and food
	Mongolia	natural disaster	financial aid
	Afghanistan	armed conflict, refugees	delivery of flour and clothers
1997	Ruanda, Zaire	international conflict	technical assistance, drivers training

Sources: (Yakov, 1996; *Rossiiskaia Gazeta*, 27 February 1997).

REFERENCES

The following list includes referencesto the cited literature and follows alphabetical order. Russian names, titles, places of publications and publishers are given in Latin transcription accompanied by English translation of the titles in parenthesis. Titles of the publications originally published in English are presented immediately after the author's name (if any) without parenthesis. Titles of the sources (books, journals, newspapers, proceedings and reports) are given in italics. Volumes are indicated by Arabic figure without any specifications (except those for books) while numbers or issues are specified as No (Issue or *Vipusk*), respectively.

Abalkin, L.I. 1988. Chto Poseesh, To I Pozhnesh. (You Will Reap What You Will Sow). *Argumenti I Fakti*, No 26: 1-2

Ackoff, R. 1985. *Planirovaniye Buduschego Corporatsii.* (Creating the Corporate Future: Planned or Be Planned For). (Transl. from English). Moskva, Progress.

Aiszenberg, Ya., Koff, G., Rogozhin, E. and Sidorin, A. 1995. Predvaritelniy Analiz Resultatov Kompleksnogo Izucheniya Neftegorskogo Zemletriaseniya I Ego Possledstviy. (Preliminary Analysis of the Results of the Comprehensive Survey of the Neftegorsk Earthquake). *Federalnaia Sistema Siesmologicheskikh Nabliudenii I Prognoza Zemletriasenii. (Informatsionno-Analyticheskii Bulleten). Spetsialniy Vipusk 'Neftegorskoye Zemletryaseniye 27 (28) Maya 1995':* 225-234

Agafonov, S. 1996. Dazhe iz katastrofi yapontsi umeyut izvlech vigodu. (Even Disasters are Profitable in Japan). *Izvestiya*, January 18.

Alexander, D., 1991. *Natural Disasters.* Amherst, MA: University of Massachusetts (mimeo).

Akt Sostoiania Radiatsionnoi Obstanovki v Raione Avarii Na Sibirskom Khimicheskom Kombinate (Tomsk-7). 1993. (The Act on the Radiation Situation in the Area of the Accident at the Siberian Chemical Complex in Tomsk-7). Moskva, GKCS.

Ansoff, I. 1989. *Strategicheskoye Upravleniye.* (Strategic Management). (Transl. from English). Moskva, Ekonomika.

Antony, R., Dearden, J. and Vancil, R. 1965. *Management Control Systems.* Homnewood, Illinois.

Arab-Ogli, E.A. 1986. *Obozrimoye Buduschee: Sotsialniya Posledstviia NTR, God 2000.* (The Foreseeable Future: The Social Consequences of the Scientific and Technological Revolution, The Year 2000). Moskva, Mysl.

Arifdzhanov, R. 1993. KamAZ Viyezhaet iz Krizisa na Amerikanskom Motore. (KamAZ is Using Americam Engine to Cope With the Crisis). *Izvestiya,* October 5.

Arnold, R.L. 1995. The Kobe quake. *Disaster Recovery Journal* (Special Issue of Electronic Journal).

Arutiunian, R., Gorshkov, V., Maximenko, B. and Tkalia, E. 1993. *Radiatsionnaia Avariia Na Sibirskom Khimicheskom Kombinate. (Obzor Operativnoi Informatsii i Predvareniy Analiz).* (Radiation Accident at the Siberian Chemical Complex. An Overview of Operative Information and Preliminary Analysis). Preprint NSI-29-93. Moskva: Institut Bezopasnogo Razvitiya Atomnoi Energetiki Rossiiskoi Akademii Nauk.

Azimov, S. 1986. Spasti Aral? (To Save the Aral Sea?). *Literaturnaia Gazeta*, No 48.

Babintsev, V.S. 1988. *SShA: Prioriteti NTP*. (The USA: Priorities of the Scientific and Technological Progress). Moskva, Nauka.

Babourin, V. 1990. Sotsialno-Ekonomicheskaia Otsenka Opasnikh Prirodnikh Iavlenii. (Social and Economic Assessment of the Natural Hazards). Pp. 21-29 in: *Sbornik Trudov Konferentsii "Opasniye Prirodniye Yavleniya", Moskva, MGU, 19-20 Maia 1989 Goda*. (Proc. of the Conference 'Natural Hazards' Held at the Moscow State University, Moscow, 19-20 May 1989). Moskva, VINITI (Dep.)

Baiduzhyi, A. 1993. Pol-Rossii Piet Nekachestvennuiu Vodu. (Half of Russians drink Water of Poor Quality). *Nezavisimaia Gazeta*, August 3.

Barton, A.H., 1969. *Communities in Disaster: A Sociological Analysis of Collective Stress Situation*. Garden City, N.Y.: Doubleday.

Baskaev, K. 1996. Gazifikatsiya Dalnego Vostoka Pomozhet Preodolet Posledstviya Sakhalinskogo Zemletriaseniya. (Gazification of the Far East Region Would Help to Overcome the Sakhalin Earthquake's Aftermath). *Finansoviye Izvestiya*, May 24.

Bates, F. and Peacock, W. 1987. Disaster and Social change. Pp. 291-330 in: Dynes, R., De Marchi, B. and Pelanda, C. (Eds.) *Sociology of Disasters*. Milano, Franco Angeli.

Belianinov, K. 1993. V Tomske Vzorvalis Frantsuzskiye Yaderniye Otkhodi. (French Nuclear Wastes Exploded in Tomsk). *Novaia Ezhenedelnaia Gazeta*, May 27.

Beliayev, S.T. (Ed.) 1991. *Mezhdunarodniy Chernobylskiy Proekt. Otsenka Radiologicheskikh Posledstviy I Zaschitnikh Mer. Doklad Mezhdunarodnogo Consultativnogo Comiteta*. (The International Chernobyl Project. The Assessment of Radiological Consequences and Protection Measures. The Report of the International Consultative Committee). Moskva: Izdat.

Bell, D. 1973. *The Coming of Post-Industrial Society. A Venture in Social Forecasting*. N.Y., Basic Books.

Bella, D.A. 1987. Organization and Systemic Distortion of Information. *Journal of Professional Issues in Engineering*, 113, No 4: 358-363.

Berz G. 1991. Global Warming and the Insurance Industry. *Nature and Resources*, 27, No 2: 13-19

_____. 1993. The Insurance Industry and INDR: Common Interests and Tasks. *Stop Disasters*, No 15: 8-10.

Biychaninova, A. and Nekrasov, B. 1993. Uroki Chernobylia ne Poshli Vprok. (Zametki s Press-Konferentsii Pravitelstvennoi Komissii 9 Aprelia). (Chernobyl Lessons Turned to be of No Value. Notes from the Press Conference of the Governmantal Commission Held on April 9). *Narodnaia Tribuna*, April 13.

Bobrov, G. 1993. Vzriv v Tomske-7 Glazami "Greenpeace". ("Greenpeace" View on the Explosion at Tomsk-7). *Spaseniye*, April 16.

Bolshoi Entsiklopeditcheskiy Slovar. 1991. (Large Encyclopedic Dictionary). Volumes 1 and 2I. Moskva, Sovetskaia Entsiklopediya.

Boltachev, A. 1993. Vozle Radioactivnogo Sleda. (Near the Radioactive Trace). *Dialog*, April 22.

Borisov, G., Buturlin, V. and Maleev, S. 1993. Rezultati Issledovaniy Radiatsionnoi Obstanovki v Rayone Vibrosa Radioactivnikh Productov pri Avarii 06.04.1993 na RCHZ Sibirskogo Khimicheskogo Kombinata Metodami Polevoi Poluprovodnikovoi Spectrometrii. (The Results of the Field Research of the Situation in the Area of Radioactive Fallout Caused by the Accident Occurred on April 6, 1993 at Sibirski Chemical Complex Using Methods of Semiconductor Field Spectrometry). Moskva: RNC "Kurchatovki Instiut". (Mimeo).

Borodenkov, A. 1993. Pepel i KamAZ. (Ashes and KamAZ). *Moscow News*, May 16

Borunov, A.K., Kandelaki, V.V., Koshkarev, A.V. and Trifonov, T.A. 1990. Nekotoriye Ekologicheskiye i Geographicheskiye Aspekti Spitakskogo Zemletriaseniya. (Some Ecological and Geographical Aspects of the Spitak Earthquake). *Izvestiya Akademii Nauk, Seriya Geographicheskaia*, No 2: 123-139.

Britton, N. 1987. Toward a Reconceptualization of Disaster for the Enhancement of Social Preparation. Pp. 31-56 in: Dynes, R., De Marchi, B. and Pelanda, C. (Eds.) *Sociology of Disasters*. Milano, Franco Angeli.

Bronshtein, B. 1993a. KamAZ Posle Pozhara. (KamAZ After the Fire). *Izvestiya*, April 28.

_____. 1993b. KamAZ Posle Pozhara. (KamAZ After the fire). *Izvestiya*, September 10.

_____. 1994. KamAZ: God Posle Pozhara. (KamAZ: A Year After the fire). *Izvestiya*, April 13.

Brown, L.R., Flavin, Ch. and Postel, S. 1991. *Saving the Planet. How to Shape an Environmentally Sustainable Global Economy*. New York, London, 1991.

Broushlinskiy, N. and Semikov, V. 1990. Problemi Sozdaniya I Funktsionirovaniya Avariinikh Sluzhb. (The Problems of Organization and Functioning of Emergency Servicies). *Problemi Bezopasnosti Pri Chrezvichainikh Situatsiakh*, No. 1: 17-42.

Brown, M. and Golding, A. 1973. *Collective Behavior: A Review and Reinterpretation of the Literature*. Pacific Palisades, CA, Goodyear Publishing Company.

Buriakov, V. Yu., Naumov, A.D. 1991. Antropogennaia Katastrofa ili Redkoie Prirodnoye Yavleniye? (A Man-Made Disaster or A Rare Natural Phenomenon?). *Priroda*, No 6: 30-31.

Burtseva, T. and Motova, M. 1996. Rossiiskiye Ucheniye Vibrosheni na Obochinu Reform. (Russian Researchers are Forced to the Roadside of Reforms). *Finansoviye Izvestiya*, December 26.

Chechetkin, V., Khotuleva, M. and Dmitrieva, N. 1993. Informatsionnoie Pismo Sovetniku Presidenta RF po Politike v Oblasti Ekologii i Zdravoochraneniya, v Sotsialno-Ecologicheskii Soyuz. (Information Letter to the Advisor of the President of the Russian Federation for Environmental and Health Care Issues and to the Social and Ecological Union). *Narodnaia Tribuna*, April 13.

Chelikov, V. 1993. Chernobyl Sibirskoi Propiski. (Chernobyl with the Siberian Address). *Moskovskiye Novosti*, May 19.

Chrezvichainiye Situatsii: Statistika I Analiz. 1994. (Emergencies: Statistics and Analysis). *Grazhdanskaia Zaschita*, No 3: 8-11

Cities At Risk. 1996. A Supplement to *Stop Disasters*, No 2: 6-7

Clarke, C. and Munasinghe, M. 1995. Economic Aspects of Disasters and Sustainable Development. Pp. 2-10 in: Clarke, C. and Munasinghe, M. (Eds.). *Disaster Prevention for Sustainable Development: Economic and Policy Issues*. International Bank for Reconstruction and Development / World Bank, Washington, D.C.

Clarke, L. and. Short, J. 1993. Social Organization and Risk: Some Current Controversies. *Annual Review of Sociology*, 19: 375-399.

Clement, R., 1989. The Characteristics of Risks of Major Disasters. *Proc. of the Royal Society. A 242*: 439-459.

Coburn, A., Pomonis, A. and Spencer, R. 1995. Seismic Vulnerability Mitigation of Human Casualties and Guidelines for Low-Cost Earthquake Resistant Housing. *Stop Disasters*, No 12: 6-8

Comfort, L.K. 1988. Designing Policy for Action: The Emergency Management System. Pp. 3-21 in: Comfort, L. K. (Ed.) *Managing Disasters: Strategies and Policy Perspectives*. Durham, Duke University Press

_____. 1994. Risk and Resilience: Inter-Organizational Learning Following the Northridge Earthquake of 17 January 1994. *Journal of Contingencies and Crisis Management*, 2. No 3, pp. 156-170

Commission Recommends Delay for NPP Suspension. 1995. *NucNet News*, No 586: 1-2.

Constitutsiya Rossiiskoi Federatsii. 1993. (Constitution of the Russian Federation). Moskva, YuridicheskaiaLiteratura.

Cuny, F. 1983. *Disasters and Development*. New York, Oxford University Press.

De Marchi, B. 1991. EffectiveCommunication Between the Scientific Community and the Media. *Disasters*, 15, No 3: 237-243

Dedikov, V. 1993. S Veroi v Uspekh. (Trusting in Success). *Bezopasnost I Srtrakhovaniye*, October 4.

Deryugin, Yu. I. 1989. Nekotoriye Psikhologicheskiye Problemi Likvidatsii Posledstvii Zemletriaseniya v Armenii. (Some Psychological Problems of Response to and Recovery From the Earthquake Disaster in Armenia). *Psikhologicheskii Zhurnal*. No. 4 (10): 129-134.

Dibskiy, K. 1995a. Sakhalinskii Razlom. (The Sakhalin Brake). *Segodnia*, May 30.

_____. 1995b. U Spasatelei Ostaetsia Vse Menshe Nadezhdi. (The Hope of the Rescueres is Shrinking). *Segodnia*, June 6.

_____. 1995c. Rossiiskiye Experti Izuchayut Uroki Nefegorska. (Russian Experts Study the Lessons of Neftegorsk). *Segodnia*, October 25.

Dibskiy, K. and Trofimov, A. 1995. Srazheniye za Neftegorsk: Viigrali Mi Ego ili Proigrali? (The Fight for Neftegorsk: Was is Won or Lost?). *Segodnia*, June 28.

Disasters Around the World. Global and Regional View. 1994. World Conference on Natural Disaster Reduction. 23-27 May, 1994. Information Paper No 4. Yokohama.

Dmitrenko, O. 1996. Kosmos Nanes Sokrueshitelnii Udar Obeskrovlennoi Nauke. (The Space Inflicted Disastrous Damage to the Despaired Science). *Finansoviye Izvestiya*, November 19.

Dollezhal, N.A. and Koriakin, Yu.I. 1979. Yadernaia Energetika: Dostizheniia I Problemi. (Nuclear Power Energy: Gains and Problems). *Kommunist*, No 14: 19-28.

Domeisen, N. 1995. Disasters: Threat to Social Development. *Stop Disasters*, No 23: 7-9.

Douglas, M. and Wildavsky, A. 1982. *Risk and Culture: An Essay on the Selection of Technological and Environmental Dangers*. University of California Press, Berkley and Los Angeles

Drabek, T. 1986a. *Emergency Management: The Human Factor*. Emmitsburg, MD.: National Emergency Training Center.

_____. 1986b. *Human System Responses to Disasters: An Inventory of Sociological Findings*. Springer-Verlag, New York.

Drouzhinin, A. 1995. Pomosch Neftegortsam Idet, no Slishkom Medlenno. (The Relief Flows to the Neftegorsk Residents but Too Slow). *Finansoviye Izvestiya*, October 20.

Dubrovskaia, L. 1992. Strategiya Sotsialnoi Zaschiti ot Promishlennikh Opasnostei. (A Strategy of Social Protection Against Industrial Hazards). *Problemi Bezopasnosti pri Chrezvichainikh Situatsiyakh*, No 3: 33-47

Dynes, R. R.. 1974. *Organized Behavior in Disaster*. Newark, DE, Disaster Research Center, University of Delaware.

_____. 1988. Cross-Cultural International Research: Sociology and Disaster. *International Journal of Mass Emergencies and Disasters*, No 6: 101-129.

_____. 1989. *Conceptualizing Disasters in Ways Productive for Social Science Research*. Working Paper # 80. Newark, DE, Disaster Research Center, University of Delaware.

_____. 1993. Disaster Reduction: The Importance of Adequate Assumptions About Social Organization. *Sociological Spectrum*, 13: 75-192

Dynes, R.R. and Quarantelli, E.L. 1968. Group Behavior Under Stress: A Required Convergence of Organizational and Collective Behavior Perspectives. *Sociology and Social Research*, No 52: 416-429.

Engels, F. 1961. Proiskhozhdeniye Semyi, Chastnoi Sobstvennosti I Gosudarstva. (The Origin of Family, Private Property and State). (Transl. from German). Pp. 23-178 in : Marx, C.

and Engels, F. *Sochineniya*. (Collection of Publications). 2nd Edition, Vol. 21, Moskva, Politizdat.

Evseev, P. 1994. KamAZ Orientiruetsa na Dostizheniya Mirivoi Avtoindustrii. (KamAZ Chooses the World-Level Car Industry as a Model). *Finansoviye Izvestiya*, August 23.

Experti Vozrazhaiut. 1989. (The Experts Are Against). *Pravitelstvennii Vestnik*, No 20: 2

Federalnii Zakon Rossiiskoi Federatsii 'O Dopolnitelnikh Garantiyakh I Compensatsiyakh Voennosluzhaschim, Prokhodiaschim Voennuiu Sluzhbu na Territoriakh Gosudarstv Zakavkazia, Pribaltiki I Respubliki Tadzhikistan, A Takzhe Vipolniayuschim Zadachi v Usloviakh Cherzvichainogo Polozheniya I Pri Vooruzhennikh Confliktakh'. 1993a. (The 1993 Federal Act for Providing Additional Guarantees and Compensations to the Servicemen Involved in the Military Service in the Caucasian and Baltic States and at Republic of Tadzhikistan and to Those Performing Their Mission While the State of Emergency and Armed Conflicts). *Vedomosti S'ezda Narodnikh Deputatov Rossiiskoi Federatsii I Verkhovnogo Soveta Rossiiskoi Federatsii*. No. 34, St. 1395.

Federalnii Zakon Rossiiskoi Federatsii 'O Sotsialnoi Zaschite Grazhdan, Podvergshikhsia Vozdeistviyu Radiatsii Vsledstviye Avarii v 1957 godu na Proizvodstvennom Ob'edinenii 'Maiak' I Sbrosov Radioaktivnikh Otkhodov v Reku Techa'. 1993b. (The 1993 Federal Act for Social Protection of the Persons Affected by Radiation as a Result of the Accident Occured in 1957 at the Industrial Complex 'Maiak' and Radioactive Effluents Discharge Into Techa River). *Vedomosti S'ezda Narodnikh Deputatov Rossiiskoi Federatsii I Verkhovnogo Soveta Rossiiskoi Federatsii*. No. 21, St. 901.

Federalnii Zakon Rossiiskoi Federatsii 'O Zaschite Naseleniia I Territorii otChrezvichainikh Situatsii Prirodnogo I Tekhnogennogo Kharactera'. 1994. (The 1994 Federal Act of the Russian Federation for Communities and Regions Protection in Natural and Technological Emergencies). *Sobraniye Zakonodatelstva Rossiiskoi Federatsii*, No 36, St.3648.

Federalnii Zakon Rossiiskoi Federatsii 'Ob Avariino-Spasatelnoi Sluzhbe I Statuse Spasatelei'. 1995a. (The 1994 Federal Act for Emergency and Rescue Service and the Status of a Rescurer in the Russian Federation). *Vedomosti Federalnogo Sobraniya Rosiiskoi Federatsii*. N 27: 2194-2216.

Federalnii Zakon Rossiiskoi Federatsii 'O Bezopasnosti Dorozhnogo Dvizheniya'. 1995b. (The 1995 Road Safety Act). *Sobraniye Zakonodatelstva Rossiiskoi Federatsii*, No 50, St. 4873.

Federalnii Zakon Rossiiskoi Federatsii 'Ob Ispolzovanii Atomnoi Energii'. 1995c. (The 1995 Federal Act for Using Atomic Energy). *Sobraniye Zakonodatelstva Rossiiskoi Federatsii*, No 48, St. 4552.

Federalnii Zakon Rossiiskoi Federatsii 'O Pozharnoi Bezopasnosti'. 1995d. (The1994 Fire Safety Federal Act). *Vedomosti Federalnogo Sobraniya Rosiiskoi Federatsii*. N 1: 18-43.

Federalnii Zakon Rossiiskoi Federatsii 'O Radiatsionnoi Bezopasnosti Naseleniya'.1995e. (The 1995 Federal Act for Radiation Safety of the People). *Rossiiskaia Gazeta*, January 17.

Federalnii Zakon Rossiiskoi Federatsii 'O Rasprostranenii Deistviya Zakona Rossiiskoi federatsii 'O Dopolnitelnikh Garantiyakh I Compensatsiyakh Voennosluzhaschim, Prokhodiaschim Voennuiu Sluzhbu na Territoriakh Gosudarstv Zakavkazia, Pribaltiki I Respubliki Tadzhikistan, A Takzhe Vipolniayuschim Zadachi v Usloviakh Cherzvichainogo Polozheniya I Pri Vooruzhennikh Confliktakh' na Voennosluzhaschikh, A Takzhe Lits Riadovogo I Nachalstvuyuschego Sostava, Kursantov I Slushatelei Uchebnikh Zavedenii Ministerstva Vnutrennikh Del Rossiiskoi federatsii, Vipolniayuschikh I Vipolniavshikh Zadachi v Usloviyakh Vooruzhennogo Conflikta v Chechenskoi Respublike. 1995f. (The 1995 Federal Act for Spreading the Power of the 'Act of the Russiian Federation Providing Additional Guarantees and Compensations to the Servicemen Involved in the Military Service in the Caucasian and Baltic States and at Republic of Tadzchikistan and to Those Performing Their Duty While the State of Emergency and Armed Conflicts' on the Servicemen, Soldiers and Officers, Students of the

Schools of the Ministry of Internal Affairs of the Russian Federartion Who Were and Are Carrying Their Mission While the Armed Conflict in Chechen Republic). *Sobraniye Zakonodatelstva Rossiiskoi Federatsii*, No. 21, St. 1923.

Federalnii Zakon Rossiiskoi Federatsii 'O Sotsialnoi Zaschite Grazhdan, Podvergshikhsia Vozdeistviyu Radiatsii Vsledstviye Karastrofi na Chernobylskoi AES'. 1995g. (The 1992 Federal Act for Social Protection of the Persons Affected by Radiation as a Result of Chernobyl Catastrophe As Amended in 1995). *Rossiiskaia Gazeta*, December 1.

Federalnii Zakon Rossiiskoi Federatsii 'O Vnutrennikh Voiskakh Ministerstva Vnutrennikh Del Rossiiskoi Federatsii". 1997. (The 1997 Federal Act for Internal Troops of the Ministry of Internal Affairs of the Russian Federation). *Rossiiskaia Gazeta*, 12 February.

Feitelman, N.G. and Vozniak, V.Ya. (Eds.). 1995. *Ecologicheskoye Ozdorovleniye Economiki.* (Environmental Rehabilitation of the Economy). Moskva, Nauka.

Fentisov, N. 1995. I Opiat - Esli bi... (And Again If...). *Grazhdanskaya Zaschita*, No 8: 38

Fink, S. 1986. *Crisis Management: Planning for the Inevitable*. N.Y., AMACOM.

Foster, H.D., 1990. *Disaster Mitigation for Planners: The Preservation of Life and Property.* N.Y.: Springer Verlag.

Fritz, C.E., 1961. Disasters. Pp. 651-694 in: Merton, R.K. and Nisbet, R. (Eds.). *Contemporary Social Problems.* N.Y.: Harcourt, Brace and World.

Gagarinskiy, A. and Gagarinskaia, I. 1996. Obschestvennoye Mneniye Posle Desiatiletiya Chernobylia. (Public Opinion a Decade After Chernobyl). *Nauchno-Informatsionnii Metodicheskii Bulleten Yadernogo Obschestva Rossii*, No 2: 2-6

Gaidar, Ye. and Yaroshenko, V. 1988. Nulevoi Tsikl. (The Start). *Kommunist*, No 8: 74-86.

Galkina, L 1993. Istoriya Balakvskoi AES Izobiluet Avariyami. (The History of the Balakov Nuclear Power Plant is Abundant with Accidents). *Segodnia*, April 20.

Galushkin, V.A., Gorbunov, S.V., Goriachenkova, T.A. and Cherkezian, V.O. 1993. Osobennosti Radioactivnogo Zagriazneniya Territorii v Resultate Avarii na Sibirskom Khimicheskom Kombinate (Gorod Tomsk-7, Aprel 1993). (Peculiarities of the Radioactive Contamination of the Land Resulting From the accident at the Siberian Chemical Complex (the Town of Tomsk-7, April 1993). *Problemi Bezopasnosti Pri Chrezvichainikh Situatsiakh*, No 2: 64-70

Gapeevtsev, A. 1995. KamAZ Poluchil 100 Millionov Dollarov bez Gosgarantii I Proekta. (KamAZ Received US$100 million Without the State Guarantees and the Project). *Izvestiya*, Septembr 2.

Gazovaia Ataka. 1989. (A Gas Attack). *Sovetskaia Rossiia*, September 28.

Gilbert, C., 1991. Politique et Compexite: Les Crises Sans Ennemi. Colloque International: Le Cadre Therique de la Gestion des Crises dans les Societes: Etat de la Question. CDR CNRS "Crise", Ecole Nationale d'Administration Publique de Quebec, dans le Cadre des Quatriemes Entretiens du Centre Jacques Cartier, Grenoble, 5-6 Decembre 1991.

_____. 1995. Studying Disaster: A Review of the Main Conceptual Tools. *International Journal of Mass Emergencies and Disasters*, 13, No. 3: 231-240.

Glazovskiy, N.F. 1990. Aralski Crisis. (The Aral Crisis). *Priroda*, 10: 10-20.

Goncharov, S. and Melnikov, V. 1995. Za Zhizn i Zdorovie Postradavshikh Borolas Meditsinskaia Sluzhba v Neftegorske. (The Medical Care Service Struggled for Saving the Life and Health of the Affected). *Grazhdanskaya Zaschita*, No 10: 36-38.

Gosudarstvennii Doklad o Sostoianii Okruzhayuschei Prirodnoi Sredi v Rossiiskoi Federatsii v 1995 Godu. 1996. (The Governmental Report on the State of Environment in the Russian Federation in 1995). *Zeleniy Mir*, No 26-29.

Gosudarstvennii Doklad o Sostoianii Zaschiti Naseleniia I Territorii Rossiiskoi Federatsii ot Chrezvichainikh Situatsii Prirodnogo I Tekhnogennogo Kharaktera. 1996. (The Governmental Report on the State of Protection of the Population and Territories in the Russian Federation

Against Natural and Technological Emergencies). *Problemi Bezopasnosti pri Chrezvichanikh Situatsiakh*, No 4: 3-87.

Great Hanshin-Awaji Earthquake: Damages and Response,The. 1995. *Stop Disasters,* No 23 (Winter): 10-13

Grigoriev, E. 1993. KamAZ Vipuskaet Avtomobili. Bez Dvigatelei. (KamAZ is Producing Trucks. Without Engines). *Trud*, April 22.

Grousha, N. 1996. Kak Nastroena Obschestvennost Belaruesi? (What Does the Public Feel in Byelarus?). *Nauchno-Informatsionnii Metodicheskii Bulleten Iadernogo Obschestva Rossii*, No 2: 7-12.

Guriev, N. 1933. "Vezuvii"-15? (vezuvi No 15?). *Rossiiskiye Vesti,* May 21.

Gusev, M. 1989a. Peredozirovka. (Overdosing). *Sovetskaia Rossiia*, March 24.

_____. 1989b. Ozhogi Na Poliakh. (Burns in the Fields). *Sovetskaia Rossiia*, May 24.

Gvozdikov, V. 1995a. V Neftegorske Otmechayut Deviat Dnei. (Nine Days After the Tragedy are Commemorated in Neftegorsk). *Izvestiya*, June 6.

_____. 1995b. Neftegorsk... 40 Dnei. (Neftegorsk: 40 Days After). *Izvestiya*, July 7.

Gvozdikov, V., Ostrovskaia, N. and Litovkin, V. 1995. "'Chas Tishini" Pomog Uslishat Golosa Zhivikh. (Voices of Survivors were Heard Thanks to a 'Quietness Hour'). *Izvestiya,* May 31.

Harris, R., Hohenemser, Ch. and Kates, R. Human and Nonhuman Mortality. 1985. Pp. 129-155 in: Kates, R., Hohenemser, Ch. and Kasperson, J. (Eds.) *Perilous Progress: Managing the Hazards of Technology.* Westview Press, Inc., Boulder, Colorado.

Hawkes, N., Lean, G., Leigh, D., McKie, R., Pringle, P. and Wilson, A. 1986. *The Worst Accident in the World. Chernobyl: The End of the Nuclear Dream.* London, Heinemann and Pan Books.

Hohenemser, Ch., Kates, R. and Slovic, P. 1983. The Nature of Technological Hazard. *Science,* No. 220: 371-383.

Horlick-Jones, T., Fortune, J. and Peters, G., 1991a. Measuring Disaster Trends. Part 1: Some Observations on the Bradford Fatality Scale. *Disaster Management*, 3 (3): 144-148

_____. 1991b. Measuring Disaster Trends. Part 2: Statistics in the Underlying Processes. *Disaster Management,* 4 (1): 41-45

_____. 1993. Vulnerable Systems, Failure and Disaster. Pp. 86-92 in: Stowell, F., West, D. and Howell, J. (Eds.). *Systems Science Addressing Global Problems.* New York, Plenum.

Hewitt, K. (Ed.), 1983. *Interpretations of Calamity.* Boston: Allen and Unwin.

Illesh, A. 1993a. Tomsk-7: Yadernaia Katasrofa ili Dosadnoie Nedorazumeniye? (Tomsk-7: A Nuclear Disaster or an Occasional Incident?). *Izvestiya,* April 17.

_____. 1993b. Tomsk-7: I Zdes Budet Svoi Sarkofag. (Tomsk-7: And Here There Will Be the Sarcophagus). *Izvestiya,* April 22.

_____. 1993c. Yadernaia Vesna: Chto Obzschego Mezhdu Chernobylem i Tomskom-7? (Nuclear Spring: What is Common Between Chernobyl and Tomsk-7?). *Izvestiya,* April 27.

Illesh, A. and Kostyukovskiy, V. 1993a. Yadernii Monstr Zagovoril v Sibiri, Opasnost Pochuvstvovali vo Vsem Mire. (The Nuclear Monstre Emerged in Siberia, the Danger Has Spread All Over the World). *Izvestiya,* April 8.

_____. 1993b. Posle Tomskoi Avarii Ucheniye Slediat za Radioactivnim Oblakom. (After the Tomsk Accident Scientists are Monitoring the Radioactive Cloud). *Izvestiya,* April 9.

_____. 1993c. Nad Tomskom Radioactivnogo Oblaka ne Bilo, No Obstanovka v Zone Daleka ot Idealnoi. (There Was no Radioactive Cloud Over Tomsk But the Situation in the Affected Area is Far From Ideal). *Izvestiya,* April 10.

Illesh, A. and Yakov, V. 1993. Avariia v Tomske-7: Plutoniy v Vibrose ne Obnaruzhen. (Accident in Tomsk-7: No Plutonium Detected). *Izvestiya,* April 13.

Instruktsiya o Poriadke Obmena v Rossiiskoi Federatsii Informatsiyei o Chrezvichanikh Situatsiakh. 1992. (Instruction for Emergency Information Exchange Regulation in the Russian Federation). *Problemi Bezopasnosti pri Chrezvichanikh Situatsiakh*, No 7: 19-22.

International Commission on Radiological Protection (ICRP). 1985. *A Compilation of the Major Concepts and Quantities in Use by ICRP*. ICRP Publication No.

42. Pergamon Press, Oxford and New York.

Ioyrish, A.I. and Choporniak, A.B. (1990). *Atomnoye Zakonodatelstvo Capitalisticheskikh Stran: Sravnitelno-Pravovoi Analiz*. (Nuclear Law in the Capitalist Countries: A Comparative Law Study). Moskva, Nauka.

Ioyrish, A. and Rogozhin, Yu. 1995. Rossii ne Oboitis bez Zakona o Yadernom Strakhovanii. (Russia Can Not Do Without Nuclear Insurance Act). *Finansoviye Izvestiya*, October 20.

Isk k "Kominefti" 311 Milliardov Rublei. 1995. (Komineft is Sued 311 Billion Rubles). *Zeleniy Mir*, No 2: 4

Ivanchenko, L. 1993. Epidemiologi Vozvraschaiutstia v Bolnitsi. (Epidemiologists Return to Hospitals). *Izvestiya*, December 21.

Kapitsa, P.L. 1987. *Experiment. Teoriya. Praktika*. (Experiment. Theory. Practice). Moskva, Nauka.

Kariakina, T. 1993. Tomsk-7: Tam Stolko Lzhi i Podloga. (Tomsk-7: So Much Lies and Forgery There). *Rossiyskaia Gazeta*, April 8..

Kasperson, R. and Kasperson, J. 1988. Emergency Planning for Industrial Crises: An Overview. *Industrial Crisis Quarterly*, 2: 81-88.

Kates, R., Hohenemser, C. and Kasperson, J. (Eds.) 1985. *Perilous Progress: Managing the Hazards of Technology*. Boulder, CO.: Westview Press.

Kapeliushniy, L. 1989. Vzriv na "Azote". (An Explosion at the 'Azot' Plant). *Izvestiya*, 21 March.

Kazantsev, V. 1993. Eto Zdes. (It is Here). *Narodnaia Tribuna*, April 10.

Kaznacheev, N.V. 1995. Problemi Sviazi I Opovescheniya pri Razrushitelnikh Zemletriaseniyakh i Drugikh Prirodnikh Katastrofakh. (Problems of Communication and Warning While Earthquakes and Other Natural Disasters). Pp. 103-106 in: *Uroki I Vivodi Sakhalinskogo Zemletriaseniya. Sbornik Materialov Nauchno-Practicheskoi Konferentsii, Moskva, 23-24 Octiabria 1995*. (The Lessons and Conclusions From the Sakhalin Earthquake. Proceedings of the Scientific and Practical Conference, Moscow, 23-24 October 1995). Moskva, MES.

Kharichev, I. 1989. Do I Posle Zemletriaseniya. (Before and After the Earthquake). *Literaturnaia Gazeta*, No. 39: 12-13

Khrnoika Sobitii 6 Aprelia. 1993. (April 6: The Chronology of Events). *Narodnaia Tribuna*, April 10.

King, W. and Kliland, D. 1982. *Strategicheskoye Planirovaniye I Khoziastvennaia Politika*. (Strategic Planning and Economic Policy). (Transl. from English). Moskva, Progress.

Kirillov, A. 1995. Beznadezhno Zhiviye. (Alive Without Hope). *Rossiiskaia Gazeta*, June 2.

Kishkurko, V. 1993. Gladko Tolko na Bumage. (It is Smooth Only in Paper). *Pozharnoie Delo*, No 7-8: 41-43.

Koff, G. 1995. Oshibki Stoyat Dorogo. (Mistakes Cost a Lot). *Grazhdanskaya Zaschita*, No 11: 40-43

Kolbasov, O.S. (Ed.). 1992. *Pravo I Chrezvichayniye Situatsii*. (Law and Emergencies). Moskva, Institut Gosudarstva I Prava Rossiyskoy Akademii Nauk.

Kollier, J. and Hewitt, J. 1989. *Vvedeniye v Yadernuyu Energetiku*. (Introduction to the Nuclear Power Energy). (Transl. from English). Moskva, Energoatomizdat.

Komandirov, A.V. 1995. O Sostoianii Sviazi i Opovescheniya Sakhalinskoi Oblasti i Rayonov Zemletriaseniya. (The State of Communication and Warning in Sakhalin oblast and the Areas Affectedby the Earthquake. Pp. 65-68 in: *Uroki I Vivodi Sakhalinskogo Zemletriaseniya*.

Sbornik Materialov Nauchno-Practicheskoi Conferencii, Moskva, 23-24 Octiabria 1995. (The Lessons and Conclusions From the Sakhalin Earthquake. Proceedings of the Scientific and Practical Conference, Moscow, 23-24 October 1995). Moskva, MES.

Kondratiev, A. 1993. Na 29-om Kilometre - V Zone Bedstviya. (At the 29th kilometer, in the Disaster Area). *Narodnaia Tribuna,* April 9.

Konventsii I Rekomendatsii Mezhdunarodnoi Organizatsii Truda. 1919-1956. T. 1.. 1991. (International Labor Organization. Conventions and Recommendations. 1919-1956. Vol. 1). Geneva: International Labor Bureau.

Koriakin, Yu. 1990. Skolko Stoit Chernobyl. (How Much Does Chernobyl Cost). *Priroda,* 10: 65 - 74.

Kornev, V. 1997. Prizrak Chernobylia Promelknul nad Volgogradom. (The Gost of Chernobyl Passed Over Volgograd). *Izvestiya,* 22 March.

Kostyukovskiy, V. 1993. Tomsk-7: Yaderniye Budni Posle Vzriva. (Tomsk-7: Working Days After the Radiation Accident). *Izvestiya,* May 12.

_____. 1996. Rasplata Smertyu. (The Payment by Death). *Izvestiya,* December 27.

Kostyukovskiy, V. and Perepletkin, Yu. 1991. Taini Zakritogo Goroda. (Mysteries of the Closed Town). *Izvestiya,* 1 August.

Kotik, M. 1987. *Psykhologiya I Bezopasnost.* (Psychology and Safety). 2nd edition. Talliinn, Valgus.

Kozlova, N. 1995. Zhiviye Uzhe ne Plachut. (Those Who are Alive Do Not Cry). *Rossiiskaia Gazeta,* June 6.

Kreps, G., 1984. Sociological Inquiry and Disaster Research. *Annual Review of Sociology,* 10: 309-330.

_____. 1989a. *Social Structure and Disaster.* Newark, Toronto and London: University of Delaware and Associated University Presses.

_____. 1989b. Future Directions in Disaster Research: The Role of Taxonomy. *International Journal of Mass Emergencies and Disasters,* 7: 215-241

Krivolutskiy, D. and Porfiriev, B. 1990. Ekho Chernobilskoi Grozi. (The Echo of Chernobyl's Thunder). *Sovetskaia Rossiya,* April 1.

Kriterii Otsenki Ecologicheskoi Obstanovki Territoriy dlia Viyavlenia Zon Chrezvichanoi Ekologicheskoi Situatsii i Zon Ecologicheskogo Bedstviya. 1994. (Assessment Criteria for Defiining the Ecological Emergency and Ecological Disaster Areas). *Zeleniy Mir,* No 11-12.

Kroll-Smith, J.S. and Couch, S.R., 1990. *The Real Disaster is Above the Ground: A Mine Fire and the Social Conflict.* Lexington: The University Press of Kentucky.

_____. 1991. What is a Disaster? An Ecological-Symbolic Approach to Resolving the Definitial Debate. *International Journal of Mass Emergencies and Disasters,* 9: 355-366.

Kunitsina, Z. 1993. Serioznoie Proischestvie, No Daleko ne Chernobyl. (A Serious Incident But Far From be Labled as Chernobyl). *Krasnoye Znamia,* April 10.

Kuzminskaia, M. 1993. Avarii kak Sposob Zhizni. (Accidents as a Way of Living). *Deloviye Lyudi,* No 1-2 (30): 18-22

Lagadec, P. 1991. *La Gestion des Crises.* Paris: McGraw-Hill.

_____. 1990. *Major Technological Risks.* Oxford, England, Pergamon.

_____. 1990. *States of Emergency: Technological Failures and Social Destablization.* London: Butterworth-Heinemann.

Larichev, O.I. and Mechitov, A.I. 1988. Metodologicheskiye Problemi Analiza Riska I Bezopasnosti Ispolzovaniya Novikh Technologii. (Methodological Problems of Risk and Safety Analysis for Implementing New Technologies). Pp. 26-44 in: *Systemniye Issledovaniya. Metodologicheskiye Problemi. Yezhegodnik.* (Systems Studies. Methodological Problems. A Yearbook). Moskva, Nauka.

Lave, L. (Ed.) 1987. *Risk Assessment and Management*. Plenum Publ. Corp., N.Y. and London.

Legasov, V. 1987a. Iz Segodnia - V Zavtra. (From Today to Tomorrow). *Pravda*, October 5.

_____. 1987b. Problemi Bezopasnogo Razvitiya Technospheri. (Issues of Technologically Safe Development). *Kommunist*, 8: 92-101.

_____. 1988. Moi Dolg Rasskazat Ob Etom. (It is My Duty to Tell Everybody About That). *Pravda*, May 20.

Leskov, S. 1997. Risk na Starte. Risk na Finishe. (Risk at the Start. Risk at the Finish). *Izvestiya*, February 7.

Litovkin, V. 1996. Adskoye Peklo. (Terrible Fire). *Izvestiya*, November 26.

Liutiy, A. 1988. Riadom s iadernim diavolom. (Close to the nuclear devil). *Pravda* February 19.

Losoto, A. 1995. Tiumenskaia "Maslennitsa" (The Tumen 'Pancacke Week'). *Izvestiya*, 16 May.

Lowenhardt, J. and Berg, van den G. P. 1989. Disaster at the Chernobyl Nuclear Power Plant: A Study of Crisis Decision Making in the Soviet Union. Pp. 37-65 in: Rosenthal, U., Charles M.T. and t'Hart, P. (Eds.) *Coping With Crisis: The Management of Disasters, Riots and Terrorism*. C.C. Thomas Publisher, Springfield (Illinois): 37-65.

Malash, L. 1993. Tomsk-7: Vnachale Bila Lozh. (Tosk-7: the Lies Come First). *Megapolis Express*, June 2.

Mansurov, V. 1987. O Resultatakh Odnogo Oprosa Obschestvennogo Mneniya. (About the Results of a Public Opinion Poll). *Argumenti I Fakti*, No. 48: 6

Marshall, V. C. 1989. *Osnovniye Opasnosti Chimicheskikh Proizvodsv*. (Major Chemical Hazards). (Transl. from English). Moskva, Mir.

Marzeeva, S. 1997. Chumu Zakazivali? (Did You Order A Plague?). *Izvestiya*, March 20.

Meadows, D.H., Meadows D.L. and Randers, I. 1994. *Beyond the Limits to Growth*. (Transl. into Russian). ?oskva.: Progress, Pangeia.

Mechitov, A.I. and Rebrik, S.B. 1990. Vospriyatiye Riska. (Risk Perception). *Psikhologicheskii Zhurnal*, No. 3 (11): 87-95.

Medvedev, Z. A. 1979. *Nuclear Disaster in the Urals*. W.W. Norton & Co., New York.

_____. 1990. *The Legacy of Chernobyl*. Basil Blackwell Ltd., Oxford (UK).

Meshkati, M. 1991. Human Factors in Large Scale Technological Systems' Accidents: Three Mile Island, Bhopal, Chernobyl. *Industrial Crisis Quarterly*, 5: 133-154.

Miagkov, S.M. 1995. *Georaphiya Prirodnogo Riska*. (Geography of Natural Risk). Moskva: Izdatelstvo Moskovskogo Gosudarstvennogo Universiteta.

Mikeev, A. K. 1990. Noviye Podkhodi k Ispolzovaniyu Podrazdeleniy Pozharnoi Okhrani pri Provedenii Avariino-Spasatelnikh Rabot. (New Approaches To Fire Units Involvement in Emergency and Rescue Works). *Problemi Bezopasnosti Pri Chrezvichainikh Situatsiakh*. No. 1: 61-78.

_____. 1993. *Upravleniye Silami I Sredstvami Organov Vnutrennikh Del Pri Likvidatsii Posledstvii Kruepnikh Proizvodstennikh Avariy I Katastrof*. (Managing Police Means and Forces While Liquidation the Aftermath of Large Scale Industrial Accidents and Catastrophes). Moskva, Akademiya MVD Rossii.

_____. 1994. *Pozhar: Sotsialniye, Ekonomicheskiye, Ekologicheskiye Problemi*. (Fire: Social, Economic and Environmental Issues). Moskva, Assotsiatsiya "Pozhnauka".

_____. 1996a. Private communication.

_____. 1996b. *Upravleniye Silami I Sredstvami Organov Vnutrennikh Del I Vnutrennimi Voiskami Pri Likvidatsii Posledstvii Kruepnikh Proizvodstennikh, Transportnikh Avarii I Katastrof*. (Managing Means and Forces of Police and Internal Troops While Liquidation the Aftermath of Large Scale Industrial, Transportation Accidents and Catastrophes). Moskva, Akademiya MVD Rossii.

Mikhailov, A., Paschenko, N. and Souldin, Yu. 1991. Klassificatsiaa Chrezvichanikh SDituatsii. (Classification of Emergencies). *Problemi Bezopasnosti Pri Chrezvichainikh Situatsiakh.* No. 6: 24-47.

Mitin, S. 1993. Promishlenniye Giganti Lutche Strakhovat za Valiutu. (Industrial Giants Should be Insured in Foreign Currency). *Finansoviye Izvestiya,* May 21.

Mitroff, I., Pouchant, T. and Shrivastava, P. 1988. The Structure of Man-Made Organizational Crises. Conceptual and Empirical Issues in the Development of a General Theory of Crisis Management. *Technological Forecasting and Social Change,* 33: 83-107.

Monroe, S. D. 1992. Cheliabinsk: The Evolution of Disaster. *Post-Soviet Geography*, 33, No 8: 533-545.

Morozov, N. 1993a. KamAZ Vozrozhdaietza iz Pepla. (KamAZ is Reviving From the Ashes). *Pravda,* May 12.

_____. 1993b. Somnenii Net: KamAZ Vistoit. (No Doubt: KamAZ Will Revive). *Pravda,* April 29.

Mozgovaya, A.V. (Ed.). 1992. *Sotsialnii Posledstviya Chernobylskoi Avarii. (Po Materialam Sotsiologicheskikh Issledovaniy).* (Social Consequences of the Chernobyl Accident: Analyzing Materials of Sociological Studies). Seriya "Sotsialniye Problemi Ecologii". Vipusk No 4. Moskva: Institut Sotsiologii Rossiiskoi Academii Nauk.

_____. 1993. *Osobennosti Sotsialnogo Povedeniya Naseleniya Regiona, Postragavshego ot Chernobylskoy Katastrofi. (Po Materialam Sotsiologicheskogo Oprosa).* (Peculiarities of Social Behavior of the Population in the Region Affected by the Chernobyl Disaster: Analyzing Materials of a Sociological Survey). Seriya "Sotsialniye Problemi Ecologii". Vipusk No 7. Moskva: Institut Sotsiologii Rossiiskoi Akademii Nauk. 98 pp.

_____. 1996. *Sotsialnaia I Psikhologicheskaia Reabilitatsiya Postradavshikh ot Chernobilskoi Katastrofi: Opit I Perspektivi.* (Social and Psychological Rehabilitation of the Persons Affected by Chernobyl Disaster: Results and Perspectives). Moskva: Institut Sostiologii Rossiiskoi Akademii Nauk.

Naisbitt, J. 1982. *Megatrends: Ten New Directions Transforming Our Lives.* N.Y., Warner Books.

Narodi Mira: Istoriko-Etnographicheskii Spravochnik. 1988. (Peoples of the World: A Historical and Ethnological Reference Book). ?oskva: Sovietskaia Entsiklopediya..

Narodnoye Khoziaistvo RSFSR v 1992 Godu. 1993. (RSFSR National Economy in 1992. Statistical Yearbook). Moskva: Goskomitet Rosiiskoi Federatsii po Statistike.

Narodnoye Khoziaistvo SSSR v 1917-1987 Godakh. 1987. (The National Economy of the Soviet Union in 1917-1987. Statistical Yearbook). Moskva, Goskomitet SSSR po Statistike.

Naumov, N. 1996. Sobirayetsia li Atomnaia Energetika Rossii Viigrivat? (The Nuclear Power Industry in Russia: Is It Going to Win?). *Nauchno-Informatsionnii Metodicheskii Bulleten Yadernogo Obschestva Rossii,* No 2: 26-27.

Nazarov, A.G. (Ed.). 1991. *Rezonans: Yuzhno-Uralskaia Atomnaia: Bit ili ne Bit?.* (Resonance: Yuzhno-Uralskaia Nuclear Power Plant: To Be or Not to Be?). Cheliabinsk, Yuzhno-Uralskoye Knozhnoye Iztatelstvo.

Nazarov, Yu. 1993. Chei Teper Nastal Chered? (Whose Turn is it Now?). *Bezopasnost i Strakhovaniye,* June 6.

Neftegorsk: Pochti 1500 Zhertv Zemletriaseniya. 1995. (Neftegorsk: Nearly 1,500 Killed by the Earthquake). *Pravda,* June 2.

Neftegorsk: Poselok, Kotorogo Net. 1995. (Neftegorsk: a Nowhere Town). *Grazhdanskaya Zaschita,* No 7: 4-6

Nesterenko, V. B. (Ed.). 1993. *Chernobilskaya Katastrofa: Prichini I Posledstviya.* (Chernobyl Disaster: Causes and Aftermath). Volumes 1-4. Minsk,Test.

Nesvetailov, G. A. 1992. Chernobyl s Tochki Zreniya Sotsiologii Katastrof. (Chernobyl From the Viewpoint of Sociology of Disasters). *Vestnik Rossiiskoi Akademii Nauk*, No 4: 54-65.

Nikipelov, B.V, Romanov, G.N., Buldakov, L.A.Babyev, N.S. and Kholina, Yu.B. 1989. Radiatsionnaia Avariia na Yuzhnom Urale v 1957 Godu. (Radiation Accident in the South Urals in 1957). *Atomnaia Energetika*, 67, No 2: 74-86.

Nikitin, S. and Feofanov, K. 1992. Sotsiologicheskaya Teoriya Riska v Poiskakh Svoiego Subyekta. (Sociological Theory of Risk in Search of its Own Subject). *Sotsiologicheskiye Issledovaniya*, No 3: 120-127.

Nikolayev, A.V. 1993. Initsiirovaniye Zemletriasenii Podzemnimi Yadernimi Vzrivami. (Provoking Earthquakes by Underground Nuclear Tests). *Vestnik Rossiikoi Akademii Nauk*, No. 63 (2): 113-117.

_____. 1995. Problemi Navedennoi Seismichnosti v Sviazi s Sakhalinskim Zemletriaseniyem. (Problems of Induced Seismicity Related to the Sakhalin Eathquake). Pp. 144-146 in: *Uroki I Vivodi Sakhalinskogo Zemletriaseniya. Sbornik Materialov Nauchno-Practicheskoi Conferencii, Moskva, 23-24 Octiabria 1995.* (The Lessons and Conclusions From the Sakhalin Earthquake. Proc. of the Scientific and Practical Conference, Moscow, 23-24 October 1995). Moskva, MES.

Normi Radiatsionnoi Bezopasnosti NRB-76/87 I Osnovniye Sanitarniye Pravila Raboti s Radioactivnimi Vezchestvami I Drugimi Istochnikami Ioniziruyuschikh Izlucheniy OSP-72/87. 1988. (The Radiation Safety Standards RSS-76/87 and Basic Sanitary Regulations for Handling Radioactive Substances and Other Sources of IIonizing Emission BSR-72/87. Moskva, Energoatomizdat.

Osipov, V.I. 1993. Metodika Otsenki Opasnosti Prirodnikh Katastrof. (The Methodology of Natural Hazards Assessment). *Problemi Bezopasnosti pri Tchrezvitchainikh Situatsiakh*, No 10: 23-38.

_____. 1995. Prirodniye Katastrofi v Tsentre Vnimaniya Uchenikh. (Natural Disasters Are In the Focus of Researchers). *Vestnik Rossiiskoi Akademii Nauk*, 65, No 6: 483-495.

Osnovi Zakonodatelstva Rossiiskoi Federatsii ob Okhrane Truda. 1993. (The Fundamentals of the Labor Protection Law of the Russian Federation). *Rossiiskaia Gazeta*, September 1.

Osnovi Zakonodatelstva Rossiiskoi Federatsii ob Okhrane Zdorovia Grazhdan. 1993. (The Fundamentals of the Health Law of the Russian Federation). *VedomostiS'ezda Narodnikh Deputatov Rossiiskoi Federatsii I Verkhovnogo Soveta Rossiiskoi Federatsii*. No. 33, St. 1318

Osoboye Mnenie ob Avarii. 1993. (A Different Opinion on the Accident). *Pravda*, May 13.

Ostrovskaia, N., Zheludkov, A., Mikheev, V. and Urigashvili, B. 1995. Chislo Zhertv na Sakhaline Prodolzhaet Rasti. (The Number of Victims at Sakhalin Keeps Increasing). *Izvestiya*, May 30.

Ostrovskaia, N. 1996. Esche 800 Sakhalinskikh Semei Lishilis Zhilia. (800 Families are Added to the Homeless). *Izvestiya*, January 10.

Pavlov, S. 1996a. Gosudarstenniye Inyektsii Bolnomu KamAZu Poka ne Pomogaiut. (State Loans are Still Useless for KamAZ). *Finansoviye Izvestiya*, March 5.

_____. 1996b. KamAZ Ozhidaet Ocherednoi Ubitochnii God. (KamAZ is Expecting the Next Unprofitable Year). *Finansoviye Izvestiya*, April 23.

Paton, B.O. 1986. Bezopasnost Progressa. (The Safety of the Progress). *NTR: Problemi I Resheniia*, No 18: 4-5

Pelanda, C., 1982a. Disaster and Order: Theoretical Problems in Disaster Research. Paper presented at the 10th World Congress of Sociology. Mexico City, Mexico, August 16-21.

_____. 1982b. Disaster and Sociosystemic Vulnerability. Pp. 67-91 in: *B.G. Jones and M. Tomazevic (Eds.). Social and Economic Aspects of Earthquakes*. Skopje: Institute of Earthquake Engineering and Engineering Seismology, University of Kiril and Metodiy. Preliminary paper No 68. Disaster Research Center, Ohio University.

Pereubedit ne Predstavliaetsa Vozmozhnim. 1993. (There Seems no Chance to Change the Opinion). *Tomskii Vestnik,* April 9.

Perrow, C. 1984. *Normal Accidents: Living with High Risk Technologies.* New York: Basic Books.

Pertsevaia, L. 1993. Goreli, Gorim i Budem Goret. (There were, There are and There will be Fires). *Moscow News,* May 16.

Petak, W. 1985. Emergency Management: A Challenge for Public Administration. *Public Administration Review*, 45, Special Issue: 3-6.

Pisano, F. 1995. Natural Disaster Reduction and Insurance Markets. *Stop Disasters*, No 24: 21-22.

Poiasnitelnaia Zapiska. 1993. (Comment to Information and Normative Materials). Pp. 2-18 in: *Sbornik Informatsionno-Analiticheskikh Materialov po Voprosam Preodoleniya v Rossiiskoi Federatsii Posledstviy Chernobylskoi Katastrofi. Chast 1.* (Collection of Information and Analitical Materials on Coping With Chernobyl Disaster Aftermath in the Russian Federation. Part 1). Moskva: IBRAE RAN, MES.

Pokrovskiy, A. 1993. Proizoshla Avariia. Naznachena Komissiia. (An Accident Occurred. A Commission Appointed). *Pravda*, June 8.

Pokrovskiy, N. 1992. Vtoraia Zapoved Funktsionalizma Roberta Mertona. (The Second Commandment of the Robert Merton's functionalism). *Sotsiologicheskiye Issledovaniya*, No 2: 114-117.

Popov, D. 1993. Ogni Moskvi. (The Fires in Moscow). *Moskovski Komsomolets*, December 18.

Popov, N., Sazonov, V. and Farberov, A. 1993. Otnosheniye Naseleniya Altaiskogo Kraia k Problemam Zagriazneniya Okruzhaiuschei Sredi. (The Attitute of the Population of the Altai Region To Environmental Contamination Problems). *Problemi Bezopasnosti pri Chrezvitchainikh Situatsiakh,* No 6: 86-101.

Porfiriev, B. N. 1988. Chrezvichainiye Situatsii kak Sledstviye NTR (Metodologicheskii Aspekt). (Disasters and Emergencies as an Outcome of Scientific and Technological Revolution). *Sbornik Trudov VNIISI,* Vipusk 5, Moskva: 48-52.

_____. 1989. *Organizatsiya Upravleniya v Chrezvichanikh Situatsiyakh: Problemi Predotvrascheniia I Sokrascheniia Masshtabov Posledstvii Technologicheskikh I Prirodnikh Katastrof.* (Organization OF Emergency Management : Problems of Prevention and Mitigation of Technological and Natural Disasters). Moskva, Znanie.

_____. 1990. *Ekologicheskaia Expertiza I Risk Tekhnologii.* (Environmental Impact Assessment and Technological Risk). Moskva, VINITI.

_____. 1991a. *Gosudarstvennoye Upravleniye v Chrezvichanikh Situatsiyakh.* (Public Administration in Disasters and Emergencies). Moskva, Nauka.

_____. 1991b. Boris Porfiriev: Premieres Victimes, Les Infantes. *La Croix.* No 3288. 26 Avril

_____. 1991c. Systemnaia Kontseptsiia Natsionalnoi Bezopasnosti. (Systems Concept of National Security). *Problemi Bezopasnosti pri Chrezvichainikh Situatsiyakh,* No 4: 1-14

_____. 1991d. *Upravleniye v Chrezvichanikh Situatsiyakh: Problemi Teorii I Praktiki.* (Disaster and Emergency Management: Problems of Theory and Practice). Seriya "Itogi Nauki I Tekhniki. Bezopasnost pri Chrezvichainikh Situatsiyakh". (Series "Results of the R&D. Safety in Emergencies"). Moskva: VINITI.

_____. 1992a. The Environmental Dimension of National Security: A Test of System Analysis Method. *Environmental Management,* 16, No 6: 735-742

_____. 1992b. Policy Responses to Large Scale Accidents in the Soviet Union. *International Journal of Mass Emergencies and Disasters,* 10, No 1: 179-188.

_____. 1993a. Strategiya Protivodeistviya Posledstviyam Kyshtymskoi Avarii s Tochki Zreniya Kontseptsii Riska. (The Strategy of Response to and Recovery From the Kyshtym Disaster From the Viewpoint of A Risk Concept). Pp. 315-323 in: Krivolutskiy, D.A. and Sokolov, V.E. (Eds.). *Ekologicheskiye Posledstviya Radioaktivnogo Zagriazneniya na Yuzhnom Urale.* (Ecological Impact of the Radioactive Contamination of the Southern Urals). Moskva, Nauka.

_____. 1993b. Uncertainties in Natural Hazards Prediction and Its Effect on the User Communities Perception: Soviet Union Case Study. Pp. 49-56 in: Nemec, J., Nigg, J.M. and Siccardi, F. *Prediction and Perception of Natural Hazards.* Dordrecht / Boston / London, Kluwer Academic Publishers.

_____. 1995. Disaster and Disaster Areas: Methodological Issues of Definition and Delineation. *International Journal of Mass Emergencies and Disasters,* 13, No 3: 285-304.

_____. 1996a. Environmental Aftermath of the Radiation Accident at Tomsk-7. *Environmental Management,* 20, No 1: 25-33.

_____. 1996b. Social Aftermath and Organizational Response to a Major Disaster: The Case of the 1995 Sakhalin Earthquake in Russia. *Journal of Contingencies and Crisis Management,* 4, No 1: 218-227.

_____. 1996c. Sotsialno-Economicheskaia Reabilitatsiia Territorii, Postradavshikh ot Radiatsionnogo Vozdeistviia, s Tochki Zrenia Kontseptsii Riska. (Social and Economic Rehabilitation of the Areas Affected by Radiation Impact From the Risk Conception Viewpoint). *Problemi Bezopasnosti pri Chrezvichainikh Situatsiyakh,* No 11: 27-44

_____. 1997. Environmental Policy in Russia: Economic, Legal and Organizational Issues. *Environmental Management,* 21, No 2: 147-157

Porfiriev, B.N., Evtin Yu., Koriakin, Yu.I., Orlov, V.V. and Chernilin, Yu.F. 1993. Analiz Strategii Razvitiya Otechestvennoi Yadernoi Energetiki v Svete Chernobylskoi Katastrofi. Pp. 13-43 in: Nesterneko, V. B. (Ed.). *Chernobilskaya Katastrofa: Prichini I Posledstviya.* (Chernobyl Disaster: Causes and Aftermath). Volumes I-IV. Volume 1. "Neposredsvenniye Prichini Avarii na Chernobylskoi AES. Dozimetricheskiy Control. Meri Zaschiti i Ich Effecivnost": (Direct Causes of the Accident at Chernobyl NPP. Dozemetrical Control. Protection Measures and Their Effectiveness). Minsk, Test,

Portnoff, A.-I. 1989. Accidents Industrielles: Records a Abbatre. *Science et Technologie,* No 16: 39-41

Pozhar kak dvigatel progressa. (1993a). (Fire a catalyst of progress). *Trud,* April 30.

Pozhar na KamAZe: Fakti l Kommentarii. (1993b). (Fire at KamAZ: facts and commentaries). *Pozharnaia Bezopasnost, Informatika l Tekhnika,* 2: 131-141.

Pravitelstvo Rossiiskoi Federatsii. Postanovleniye ot 18.04.1992 No 261. "O Sozdanii Rossiiskoi Sistemi Preduprezhdeniya I Deistviy v Chrezvichainikh Situatsiakh. Polozheniye o Rossiiskoi Sistemi Preduprezhdeniya I Deistviy v Chrezvichainikh Situatsiakh". 1992. (The Government of the Russian Federation. Regulation 'Establishing the Russian System for Prevention of and Actions in Emergencies. The Status of the Russian System for Prevention of and Actions in Emergencies'). *Sbornik Normativnikh Aktov Rossiiskoi Federatsii.* No 13: 27-28

Pravitelstvo Rossiiskoi Federatsii. Postanovleniye ot 25.12.1992 No 1011. "Ob Utverzhdenii Polozheniya o Federalnoi Sluzhbe Rossii po Gidrometeorologii I Monitoringu Okruzhayuschei Sredi". 1993. (The Government of the Russian Federation. Regulation 'Confirming the Statute of the Federal Service Hydrometeorology and Environmental Monitoring'). *Sobraniye Aktov Prezidenta Rossiiskoi Federatsii I Pravitelstva Rosiiskoi Federatsii.* No 4:. 303

Pravitelstvo Rossiiskoi Federatsii. Postanovleniye ot 11.05.1993 No 444 "O Federalnoi Systeme Seismologicheskikh Nabliudenii I Prognoza Zemletriasenii". 1994. (The Government of the Russian Federation. Regulation 'The Federal System for Seismological Monitoring and

Forecasting). *Federalnaia Sistema Siesmologicheskikh Nabliudenii I Prognoza Zemletriasenii. (Informatsionno-Analiticheskii Bulleten)*. No 1: 3-5.

Pravitelstvo Rossiiskoi Federatsii. Postanovleniye ot 2.06.1995 No 539 "O Poriadke Predostavleniya Edinovremennoi Materialnoi Pomoschi I Kompensatsionnikh Viplat Grazhdanam, Postradavshim v Resultate Zemletriaseniya v Sakhalinskoy Oblasti". 1995a.(The Government of the Russian Federation. Regulation 'Procedure of Providing Allowances and Compensations to the Citizens Sufferedas a Result of the Earthquake in Sakhalin Region'). *Rossiyskaia Gazeta*, June 6.

Pravitelstvo Rossiiskoi Federatsii. Postanovleniye ot 2.06.1995 No 541 "O Finansovoi Pomoschi na Likvidatsiyu Posledstvii Zemletriaseniya v Okhinskom Rayone Sakhalinskoy Oblasti". 1995b.(The Government of the Russian Federation. Regulation 'Providing Financial Aid for Recovery From the Earthquake in Okha Rayon of the Sakhalin Region'). *Rossiiskaia Gazeta*, June 6

Pravitelstvo Rossiiskoi Federatsii. Postanovleniye ot 5.06.1995 No 559 "O Merakh po Likvidatsii Posledstvii Zemletriaseniya v Sakhalinskoi Oblasti". 1995c. (The Government of the Russian Federation. Regulation 'Measures to Recover From the Earthquake in Okha Rayon of the Sakhalin Region'). *Rossiiskaia Gazeta*, June 9.

Pravitelstvo Rossiiskoi Federatsii. Postanovleniye ot 5.11.1995 No 1113 "O Yedinoi Gosudarstvennoi Systeme Preduprezhdeniya I Liquidatsii Chrezvichainikh Situatsii". 1995d. (The Government of the Russian Federation. Regulation 'The Unified State System for Emergency Prevention and Response of the Russian Federation'). *Sobraniye Zakonodatelstva Rosiiskoi Federatsii*, No 46, St. 4459.

Pravitelstvo Rossiiskoi Federatsii. Postanovleniye ot 24.07.1995 No 738 "O Poriadke Podgotovki Naseleniia v Oblasto Zaschiti ot Chrezvichainikh Situatsii". 1995e. (The Government of the Russian Federation. Regulation 'On Procedure of Communities Preparedness to Emergencies and Disasters'). *Rossiiskaia Gazeta*, July 31.

Pravitelstvo Rossiiskoi Federatsii. Postanovleniye ot 03.08.1996 No 924. "O Silakh I Sredstvakh Yedinoi Gosudarstvennoi Systemi Preduprezhdeniya I Liquidatsii Chrezvichainikh Situatsii". 1996a. (The Government of the Russian Federation. Regulation 'On Means and Forces of the Unified State System for Emergency Prevention and Response of the Russian Federation'). *Rossiiskaia Gazeta*, August 14.

Pravitelstvo Rossiiskoi Federatsii. Postanovleniye ot 13.09.1996 No 1094. "OKlassificatsii Chrezvichainikh Situatsii Prorodnigi I Tekhnogennogo Kharactera".1996b. (The Government of the Russian Federation. Regulation 'Classification of Natural and Technological Emergencies and Disasters in the Russian Federation'). *Rossiiskaia Gazeta*, September 24.

Pravitelstvo Rossiiskoi Federatsii. Postanovleniye ot 14.02.1997 No 171. "O Sostave Mezhvedomstvennoi Comissii po Preduprezhdeniyu I Likvidatsii Chrezvichainikh Situatsii". 1997. (The Government of the Russian Federation. Regulation 'The Staff of the Intergovernmental Commission for Emergency Prevention and Response'). *Rossiiskaia Gazeta*, February 27.

Pravitelstvo Rossiiskoi Federatsii. Rasporiazheniye ot 7.10.1993 No 1770-p. 1993. (The Government of the Russian Federation. Executive Order # 1770-p of 7 October 1993.). *Rossiiskiye Vesti*, October 11.

Pravitelstvo Rossiiskoi Federatsii. Rasporiazheniye ot 28.05.1995 No 734-p. 1995a. (The Government of the Russian Federation. Executive Order # 734 of 28 May 1995). *Rossiiskiye Vesti*, May 30.

Pravitelstvo Rossiiskoi Federatsii. Rasporiazheniye ot 3.06.1995 No 739-p. 1995b. (The Government of the Russian Federation. Executive Order # 739-p of 3 June 1995). *Rossiiskiye Vesti*, June 6.

Prezident Rossiiskoi Federatsii. Ukaz ot 17.03.1997 No 249 "O Sovershenstvovanii Structuri Federanikh Organov Ispolnitelnoi Vlasti". 1997. (The Presidential Decree 'On

Improving the Structure of the Federal Executive Authority Bodies'). *Rossiiskaia Gazeta*, March 19.

Prigozhin, A. I. 1989a. *Novovvedeniia: Stimuli I Prepiatstviia: Sotsialniya Problemi Innovatiki*. (Innovations: Stimulators and Obstacles: Social Issues of Innovatics). Moskva, Politizdat.

_____. 1989b. Sotsiodinamica Karastrof. (Sociodynamics of disasters). *Sotsiologicheskiye Issledovaniya*, No 3: 35-45.

Programma Deistvii: Povestka Dnia na XXI Vek I Drugie Dokumenti Konferentsii v Rio de Janeiro). 1993. (Action Program: Agenda for the 21st Century and Other Documents of the Conference in Rio de Janeiro). Geneva: "Our Common Future" Center.

Quarantelli, E.L. 1966. Organization Under Stress. Pp. 3-19 in: Bricston, R. (Ed.), *Symposium on Emergency Operations,* System Development Corporation, Santa Monica

_____. 1981. The Command Post Point of View in Local Mass Communication Systems. *Communications: International Journal of Communication Research*, 7: 57-73.

_____. 1985. What is a Disaster? The Need for Clarification in Definition and Conceptualization in Research. In: *Disaster and Mental Health: Selected Contemporary Perspectives.* Washington DC: US GPO.

_____.1987a. Disaster Studies: An Analysis of the Social Historical Factors Affecting the Development of Research in the Area. *International Journal of Mass Emergencies and Disasters*, 5: 285-310

_____. 1987b. What Should We Study? Questions and Suggestions for Research About the Concept of Disasters. *International Journal of Mass Emergencies and Disasters*, 5: 7-32.

_____. 1990. *Emergency.* Preliminary Paper No. 143. Newark, DE, Disaster Research Center, University of Delaware.

_____. 1991. Disaster Response: Generic or Agent Specific? Pp. 97-105 in: Kreimer, A. and Munasinghe, M. (Eds.). *Managing Natural Disasters and the Environment.* Washington, D.C., The World Bank.

_____. 1992a. Disaster Research. Pp. 492-497 in: Borgatta, E. and Borgatta, M. (Eds.). *Encyclopedia of Sociology.* Macmillan Publ.Co.

_____. 1992b. *Organizational Response to the Mexico City Earthquake of 1985: Characteristics and Implications.* Preliminary Paper No. 187, Disaster Research Center, University of Delaware, Newark.

_____. 1992c. Urban Vulnerability and Technological Hazards in Developing Societies. Pp. 187-236 in: Kreimer, A. and Munasinghe, M. (Eds.) *Environmental Management and Urban Vulnerability.* Washington, D.C., World Bank:.

_____.1993. The DifferentWorlds of Science and Mass Communication; Implications for Information Flow From the Former to the Latter. Pp. 175-182 in: Nemec, J., Nigg, J.M. and Siccardi, F. (Eds.) *Prediction and Perception of Natural Hazards.* Dordrecht, Kluwer Academic Publishers:.

Quarantelli, E. L. and Dynes, R. R. 1977. Response to Social Crisis and Disaster. *Annual Review of Sociology*, No 2: 23-49.

Quarantelii, E.L. and Popov, K.N. (Eds.) 1993. *Proceedings of the United States - Former Soviet Union Seminar on Social Science Research on Mitigation Of and Recovery From Disasters and Large Scale Hazards.* (Meeting Held in Moscow, Russia at the Institute for Systems Analysis of the Russian Academy of Sciences, on April 19-26, 1993). Volume 1: The American Participation. Newark: Disaster Research Center, University of Delaware.

Quarantelii, E.L. and Mozgovaya, A.V. (Eds.). 1995. *An Annotated Inventory of the Social Science Research Literature in the Former Soviet Union and Contemporary Russia.* Newark: Disaster Research Center, University of Delaware.

Rabotnikov AES Vinudili Poiti na Krainiye Meri. (1996). (NPP Personnel was Forced to Undertake Extraordinary Measures). *Atom-Pressa*, 36 (228), October.

Radiatsiya I Risk. 1992. *Broshura Rossiiskogo Gosudarstvennogo Medico-Dozimetricheskogo Registra*. (Radiation and Risk. Brochure of the Russian State Medical Dosimeter Register), Issue 1. Moskva.

Radi Zdoroviia Liudei. 1989. (In the Sake of Human Health). *Pravda*, May 17.

Riabchikov, V. 1995. Kto Zakril Seismostantsii. (Who Closed the Seismological Stations). *Pravda*, June 7.

Risk Assessment in the Federal Government: Managing the Process. 1983a. National Academic Press, Washington, D.C.

Risk Assessment: A Study Group Report. 1983b. The Royal Society of Science, London.

Rogozhin, Yu. 1993a. Radioactivni Vzriv v Secretnom Tomske-7. (Radiation Explosion at the Secret Town of Tomsk-7). *Izvestiya*, April 7.

──────. 1993b. VPK Po-Prezhnemu ne Podchiniaetsa Nikomu. Dazhe Prezidentu. (Military and Industrial Complex Has Been Still Not Subordianted to Anybody, Even to the President). *Izvestiya,*: October 17.

Romanenko, V. 1993. Iz-Pod Nog Moskvichei Ukhodit Zemlia. (Muscovites Loose the Ground). *Segodnia*, July 6.

Romanov, G. 1993. *Likvidatsiya Posledstviy Radiatsionnikh Avariy: Spravochnoie Rukovodstvo*. (Liquidqtion of the Consequences of Radiation Accidents: A Manual). Moskva, Izdat.

Romanov, G.N., Tepliakov, I.G. and Shilov, V.P. 1990a. Kyshtymskaia Avariya Krupnim Planom: Vosstanovleniye Khoziaistvennoi Deiatelnosti. (The Kyshtym Disaster at Large: Economic Rehabilitation). *Priroda*, No 5: 67-72.

Romanov, G.N., Drozhko, E.G. and Nikipelov, B.V. 1990b. Kyshtymskaia Avariya Krupnim Planom: Podvodia Itogi. (The Kyshtym Disaster at Large: Summing Up the Results). *Priroda*, No 5: 75-77.

Romanov, G.N., Drozhko, E.G., Nikipelov, B.V., Tepliakov, I.G. and Shilov, V.P. 1993. Podvodia Itogi: Vosstanovleniye Khoziaistvennoi Deiatelnosti. (Summing Up the Results: Economic Rehabilitation). Pp. 324-332 in: Krivolutskiy, D.A. and Sokolov, V.E. (Eds.). *Ekologicheskiye Posledstviya Radioaktivnogo Zagriazneniya na Yuzhnom Urale.* (Ecological Impact of the Radioactive Contamination of the Southern Urals). Moskva, Nauka.

Rosenthal, U., 1986. Governmental Decision Making in Crisis Situation: Decisions at Hectic Moment. Paper presented at XI World Congress of Sociology. New Delhi, India, August 18-22.

──────. 1990. Cross-National Approaches to Disasters and Disaster Research. Paper prepared for Research Committee on Disasters, World Congress of Sociology, Madrid, 9-13 July 1990, Leiden University.

Rosenthal, U., Charles, M.T., t'Hart, P., Kouzmin, A. and Jarman, A. 1989. From Case Studies to Theory and Recommendations: A Concluding Analysis. Pp. 436-472 in: Rosenthal, U., Charles, M.T. and t'Hart, P. (Eds.). *Coping with Crisis: The Management of Disaster, Riots and Terrorism.* C.C. Thomas, Springfield,.

Rosenthal, U., Charles, M.T. and t'Hart, P. (Eds.) 1989. *Coping With Crisis: The Management of Disasters, Riots and Terrorism.* Springfield, Illinois: Chrles C. Thomas Publisher.

Rosenthal, U., t'Hart, P., van Duin M.J., Boin, R.A., Kroon, M.B.R., Otten, M.H.P. and Overdijk, W.I.E. 1994. *Complexity in Urban Crisis Management: Amsterdam's Response to the Bijlmer Air Disaster*. L.:James & James.

Roubtsov, A. 1994. KamAZ Nashel Sposob Privletch Zapadnikh Investorov. (KamAZ Found the Way to Attract Investors From the West). *Finansoviye Izvestiya*, September 22-28.

Rudashevskiy, V.D. 1987. Metodologicheskiye Predposilki Razvitiya Teorii Koordinatsii. (Methodological Prerequisites for Coordination Theory Development). Pp. 223-242 in: *Systemniye*

Issledovaniya. Metodologicheskiye Problemi. Yezhegodnik. (Systems Studies. Methodological Problems. A Yearbook). Moskva, Nauka.

Sasayama, K. 1996. Keynote Speech of the Mayor of Cobe City at the 2nd International Conference 'Local Authorities Confronting Disasters and Emergencies', Amsterdam, the Netherlands, 21-24 April 1996.

Scanlon, J., Luukko, R. and Morton, G. 1978. Media Coverage of Crisis: Better Than Reported, Worse Than Necessary. *Journalism Quarterly,* 55: 66-72.

Semenchenko, M. 1993. Pozharniye Idut Pervimi. (Firemen Come the First). *Dialog*: April 22.

Sergeev, G. and Pegov, S. 1992.Upravleniye Riskom: Rol Sotsialnikh Factorov v Krupnomaschtabnikh Avariyakh. (Risk Management: The Role of Social Factors in Large Industrial Accidents). *Problemi Bezopasnosti pri Chrezvichainikh Situatsiyakh,* No 10: 1-12.

Shestakov, S. 1992. Printsipi Klassifikatsii Ekologo-Geographicheskikh Situatsii. (Principles of Typology of Environmental and Geographic situations). *Izvestiya Russkogo Georaphicheskogo Obschestva,* No. 3 (124): 241-249.

Shirokovskikh, G. 1997. Normi Radiatsionnoi Bezopasnosti. (Radiation Safety Standards). *Grazhdanskaia Zaschita,* No 4: 83-84.

Shoigu, S. 1993. Situatsia Normalnaia. Nikakogo Sravneniya s Chernobylem ne Mozhet Bit. (Situation is Normal. Nothing to be Compared with Chernobyl). *Tomskiy Vestnik*: April 14.

_____. 1996. Schit Bezopasnosti. (Safety Shield). *Grazhdanskaia Zaschita,* No. 10: 5-9.

Shoigu, S. and Vorobyev, Yu. 1995. Likvidatsiya Katastrophicheskikh Posledstvii Zemletriaseniya v Neftegorske. (Recovery From the Earthquake Disaster in Neftegorsk). *Federalnaia Systema Seismologicheskikh Nabluidsenii I Prognoza Zemletriasenii. Informatsionno-Analiticheskii Bulleten. Spetsialnii Vipusk "Neftegorskoye Zemletriaseniye. 27 (28). 05. 1995":* 5-17.

Shrivastava, P. 1992. *Bhopal: Anatomy of a Crisis.* 2nd Edition. London: Paul Chapman Publishing Ltd.

Simenons, Ch. 1985-1986. Accidents: Information and Response. *Toxic Substances Journal,* 1, No 1-4: 29-32

Siniavskiy, B. 1997. Uran na Sei Raz Okazalsia Dobrodushnim. (This Time Uranium Turned to be Kind). *Izvestiya,* January 21.

Sivard, R.L. 1991. *World Military and Social Expenditures.* World Priorities, Washington, D.C.

Sivintsev, Yu.V. and Kachalov, V.A. (Eds.). 1992. *Chernobyl: Piat Trudnikh Let.* (Chernobyl: Five Hard Years). Moskva, Izdat.

Smirnov, N.N. 1988. *Ekologia Biosfernoi Katastrofi.* (Ecology of a Biosphere Catastrophe). Moskva, Znaniye.

Solarev, A. 1989. Yadovitoie Oblako Rasseyano. (The Poisenous Cloud Is Dissolved). *Sovetskaia Rossiia,* March 24.

Sorokin, P. A. 1920. (Reprinted in 1993). *Sistema Sotsiologii.* Volumes 1 and 2I. (System of Sociology). Moskva, Nauka.

_____. 1942. *Man and Society in Calamity.* New York, Dutton.

_____. 1992 *Chelovek. Tsivilizatsiya. Obschestvo.* (Man. Civilisation. Society). (Transl. from English). Moscow, Politizdat.

_____. 1993. Chelovek i Obschestvo v Bedstvii. (Man and Society in Calamity). *Problemi Sotsiologii,* No 3: 53

Sources, Effects and Risk of Ionizing Radiation. 1988. United Nations Scientific Committee on the Effects of Atomic Radiation Report to the General Assembly. United Nations, New York.

Sotnikova, T. 1993. Mi Vse - Gruppa Riska. (We are All a Risk Group). *Segodnia,* December 9.

Sovet Ministrov SSSR. Postanivleniye ot 15.12.1990 No 1282 "O Sozdanii Gosudarstvennoi Obschesoyuznoi Sistemi Po Preduprezhdeniyu I Deistviiam v Chrezvichainikh Situatsiakh". 1990. (The USSR Council of Ministers. Regulation #1282 'On Establishing the State All-Union System for Prevention of and Actions in Emergencies'). *Pravda,* December 17.

Starr, Ch. 1969. Social benefit versus technological risk. *Science.* No. 165: 183-197.

Stroganov, Yu. 1989. Sluchilos v Ionave. (It Occurred in Ionava). *Pravda,* March 24.

Sturua, M. 1996. Nadlomlennaia Chetvertaia Vetv. (The Cracked Fourth Branch of Power). *Izvestiya,* December 27.

A Summary of Federal Emergency Preparedness in Canada. 1995. Ottawa, Emergency Preparedness Canada (EPC).

Suverov, S. 1997. KamAZ Gotov Prodat Aktsii Pravitelstvu Tatarii. (KamAZ is Ready to Sell Its Stocks to the Tatarstan's Government). *Izvestiya,* February 4.

Sweet, W. 1996. Chernobyl Stressful After-Effects. *IEEE Spectrum,* 33, No 11: 27-34.

Tarasenko, V. and Poliakov, V. 1992. Nekotoriye Problemi Zaschiti Naseleniya v Avariyakh, Katastrofakh I Stikhiynikh Bedstviyakh. (Some Problems of Protection of Population in Accidents, Catastrophes and Natural Calamities). *Problemi Bezopasnosti pri Chrezvichainikh Situatsiyakh,* No 5: 20-25

Tarasov, A. 1993. Bolshaia Lozh i Posle Tomskoi Avarii. (Big Lies Also Escort the Accident at Tomsk). *Izvestiya,* June 9.

Tchernikh, A. 1993a. Avariya v Tomske-7. (Accident in Tomsk-7). *Rossiyskaia Gazeta,* April 8.

_____. 1993b. Avariya v Tomske-7: Noviye Podrobnosti. (Accident in Tomsk-7: new details). *Rossiyskaia Gazeta,* April 10.

_____. 1993c. Tomsku-7 Krupno Povezlo. (Tomsk-7 was Very Lucky). *Rossiyskaia Gazeta,* April 14.

Teyes, J. 1987. 21st Century: Environment and Resources. *European Environment Review,* 1, No 5: 7-10

t'Hart, P., Rosenthal, U. and Kouzmin, A. 1993. Crisis Decision Making: The Centralization Thesis Revisited, *Administration and Society,* 25, No 1: 12-45.

Thournburg, R. 1986. *The Three Mile Island Experience: Ten Lessons in Management.* An Address to the International Conference on Industrial Crisis Management. N.Y., New York University (mimeo).

Tierney, K.J. 1989. Improving Theory and Research on Hazard Mitigation: Political Economy and Organizational Perspectives. *International Journal of Mass Emergencies and Disasters,* 7: 367-396.

Toffler, A. 1980. *The Third Wave.* N.Y., Morrow.

Tolerability of Risk from Nuclear Power Stations, Health and Safety Executive, The. 1992. London.

Tomsk-7. 1993. (Tomsk-7). *Sovershenno Otkrito,* No 1: 28-29.

Tomsk-7 Schitaet Izotopi. 1993. (Tomsk-7 Counts Isotopes). *Trud,* April 10.

Treschina. 1995. (A rupture). *Grazhdanskaya Zaschita,* No 8: 25.

Tsarev, I. 1993. Zakriti Gorod Mozhet Spat Spokoino? Atomnii Dzhinn Snova Virvalsia na Svobodu. (Can the Closed Town Sleep Calmly? The Nuclear Jinni is Free Again). *Trud,* April 9.

Tsarev, I. and Zolotov, O. 1995a. Nu Chto Teper Skazat pro Sakhalin? (What Can we Say About Sakhalin Now?). *Trud,* May 30.

_____. 1995b. Ostrov Skorbi i Nadezhdi. (The Island of Sorrow and Hope). *Trud,* June 1.

Turner, B.A., 1978. *Man-made Disasters.* London: Wykeham.

_____. 1979. The Social Aethiology of Disasters. *Disasters,* 3, No 1: 53-59.

Turner, R., Nigg, J. and Paz, D. 1986. *Waiting for Disaster: Earthquake Watch in California*. Los Angeles, CA, University of California Press.

Ukhov, E. 1993a. Zavoda Net. Paniki Odnako Tozhe. (No plant, However no Panics). *Trud*, May 14.

_____. 1993b. Pozhar Busheval Vsiu Notch. (The Fire Raged All the Night). *Trud*, April 16.

Ulomov, V.I. 1995. Otsenka Seismicheskoi Opasnosti I Vremennaia Skhema Seismicheskogo Rayonirovaniya Sakhalina. (The Seismic Risk Assessment and the Interim Scheme of Sakhalin Seismological Zoning). *Federalnaia Systema Siesmologicheskikh Nabliudenii I Prognoza Zemletryasenii. Informatsionno-Analyticheskii Bulleten. Spetsialnii Vipusk 'Neftegorskoye Zemletryaseniye 27 (28) Maia 1995'. Moskva, MCS*: 18-26.

UNDRO, 1982. *Natural Disasters and Vulnerability Analysis*. Geneva: Office of United Nations Disaster Relief Co-ordinator.

US Congress. House. Committee on Government Operations. *Reorganization Plan No 3 of 1978*, Message from the President of the United States. 95th Congress, 2nd session. 1978. H. Doc. 95-356

Usoltsev, A. and Kharitonova, N. 1988. Beda Nazrevala Davno. (The Disaster Was Expected Long Ago). *Sovetskaia Rossiia*, 5 May.

Vasilkevich, Ya.I. 1991. Chrezvichainiye situatsii: opredeleniya I suschnost. (Emergencies: Definition and Essence). *Problemi Bezopasnosti Pri Chrezvichainikh Situatsiakh*. No. 9: 112-123.

Verkhovnii Sovet Rossiiskoi Federatsii. Postanovleniye "O Merakh po Liquidatsii Posledstvii Avarii v Tomskoi Oblasti na Sibirskom Khimicheskom Kombinate (gorod Seversk) 6 Aprelia 1993 goda". 23 Iyulia1993 goda. (1993). (The Russian Federation Supreme Soviet. Regulation 'On Measures for Liquidation in the Tomsk Region the Consequences of the Accident Occurred on 6 April 1993 at the Siberian Chemical Complex (Tomsk-7)' of 23 July 1993). Moskva.

Vibros Gaza. 1989. (Gas Emission). *Pravda*, September 15.

Vigon, S. (1993). Tomsk-7: Svezhaia Informatsiya. (Tomsk-7: A New Piece of Information). *Krasnoye Znamia*, April 13.

Vikulin, A. 1996. Kamchatka Izuchaet Uroki Neftegorska. (Kamchatka Draws Lessons From Neftegorsk). *Grazhdanskaia Zaschita*, No 8: 92-93.

Vishnevski, B.1993a. Mi Vse Estche Edem v Odnom KamAZe! (We Still are Driving Our Common KamAZ). *Komsomolskaia Pravda*, May 20.

_____. 1993b. Bottichelli ne Katalsia na KamAZe. (Botichelli Did Not Drive KamAZ). *Komsomolskaia Pravda*, June 24.

Vorobyov, Yu. 1996. Rossiiskaia Sluzhba Spaseniya. (Rescue Service in Russia).*Systemi Bezopasnosti, Sviazi I Telecommunicatsii*, No 5: 68-71.

_____. 1997. Poiskovo-Spasatelnaia Sluzhba MChS Rossii. (Search and Rescue Service of the MES of Russia). *Grazhdanskaia Zaschita*, No 2: 73-75.

V Rossii Resheno Ostanovit Rost Proizvodstvennogo Travmatizma. 1996. (Russia Takes the Decision to Stop Industrial Traumas Increase). *Izvestiya*, May 29.

Vzriv v Tomske Bil Predskazan. 1993. (The Explosion in Tomsk was Predicted). *Trud*, April 28.

Walters, L.M., Wilkins, L. and Walters, T. (Eds). 1989. *Bad Tidings: Communication and Catastrophe*. Hilsdale, Lawrence Erlbaum Associates Publishers.

World Map of Natural Hazards. 1987. Munich: Munich-Re Co.

World Disasters Report 1995. International Federation of Red Cross and Red Crescent Societies, Geneva.

Wyllie, L.A. and Filson, J.R. (Eds.). 1989. Armenia earthquake reconnaissance report. *Earthquake Spectra* (Special Supplement). August.

Yakov, V. 1995. Est Kto Zhivoy? Otzovis. (Is Anybody Alive Here? Reply). *Izvestiya*, June 1.

_____. 1996. Polet Cherez "Zonu Molchaniya". (The Flight Over the 'Soundless Zone'). *Izvestiya*, December 15.

Yarigin, S.V. 1996. Povisheniye Effectivnosti Upravleniya Silami i Sredstvami Preduprezhdeniya i Likvidatsii Chrezvichainikh Situatsii. (Increasing Effectiveness of Management of Means and Forces for Prevention and Response to Emergencies. Abstract of the Candidate of Science Dissertation). Moskva, Academia Narodnogo Khoziaistva pri Pravitelstve Rossiiskoi Federatsii.

Yaroshinskaya, A.A. 1992. *Chernobyl: Sovershenno Sekretno*. (Chernobyl: Top Secret). Moscow: Drugiye Berega.

Yekaterinoslavskiy, Yu. Yu. 1988. *Upravlencheskiye Situatsii: Analiz I Resheniya*. (Management Situations: Analysis and Solutions). Moskva, Ekonomika.

Yelkov, I. 1996. Zarazhennoye Miaso Mozhet Bit Prodano v Liubom Gorode Rossii. (Contaminated Meat May be Sold in Any Russian Town). *Komsomolskaia Pravda*, July 24.

Yelokhin, A.N. and Chernopliokov, A.N. 1994. Opit I Otsenka Potentsialnoi Opasnosti Promishlennikh Ob'ektov I Vnedreniia Elementov Sistemi APELL v Gagarinskom Raione Moskvi. (The Experince and Assessment of Hazards From Industrial Facilities and of the Use of Elements of the APELL System in the Gagarinskii Distric of Moscow City). *Problemi Bezopasnosti Pri Chrezvichainikh Situatsiakh*, No. 11: 44-78

Yermolayev, O. (1996). "Sakhalinmorneftegaz" Ischet u Pravitelstva Podderzhku. ('Sakhalinmorneftegaz' Seeks Governmental Support). *Finansoviye Izvestiya*, May 30.

Yevin, I.A. and Yablonsky, A.I. 1992. Modeli Razvitiya i Teoriya Katastrof. (Models of Development and Catastrophe Theory). Pp. 98-130 in: *Systemniye Issledovaniya. Metodologicheskiye Problemi. Yezhegodnik.* (Systems Studies. Methodological Problems. A Yearbook). Moskva, Nauka.

Yudin, P. 1995. Nesmotria na Pozhar, KamAZ ne Progorel. (KamAZ is Not a Bankrupt Despite the Fire). *Kapital*, June 16.

Yurin, D. 1995. Pervimi na Pomosch Prishli Neftianiki. (Oil Workers were the First to Come to Help). *Sakhalinskiy Neftianik*, June 1.

Zaitsev, A. 1995. Neftegorsk - Nasha Bol. (Neftegosk is Our Pain). *Grazhdanskaya Zaschita*, No 10: 36-38.

Zakharov, A. 1993. Rukovodstvo Poznaetsa v Bede. (Administration Proves in Disaster). *Narodnaia Tribuna*: April 14.

Zakon Rossiiskoi Sovetskoi Federativnoi Sotsialisticheskoi Respubliki 'OChrezvichainom Polozhenii'. 1991a. (1991 State of Emergency Act of the Russian Soviet Federative Socialist Republic). *Vedomosti S'ezda Narodnikh Deputatov RSFSR i Verhovnogo Soveta RSFSR*. No. 22, St. 773.

Zakon Rossiiskoi Sovetskoi Federativnoi Sotsialisticheskoi Respubliki 'O Militsii". 1991b. (The 1991 Militia Act of the Russian Soviet Federative Socialist Republic). *Vedomosti S'ezda Narodnikh Deputatov RSFSR i Verhovnogo Soveta RSFSR*. No. 16, St. 503.

Zakon Rossiiskoi Sovetskoi Federativnoi Sotsialisticheskoi Respubliki 'O Sanitarno-Epidemiologicheskom Blagopoluchii Naseleniia. 1991c. (1991 Act of Sanitary and Epidemiological Welfare of People). *Vedomosti S'ezda Narodnikh Deputatov RSFSR i Verhovnogo Soveta RSFSR*. No 20, St. 641.

Zakon Rossiiskoi Federatsii 'O Bezopasnosti'. 1992a. (1992 Security and Safety Act of the Russian Federation). *Vedomosti S'ezda Narodnikh Deputatov Rossiiskoi Federatsii Verkhovnogo Soveta Rossiiskoi Federatsii*. No. 15, St. 769.

Zakon Rossiiskoi Federatsii 'Ob Oborone'. 1992b. (1992 Defence Act of the Russian Federation). *Vedomosti S'ezda Narodnikh Deputatov Rossiiskoi Federatsii I Verkhovnogo Soveta Rossiiskoi Federatsii*. No. 42, St. 2331.

Zakon Rossiiskoi Sovetskoi Federativnoi Sotsialisticheskoi Respublici 'Ob Okhrane Okruzhayuschei Prirodnoi Sredi". 1992c. (1991 Natural Environmental Protection Act). *Vedomosti S'ezda Narodnikh Deputatov RSFSR i Verhovnogo Soveta RSFSR*. No. 10, St. 457.

Zakon Rossiiskoi Federatsii 'O Strakhovanii'. 1992d. (1992 Insurance Act of the Russian Federation). *Vedomosti S'ezda Narodnikh Deputatov* ^{Rossiiskoi} *Federatsii I Verkhovnogo Soveta Rossiiskoi Federatsii*. No., St..

Zakon Rossiiskoi Federatsii 'O Zaschite Prav Potrebitelei. 1992e. (1992 Consumer Rights Protection Act of the Russian Federation). *Vedomosti S'ezda Narodnikh Deputatov Rossiiskoi Federatsii I Verkhovnogo Soveta Rossiiskoi Federatsii*. No. 15, St. 766.

Zakon Rossiiskoi Federatsii 'O Statuse Voennosluzhaschikh". 1993. (The 1993 Servicemen Status Act of the Russian Federation). *Vedomosti S'ezda Narodnikh Deputatov Rossiiskoi Federatsii i Verhovnogo Soveta Rossiiskoi Federatsii*. No. 6, St. 188.

Zinchenko, V.P. 1989. Chelovecheskii Intellekt I Tekhnokraticheskoye Mishleniye. (Human Intellect and Technoctratic Thinking). *Kommunist,* No 3: 97-99.

Zubacheva, V.Ya. 1991. Metodicheskiye Podkhodi k Economicheskoi Otsenke Uscherba ot Katastrofi na Chernobylskoi AES. (Methodological Approaches to Evaluation of Economic Losses Due to the Chernobyl Catastrophe). Pp. 103-110 in: *Ecologicheskiye I Ekonomicheskiye Problemi v Byelorussii I Puti Ikh Resheniya*. (Ecological and Economic Problems of Byelorussia and the Ways to Solve Them). Minsk.

Index

A

Africa, 4, 7, 18, 128
agriculture, 117, 153, 159
alcoholism, 27
America, 7, 18, 19, 128
armed conflict, 1, 2, 3, 36, 46, 63, 71, 91, 105, 106, 110, 199, 200
armed conflicts, 1, 2, 3, 46, 63, 71, 91, 105, 106, 110
Armed Forces, 113
Armenia, 41, 92, 93, 173, 220
arsenic, 13
Asia, 7, 18, 19, 39, 128
Astrakhan gas complex, 44

B

banks, commercial, 164, 165
Bhopal, 13, 15, 19, 210, 218
Bosnia, 199
Brazil, 7, 15, 19
Byelorus, 17, 77, 88, 92, 93

C

California, 11, 72, 204, 220
Canada, 18, 101, 105, 219
cesium, 17, 143
Chechnia, 46, 85, 106
Cheliabinsk, 13, 15, 17, 46, 87, 105, 111, 132, 133, 134, 136, 139, 148, 211
chemical industry, 14, 15
Cherniye Zemli, 46
Chernobyl radiation disaster, 13, 14, 17, 34, 40, 63, 76, 87, 92, 93, 95, 96, 105, 112, 139
China, 3, 7, 10, 15, 199, 200
chlorofluorocarbons, 37
civil defense, 84, 94, 98, 99, 101, 102, 103, 109, 112, 114, 120, 123, 125, 126, 127, 128, 129, 148, 161
civil disturbances, 41, 47
Cold War, 2, 98, 112
Colorado, 207
Communist Party, 98
communities, 1, 2, 11, 12, 19, 28, 34, 37, 39, 40, 44, 45, 61, 62, 63, 76, 82, 84, 85, 87, 91, 94, 97, 98, 99, 100, 102, 104, 106, 107, 108, 109, 111, 112, 113, 114, 115, 117, 119, 120, 121, 125, 128, 132, 133, 134, 135, 143, 144, 146, 147, 149, 151, 152, 155, 161, 165, 166, 172, 173, 175, 177, 187, 188, 191, 192, 193
contamination, 1, 11, 15, 17, 42, 44, 46, 88, 99, 106, 111, 139, 140, 143, 144, 146, 149, 150
corruption, 39, 91, 186
crisis response, 36

D

decentralization, 181
Delaware, 204, 209, 216
diphtheria, 26
droughts, 3, 7

E

earthquakes, 3, 4, 10, 11, 19, 37, 41, 45, 47, 48, 72, 99, 101, 108, 170, 172, 173, 175, 179
economic crisis, 3, 27, 40, 46, 77, 83, 84, 92, 136, 151, 156, 162, 164, 165, 170, 173, 186, 187, 188, 192
economic damages, 2, 3, 4, 7, 11, 14, 17, 18, 48
economic development, 7, 17, 34, 45, 46, 65, 72
economic stability, 1
education, 197
Egypt, 199
emergency management, 12, 27, 35, 36, 42, 47, 63, 64, 65, 68, 69, 74, 78, 82, 88, 89, 90, 91, 92, 93, 94, 95, 96, 97, 98, 99, 100, 101, 102, 103, 104, 109, 110, 112, 114, 117, 120, 127, 131, 133, 154, 188, 191, 192
emergency prevention, 78, 104, 107, 108, 114, 117, 120, 187, 192
emergency workers, 17, 45, 108
environmental protection, 92, 126
equipment design, 42
Ethiopia, 200
Europe, 2, 3, 7, 15, 19, 28, 98, 128, 135, 153
evacuation, 15, 34, 44, 72, 73, 83, 84, 85, 109, 114, 115, 126, 128, 149, 153, 160, 177, 179, 183

F

Far East, 10, 11, 34, 131, 173, 174, 178, 180, 181, 183, 202
financial support, 136
fire prevention, 154, 155, 156, 157, 162, 170
floods, 3, 4, 7, 10, 47, 72, 99, 101, 106, 108, 199
forest fires, 19, 143
France, 15, 109, 138

G

gas explosions, 27
Gaza, 44, 220
geography, 210, 211
Germany, 27, 37, 77, 92, 109, 133
goods and services, 62, 92
governmental policy, 46
Great Britain, 15, 37, 92, 100, 101, 107, 108, 150
Greenpeace, 17, 202
gross national product, 3, 7, 10, 15, 93
Guatemala, 10

H

health care, 101, 183
human factor, 42, 62, 74, 135, 147, 188
human factors, 135
human resources, 93, 96

I

Illinois, 201, 210, 217
India, 7, 13, 15, 19, 98, 217
industrial accidents, 1, 11, 42, 155
industrialization, 17, 191
International Atomic Energy Agency, 99, 132, 150, 196
International Bank for Reconstruction and Development (IBRD), 203
Iran, 3, 10
Italy, 10, 15, 111

J

Japan, 3, 10, 11, 27, 48, 77, 93, 98, 99, 107, 109, 170, 172, 178, 185, 188, 199, 201

K

Kalmik Republic, 46
KamAZ, 34, 44, 45, 84, 153, 154, 155, 156, 157, 158, 159, 160, 161, 162, 163, 164, 165, 166, 167, 168, 169, 170, 171, 186, 187, 201, 202, 203, 205, 206, 207, 211, 212, 214, 217, 219, 220, 221
Kazakhstan, 93, 111
Kentucky, 209
Khazakhstan, 157, 163
Kobe, 3, 11, 48, 93, 95, 170, 172, 175, 178, 179, 181, 182, 185, 188, 201
Korea, 199

L

Latin America, 18
legislation, 98, 99, 100, 102, 103, 104, 105, 106, 109, 110, 111, 113, 127
licensing, 94
life expectancy, 144
Lithuania, 15
living standard, 27

M

management strategy, 42, 62, 63, 69, 78, 82, 88, 89, 90, 91, 94, 96, 103, 113
mass destruction weapons, 46, 71, 86
mass disturbances, 72, 104, 105
mass media, 30, 41, 45, 76, 88, 92, 93, 139, 147, 152, 166, 167, 170
Massachusetts, 201
Mexico, 15, 19, 175, 179, 212, 216
military plants, 71, 159
military power, 37
modernization, 27, 42, 129, 164, 165

N

natural disasters, 3, 4, 7, 10, 11, 14, 17, 18, 26, 47, 48, 74, 91, 106, 175, 187

natural hazards, 1, 2, 3, 4, 7, 10, 11, 12, 13, 14, 82, 85
natural science, 28
Nefegorsk, 41
Neftegorsk, 3, 11, 19, 34, 41, 45, 48, 84, 87, 94, 95, 108, 128, 170, 172, 173, 174, 175, 176, 177, 178, 179, 180, 181, 182, 183, 184, 185, 186, 187, 201, 204, 207, 211, 218, 220, 221
Netherlands, 101, 218
New York, 132, 203, 204, 207, 208, 210, 213, 218, 219
nitrates, 107
nitrogen, 15, 136, 137
Northridge, 3, 11, 172, 203
nuclear industries, 15
nuclear missiles, 71
nuclear plants, 134, 135, 136, 138, 189
nuclear power plants, 45, 76, 77, 92, 93, 99, 119, 129, 132, 136, 156, 189

O

Oceania, 18
OECD, 14, 18, 99
of environmental monitoring, 126
Ohio, 212
oil spills, 44

P

Pacific, 203
peat fires, 19, 85
Perestroika, 136
Peru, 7, 10
pipelines, 14, 19, 39, 172, 174
political security, 1
pollution, 92, 99, 140
polystyrene, 154, 155, 156, 157, 158, 162
population density, 40, 172
population growth, 11
power plants, 19, 40, 45, 76, 77, 92, 93, 98, 99, 119, 129, 132, 136, 156, 189
privatization, 102, 152
psychological stress, 45
public opinion, 76, 77, 151, 165, 170, 206, 210
public order, 105

R

radiation accident, 12, 13, 27, 34, 42, 44, 45, 47, 92, 131, 133, 134, 135, 167, 170, 186, 187, 188
radiation exposure, 139, 140, 143, 144, 146, 152
radiation safety, 98, 105, 133, 134, 135, 140
radioactive, 13, 15, 17, 45, 46, 62, 77, 87, 88, 132, 137, 138, 139, 140, 143, 144, 146, 147, 149, 150, 152
radioactive fallout, 17, 62, 77, 87, 88, 146, 149, 150, 152
recession, 27
recovery, 3, 11, 12, 17, 29, 35, 43, 46, 47, 48, 68, 74, 78, 86, 87, 88, 89, 91, 92, 93, 94, 96, 97, 99, 100, 103, 104, 109, 111, 115, 117, 119, 123, 125, 126, 127, 128, 129, 133, 147, 149, 150, 152, 153, 154, 158, 160, 162, 163, 164, 165, 167, 170, 185, 186, 187, 188, 192
reforms, economic, 34, 40, 173
regional armed conflicts, 46, 63, 110
regional security, 117
rehabilitation, 3, 43, 46, 86, 87, 93, 94, 99, 100, 109, 153, 174, 186, 188
response and recovery policy, 17
riots, 47, 72, 104
risk factors, 18, 36, 45, 46, 62, 72
Royal Society, 203, 217
rural areas, 117
RUSPRE, 97, 104, 105, 106, 112, 113, 114, 115, 116, 117, 118, 119, 120, 121, 123, 125, 126, 127, 128, 129, 188, 192, 196, 197
RUSPRE system, 127, 128

S

sabotage, 42
safety standards, 94, 109, 156
safety system, 103, 134, 135, 137, 138
safety, industrial, 27, 84, 107, 114, 156
Sakhalin Island, 3, 11, 34, 37, 41, 87, 172, 173, 177, 186
Sandoz chemical disasters, 18
Security Council, 113, 121
Semipalatinsk, 111, 146, 151
Seversk, 27, 34, 41, 42, 45, 131, 132, 133, 134, 144, 146, 147, 148, 149, 150, 153, 167, 220
Shanghai, 15
sheltering, 72, 85, 114, 126, 128
Shibenik, 15

social protests, 92
social security, 46, 115, 148, 162
social system vulnerability, 1, 15, 17, 26, 40, 44
social welfare, 95, 105
sovereignty, 65, 105
Soviet Union, 1, 2, 7, 10, 11, 13, 15, 17, 18, 19, 26, 30, 34, 35, 37, 39, 40, 41, 44, 63, 71, 72, 76, 77, 83, 84, 88, 89, 91, 92, 93, 95, 96, 98, 99, 104, 107, 109, 110, 111, 112, 119, 133, 134, 136, 146, 153, 154, 155, 156, 160, 166, 170, 173, 174, 177, 187, 191, 192, 210, 211, 213, 214, 216
Spitak, 10, 19, 41, 45, 46, 108, 172, 173, 181, 188, 203
state of emergency, 103, 104, 110, 127
state ownership, 109
state policy, 39, 100, 103, 112
strategic management, 42, 68, 69, 73, 77
strontium, 17
sulfur dioxide, 44
Sweden, 93, 100
Switzerland, 15, 18, 109

T

Technological Accidents, 2, 13, 16, 25
terrorism, 42, 92, 105
Third World countries, 10
thorium, 137, 146
thyroid cancer, 17
toxic spills, 14, 101
toxic substances, 36, 45, 99, 154
transportation, 14, 15, 19, 39, 40, 84, 94, 98, 106, 109, 110, 117, 123, 125, 126, 128, 159, 178, 181, 185, 186, 188
tuberculosis, 26
Turkey, 10

U

Uganda, 200
Ukraine, 17, 88, 92, 93, 156, 157, 163
United Kingdom, 76, 134

United Nations, 150, 218, 220
United States, 11, 15, 30, 71, 76, 85, 92, 93, 98, 99, 101, 106, 107, 108, 109, 110, 111, 216, 220
uranium, 132, 133, 136, 137, 138, 146, 152
urbanization, 11, 12, 17
USSR, 2, 10, 27, 99, 109, 132, 133, 134, 152, 155, 175, 196, 219

V

vaccinations, 27

W

warning, 42, 43, 44, 73, 82, 84, 85, 87, 96, 99, 119, 125, 134, 138, 147, 148, 149, 150, 151, 152, 153, 156, 160, 173, 175, 177, 178, 187, 188, 191, 192
warning system, 82, 84, 85, 147, 148, 173, 177
wars, 1, 2, 3, 46, 71, 91, 98, 105, 106
wastewater, 39
wastewater treatment facilities, 39
water contamination, 15
water supply, 161
weapons of mass destruction, 105
Western Europe, 98, 99
windstorms, 3, 4, 11, 143
World Bank, 203, 216

Y

Yugoslavia, 2, 15, 199

Z

Zaire, 199, 200
zero risk, 42, 76, 77, 78